Buddhism in the Global Eye

Also available from Bloomsbury:

A Critique of Western Buddhism, Glenn Wallis
Dynamism and the Ageing of a Japanese "New" Religion, Erica Baffelli and Ian Reader
Language in the Buddhist Tantra of Japan, Richard K. Payne
Methods in Buddhist Studies, edited by Scott A. Mitchell and Natalie Fisk Quli

Buddhism in the Global Eye

Beyond East and West

Edited by
John S. Harding, Victor Sōgen Hori,
and Alexander Soucy

BLOOMSBURY ACADEMIC
LONDON • NEW YORK • OXFORD • NEW DELHI • SYDNEY

BLOOMSBURY ACADEMIC
Bloomsbury Publishing Plc
50 Bedford Square, London, WC1B 3DP, UK
1385 Broadway, New York, NY 10018, USA
29 Earlsfort Terrace, Dublin 2, Ireland

BLOOMSBURY, BLOOMSBURY ACADEMIC and the Diana logo are trademarks of Bloomsbury Publishing Plc

First published in Great Britain 2020
This paperback edition published in 2021

Copyright © John S. Harding, Victor Sōgen Hori, Alexander Soucy and Contributors, 2020

John S. Harding, Victor Sōgen Hori, & Alexander Soucy have asserted their right under the Copyright, Designs and Patents Act, 1988, to be identified as Editors of this work.

Cover image: Tian Tan Buddha, Big Buddha (© Pierre Ogeron/Getty Images)

For legal purposes the Acknowledgments on p. viii constitute an extension of this copyright page.

All rights reserved. No part of this publication may be reproduced or transmitted in any form or by any means, electronic or mechanical, including photocopying, recording, or any information storage or retrieval system, without prior permission in writing from the publishers.

Bloomsbury Publishing Plc does not have any control over, or responsibility for, any third-party websites referred to or in this book. All internet addresses given in this book were correct at the time of going to press. The author and publisher regret any inconvenience caused if addresses have changed or sites have ceased to exist, but can accept no responsibility for any such changes.

A catalogue record for this book is available from the British Library.

A catalog record for this book is available from the Library of Congress.

ISBN: HB: 978-1-3501-4063-9
PB: 978-1-3502-8317-6
ePDF: 978-1-3501-4064-6
eBook: 978-1-3501-4065-3

Typeset by Deanta Global Publishing Services, Chennai, India

To find out more about our authors and books visit www.bloomsbury.com and sign up for our newsletters.

Contents

Notes on Contributors	vi
Acknowledgments	viii
Spelling Conventions	ix
Introduction *John S. Harding, Victor Sōgen Hori, and Alexander Soucy*	1
Part One World Religions	9
1 Buddhism and the Secular Conception of Religion *Victor Sōgen Hori*	11
2 Mapping Buddhism beyond East and West *John S. Harding*	26
3 Buddhism and Global Secularisms *David L. McMahan*	42
4 Women and Vietnamese Buddhist Practice in the Shadow of Secularism *Alexander Soucy*	56
Part Two Global Flows	69
5 Socialism, Russia, and India's Revolutionary Dharma *Douglas Ober*	71
6 D.T. Suzuki and the Chinese Search for Buddhist Modernism *Jingjing Li*	87
7 Recent Emergence of Theravāda Meditation Communities in Contemporary China *Ngar-sze Lau*	103
Part Three Asian Agencies	121
8 Shin Buddhism in Chōshū and Early Meiji Notions of Religion-State Relations *Mick Deneckere*	123
9 Nanjō Bunyū's Sanskritization of Buddhist Studies in Modern Japan *Paride Stortini*	137
10 An Alternative to the "Westernization" Paradigm and Buddhist Global Imaginaires *Lina Verchery*	150
11 Glocalization in Buddhist Food Ventures on a Small Canadian Island *Jason W. M. Ellsworth*	163
Notes	177
Bibliography	186
Index	208

Contributors

Editors

John S. Harding, **Victor Sōgen Hori**, and **Alexander Soucy** have collaborated on a series of conferences, research projects, and publications since 2006. Harding, Hori, and Soucy are coinvestigators for a multiyear Social Sciences and Humanities Research Council (SSHRC) of Canada-funded research project on "The Modernization of Buddhism in Global Perspective" and coeditors of *Wild Geese: Buddhism in Canada* (2010) and *Flowers on the Rock: Global and Local Buddhisms in Canada* (2014).

John S. Harding is an associate professor in East Asian Religions at the University of Lethbridge, the author of *Mahayana Phoenix: Japan's Buddhists at the 1893 World's Parliament of Religions* (2008), and the editor of *Studying Buddhism in Practice* (2012).

Victor Sōgen Hori, a former Buddhist monk, is an associate professor (retired) in Japanese Religion in the School of Religious Studies at McGill University and the author of *Zen Sand* (2003).

Alexander Soucy is a professor and chair of the Religious Studies Department at Saint Mary's University (Halifax) and the author of *The Buddha Side: Gender, Power, and Buddhist Practice in Vietnam* (2012).

Contributors

Mick Deneckere (PhD Cantab 2015) is Visiting Professor of Japanese Studies and a postdoctoral fellow of the Flanders Research Foundation (FWO) at Ghent University, Belgium. She is currently working on a book project tentatively titled *Buddhism and the Japanese Enlightenment: The Role of True Pure Land Buddhism in the Early Stages of Japan's Modernization*.

Jason W. M. Ellsworth is a doctoral candidate in social anthropology at Dalhousie University. Current and past research interests include the anthropology and sociology of religion, Buddhism in North America, food movements, political economy, marketing, transnationalism, orientalism, identity construction, and discourses on classification.

Ngar-sze Lau completed her MPhil (Oxford) in Social Anthropology and PhD (Lancaster) in Religious Studies. She has been studying the emergence of Theravāda meditation and mindfulness communities in contemporary China, Taiwan, and Hong Kong. She is now a full-time lecturer at the Education University of Hong Kong and affiliated to CUHK's Centre for the Study of Chan Buddhism and Human Civilization.

Jingjing Li received her doctorate from McGill University and is currently an assistant professor in the Institute for Philosophy at Leiden University. Her research interests include Yogācāra Buddhism, phenomenology, comparative philosophy, and the modernization of Buddhism and Confucianism in China.

David L. McMahan is the Charles A. Dana Professor of Religious Studies at Franklin and Marshall College in Pennsylvania. He is the author of *The Making of Buddhist Modernism* and *Empty Vision: Metaphor and Visionary Imagery in Mahāyāna Buddhism* and editor of *Buddhism, Meditation and Science* and *Buddhism in the Modern World*.

Douglas Ober (PhD UBC) is a research associate in the Centre for India and South Asia Research (CISAR) at the University of British Columbia. His interests include Buddhist modernity and Buddhism in colonial contexts. His writings have appeared in *Modern Asian Studies*, *Contemporary Buddhism*, *Himalaya*, and the *Journal of Buddhist Ethics*.

Paride Stortini is a doctoral candidate in the History of Religions at the University of Chicago. His main interests are Japanese Buddhism, Orientalism and the study of religion, transnational approaches to religion and modernity. In his current research, he is analyzing ideas and images of India in modern Japanese Buddhism, using a transnational perspective on the history of Buddhism in the late nineteenth and early twentieth centuries.

Lina Verchery is scheduled to receive her PhD in Buddhist Studies from Harvard University in May 2020 and is currently Visiting Assistant Professor of Religion at Union College. Her research considers issues in Buddhist ethics—questions of selfhood, agency, discipline, and community—through the study of modern Buddhist monastic life in China and throughout the Chinese diaspora. She is also an award-winning filmmaker.

Acknowledgments

We first wish to thank the Social Science and Humanities Research Council of Canada for funding our research project, "The Modernization of Buddhism in Global Perspective." In addition to funding research trips and conference travel, the SSHRC research project fund allowed us to organize a conference in 2016, "Buddhism in the Global Eye: Beyond East and West," with travel scholarships for graduate students to attend. The conference was held at the University of British Columbia hosted by the Robert H. N. Ho Family Foundation Program in Buddhism and Contemporary Society. We wish to thank Jessica L. Main, the director of the Program in Buddhism and Contemporary Society, for agreeing to co-sponsor the conference and for exercising on our behalf her formidable talent at organizing panels, managing conference logistics, and attending to the needs of conference participants. We would also like to thank the Robert H. N. Ho Family Foundation Program for providing the opportunity for such conferences to take place.

We would each like to thank our universities—University of Lethbridge for John Harding, McGill University for Victor Sōgen Hori, and Saint Mary's University for Alexander Soucy—for supporting our research project and for hosting research project meetings. In addition, Hori wishes to thank the Centre for Studies in Religion and Society (and Paul Bramadat, director) of the University of Victoria for allowing us to hold research project meetings on the University of Victoria campus.

Spelling Conventions

For romanization of Chinese, in general this volume uses the Pinyin system. However, there are several instances where the older Wade-Giles system may be used, for example, in personal names and in organizational titles. Throughout this book, we have tried to follow a policy of being faithful to the source. However, the editors also found it impossible to maintain a consistent policy on the use of diacritical marks. Scholars use Buddhist technical terms indicating pronunciation with diacritical marks, but practicing Buddhists use the same terminology usually without the diacritical marks. Complicating matters, many Buddhist terms have been accepted into the English language where they appear without diacritical marks. Depending on the subject matter, it may be appropriate for a particular scholar to use diacritical marks or to omit them. We try to follow whatever convention a Buddhist organization has accepted for itself. Names of well-known places are written without diacritical marks, thus, Kyoto not Kyōto, Tokyo not Tōkyō. Names of persons are written as the person himself or herself normally writes it or as normally appears on the person's publications, whatever the system of romanization and whatever the convention on diacritical marks and name order.

Introduction

John S. Harding, Victor Sōgen Hori, and Alexander Soucy

Within the academic discipline of Buddhist Studies today, a significant proportion of the research is focused on the relatively new subfield of modern Buddhism. But over the past decade, the content of the research on modern Buddhism has been changing. The first wave of writers included authors such as Lama Surya Das, Rick Fields, and James Coleman, who identified modern Buddhism with Western Buddhism. They focused their attention on the Buddhism that had been transplanted to the West and was starting to spread among native-born Westerners. The new Buddhism looked quite different from traditional Asian Buddhism. These authors made similar lists of the features that the new modern Buddhism would have. The new transplant Buddhism would display the features of Western culture: it would be democratic, egalitarian, lay-oriented, gender-neutral, socially engaged, and so on (Fields 1987; Lama Surya Das 1997; Coleman 2001). They also implied that this Westernized Buddhism was authentic Buddhism, the same as originally taught by the Buddha. Said Coleman, "Buddhism as refracted through the prism of late Western modernity certainly bears a family resemblance to all its Asian ancestors, but the most striking likeness is to the original 'Buddhism' Siddhartha Gautama first taught in India over two millennia ago" (Coleman 2001: 218). With this claim, we are confronted by a pernicious East-West binary trope that views the "new" Buddhism of the West (and of Westerners) as paradoxically more authentic than the Buddhism of Asia.

In his concept of Orientalism, Edward Said taught us how the West's fixed images and stereotypes about the Orient not only carry ideological import but also rationalize Western hegemonic control of Asia (Said 1978). The East-West binary trope is the most basic of those cultural stereotypes. The West is depicted as the motor force for progress and modernity while Asia, the East, is depicted as stuck in a retrograde tradition that stands in the way of progress. East and West are contrasted in numerous ways with the West almost always assumed to be more modern, rational, dynamic, organized, and active. As the Coleman example illustrates, even Buddhism transplanted a few decades in the West is portrayed as surpassing centuries of Buddhist tradition in Asia in terms of adhering to the original teachings of the Buddha.

The next wave of scholars has corrected this biased understanding by focusing their attention not on Buddhism transplanted to the West but on Buddhist modernization movements in Asian countries. These scholars are dissatisfied with the East-West binary trope, and they are seeking a better template for research. In a recent book, *The Invention of Religion in Japan*, Jason Josephson makes this stance explicit: "This book contests the narrative that understands modernity to be simply the product of

Euro-American culture exported to an imitative or passive 'Asia'" (Josephson 2012: 3). Erik Hammerstrom's book, *The Science of Chinese Buddhism*, takes a similar posture. He writes, "An older approach to studying Chinese-Western interactions viewed Chinese engagement with modern thought as a process of stimulus-response in which modernity and the West act and China and Chinese thinkers merely react. In this approach, it is imagined that modernity and elements of modern thought ... are foisted upon a passive subject who can only accept them" (Hammerstrom 2015: 5). Justin Ritzinger, in *Anarchy in the Pure Land*, calls this the "push" model of the modernizing process, and in his study of the Chinese reformist monk Taixu (太虛 1890–1947), he proposes "a pull model, one that approaches modernity as a source of attraction rather than compulsion" (Ritzinger 2017: 2–7). The title of this volume, *Buddhism in the Global Eye: Beyond East and West*, expresses our agreement with these scholars that the forms of Buddhism that we see today cannot be understood without taking a global perspective and that globalization, following Appadurai (1996), needs to be understood as consisting of flows that not only connect East and West but also bounce between nodes located around the world.

A global approach to Buddhism that we use in this volume acknowledges that because the idea of "religion" emerged from the European Age of Enlightenment, it takes Christianity as the ideal prototype (Beyer 2006: 70–71). In the fifteenth and sixteenth centuries, the European states sent forth sailing vessels to discover new resources in the Americas, Africa, and Asia. The discovery of new religions did not shake their faith in Christianity, which for them represented supreme truth. The West judged other world religions against the standard of Christianity and always found the other religions wanting. For any tradition that they categorized as "religion," Western scholars (and others) would measure in relation to the yardstick of Christianity: Is it monotheistic? Does it have a founder? Has it a sacred text or scripture? What is its code of ethics? Was it divinely revealed? These are the features that characterize Christianity. So, Hinduism and Shintō would be faulted for having too many gods and would lose additional points for having no founder. Confucianism would be considered inferior for not being divinely revealed. And so on.

A global approach to world religions recognizes the Western roots of the idea of religion and the impact that it had on non-Christian traditions as they reinvented their traditions as religions. This means that the global approach takes into account the role that secularism plays in framing religion as a distinct form of communication. Secularism was formulated as a way to make room for multiple faiths following the European wars of religion in the sixteenth to eighteenth centuries (Roetz 2013: 10–11). In some countries, like Germany and Austria, this view still informs public policy regarding religions, but in places like France and Quebec, *laïcité* (secularism) tends to connote more the prohibition of religion in state affairs and public spaces. Approaching Buddhism through a global lens takes into account the multiple discourses of secularism that form the local contexts of where Buddhism is lived. It pays attention to how Buddhism as a "world religion" has been variously constructed and the consequences of these ongoing restructurings.

A global approach interrogates "East" and "West." The East-West binary reifies and essentializes "East" and "West." Both need deconstruction, since they are not monolithic. They contain many lines of fracture, and spokespersons for East and West did not all speak with the same voice. For example, Asians had a difficult time understanding Christianity because while some colonial representatives declared it the pinnacle of civilization, others derided it as a collection of myths and superstitions. When we talk of the West, most of the time we are thinking of Western Europe and America despite the fact that Buddhists in Asia also encountered Russian ships and Karl Marx's communism. East and West as rhetorical constructions suggest that they are inert, but in fact they are constantly changing, since in space and history they are contextually dependent. European Sinophilia during the 1700s turned to Sinophobia during the 1800s. On a spherical globe, East and West are directions or lines of travel rather than fixed entities. As terms to categorize alleged cultural characteristics, Eastern and Western are even more variable and problematic.

A global approach recognizes Asian agency and takes into account both sides of the East-West encounter. A global approach sees Buddhism through a global eye, beyond East-West, aware of how the constructions of religion and secularity are co-constitutive, and perceives Asian agency as integral to dynamic transformations. Starting in the mid-1800s, Asian countries modernized under pressure from the advance of the colonial West. However, as part of this process of modernization, there was also Asian agency that strongly influenced the final outcome. For one thing, there were significant domestic tensions and diverse debates about how best to respond. In the early years of the Meiji Restoration (1868–1912), for example, the Japanese deliberately sent envoys to the advanced nations of the West to identify "best practices" with the intention of adopting them in Japan. In 1889, Japan promulgated its Constitution, laying out the structure of its government. Consistent with the Western concept of religion, the Japanese Constitution implemented freedom of religious belief and separation of religion and government. Despite the insertion of these elements of modern religion, the Japanese Constitution also resurrected the ancient emperor system as part of its system of government. The Emperor was said to be a sacred person, the direct descendant of Amaterasu Ōmikami, the goddess of the sun, in an unbroken line of descent. The Constitution reverted to the most ancient of Japan's mythical traditions. Despite this, or because of it, Japan's modernization was spectacularly successful. Japan was the first Asian country to defeat a modern Western power militarily. In 1905, Japan humiliated Russia in a dramatic sea battle that destroyed the Russian navy. This shows that the modernization of Asia is not a simple story of imposing Western cultural characteristics onto a passive Asian recipient. The decisions the Asian actors made reflect their own worldviews, agendas, and solutions to the problems they faced as they saw them. A global approach shows all sides of that encounter.

A global approach is not linear; it emphasizes nodes that radiate into networks extending in all directions. The lines of influence and communication run not only from West to East but also from East to West and East to East. Investigate the history of Europe's contact with Asia, and one will learn how in the reverse direction, at first it was Europe that changed in response to stimulus from the East. In the sixteenth and seventeenth centuries, the Jesuits sent back detailed descriptions of China, a culture that had a civilization older than that of the West. Chinese accounts of history challenged the authority of the Biblical account and caused Europeans to rethink their position in world history (Mungello 2005: 89).

The intra-Asian lines of communications and causality are important points to consider in understanding the development of Buddhism in the modern period. Asians traded information with other Asians and gave each other mutual support and ideas about the shape of Buddhism. The career of Yang Wenhui (楊文會 1837–1911), the father of the Chinese Buddhist reform, clearly displays the Asia-to-Asia network-node structure. Ngar-sze Lau, in this volume, describes how Yang Wenhui communicated with Nanjō Bunyū (南条文雄 1849–1927) and through him learned of the "modern" way of doing Buddhist Studies based on the close study of Pāli and Sanskrit texts as exemplified by Max Müller. Yang left behind several disciples, notably Taixu, who carried on his reforms. Taixu was hugely influential in the Buddhist reform movement in Vietnam (DeVido 2009). The Ceylonese Buddhist reformer Anāgārika Dharmapāla (1864–1933) spent an enormous amount of effort traveling around Asia (and the West) to get support for constructing Bodhgaya as the global center of Buddhism. In 1893, Anāgārika Dharmapāla met Yang to discuss cooperation about reviving Buddhism in India and spreading it throughout the world. Yang Wenhui did not spend his life facing West and waiting for instruction but instead created a network that spanned China, England, Japan, and Ceylon, and connected Max Müller, Nanjō Bunyū, and Anāgārika Dharmapāla.

The editors of this volume—John S. Harding (University of Lethbridge), Victor Sōgen Hori (McGill University), and Alexander Soucy (Saint Mary's University)—received a five-year Insight Grant from the Social Sciences and Humanities Research Council of Canada under the project title "The Modernization of Buddhism in Global Perspective" to reexamine modern Buddhism worldwide and dispel distortions caused by the East-West binary trope. In 2016, in collaboration with Jessica Main at the University of British Columbia (UBC), the three coinvestigators organized a conference "Buddhism in the Global Eye: Beyond East and West" designed to bring scholars together to map out a better paradigm for the modernization of Buddhism. This conference was instrumental for interrogating key themes, case studies, and global and modernist Buddhist developments addressed in this volume. In addition to the authors in this volume, Jessica Main, Richard Jaffe, Erik Hammerstrom, and a number of other scholars from North America, Europe, and Asia contributed to the lively and productive discussion held on the UBC campus. This book is not a conference proceeding, but it has benefited from the engagement and insights of many of the participants at that conference as well as from the proliferating scholarship on modern and global Buddhism in recent years.

Buddhism in the Global Eye is divided into three parts: World Religions, Global Flows, and Asian Agencies. The chapters on world religions track the evolution of the modern concept of religion, the recognition of Buddhism as a world religion, and some of the implications of this process as well as ongoing reconfigurations of Buddhism. They recognize that an essential element of modern religion is the codependent relationship with secularism. Victor Sōgen Hori, in his chapter "Buddhism and the Secular Conception of Religion," focuses on a single large-scale event: at the end of the nineteenth century, Buddhism became a world religion. He argues, in order for Buddhism to be recognized as a world religion, two things had to happen: Buddhism in Asian countries needed to modernize to conform to the new Western concept of religion, and the old premodern concept of religion in the West needed to modernize to accommodate non-Western, non-Christian religions, such as Buddhism. Modernization is revealed to be a two-way process in which Asia and the West mutually influence each other.

John Harding's chapter, "Mapping Buddhism beyond East and West," explores the utility and limitations of East and West for representing Buddhist developments. Examples range from early transmissions of the tradition in Asia to modernist Buddhism emerging in the late nineteenth century. He asserts that these terms functioned earlier as relatively simple indicators of direction and contextual symbols of identity but have become often misleading constructions. We need to look to global flows beyond these rhetorical notions of East and West because ultimately these binary terms correspond neither to a simple East-West division nor to actual and stable essentialized characteristics of Eastern and Western values, traits, and modes of thinking.

In his chapter "Buddhism and Global Secularisms," David L. McMahan skillfully summarizes the recent scholarship on the religious-secular binary emphasizing the diversity, fluidity, and constructedness of the categories of religious and secular. He then focuses attention on several examples of Buddhist secularity: S. N. Goenka's de-religioned meditation, meditation that has been secularized into stress reduction mindfulness, and Buddhism reconfigured in China and Tibet. The three very different examples show that secularization is not a uniform process.

Alexander Soucy's chapter, "Women and Vietnamese Buddhist Practice in the Shadow of Secularism," shows that the restructuring of Buddhism as a religion had unintended consequences. The Buddhist reform movement and the hegemonic secular state simultaneously created and tried to enforce new orthodoxies in a way that created distinctions between Buddhism and superstition. In the process, they marginalized women's Buddhist practices. Nonetheless, these practices have persisted in the face of official condemnation, because the new structures of Buddhism as a religion also unpredictably created space for subaltern women's practices that defied those orthodoxies.

Part Two, "Global Flows," tracks some of the lines of communication and causality behind the movement to modernize Buddhism. The East-West binary trope gives the impression that the lines run from the West to the East, that Western society provides the example, and that social pressure imposes the features of Western culture onto a passive Asian Buddhism. The three chapters in this part challenge that model.

Douglas Ober explores new areas of early transnational influence and dialogue between Buddhism and Marxist thought in "Socialism, Russia, and India's Revolutionary Dharma." By focusing on the global travels, politics, and intellectual crises of several of colonial India's most profound Buddhist thinkers, Ober maps the social and intellectual spaces of the Indian left in general and the transnational networks that Buddhists and Marxists shared in India, Russia, Tibet, and beyond during the first half of the twentieth century. In doing so, he identifies the central figures, social conditions, and discourses that made the Buddhist Marxist milieu so pervasive, and he demonstrates the creative synergy and influence that leftist orientations had in the reinvention of India's and, indeed, the world's modern Buddhism.

Jingjing Li, in her paper "D.T. Suzuki and the Chinese Search for Buddhist Modernism," argues that the movement to modernize Buddhism in China reflected not so much Western influence as historical China-Japan tensions. The case that she presents shows that the role played by D.T. Suzuki—the Japanese scholar credited with introducing Zen to the Western world—was not straightforward. While D.T. Suzuki argued for the superiority of Asian culture over Western culture, he also asserted the superiority of Japanese Buddhism and culture over their Chinese counterparts. Suzuki was at times criticized and at times admired by the Chinese, his reputation a barometer of ongoing China-Japan tensions.

Ngar-sze Lau, in her chapter, "Recent Emergence of Theravāda Meditation Communities in Contemporary China," brings the historical account up to date. Despite the fact that Chinese Buddhism has a long history of meditation practice, in Mainland China today a non-Chinese form of meditation—Theravāda meditation—is increasingly popular. Lau brings the reader's attention to a history, going back to the nineteenth century, of Chinese Buddhist reformers looking to the Theravāda tradition as a source of inspiration for revitalizing Buddhism in China. This has culminated in a recent trend toward engaging in Theravāda meditation practices in the PRC.

Taken together, these chapters show that the globalization of Buddhism has as much to do with intra-Asian transnational interactions as it does the transmissions of Euro-American ideas to Asia or Asian Buddhism to the West. That is, the flows of communication were global in nature. Asian Buddhists sought a variety of sources of inspiration and ideas for reforming Buddhism to confront the challenges of modernity and Orientalist discourses.

Part Three, "Asian Agencies," discusses the fact that in the modernization of Buddhism, the Asian reformers did not passively accept the Western example. They had their own points of view and agendas, which they actively pursued. The part begins with Mick Deneckere's chapter, "Shin Buddhism in Chōshū and Early Meiji Notions of Religion-State Relations." She challenges a widely accepted example of the Westernization narrative as applied to Japan. During the Meiji Period (1868–1912), Japanese officials argued about how to apply the Western concept of religion to Japan. Shimaji Mokurai wrote a document arguing for the separation of religion and state, a position often identified as secular and modern in the study of religion. Since he wrote this document while he was in Paris, it has often been assumed that his modern attitude to religion-state relations was influenced by Western ideas. But Deneckere argues that Shimaji Mokurai's attitude reflects not a French idea but his early experience in his home domain Chōshū, of relations between Buddhism and domain government. That is, his modern attitude was inspired not by the West but by Japanese historical precedent.

Paride Stortini's chapter, "Nanjō Bunyū's Sanskritization of Buddhist Studies in Modern Japan," explicitly takes up the issue of the agency of Asian Buddhists. Max Müller (1823–1900) was one of the Orientalist scholars who is credited with "inventing Buddhism" at the end of the 1800s. In the vision of the Orientalist scholars, true Buddhism was the original Buddhism taught by the Buddha before his teaching was corrupted by legend, mythology, and superstition. The Orientalist view dismissed all later Buddhism as corrupt, including the Mahāyāna Buddhism of China and Japan. The privileging of certain forms and dismissal of others also betrayed an anti-Catholic polemical bias carried out through the scholarship and evaluation of Buddhism (Almond 1988). Nanjō Bunyū was a monk of the Mahāyāna True Pure Land School of Japanese Buddhism, who was sent by his school to study with Müller at Oxford University in order to learn the modern philological methodology for studying Buddhism. Instead of passively absorbing Müller's bias against Mahāyāna Buddhism, however, Nanjō used his Western learning to reconceptualize Pure Land Buddhism as a modern universal religion.

Lina Verchery, in her chapter, "An Alternative to the 'Westernization' Paradigm and Buddhist Global Imaginaires," reverses the gaze of much post-Orientalist Buddhist Studies scholarship and considers how a Chinese Buddhist agent has appropriated "the West." To an extent, it could be said that the former hegemonic power of the West is no longer as predominant as it was and is now being reversed. Her study of the Dharma Realm Buddhist Association (DRBA) founded by the Master Hsuan Hua (1918–95) explores the idea of the "West" in the Chinese Buddhist imaginaire and shows that Chinese agents—like Hsuan Hua and his followers—have also been appropriating, redefining, and inventing new discursive categories for thinking of cultural difference.

Finally, Fu Chih (Bliss and Wisdom)—a Taiwanese Buddhist NGO in a Western context—is explored by Jason Ellsworth, in "Glocalization in Buddhist Food Ventures on a Small Canadian Island." On Prince Edward Island (P.E.I.), Canada, it has set up the Great Enlightenment Buddhist Institute Society (GEBIS) under the leadership of the female lay Master Zhen-Ru. GEBIS now operates two animal sanctuaries, a vegetarian restaurant, local charitable food programs, a grocery store in downtown Charlottetown, and an organic agriculture business. Local P.E.I. farmers benefit economically from the business that GEBIS activities generate. Under colonialism, the Western power went to Asia and exploited the local economy impoverishing the local people. In the case of GEBIS, it is the Asian power that has come to the West. Instead of impoverishing the local people, its business activities support the local economy.

Scholars in the subfield of modern Buddhism have moved the focus of contemporary research to the study of modernization movements in Asian countries. With their more global focus, they are challenging the East-West binary trope, which overhangs the field. Their studies challenge Western notions of modernity, which privilege the West. The next great question is, will the modernization of Asian Buddhism reject the hegemony of the West or will modernization subtly reimpose it? That is a good topic for another research project.

Part One

World Religions

One feature of modernity is that religion as a category came into existence. This process involved, in the first instance, distinguishing the religious from the secular. The religious involved human activities and thought that dealt with the other world, the supernatural, the numinous, salvation, and morality. The secular, on the other hand, was seen as the realm of human endeavor, focused on this world: politics, economics, and so on. Another major distinction that came about was the recognition that religion, as a category, grouped together cross-cultural phenomenon that dealt with these issues but in different ways.

The concept of "religion," or rather "the religious," in the premodern period referred almost entirely to Christian monastic life (Beyer 2006: 70–71; Calhoun, Juergensmeyer and VanAntwerpen 2011: 7–8). This meaning of "religious" still holds as one (though infrequently used) meaning of the word but has been expanded. As Christian kingdoms started to explore the unknown worlds, particularly Asia, they encountered and attempted to understand sophisticated systems of philosophy and practice (Mungello 2005: 77–106). As part of the Age of Enlightenment and the application of the burgeoning scientific process, they started to see beyond the myopic view of Christianity as the only religion. This entailed perceiving a range of phenomena that fit into a broad category of religion as well as the recognition that there were, in fact, several religions within this newly conceived category, of which Christianity was only one (Harrison 1990: 14).

The repercussions of this discovery, and the spread of this view to the people whom Western imperialists either subjugated or dominated in other ways, were that the traditions with which they came in contact started to assume this view and react to it. Beyer describes that these reactions were as diverse as the traditions themselves, and there was a multitude of voices within these traditions that responded to the emerging conceptual model of a unitary category called "religion," which comprised a number of religions. Hinduism was born out of this process, bringing together a dizzying mélange of beliefs, practices, ritual experts and so on, under a single label. The fit has always been an uncomfortable one, as anyone who has tried to teach a course on Hinduism will attest. Nonetheless, we see today that the process has brought into existence the notion of there being a Hinduism, so that overseas Indian communities regroup themselves in this way. The emergent models for mapping religious identity can entail distorting or damaging consequences. For example, these recently invented categories of religious identity have been the basis for an, at times, alarmingly violent Hindu nationalist movement in India.

Buddhism was similarly brought into existence by this process, as Hori surveys in this section. The Buddhist reformers in Asia in the late nineteenth and early twentieth centuries were particularly invested in restructuring Buddhism to position themselves favorably in this new category. Portraying Buddhism as a respectable world religion imparted a rational and modern validity that could usefully defend the tradition from domestic critics while also fending off the onslaught of Christian missionary campaigns. Harding explores some examples in the promotion of Buddhism while problematizing misleading constructions of East and West in the representation and spread of the tradition. McMahan's analysis of the similarly co-constitutive religious-secular binary elucidates a range of Buddhist reconfigurations including some that de-emphasize the religious tradition itself. The formative role of secularity informs all the studies in this section, from Hori's investigation of the origins of Buddhism as a world religion to Soucy's analysis of how Vietnamese women's practices resist new Buddhist orthodoxy, shaped by secular influence.

Throughout, the globalization of Buddhism is intertwined with the recognition of Buddhism as a world religion, its restructuring in relation to this modern category, and ongoing developments through which dynamic forms and select representations of Buddhism navigate shifting influences. The chapters in this part move from the origins of world religions to a variety of global Buddhist examples while challenging assumptions about East and West, engaging the interconnection between religion and secularism, and analyzing competing Buddhist practices and conceptions that construct new models of authority.

1

Buddhism and the Secular Conception of Religion

Victor Sōgen Hori

Discussions about the modernization of Buddhism immediately run into a problem. In Asia-related academic fields, there is an East-West binary trope at work that skews the discussion of modernization. This is the Orientalist stereotype (in Edward Said's sense) that depicts Asia as backward and the West as progressive. J. M. Hobson put it bluntly. In the study of economic development, he noted, "the West is generally thought to be the prime mover of the international system and of progressive economic development in the last 500 years while the East is demoted to the status of passive recipient of Western actions—whether these take the form of either Western largesse or exploitation" (Hobson 2005: 1). In this picture, to modernize is to Westernize.

In this chapter, I propose to set aside the East-West binary stereotype and instead view the modernization of Buddhism as a two-sided process in which both East and West mutually influence each other. "The West" is not a static entity (App 2010: xiii). The West, too, is constantly changing and evolving. In fact, it is evolving partly in response to stimulus from the East. Both East and West evolve in response to the other. Each side is "Other" to the other. This is a complicated story and to tell it, I suggest we focus on an example, the historical moment when Buddhism gained the rank of a "world religion." To make possible this new category of "world religion," the concept of "religion" itself had to modernize. If we track the evolution of the word "religion," we will see that the encounter with Asia helped Europeans modernize their conception of religion.

"Religion," "World Religion," Secularity

Before the advent of empirical science in the sixteenth century, "religion" in its premodern meaning referred to the adherents of Christianity, Mosaism, Mahometanism, and heathenism (App 2010: 101–2; Masuzawa 2005: xi). The four were not equals. When Western churchmen and scholars used the word "religion" in its premodern sense, they were thinking of Christianity convinced of its supremacy and its exclusive possession of truth. They made no strong distinction between "religion" and their own faith, which they took to be "true religion." "Religion," in effect, was a class with one member. Christianity in premodern Europe provided an entire world view that included a historical account of mankind, a geography of the then known physical world, and a revelation from God bespeaking its divine origin. Premodern religion was also closely associated with membership in an ethnic or national group. The conviction that one's group had the only true religion encouraged an attitude of intolerance toward other groups and their religious convictions. This was a time when a person could be imprisoned for avowing atheism or punished for holding heretical opinions. The bloody and brutal Thirty Years' War, 1618–48, testified to the viciousness of the fight over religious difference. This premodern conception of religion persisted into the modern period. Even in today's modern world, there are premodern voices, which equate "religion" with "true religion."

The modern concept of religion, on the other hand, is a product of powerful historical movements. In the early sixteenth century, the Reformation made a sweeping critique of the Roman Catholic Church's dogma, institutions, and social position. Protestants challenged the authority of the Pope and the intermediary role of priests. One relied instead on scripture and attained salvation through faith, not good works. Numerous Protestant groups emerged seeking freedom from both the Catholic Church and the state monarchs aligned with the church.

The Reformation overlapped with the scientific revolution. In the sixteenth century, Copernicus published his theory, which placed the sun, not the earth, at the center of the universe and thereby radically revised the European conception of the position of the human being in the universe. The revolution in science also created a methodology for making scientific discovery and redefined who had the authority to declare what is factual truth.

The eighteenth-century Enlightenment continued these developments. In the Enlightenment, Europeans idealized the rational and the natural. Human beings endowed with the power of reason did not need to rely on divine revelation and felt no necessity to invoke a supernatural being who created the universe. Rationality promised a way of seeing the world free of religious and political strife. The power of reason was natural, part of the original endowment of all human beings everywhere. People came to understand religion as a natural faculty of the human being, not a divine revelation given to humans by God. This implied that the term "religion" could be used in a plural sense and that religion could be understood as a general class with many particular religions.

Secularity is an essential part of the modern concept of religion. The word "secular," however, can be used with different meanings. "Secular" sometimes indicates the complete absence of religion. For example, the secularization thesis claims that as societies modernize, they become more rational and less religious, until religion atrophies and disappears altogether. So too, when people advocate the secular separation of church and state, they mean that there should be no element of religion influencing the government of the state. The weakness of this interpretation of "secular" is that it is as totalistic and exclusive as the concept of religion it claims to modify. Just as premodern "religion" was associated with Christianity's claim to exclusive possession of religious truth, so also this hard interpretation of "secular" seeks for the total exclusion of religion. The two, "religion" and "secular," share an extremist fervor, both seeking to claim exclusive possession of truth.

There is, however, a softer understanding of "secular." In this meaning, "secular" indicates the presence of religion but under a system of rights and regulation, which protects and regulates the expression of religious opinion. According to Roetz, this is what George Holyoake (1817–1906) meant when he first coined the term "secularism." The secularist project is not "primarily a program of fighting religion ... [but] rather a struggle for a system of rights that would allow the free expression of all ... opinions" (Roetz 2013: 10–11). The modern concept of religion contains the element of secularity understood as the fair and open regulation of religious expression. In this chapter, we understand the secular to be that zone where a religion gives up its claim to exclusive possession of truth and concedes a place for the "Other."

Starting in the fifteenth century, explorer ships set out from Europe to Africa, Asia, and the newly "discovered" Americas. The encounter with the Other in foreign cultures caused Europeans to question their own heritage especially when they examined cultures, such as China, which claimed to be just as ancient and civilized as the West. The East-West binary typically emphasizes how the West influenced Asia. However, Asia also influenced the West. Europe imported both material goods and philosophical ideas from Asia. The impact of the foreign Other on Europe was so strong that some scholars call the European Enlightenment "an intercultural phenomenon" (Roetz 2013: 12–13).

Tolerance for other religions was not always the case. In the beginning, the European Christians looked down upon "heathen" religion as primitive savagery and felt confirmed in their belief in the unique truth of Christianity (Hunt, Jacob and Mijnhardt 2010: 1–20). But where most Europeans emphasized their difference from the strange peoples of foreign lands, some few Europeans were impressed by the apparently universal presence of religion in these foreign lands, primitive though it may have been. In 1723–37, Jean Frederic Bernard and Bernard Picart published *Cérémonies et coutumes religieuses de tous les peuples du monde* (Religious Ceremonies and Customs of All Peoples of the World). This tome has been called "the book that changed Europe" because of its great influence in altering European attitudes to religions other than Christianity (Hunt, Jacob and Mijnhardt 2010). Bernard's opening essay "Dissertation sur le culte religieux" did not distinguish between true and false religion. Under religion, it included every kind of worship (Hunt, Jacob and Mijnhardt 2010: 15–16). Picart's illustrations emphasized what the savage foreign peoples shared with civilized Europe, not what made them different. He put together Inca sun worshippers with Catholics in procession, a Jewish synagogue with a Buddhist temple. The "analogies could only be unsettling to those accustomed to thinking of their own religion, or Christianity, or monotheistic religions more generally, as superior in their difference and separateness" (Hunt, Jacob and Mijnhardt 2010: 156). The book sowed the radical idea that religions could be compared on equal terms and that all religions were equally worthy of respect and equally open to criticism (Hunt, Jacob and Mijnhardt 2010: 1). The tolerant and respectful attitude toward other religions would develop centuries later into a modern conception of religion.

The Jesuits in China

In the mid-1500s, priests of the Society of Jesus—the Jesuits—began missionary work in Asia, intending to convert its peoples to Christianity. The Jesuits' mission in Japan was shut down by the Japanese shōgunate government in the early 1600s, but the Jesuits' China mission continued into the nineteenth century. A short study of the Jesuits' China mission is extremely informative for several reasons. First, we see how knowledge of the East came to the West, how the Jesuits provided contemporary Europe with a stream of information about an Other culture, and how Europe responded. Second, in the Jesuit policy of cultural accommodation, we see Jesuit attempts to define secularity before the term "secular" had been created. Third, the Jesuits taught Europe about Confucius. We see that different European groups appropriated the figure of Confucius for quite different political reasons.

Not in the Bible

Through their translations and writings, the Jesuits created a place for China in the European worldview. The Jesuits made the serious study of local language an integral part of their missionary effort in foreign countries. They created in-house Latin translations of Chinese texts, the Confucian Four Books—*The Analects of Confucius, Great Learning, Doctrine of the Mean,* and *Mencius*. They used these translations as language textbooks for teaching missionary priests newly arrived in Asia. Over the years, these translations were revised and improved until finally they were taken to Europe and published in 1687 as *Confucius Sinarum Philosophus* (Confucius, Philosopher of the Chinese) (Mungello 2005: 82). The book contained a biographical essay, "The Life of Confucius," and Latin translations of the Confucian *Analects, The Great Learning* and *The Doctrine of the Mean*. Translated again from Latin into the languages of Europe, the tome became a philosophical sourcebook for Europeans allowing them direct access to Chinese Confucian philosophical thought.

Europe learned about China on several fronts. The Jesuit priest Martino Martini published a detailed atlas of China in 1685. Other Jesuits produced books, translations, maps, essays, and letters. Although he himself had not been to China, the Jesuit priest Jean-Baptiste du Halde (1674–1743) collated missionary reports written by other Jesuits and created the 1735 four-volume *Description Geographique, Historique, Chronologique, Politique, et Physique de l'Empire de la Chine et de la Tartarie Chinoise* (Jones 2001: 18–19). This became the standard reference work on China.

This newly acquired knowledge of China challenged the European worldview based on the Bible. In 1650 to 1654 in London, the Anglican archbishop James Ussher published a chronology of the Christian world based on Biblical sources. According to this chronology, God completed his creation in 4004 BC and the Noachian flood took place in 2349 BC (Mungello 2005: 89). The Italian Jesuit priest Martino Martini (1614–61) entered China in 1643 and immersed himself in Chinese historical and geographical documents. In 1658, he published a chronology of the world based on Chinese sources (Mungello 2005: 89). The historical record in Chinese scholarship started 2,697 years before Christ significantly preceding the Christian account (Jones 2001: 14). The publication of the Chinese histories set off excited speculation among European scholars. Was the Chinese historical record more accurate than Biblical history? Were the Chinese people unrelated to the sons of Noah? Was Chinese the language spoken by people before the flood? And so on (Jones 2001: 15). In dramatic fashion, the discovery of the Chinese historical record caused Europeans to question their understanding of themselves and the authority of the Bible.

Cultural Accommodation

As a strategy for missionizing, the Jesuits advocated cultural accommodation with the Chinese. Rather than expect the Chinese to learn Western language and culture, the Jesuits took it upon themselves to learn the Chinese language, wear the Chinese literati's robes, and in general attempt to accommodate themselves to Chinese culture (Mungello 2005: 17). The policy of accommodation meant that the Jesuits had to make many difficult choices about what was acceptable to Christian doctrine and what was not (Mungello 2005: 17). Surprisingly, the Jesuits declared that Confucianism was consistent with Christianity.

Confucianism was the ideology of the literati class. The Chinese government bureaucracy was staffed by scholar-officials, literati who had successfully passed the rigorous imperial examination system. The Jesuits had sympathy for the literati as they were similar to themselves in terms of education, social standing, and moral cultivation (Mungello 2005: 82). The Jesuits had to get European support for their strategy of accommodation, and thus they presented Chinese Confucianism in a highly favorable light and at the same time depicted Buddhism and Daoism disparagingly as gross superstitions (Mungello 2005: 47, 82). In the Jesuit account, the imperial court and the literati scholar-officials followed the rule of reason, worshipped heaven, and practiced Confucian morality (Jones 2001: 17). Confucianism, they said, was primarily an ethical system meant for the moral cultivation of human beings, not a religion concerned with spirits and the afterworld (Mungello 2005: 47). The Jesuit priest Matteo Ricci (1552–1610), one of the chief architects of cultural accommodation, distinguished early Confucianism prior to 220 CE (the end of the Han dynasty) from revived Confucianism after 960 CE (the Song dynasty), and he much favored early Confucianism. Early Confucianism was portrayed as a pure monotheistic reverence for Heaven, untainted by Buddhism imported from India (Mungello 2005: 97). Thus, the Jesuits argued that the religiosity inherent in early Confucianism—a monotheistic natural religion—remained undeveloped, and this fact meant that early Confucianism could be paired with Christianity. Specifically, Chinese Confucianism lacked the element of divine revelation, precisely the element that Christianity could provide (Mungello 2005: 83). Thus, in proselytizing among the Chinese, the Jesuits could tell the Chinese that in accepting Christianity, they were not accepting a totally foreign religion; they were bringing to completion the religion undeveloped and implicit in early Chinese Confucianism. And to their European audience, they could claim that early Confucianism was not a pagan heathenism but an early stage natural religion, which could be nurtured to conform to Christianity (Jones 2001: 18).

The missionary tactic of cultural accommodation led to what is called the Chinese Rites Controversy. The Jesuits claimed that Chinese Christians could still continue to perform ancestor rituals and rituals honoring Confucius since these rituals were not religious in nature; they were merely cultural custom, nothing more than moral or civic ritual (Jones 2001: 18–19). However, the Dominicans, another Catholic order also doing missionary work in China, claimed that Chinese ancestor rituals were indeed religious; they were idolatrous and inconsistent with Christianity. The Dominicans took their disagreement to the Roman Curia, which after many decades decided against the Jesuits. The Jesuit interpretation of Confucianism was refuted, and cultural accommodation as a strategy for missionizing was rejected by papal decrees in 1704, 1715, and 1742 (Mungello 2005: 84).

Looking back on this controversy, we can see that the Jesuits were at this early stage arguing for a kind of secularity. Although the Jesuits never gave up their conviction in the supremacy of Christianity, they did preach respect and tolerance for Confucianism. But the Jesuits did not have the concept of secularity to express this viewpoint. The Jesuit position in the Rites Controversy was defended by the philosopher Leibniz who in 1700 wrote a treatise entitled *De cultu Confucii civili* (The civil cult of Confucius), which presented the argument that the cult of Confucius was not a religious cult but a civil or state cult (Lach 1945: 447–48). Europeans in the year 1700 did not have the concept of the secular and so used other concepts such as civil cult to indicate an area that was not the exclusive possession of a single religion.

Confucius in Europe

In the sixteenth and seventeenth centuries, Confucius became a well-known respected figure in Europe. The 1687 Jesuit text *Confucius Sinarum Philosophus* (Confucius, Philosopher of the Chinese) contained an illustration showing Confucius wearing literati robes and standing in a library. It depicted him as a human being, a "most wise master of moral philosophy" (Jones 2001: 19) and not as a religious leader or divine person (Mungello 2005: 82). As Knud Lundbaek notes, "Written in Latin it was accessible to all educated persons in Europe. Widely read and commented upon in the contemporary learned periodicals, it started the first Western wave of enthusiasm for the wisdom of Confucius, a wave that was to last for nearly a century" (1983: 19). The Journal of Savants published a review of the *Confucius Sinarum Philosophus* in which the reviewer expressed his admiration, "Apart from motive I do not see that the charity of the Chinese is different from that of Christians, so true it is that God has put even into the minds of Infidels enlightenment (*lumières*) leading them to virtues which, as far as exterior acts are concerned, are in no wise different from Christian virtues" (quoted in Rowbotham 1945: 227). The philosopher Wilhelm Leibniz (1646–1716) was even more fulsome in his praise. In his 1697 treatise, *Novissima Sinica* (The Latest News of China), he wrote that although in the contemplative sciences Europe surpassed China, in technology they were equals and in practical philosophy China surpassed Europe. He advocated the reciprocal exchange of missionaries wherein Christian missionaries would teach revealed religion to the Chinese and the Chinese would teach Europeans the practice of natural religion (Mungello 2005: 90–91; Lach 1945: 440–41).

The wave of enthusiasm for Confucius spread to include all things Chinese. Europeans drank Chinese tea and wore Chinese silk clothing. The word "china" became synonymous with fine porcelain. In European art and design, China-inspired themes became so common that the word *chinoiserie* was coined to refer to them (Mungello 2005: 99). Although there were critics of the enthusiasm for China, the European attitude to Chinese culture was mostly laudatory. A sign of approval—during this early period, the seventeenth century, European writings frequently referred to the Chinese people as white in skin color (Mungello 2005: 123; Kowner and Demel 2013: 47–48).

But then came the eighteenth century and with it the turmoil of the European Enlightenment. A second wave of enthusiasm for Confucius in Europe ran until about 1800 promoted by a quite different group of actors. In the first wave, the Jesuits, as part of their strategy of missionizing through cultural accommodation, claimed that early Confucianism was compatible with Christianity. The Jesuits were clearly Christian partisans. In the second wave, some Enlightenment thinkers, like Voltaire (1694-1778), saw in Confucianism a similarity with the ideals of the European Enlightenment. These thinkers were anti-Christian partisans. They sought to replace irrational Christianity with rational religion, and they held up Confucianism as an example of such rational religion (App 2010: 61). On another front, the German philosopher Christian Wolff (1679-1754) gave a controversial lecture in 1721 praising the Chinese practical philosophy as a rational ethic, which confirmed the radical claim that it was possible to have morality without Christian religion (Mungello 2005: 117-18). During the sixteenth and seventeenth centuries, the Jesuits considered Confucianism to be Christianity's local partner in missionizing in China. But during the eighteenth century, Confucianism was brandished by the Enlightenment thinkers as a weapon in their fight against what they considered a superstitious and brutal Christianity.

The Tide Turns

If one sees the Western concept of religion against its history, one can see that over three centuries the European conception of religion changed and the change was in part stimulated by its discovery of Asian religion. The Chinese historical texts raised numerous questions that challenged the authenticity of the Bible. In addition, knowledge of the Chinese Other provided an imaginary screen on which Europeans projected their ideas of good society, correct government, ideal rulers, and true religion. European imaginary thinking about China constituted a kind of philosophical thought experiment testing to see which hypotheses worked and which did not. During this early period, one can see an East-West binary trope in operation, but one that privileged the East over the West. In the beginning, it is the Chinese who are assumed to be more rational, ethical, and civilized, not the Europeans.

By 1800, the first great encounter between Europe and China was over (Mungello 2005: 130). The European love affair with the East had come to an end. A second great encounter between East and West was building, and this time the confrontation would happen on Asian ground. From the latter half of the 1700s in Europe, increasingly Sinophilia turned to Sinophobia. Now China was depicted as a stagnant and despotic society lacking life and incapable of change, an "embalmed mummy" (Zhang 2008: 98). A sign of this new attitude was the newly created theory of race. In the 1800s, ideas about race coalesced into a "scientific" theory, which divided the people of the world into a hierarchy of four or five races. Where once the Chinese and Japanese had been classed as white, after 1800 they were classed as yellow and positioned as inferior to the European white race, which was placed at the top of the hierarchy (Kowner and Demel 2013: 22).

Many of the nations of Europe had powerful navies for centuries. Enhanced industrial and military power now allowed those countries to create colonial empires in America, Africa, and Asia. Massive trading companies controlled great areas where they exported local resources, exploited the local populations, and functioned as the virtual government.

The Opium Wars were symptomatic of the new relationship between East and West. China sold vast quantities of tea, silk, and porcelain to the West, for which the Western powers paid in Mexican silver dollars, the standard international currency at the time. The problem for the Western powers was that while China exported goods to the West, it did not import anything. This meant that the flow of silver only went one way, to China, making international trade difficult. The Western powers needed to find some Western commodity that China wanted to import. They found that Western commodity in opium. The British East India Company had cultivated opium in India for more than a century. The British sold their opium to traders who transported the opium up the coast to Canton in southern China and smuggled it into the country. The Qing emperor issued edicts forbidding trafficking in opium but to no avail. Opium addiction among the Chinese continued to increase, and opium smuggling continued to boom. "Opium . . . flowed freely from all of India to Canton, and by 1836, total imports came to $18 million, making it the world's most valuable single commodity trade of the nineteenth century" (Wakeman 1978: 172).

In 1839, the Qing emperor confiscated the opium that the foreign traders were smuggling into the country and incinerated it. Britain responded with warships whose cannonfire destroyed the Chinese navy and coastal defenses. Britain fought the First Opium War from 1839 to 1842. The Second Opium War was fought from 1856 to 1860, with France involved. In the treaties that ended these wars, China was forced to pay large cash indemnities, cede the island of Hong Kong, open five ports for trade, and concede extraterritoriality for Westerners (Wakeman 1978: 212). The treaties, called "unequal treaties" by the Chinese, introduced "a century of national humiliation" (百年國恥).

The Opium Wars in China set the historical stage for the opening of Japan to the West. Japan had had a policy of national isolation for more than two centuries. But in 1853—eleven years after the First Opium War and three years before the Second, Commodore Matthew Perry of the United States sailed his "black ships" into Uraga Bay, threatening to bombard the capital if the Japanese government refused to enter into diplomatic negotiations to open the country to trade. The shōgun government acquiesced and signed the Convention of Kanagawa in 1854, the first of Japan's "unequal treaties." In short order, Japan was forced to sign similar unequal treaties with the other Western powers—the United States and Britain in 1854, Netherlands, Russia, and France in 1858, Prussia in 1861, and the Austro-Hungarian Empire and Spain in 1868.[1] The unequal treaties symbolized the subjugation of Japan to the Western powers.

At the end of the nineteenth century, to structure international diplomacy, the European powers had created a typology of nation-states, which classified them into ranks: "civilized," "barbarous," and "savage" (Lorimer 1893: 101). Japan was classed as "barbarous." The treaties stipulated that citizens of a "civilized" state had the right of extraterritoriality in a "barbarous" state (Lorimer 1893: 217). If a Westerner committed an act considered criminal by Japanese law, the Japanese police could not arrest that Westerner and try him in a local court. Extraterritoriality meant that the Westerner was subject only to Western law, not Japanese law. The Japanese considered this a national dishonor.

The four religions, the four/five races, the three ranks of nation-states—by these hierarchies, the Western nation-states ordered their relations with the peoples of the East and the world at large. Western powers placed themselves at the highest rank of these hierarchies and the other countries of the world all at various levels of inferior rank. It is in this context that the East-West binary trope came to privilege the West.

Japan Reconstructs "Religion"

Japan was the first state in East Asia to modernize. 1868 marks the first year of the Meiji Restoration, the beginning of Japan's modern period. The Japanese explicitly set out to copy and adapt Western institutions and practices. At first glance, Japan seems to be a model case study exemplifying the principle that to modernize is to Westernize. But a second glance reveals more.

The new Meiji government sent observers to the nations of the West in a systematic effort to identify and adopt the best practices then current. The most prominent of these missions was the Iwakura Embassy sent to the United States, Britain, Europe, and the Middle East in 1871 to 1873 (Nish 1998). Among other investigations, these observers saw Western religion in its home setting, and their reports intensified a vigorous debate then current in Japan about what "religion" meant in the West, what could be classified as religion in Japan, how much freedom it should be allowed, whether Japan should adopt Christianity as a national religion, and what Japanese word should be used to translate "religion" (Josephson 2012: 196–218; Maxey 2014: 95–108). The debate about what Westerners called "religion" had got started a few years earlier in the 1850s during the treaty negotiations. The Western powers had demanded the opening of the country to foreign trade, extraterritorial protection for its citizens, and "freedom of religion." The problem was that the Japanese did not have the Western concept of religion and the translators for the treaty negotiations struggled to find a word in the Japanese language to translate "religion." In the Meiji era, eventually the Japanese settled on the term *shūkyō* 宗教, (lit. "teaching of the sect"), an old Buddhist term, redefined to correspond to the Western concept of "religion" (Josephson 2012: 189, 199–200, 219, 236–37; Krämer 2015: 4–8, 43–45; Maxey 2014: 7–9, 232–33). The debates about religion continued for several decades until 1889 when the Japanese government promulgated a constitution that defined the structure of its government.

The Meiji Constitution applied the modern Western notion of "religion" to Japanese society, but the result was not a simple imitation of the West. Ironically, the 1889 Japanese Constitution resurrected the mythology of the emperor of Japan who was said to be the direct descendant of Amaterasu Ōmikami, the goddess of the sun. The modernization movement in Japan reinstated the most ancient of premodern Japanese traditions (Josephson 2012: 95).

The Japanese writers of the 1889 Constitution made many decisions about religion, which showed how well they had done their homework studying what "religion" meant in the West. The text that appeared in the Constitution, however, was just the tip of the iceberg compared to the long and involved complex arguments beneath the surface. Article 28 of the Meiji Constitution said, "Japanese subjects, within limits not prejudicial to peace and order and not antagonistic to their duties as subjects, have freedom of religious belief" (Itō 2003-4). The text is significant for what it says and what it does not say explicitly.

Japanese subjects have "freedom of religious belief." "Belief"—this means that religion is private to each individual person. Here the Constitution writers were influenced by Protestant Christianity, which was taken as archetype of modern religion (Maxey 2014: 56; Krämer 2013: 201).[2] The Constitution's "freedom of religious belief" silently implies that religion does not essentially need the mediation of priest or church. But the guarantee of religious freedom is limited. Religion must be "not prejudicial to peace and order and not antagonistic to their duties as subjects" (Itō 2003-4). This means that while subjects have freedom of private religious belief, the state can control any public expression of it (Josephson 2012: 226–35). The public/private line corresponds to the state/religion line, and the Constitution asserts the authority of the state over religion. Although it did not use the language of secularity, the 1889 Constitution thus defined Japan as a secular state.

What did the Constitution not say? The Constitution did not affirm Christianity as the national religion of Japan. This option was considered and rejected by the Meiji politicians. In the early 1600s, the Tokugawa government had expelled all Christian missionaries and prohibited proselytizing on behalf of Christianity. For more than two centuries, Japan had followed a policy of national isolation designed to keep out foreign influence, especially Christianity. But the members of the Iwakura Mission reported that in the West, Christianity was considered the peak of civilization and that Japan would never be accepted as a civilized nation until it gave up its prohibition of Christianity (Maxey 2014: 160, 164–65). In addition, the members of the Iwakura Embassy observed the tension in Western countries between religious bodies and the state. This strengthened their conviction that the Japanese state should be clearly beyond the reach of religion (Maxey 2014: 81). Thus, the Japanese state would allow religion, even Christianity, but the state would be secular.

The Japanese were impressed by Christianity's power to convert people. They had seen how Christianity in Western countries instilled religious fervor and intense loyalty among followers. Under the Tokugawa, the nation of Japan consisted of a collection of semiautonomous feudal domains. Ordinary people identified themselves as members of their domain and not as citizens of the nation of Japan. In addition, Japan had just fought a civil war and was left a fragmented nation. The Meiji politicians wanted religion to do for Japan what Christianity was thought to do for the Western countries—through conversion, instill a sense of national identity and create a culture of unity and loyalty (Maxey 2014: 20–22). But the Meiji politicians also feared Christianity. If they accepted Christianity as the national religion of Japan, they feared Japan would lose its sovereignty to the West. Thus, the Meiji politicians chose not to make Christianity the national religion of Japan.

The Constitution similarly did not affirm Buddhism as the national religion of Japan. Buddhism had been in the country for more than a thousand years and had become thoroughly adapted to Japanese culture. But Buddhism in Japan was fragmented into numerous sects that were given to petty quarreling with each other (Maxey 2014: 202). Buddhism was accused of having become stagnant, an archaic provider of funerals and memorial services rather than an integral part of a modernizing nation. During the Tokugawa period, to prevent people from converting to Christianity, the government monitored the populace by forcing all families to register with their local Buddhist temple. In 1868, in a short-lived persecution, pent-up anger at the Buddhist establishment caused the destruction of many temples. Then too, Buddhism needed modernizing. Many practices conducted under the name of Buddhism—faith healing, divination, casting spells, communicating with the dead, and so on—counted as "superstition" and were unacceptable in the new age of science and rationality.

The interesting case is Shintō. The Constitution did not declare Shintō the national religion of Japan. This statement may be contentious. The popular perception assumes that the Meiji Constitution established State Shintō (*kokka shintō*)—more colloquially, "emperor worship"—as the national religion of Japan. This is not (quite) correct. First of all, the term "Shintō" needs definition. One part of Shintō—the folk rituals and worship of *kami*, the local shrines devoted to ancestor worship, the taboos about purity—was called "shrine Shintō" (*jinja shintō*). But in comparison with the religion of the Western countries, *jinja shintō* was found wanting. For example, Christianity had a founder, a sacred text, and an ethical code while Shintō had none of these. Shintō seemed to be a primitive polytheistic animism with little substance. But another part of Shintō, called "State Shintō" (*kokka shintō*)—the belief in the divine emperor, descendant of Amaterasu Ōmikami, the sun goddess in an unbroken lineage of imperial succession—was national teaching, essential to Japan's identity as a nation, and far too important to be classed together with mere religion. For a citizen of Japan, allegiance to the national teaching was a civic obligation and a public commitment. Thus, many voices asserted, "Shintō is not a religion" (Josephson 2012: 129).

In accordance with the best practices observed in Western countries, the Meiji reformers on the one hand wanted to establish "the constitutional separation of state and religion" (*seikyō bunri* 政教分離) (Maxey 2014: 105), to prevent religious organizations with their sectarian agendas from interfering with government. At the same time, they envisioned Japan as a country spiritually united under the emperor, the direct descendant of Amaterasu Ōmikami, the sun goddess. This vision would in other cultures ordinarily be considered religion, "emperor worship," but in the Japanese context it was not a matter of private belief and therefore it was not considered religion. It was national teaching, and since national teaching was not private religion, the government could require schools to teach it. Thus, schools taught that the emperor was a living *kami* and practiced rituals with their children designed to inculcate obedience and loyalty.

The Japanese case teaches an important lesson about secularity. The Meiji Constitution implicitly drew a line between the religious and the secular. The imperial institution fell not in the religious half but into the secular half. Secular national teaching became the functional equivalent of a national religion. This shows that secularity can be just as ideologically charged as religion.

Original Buddhism

The West started to learn about Buddhism about the same time it first learned about Confucius. The famous *Confucius Sinarum Philosophus* of 1687 contained a 106-page introduction by the Jesuit priest Philippe Couplet (1623–93), which included several pages that summarized what the Jesuits in Asia had learned about *Foe Kiao* (Ch. *Fojiao* 佛教, i.e., Buddhism) since their arrival in Japan in 1549 (App 2010: 124). Gleaned mainly from Japanese and Chinese sources, the Introduction contained information about the history, texts, geographical presence, and teaching of Buddhism as well as a biography of the founder (App 2010: 124). At the end of the seventeenth century, two more books appeared with significant information about Buddhism, Louis Daniel Lecomte's *Nouveaux memoires sur l'état present de la Chine* (1696) and Charles Le Gobien's *Histoire de l'édit de l'empereur de la Chine* (1698). In 1727, Engelbert Kaempfer published *Heutiges Japan* (Japan Today), with detailed descriptions and illustrations of things from flowers and plants to social customs and the religious landscape of Japan. A century later, in 1817, Michel-Jean-François Ozeray published *Recherches sur Buddou*, the first Western book on Buddhism (Ozeray 2017). These writings on Buddhism alarmed the Europeans. First, the publications documented the vast geographical spread of Buddhism and the sheer size of its body of adherents, many hundreds of millions of believers. Did Buddhists outnumber Christians (App 2014: 148; Ozeray 2017: 287–99)? Second, the resemblance of Buddhism to Christianity was troubling. Jesuit reports of Buddhism in Japan, for example, described a religious culture similar to that of Christian Europe. "It featured monks and nuns, monasteries and bells, rosaries and sermons, sects and sacred texts, baptisms and funerals, processions and temple services, and even heaven and hell" (App 2010: 9–10). Could this be the work of the devil (Almond 1988: 124; Josephson 2012: 62)?

In the last quarter of the 1800s, just as there were Japanese who were arguing that Shintō is not a religion, there were also Europeans who were arguing that Buddhism is not a religion. These Europeans were the first Orientalist scholars: Western academics like Eugène Burnouf (1801–52), T. W. Rhys Davids (1843–1922), Caroline Rhys Davids (1857–1942), and Max Müller (1823–1900). All were philologists who read early Buddhist texts written in Pāli, Sanskrit, and other classical languages. Burnouf is credited with writing the first Western language history of Buddhism. T. W. Rhys Davids and his wife Caroline founded the Pāli Text Society in 1881 and published translations of the entire Pāli Canon, along with concordances, dictionaries, histories, and commentaries. Max Müller was general editor of the fifty-volume *Sacred Books of the East* series. Müller is often cited as the founder of *Religionswissenschaft*, the academic study of religion. These, the first generation of academic Buddhist Studies scholars, were so influential in imposing their particular ideas about Buddhism that it has been said they "invented Buddhism as a world religion" (McMahan 2012c: 14).

How did the Orientalist scholars conceive of Buddhism? First, they distinguished between the Buddha, a teacher whom they respected highly, and Buddhism, a religion that they criticized as debased. Consistent with a rational science conception of religion, they conceived of the Buddha as a this-world human being and not as a divine being. He was also "the Luther of Asia" opposing the corruption of institutional religion and the injustice of the caste system (Lopez 2008: 5; Almond 1988: 73). The teaching of the Buddha was rational. It required no supernatural God who created the universe nor wrathful God to punish the sinful. But the Orientalist scholars distinguished between this teaching, which they found in the earliest Pāli texts and called "original Buddhism," and later Buddhism, which they said had been corrupted by ignorant monks in later generations. Later Buddhism had degenerated into mere religion. Degenerate Buddhism included all of the Mahāyāna Buddhism of East Asia, all tantric Buddhism, and all forms of Buddhism that were then being practiced by Asians. The scholars considered "Lamaism" particularly degenerate, "the exact contrary of the earlier Buddhism" (Rhys Davids 1907: 208). Critics of the Roman Catholic Church noted the similarity between it and degenerate Mahāyāna Buddhism (Almond 1988: 123–25).

In their claim that pure "original Buddhism" had degenerated into mere religion, the Orientalist academic scholars were evincing the scientific rationalism of modernity, using it as the criterion to distinguish between authentic religion and inauthentic religion. Inauthentic religion—such as Mahāyāna Buddhism and Roman Catholicism (Rhy Davids 1891: 192–94)—believed in supernatural beings and superstitions, while authentic religion, such as "original Buddhism," was consistent with rational science. This is the attitude of the European Enlightenment. Religion should be rational and consistent with science, grounded in philosophy and ethics, eschew faith and ritual, and be tolerant of other religions. The Orientalist scholars were convinced that Original Buddhism was an example of religion in the modern Enlightenment sense.

Buddhism, the World Religion

When did Buddhism become a world religion? To see the term "world religion" being used in its modern secular meaning, we need to fast-forward to the 1870s, which sees the beginning of *Religionswissenschaft*, or the modern science of religion (Masuzawa 2005: 107). Masuzawa tells us that the term "'world religions' makes its appearance without ceremony, without explanation, and seemingly without a history" (Masuzawa 2005: 11). Nevertheless, we look for some marker event that exemplifies the meaning of the new term "world religion." When Max Müller, for example, picked out those religions that had a canonical text, he created a list—Brahmanism, Buddhism, Zoroastrianism, Mosaism, Christianity, Mohammedanism, and the traditions of Confucius and Lao-tse—that looks like an early list of world religions (Müller 1872: 30). Müller encouraged the comparative study of religion saying "He who knows one religion knows none" (Müller 1872: 11), a slogan that presupposes that the term "religion" can be used in the plural, that "religion" is a general term with several particular instances. Does this event illustrate "world religion" in its modern sense? Not quite. Although Müller promoted the study of world religions, he still conceived of religion in Christian-centered terms: "If we look but steadily into those black Chinese eyes, we shall find that there, too, there is a soul that responds to a soul, and that the God whom they mean is the same God whom we mean, however helpless their utterance, however imperfect their worship" (Müller 1872: 83).[3] Where can we find "world religion" without the assumption of a Christian prototype?

"World religion" came closest to liberating itself from the Christian prototype in 1893 when the city of Chicago organized the World's Parliament of Religions as part of the Columbian Exposition. The Parliament invited representatives from religions around the world. As much of the rhetoric prior to the event suggested that the Parliament would seek to unify the world's religions into a single religion under the banner of Christianity, many official Japanese Buddhist organizations, such as the Jōdo Shinshū Pure Land Buddhism school and the Buddhist Transsectarian Cooperative Society (*Bukkyō kakushū kyōkai*), feared they would be manipulated by the Christians and refused the invitation to attend the Parliament (Harding 2008: 62–64). Thus, for Buddhism in Japan, the delegates who did attend came not as representatives of organizations but as individuals—individuals who went to confront the Christian hosts on their home ground.

The individuals did well for themselves. The Asian delegates of the world religions spoke in their own voices without the encumbrance of Western interpreters. The Asian Other faced the Western subject directly. The delegates were various, but since they all shared a history of colonial encounter with the West, they spoke, in Seager's words, against the "triumphalist often racist celebration of the superiority of Western Christian civilization" (1989: 311). Among others, the Hindu swami, Vivekananda, the Japanese Zen priest, Shaku Sōen, and the leader of the Maha Bodhi Society, Anagārika Dharmapāla, each gave stirring defenses of their religion couched in the language of science and interreligious harmony. In an oft-repeated story, it is said that Vivekananda began his speech with "Sisters and brothers of America" and received a two-minute standing ovation from the crowd of seven thousand.[4] Seager comments that of 216 presentations at the Parliament, "forty-one were from Asians who, although as far to the fringe as one could possibly get, were in fact the real stars of the assembly, who gained much of the public's attention and most of the best press" (Seager 1989: 317).

Premodern religion equated "religion" with "true religion" and thus used "religion" as if it had no plural. Modern religion includes an element of secularity, acknowledging that there can be more than one religion. When "world religion" sufficiently liberated itself from the Christian prototype, Buddhism became a world religion.

At the Parliament, some individuals in the Western world were still ensconced in premodern attitudes. The Archbishop of Canterbury declined to attend the Parliament. He wrote, "The difficulties which I myself feel are not questions of distance and convenience, but rest on the fact that the Christian religion is the one religion. . . . I do not understand how that religion can be regarded as a member of a Parliament of

Religions without assuming the equality of the other intended members and the parity of their position and claims" (Barrows 1893: 20–22). Here the East-West binary has reversed its polarity. In this case, the West is premodern and the East is modern.

Conclusion

The East-West binary stereotype provides a ready-made explanation for the process of modernization: many assume that the West is the engine of progressive change while the East is the repository of fossilized tradition. In this picture, the modernization of Asian religion consists in its Westernization. The West is the active agent; all the East needs to do is conform. This one-sided, reified, picture fails to acknowledge that the West too evolves and changes and that the East has its own agenda, which it actively implements. This chapter has tried to show that the West evolved in part in response to stimulus from the East and that modernization was a two-sided process in which both sides East and West helped shape the other. To display the symbiotic nature of the modernization process, this chapter has scanned the historical context in which the modernization of religion took place.

For Europeans in the premodern period, "religion" meant "true religion" and it expressed the conviction of the true believer in his exclusive possession of religious truth. Modern religion, by contrast, incorporates an element of secularity. It acknowledges that there is more than one religion. Modernization of religion began with Europe's discovery of the rest of the world. Reports of lands and peoples overseas challenged the authority of the Bible and pushed Europeans to expand their concept of "religion." The discovery of China was especially disturbing because China was as civilized as the West and it had a written textual tradition whose history predated that of the West. The Jesuits in China argued that the cult of Confucius was not religion but a civic cult. This move can be seen as an early attempt to create a concept of secularity.

The nation-states of Europe established colonies in the overseas lands of America, Africa, and Asia. The subjugated peoples were forced into changing their traditional cultures and adapting the new practices of the modern West. Japan is a good case study of the modernization process in East Asia. Japan deliberately set out to modernize itself through identifying and adapting the best practices of the Western states, and in its Constitution of 1889, it adopted elements of the Western concept of religion, such as freedom of religious belief and separation of religion and state. But it also reinstated the mythology of the divine emperor who rules Japan, the direct descendant of the sun goddess, Amaterasu Ōmikami. This example makes abundantly clear that Japan adapted the Western concept of religion to serve its own purposes. In modernizing, far from being a passive recipient of Western culture, it had its own agenda.

Buddhism became a world religion at the World's Parliament of Religions in 1893. The concept of world religion presupposes a modernized secular concept of religion. When the concept "religion" got secularized enough to allow other religions to speak in their own voice, then Buddhism became a world religion.

2

Mapping Buddhism beyond East and West

John S. Harding

This study explores the relevance and use of terms "East" and "West" from early Buddhist movements in Asia to recent modernist representations. In this chapter, I use the analogy of mapping to trace the dynamic relationship of how these terms have been associated with Buddhist developments. Two case studies follow large-scale transmissions of Buddhism in Asia at the macro level as Buddhism spread into China and Japan in the first millennium CE. In surveying these encounters, East and West often function simply as indicators of direction for Buddhist influence. Closer examination reveals contextual symbolic meanings that map correspondence between geographic location and cultural identity. As Buddhism became increasingly global with modernist movements emerging in the nineteenth century, East and West became labels for notions of essentialized characteristics—a transition that marks a more ideological form of cultural mapping.

When selective cultural traits are reified and associated with terms such as "Eastern" and "Western," the resulting concepts are deployed as if they are natural reflections of a putative reality. As a result, these constructions actively shape (mis)representations and (mis)understandings that influence the development of Buddhism beyond signaling direction. Some modern examples reveal how rhetorical notions of East and West have been constructed and deployed in the promotion and transmission of Buddhism even though the mutually forming elements are variable, unstable, and often misleading. Mapping these shifting discursive meanings of East and West gives insight into the origins, objectives, agency, and ongoing patterns of representation; furthermore, it underlines the need to go beyond East and West.

Seeking a fuller awareness of global Buddhist currents beyond simple binaries discloses complex Asian agency located across a network of nodes that produce and reflect series of interrelated adaptations in the modern era. Not only does this move beyond East and West but it also keeps to the course that we set out in our 2014 work, *Flowers on the Rock: Global and Local Buddhisms in Canada*. In that volume, we contend that a focus on globalization is necessary to understand local manifestations of the tradition anywhere—even modernist forms of Buddhism in North America arise from global interactions, and often, origins developed first in Asia (Harding, Hori and Soucy 2014: 12). After an examination of the conceptual framework for mapping Buddhism in this chapter, I survey a series of examples that move from premodern dynamics within Asia to a worldwide emergence of modern Buddhism in the last century and a half. Consequential dynamics shift in the modern period with intensifying globalization and new categories of world religion. Close attention to the complex cross-cultural influences that shape individuals, relationships, events, and encounters in the formation and global circulations of modern Buddhism can be best accomplished if we are equipped with a map capable of charting the currents beyond East and West.

Terms: Metageography and Malleable Maps

A good point of departure is exploring the terms used here: "metageography," "maps," and "East and West." I am following Lewis and Wigen's critique in defining the term "metageography" as "the set of spatial structures through which people order their knowledge of the world: the often-unconscious frameworks that organize studies of history, sociology, anthropology, economics, political science, or even natural history" (1997: ix). Buddhist Studies, Asian Studies, and Religious Studies are not exempt. Moreover, the term "metageography" applies to multiple versions of East, West, Asia, and the Orient, and Lewis and Wigen chart the shifting boundaries, mythic uses, and ideological power beneath the surface of these terms (1997: xiii). Although humanly constructed mental categories, these metageographic designations are often taken for granted as objective or commonsense reflections of an actual, and natural, reality. Closer examination reveals power dynamics, biases, and inconsistencies in the various ways they are configured, contested, and deployed.

Although I will reference East and West throughout the chapter, I am positing that ultimately there is not a real, enduring, or essential East-West division—not even when Buddhists themselves are making essentializing generalizations about Eastern and Western values, strengths, and modes of thinking. I am not arguing that the associations produced and communicated through this East-West binary, such as a "rational and intellectual West," were not influential. In fact, some Asian proponents reinforced the same description of traits East and West, but at times flipped the script in terms of which traits to valorize. Despite frequent use of the East-West binary and associated traits, I maintain that modern Buddhisms emerge from global discourses, of which variations of an East-West binary are only a part, and the global circulations of these traditions' formative influences and their own spread are misrepresented by overemphasis on a single direction of transfer in either direction, East or West.

Maps are more familiar than metageography, though they are interrelated. Maps on our smartphones and our vehicles' navigation systems are digital and interactive. We commonly see and utilize actual maps, whether digital or physical. Moreover, we are frequently exposed to metaphorical language oriented around maps, directions, charting a course, and navigating various aspects of life. Sometimes we also make maps, of various types, which further reinforces that a map is a construction, relative to the specific circumstances and purpose at hand. Maps are malleable, they can be shaped into various designs for navigational use, aesthetic value, coordinating military campaigns, grouping regions with ostensibly shared characteristics, and depicting diverse types of information in correspondence with physical locations. Maps distort, even when the intention is not to mislead. Mercator projection maps of the world have been popular and beneficial for navigation since their eponymous Flemish mapmaker designed them in 1569. They also suffer from obvious distortions that magnify Greenland and Antarctica at the poles while minimizing the size of Africa and other lands in the equators. One need not throw out maps to progress forward, but it is important to understand the purposes, strengths, and limitations of each.

It is also imperative to be aware of ways in which maps, and notions of East and West, connect with real-world power and consequences. Maps can be used to project power—by positioning and naming places strategically or by unilaterally extending the boundaries of an authority's influence, jurisdiction, or recognized territorial claim. Maps are also created to maintain power, such as the convoluted political maps of gerrymandered congressional districts in the United States. They can carve out spheres of influence for colonizing powers, such as the map arising from the 1494 Treaty of Tordesillas, which divided much of the world beyond Europe between the reigning Iberian imperial powers of Portugal and the Spanish Crown of Castile. Even in colonial retreat, maps can instigate violent dispute, most notably the aftermath of the sudden partition drawn between India and Pakistan in 1947, which, regardless of its intention, delivered a parting blow from British India at the very moment it relinquished control. Although maps are constructed, sometimes delineating conceptual abstractions with limited correlation to a reality on the ground, they can nevertheless shape events and perceptions with real consequences.

So too, the discursive terms "East" and "West" have a wide range of meaning, use, and consequence. They can represent relative directions, regions, or (in the adjectival form of Eastern and Western) abstract descriptions that essentialize and reify certain characteristics that have been selectively identified with East or West. The term "metageographic" is useful for reflecting on these concepts. Metageographic terms can order our knowledge of the world, but we should not expect them to align with an actual reality apart from the constructed discourse. Similarly, maps range from detailed and careful descriptions of a domain to carelessly inaccurate sketches—or even intentionally misleading portrayals. Maps can (mis)represent any realm, but maps are not territory.[1]

Buddhism Moves East, Pilgrims Journey West

Equipped with examples and disclaimers of their limitations and dangers when not used reflectively, let us proceed anyway to map the development and dissemination of Buddhism and interrogate the related meanings attached to East and West along the way—even as close scrutiny of the instability of these metageographic categories points us beyond simple binary constructions of East and West. The idea of Buddhism as a beneficial export is common to accounts of its transmission, though not without biases and challenges to overcome in each new cultural setting. The relative positions of East and West have fluctuated in descriptions of this transfer, and the move of Buddhism from one cultural context to another has served as a significant force through history, shaping innumerable aspects of the societies that have closely engaged it for centuries.

China as Central Power, India as Buddhist West

The immense scope of the factors involved in the transmission of Buddhism from India to China is staggering. These ancient and regionally dominant civilizations were strikingly different, requiring extensive translation to bridge the gulf between their languages and their contrasting religious and philosophical worldviews. As suggested by the subtitle of the insightful 2009 work *TransBuddhism: Transmission, Translation, Transformation* (Bhushan, Garfield, and Zablocki 2009), the spread of Buddhism from India to China entailed centuries of transmission, translation, and mutual transformation. For China, the West was India—along with the trade routes and shifting central Asian powers that connected these two influential civilizations. Buddhism originated in India and came to China along those connecting corridors. Consequently, throughout this encounter and transmission, China looked to the West in several important ways linked to Buddhist connotations. For Buddhists in China, the West contains religiously rich layers of meaning: the direction of Amitābha's Pure Land, the origins of Buddhism, and the home to sacred sites where the historical Buddha had lived and taught. India is the supposed origin of Bodhidharma and the Chan/Zen school and the actual generative Buddhist source for many texts and objects of material culture. Thus, the West became the outbound direction for the heroic journeys that adventurous and devoted Chinese pilgrim monks embarked upon to travel to India, and the West is depicted in the maps, journals, translated texts, and rich descriptions of life in Buddhist India that they produced.

Faxian (法顯 337–422), Xuanzang (玄奘 602–64), and Yijing (義淨 635–713) set off at different times for the distant West of India. Faxian and Xuanzang traveled through China's western borderlands and traversed the desert trade routes that wound through central Asia to reach the Buddha's native realm. The West, for Chinese Buddhists in the early days, was the Buddha's homeland. West served as a direction and an idealized destination. These pilgrims traveled different routes (including Yijing's sea voyages through Southeast Asia), used various modes of transport (Faxian reported walking all the way to India and then traveling to Ceylon and back home to China by ship), and encountered diverse people and challenges along the way. But each visited key Buddhist sites in the West and returned to China after thirteen (Faxian) to twenty-five (Yijing) years in order to translate the texts they gathered and to transform their contemporaries' understanding of the West, and its Buddhism.

In addition to the Buddhist texts they retrieved, these travelers mapped the landscapes, routes, sites, cultures, and activities they observed. For example, the Chinese pilgrim Xuanzang's *Great Tang Records on the Western Regions* recounts his sixteen years of travel and study to India and back, replete with observations about the Buddhist world of the time. In this work, the West symbolically signifies authenticity and authority linked to the sacred sites in and around India. The appeal of such sites must have been very strong to convince monks to undertake such strenuous, and dangerous, journeys. Xuanzang's *Journey to the West* fulfilled his quest as a pilgrim, scholar, monk, and chronicler; it also inspired the popular Chinese novel of that title nearly a millennium later. This last twist, replete with fantastic characters accompanying the protagonist monk inspired by Xuanzang, further demonstrates the ongoing transformations and adaptations of earlier signifiers and referents in cultural mapping.

Another way the East-West binary serves as shorthand for this transfer is evident in a famous koan, variously phrased as, "Why did Bodhidharma come from the West?" (or, "What is the meaning of, 'Bodhidharma came from the West,'" or as in the title of the meditatively paced Korean film, *Why Has Bodhidharma Left for the East*?). I will not delve into the koan or the fascinating legends of the quasi-historical Bodhidharma, who is traditionally said to have brought the Chan (known in Japan as Zen) meditation school of Buddhism from India to China in the first half of the sixth century. Instead, I am calling attention to the use of West and East as providing not just directional reference points for the relative location of India and China but also symbolically associating India with Buddhist authority and origins to the point where the koan can be understood as a question of what is Buddhism, Chan/Zen, or Buddhist awakening itself. That Bodhidharma came from the West can signify that he came from awakening. The West, therefore, may still provide authority specific to the Buddhist tradition, whether confirming ordination and proper compliance with Buddhist monastic principles or invoking a transitional figure such as Bodhidharma to demonstrate that the authoritative lineage from India purportedly made it to China intact.

Bodhidharma and Buddhism came from the West, pilgrims travel there, and lay and monastic Buddhists alike locate the Pure Land of Amitābha as a Western Paradise. Positive early references to the West are especially significant coming from China. China is famously known as the Middle Kingdom. This name for the country combines the character 中 (meaning middle/central) with the character 國/国 (the older vs. newer/simplified versions for state/country/kingdom). This is not merely a recent term for the modern nation-state of China, 中国; instead, the older version 中國 is discernible on artefacts from three millennia ago. China's power in various eras, as well as its continuity with an impressive civilization from early times, participates in this projection of status—centrality beyond mere location—denoted by the name Middle Kingdom. Just as many modern world maps produced in Europe position Europe at the center, China designated itself as the center, replete with connotations of superiority that suggested the related correlation that links barbarism with distance from the Chinese center. To the Chinese, Bodhidharma was a barbarian. Chan/Zen cannot be attained through the methods of civilization—literacy, knowledge, and learning. Both connotations for the distant West can be mapped simultaneously, India can be perceived as relatively barbaric *and* the authoritative homeland of Buddha.

These cultural assumptions, as well as the relative geographic locations of China and India, are relevant in Chinese ambivalence about India and the West. Buddhism tests Chinese cultural assumptions of superiority. It is an impressive import with rich literature, formidable religious practices, and refined material culture. Patronage of Buddhism does not negate assumptions of Chinese cultural superiority, and although Buddhism profoundly influenced China, Buddhism in turn was transformed by

China. These important and mutually influential connections between Buddhism and China does not, of course, denote uniform or universal views. In contrast to Buddhism's many inroads, including patronage from emperors and one empress, some guardians of Chinese culture were never swayed by the allure of Buddhism. They wanted to keep the Buddhist/Indian West far away from the Chinese center. For example, the plea by the literati Han Yu (韓愈 768–824) insists that the emperor should not allow the "rotting bone" of the Buddha—a foreigner of "barbarian origin"—into the palace as a relic to be worshipped (LaFleur 1988: 56–61). Rather than East and West, LaFleur invokes ideas of center-periphery in his analysis when describing Han Yu's plaintive poem bemoaning his own subsequent exile from the capital and contrasting Han Yu's anticipated fate to the admission of the foreign relic bone into the capital:

> The bones of an Indian now lay in the heart of China's capital, and he, as loyal a Confucian as could be found in the Middle Kingdom, faced the prospect of his own bones lying on the outer region of the empire, in a wild and untamed area ... the total reversal or inversion of all that should be. (LaFleur 1988: 61)

Despite enduring notions of Chinese cultural superiority that came to claim Chinese adaptations of Buddhism as the culmination of the tradition, Buddhism deeply influenced China and vice versa. The precise balance, mechanisms, and measurements that chart China's sinicization of Buddhism as opposed to Buddhism's transformation of China have been debated for more than half a century (Ch'en 1973; Sharf 2001; Tsukamoto 1985; Zürcher [1959] 2007). In all cases, it is clear that the transmission of that tradition to the East marked an important encounter between these Asian powers, but the nuance is contested by scholars today, though less dramatically than Han Yu's protest 1,200 years ago.

Japan as Sacred East: China as Unwilling West

We now shift from China to Japan, following the spread of Buddhism as it moves from West to East proceeding from China first to Korea and then on to Japan over the course of five centuries. The subheading for this section indicates that East and West are still contextual in the direction of Buddhist movement, and in the relative geographical location of China to the west of Japan. Moreover, "China as Unwilling West" suggests that this status is contested—China may resist this binary as it implies a complementarily equal pairing at odds with its own metageographic self-identity as the Middle Kingdom. The other part of this section's subheading, "Japan as Sacred East," signals the religious and mythic dimensions underlying the epithet Land of the Rising Sun. Similar to the significance of China's name discussed earlier, here also the two *kanji* (Chinese characters) that name Japan (日本) mean sun and origin with layers of meaning formative to a religiously and politically charged identity. The correspondence between location, name, and founding myths converges in claims of status as a sacred country with an imperial lineage descending from Amaterasu, the sun goddess.

The origins of Buddhism in Japan are typically described as a political gift in the sixth century CE from a king of one of the three main powers on the Korean peninsula at that time, to Japan's Emperor Kinmei (欽明天皇 509–571). Along with "an image of Buddha and sacred writings," the Korean king sent a memorial proclamation asserting that Buddhist doctrine "is among all doctrines the most excellent, but it is hard to explain and hard to comprehend. . . . Every prayer is fulfilled and naught is wanting" (De Bary [1958] 2001: 100). The circumstances of this transfer are important, in part, because the link between Buddhism and political and protective power endured, as did the emphasis on practical, this-worldly benefits attainable through Buddhism. In this case, the direction from West to East is just an observation of relative geography with the Korean peninsula west of Japan. Although this example is not weighted with rhetorical and ideological implication, even here, carefully following the use and associations of the terms "East" and "West" can help delve into cultural relationships and ideas of identity beneath the map's surface.

The Korean king's portrayal of Buddhism traces its origins back to a point much further west, noting "from distant India it has extended hither to Korea, where there are none who do not receive it with reverence as it is preached to them" (De Bary [1958] 2001: 100). The attribution of origins to India is important, but the more influential and immediate influx of ideas, models, and even material culture from the Asian mainland at this time came predominantly from Korea followed by China, not distant India. Also, Buddhism in China significantly shaped the tradition in Korea. In short, this was a transfer from Korea to Japan, but it meaningfully participated in a larger exchange between China, Korea, and Japan with ever greater direct exchange with China in subsequent centuries.

The East-West inflected Japan-China relation is more the focus of this case study. Notions of cultural identity relative to Chinese power and influence were already more complicated around that same time between Japan and China. The operative terms mapping the relationship between the young country of Japan and the dominant, and much more established, Chinese empire to their west included these directional terms. But there are also correlative natural symbols of these relative positions that highlighted Japan's self-understanding as the place where the sun originates, a literal reading of 日本, the *kanji* for the country of Japan.

Both directional and symbolic uses are on display in letters from Prince Shōtoku (聖徳太子 574–622) to the emperor of the Sui Dynasty, circa 600 CE. These are relevant to the spread of Buddhism as the correspondence in question traveled from Japan to China less than a century after the tradition's introduction into Japan. Furthermore, Shōtoku was famously supportive of Buddhism and clearly revered multiple aspects of Chinese culture. Nevertheless, Shōtoku's use of East-West references upset the Chinese emperor as insufficiently deferential. The binaries in his opening greetings seem to imply a complementary equivalence in both salutations, with one letter from "the Child of Heaven in the Land of the Rising Sun to the Child of Heaven in the Land of the Setting Sun," and the other, the more concise, and explicitly East-West missive, in which, "The Eastern Emperor Greets the Western Emperor" (De Bary [1958] 2001: 42).

The use of the terms "East" and "West" can be controversially charged with self-serving bias, merely descriptive of direction, or shaped by a combination of these and other factors with implication of areas of relative Buddhist strength or authenticity. Some of these aspects are suggested in this Japanese example from more than 1400 years ago, but we have few records and must speculate about some of the intentions and dynamics at play. Also, it is possible that China's emperor took offense not just because of the implied equivalence of Eastern emperor and Western emperor but also as a protest of being labeled as West given China's own ambivalent associations with the West in opposition to their self-identity as the center. The first letter is particularly relevant for symbolism of self-identity because "Child of Heaven in the Land of the Rising Sun" invokes at least two meanings. The land of the Rising Sun simply names Japan (日本), but this name is imbued with mythic and religious association, not merely descriptors of geographic location. That is, this name is not simply moving from an awareness of the country's relative direction and location to forging a correspondence with the natural observation (the sun is seen to rise in the east), this identification also expresses the mythic links to the sun goddess, Amaterasu, who is portrayed as the divine ancestor of Japan's imperial lineage and the most important of all the Japanese divine *kami*.

From Premodern Metageography in Asia to Modern Global Discourse

The major transfers of Buddhism *within* Asia from more than a millennium ago appeared to move from West to East. As noted in the Asian examples, West and East indicated geographical direction and are relative terms of location that make common sense in context. At another level, East and West are mapped with corresponding symbolic associations. These shape and reflect constructions of self-identity and attitudes about relational others. Namely, China's ambivalent connotations of the Buddhist (but also barbaric) West of India relative to China's civilized centrality as the Middle Kingdom. In Japan's case, their location east of China, Korea, and all the Asian mainland dovetailed with a self-identification as the land of the rising sun with all the natural, mythic, religious, and political connotations that entailed.

The East-West binary for early Buddhist dissemination within Asia was relatively less ideological than what has transpired with modern Buddhism worldwide. The earlier examples from formative centuries of Buddhist transmission, first from India to China and then on to Korea and Japan, can be charted at several levels from mere direction, to relative location, and even to the more complex and constructed notions labeled here as premodern metageography. On the one hand, metageography can stand alone without the premodern to modify it. After all, these cases include the use of directional terms to order the world around them including the very names for China and Japan that reinforce the symbolic models that construct identity reflective of assumptions of Chinese centrality and Japanese sacrality. These examples from the early spread of Buddhism in Asia remain responsive to context and location, but they are also relatively enduring as signified by the ongoing use of the characters for each country's name and their related symbolic meanings.

Nevertheless, premodern figured into the summary of this first set of examples to draw a contrast in time period, relative global intensity of interaction, and a shift from contextual use of East and West for these earlier examples to increasingly discursive manipulations of the terms, which further reveals that they are unstable, strategic constructions that often fail to reflect or account for the complexity and deep interrelation of global flows in the modern examples we turn to next. This shift to the modern also rhetorically reverses the flow of influence, from West to East, to East to West. Unlike the early examples from Asia, most descriptions in recent centuries emphasize the movement of Buddhism from East to West. This flips the direction of the terms, though one could show a simplistic model emphasizing continuity of movement by tracing a single arc along a globe from India to China to Japan to North America and on to Europe. Charting an ongoing West to East flow in this way would be only a map of convenience. The modern examples in the next section reveal global circulations of influence beyond the capacity of the East-West binary to map. Moreover, the inversion of the terms from West-East to East-West is not just an alteration in the direction of flow, but also signals a shift in what is meant by East and by West when we turn to modern examples. What each comes to designate betrays the fluidity of the concepts, constructed for specific purposes rather than capturing some enduring core reality.

Global Flows: Submerging East and West

The designations East and West to label core cultural traits are ultimately misleading if taken as fixed, sui generis, categories. First, as exemplified in the earlier transmissions in Asia, the terms are contextual. Second, the interactions between East and West are so deeply and inextricably global that an appearance or rhetorical claim of faithfully describing either the East or West in isolation is delusory. The examples in this section survey the convergence of mutually shaping global influences to trace links between global conversations and the publications, views, and other products of the collaborative exchanges among representatives from Asia, Europe, and North America. Because of overlapping concerns and shared global context, the very attempt to follow these causal factors—and the Buddhist movements that emerge in relation to them—back to their source erodes what may have first appeared to exemplify a fixed idea of East or West. Third, the terms "East" and "West" can become empty, or floating, signifiers. The terms are used, but there is no actual object or real referent that they signify—instead, shifting and situational uses are so variable and arbitrary that the terms float on the currents of global discourse with no fixed attachment. The chapter in this volume by Lina Verchery illustrates a related observation. Her compelling study of global Buddhist imaginaires analyzes a twentieth-century case in which the Chinese Buddhist master Hsuan Hua (宣化上人 1918–95) and his Dharma Realm Buddhist Association (*Fajie Fojiao Zonghui* 法界佛教總會) followers construct a supposed West that serves their own purposes, an appropriation or reverse orientalism that exemplifies how the terms East and West can be imaginatively redefined to fit the desired content. Verchery's chapter is also instructive in its reminder that the terms used, and the categories that are constructed, still matter, imagined or not.

In fact, chapters throughout the volume provide case studies that move us beyond a typical East-West binary. This next case study is centered on the last decade of the

1800s—an era chosen to demonstrate that even at this formative stage for modern representations of Buddhism, taking East and West as reified categories is profoundly misleading. References to East and West are common, but stable referents are scarce.

The late-nineteenth-century "other" may have seemed more profoundly and mysteriously "other" than in contemporary views informed by more intensive worldwide travel and communication. However, back then too, East and West prove empty signifiers in the global currents of discourse about Buddhism. In fact, the term "empty" is relevant in at least two ways here. First, it describes the malleable imaginaires of East and West in this global discourse. Second, the term connects to the Buddhist notion of emptiness (śūnyatā) by pointing to a deeper level of profound integration (rather than a mere absence) to explain the common misperception of assuming the existence of an actual reified referent rather than what closer scrutiny reveals—a lack of truly stable, separate and dualistic states of East and West. In the examples that follow, the uses of terms vary, as do both the directions of influence and the adequacy of an East-West binary to delineate the exchange.

Early Global Collaborations: Mutual Influence beyond East and West

East-West discursive categories are simply inadequate to capture the complex global Buddhist networks created through the relationships among influential representatives from Asia and Euro-America. Close examination of their journals, letters, published writings, public talks, and travels provide insights into the complexity of their mutual influence as well as the global underpinnings of their Buddhist presentation. I find the relationship between Paul Carus (1852–1919) and Shaku Sōen (釈 宗演 1860–1919), at times mediated by Daisetsu Teitarō Suzuki (鈴木大拙貞太郎1870–1966), to be especially compelling in this regard (Harding 2008, 2016).

The correspondence of Paul Carus, including letters to and from Shaku Sōen, is preserved in the Open Court Collection, part of the Special Collections archives at the Southern Illinois University–Carbondale. Those letters portray a relationship where each shaped and promoted the other's works to the benefit of their shared advocacy of Buddhism as well as for individual aims. "On both sides, the inclusion of 'foreign' materials served to bolster a domestic agenda," often directly connected to the global promotion of Buddhism, but in the case of Sōen's March 8, 1895, letter stating he would publish something supportive that Carus had opined about Japan's war with China, this relationship was leveraged for political support of military and nationalistic objectives (Harding 2008: 131). These letters reflect intertwined agency, well beyond an East-West binary, to the point that authorship itself is not always clear. Most notably, Carus writes to Sōen indicating the need to respond to an 1896 published critique of Buddhism in the *Chicago Tribune* written by the Parliament's organizer, John Henry Barrows. Carus even supplies key points that the Zen abbot Sōen should make in his reply. Rather than write his own response to Barrows as requested by Carus, Sōen appears to have simply replied that Carus should proceed with such a response, that is, publish the reply as already constructed by Carus. Verhoeven articulates this same suspicion about authorship, writing that Sōen "was credited with the letter of response, 'Reply to a

Christian Critic,' but correspondence between the two strongly suggests that Carus initiated the exchange and penned the letter himself" (Verhoeven 2004: 41, fn. 97).

Sōen lent his name to this letter for the prestige and sense of authenticity derived from the (ostensible) view of an esteemed "Eastern" abbot of Zen Buddhism, but if Carus is the actual author of the reply to Barrows's critique, then this is at one level an exchange between two influential "Western" religious figures arguing about Buddhism. Marking East and West can be misleading. The boundaries of the East and West in the previous example are unclear, even beyond authorship, because Sōen influences the views of Carus. Furthermore, by lending his name and Japanese Buddhist clerical authority, Sōen endorses that view even if it was Carus who actually wrote the reply and emphasized certain aspects in particular that more closely reflect Carus's own understanding, rhetoric, and concerns.

The disorientation of direction and voice, East and West, continues when Japanese Shin missionaries arrive in the United States to tell Carus what a profound impact his writings on Buddhism had on them in Japan. Sonoda Shuye (1863–1922), who became a founding leader of the Shin denomination's Buddhist Mission of North America (BMNA), later known as the Buddhist Churches of America (BCA), wrote to Carus immediately upon his 1899 arrival in San Francisco. A brief survey of context for that letter, its recipient, and the already complex back and forth influences that help make sense of that exchange, illustrates the instability of the East-West distinction even in these early encounters. Sonoda reports on his "first attempt at the propagation of the new light of the truth in the New World" and also informs Carus, "I knew your name at home through your excellent writing tinted with candidness and I was especially interested in your 'Gospel of Buddha,' which I adopted as my college English text when I became the principal of the Buddhist college Honganji Bungakuryo, Kioto" (Tweed and Prothero 1999: 78–80).

Sonoda is an influential figure in his own right. Both titles of Reverend and Doctor precede his name at different times signaling his range of leadership, missionary, translation, and educational roles for Shin Buddhism in Japan and North America. For example, he was the translator of the 1893 pamphlet written by Y. Mayeda, "An Outline of the True Sect of Buddhism," and Sonoda describes in his July 27, 1893, preface to this work that it was produced "at the request of the Buddhist Propagation Society, for free distribution at the World's Fair of Chicago," as a means of additional representation at the World's Parliament of Religions. As noted in his letter to Carus, he also held a leadership role in a Shin college in Kyoto before he came to North America in 1899. In fact, after Sonoda returned to Japan following his work to launch the BMNA as part of the missionary "attempt at the propagation" of Buddhism that instigated his letter to Carus cited earlier, he later resumed leadership positions in that institution becoming "head of Bungaku-ryō (present-day Ryūkoku University) in 1905" (Williams and Moriya 2010: 75). The content of this 1899 letter raises numerous issues for Buddhism both in late-nineteenth-century North America and in Meiji Japan. These include the role of "Western" writers, such as Carus, and the influence of their works about Buddhism as read (both in English and in translation) and used by Asian Buddhists. Judith Snodgrass skillfully delineates these dynamics in her 1998 study of how Carus's *Gospel of Buddha* was deployed in Japan.

I raise this letter from Sonoda—informing Carus about his arrival in North America and plans to propagate Buddhism in the West while also telling Carus that he had used *Gospel of Buddha* back in Japan—as an example to complicate the East-West binary and to illustrate its inadequacy to unpack the actual forces at work or to adequately map their complex and mutually influential directions of travel. At minimum, East and West for the promotion of Buddhism are reciprocally constitutive, but they often obscure—more than they delineate—the complex back and forth of the global networks in play. In the example of Sonoda's letter, the layers of interrelated issues and influences in North America and Japan shape and are shaped by global Buddhist discourse, modern representations of Buddhism, and the receptions of Buddhism in both locations. One could try to chart the back and forth flows in terms of East and West, but the exercise circles back on itself.

Consider the cross-cultural complexities exemplified by the following interrelated four factors. One, these Buddhist missionaries from the East were praising Carus's *Gospel of Buddha* and used it as a textbook at a Japanese Buddhist college. Two, they used the English language version of the text—perhaps as much to become more familiar with the language and existing understanding of Buddhism for their encounter with the "West" in the role of Buddhist missionaries as to learn about their own "Eastern" tradition. Three, D. T. Suzuki was living with Carus when Sonoda sent the letter, and Suzuki had been responsible for translating that same work about Buddhism by Carus into Japanese for a Japanese audience. Four, Suzuki and his own teacher, Shaku Sōen, had also exerted considerable influence on Paul Carus's understanding of Buddhism in the first place, though this exercise of beginning to retrace circulations of influence casts doubt on the existence of a "first place."

In fact, each of these four points invites additional investigation, which in turn leads to complicating nuance that tends to further destabilize apparent East-West binaries. For example, the fourth point (that Carus was influenced by Suzuki and Sōen) suggests an East to West influence, but this is counterbalanced by evidence of the strong influence Carus exerted on Suzuki's own presentation of Buddhism, a West to East countercurrent (Sharf 1993). Moreover, Suzuki's presentation of Buddhism exerted global influence in Asia and in the West. In addition to his well-known influence in North America, Europe, and Japan, Jingjing Li's chapter in this volume also provides evidence of significant influence in China. Presentations of Buddhism by Sōen, Carus, Suzuki, and Sonoda at the turn of the century arose from a mutually influential discussion and continued to inform the global discourse of modern Buddhism with publications, lectures, letters, and personal encounters worldwide. These four were influential pioneers. Like the early Chinese pilgrim-translators, these four traveled widely, translated ideas across East-West divides, and were, in a sense, conceptual mapmakers who helped others navigate the terrain across traditions that they described and actively shaped.

Mid-Century Reflections on Global Recirculations

The spectacle of Buddhism as a newly introduced World Religion at the 1893 Parliament and the attendant intense interaction and self-conscious strategies among

Buddhist advocates of that time were especially remarkable, but of course did not mark the end of Buddhism's spread and transformation. The ongoing global exchange since this formative period has prompted observations from religious figures and scholars in Asia and in the "West" about recirculations of influence beyond initial East-West transmissions.

In 1961, four eminent Japanese Buddhist thinkers gathered on Mt. Hiei for a three-day discussion. This gathering of D. T. Suzuki, philosopher Nishitani Keiji (西谷 啓治 1900–1990), and Shin thinkers Kaneko Daiei (金子 大栄 1881–1976) and Soga Ryōjin (曽我 量深 1875–1971) embarked on a wide-ranging discussion that included an exchange that invokes East and West, but points beyond them. Their conversation also provides a fascinating example of the recirculation of influence that posits that Western interest in Zen, in combination with interest in the West among Japanese youth, might lead to a confluence where young Japanese take more interest in "their" own "Eastern" traditions when it circles back to them from the "West." Nishitani starts this portion of the dialogue and adds the supplementary dimension that interpretation is not only moving back and forth with translations East and West but also moving through time more globally as classical texts are interpreted for the contemporary world. An excerpt of some of his comments along with responses from Suzuki and Soga follows:

> *Nishitani:* Here's an opportunity to interpret these ancient works not only for contemporary Westerners but also for the Japanese, who have become highly Westernized. Furthermore, these works are not only interpreted for the contemporary reader, but are also interpreted from the standpoint of the contemporary world. We assume this standpoint naturally, whether we are conscious of it or not. New interpretations emerge. Do you agree?
> *Suzuki:* Yes, that's why this is not really translation. It's not that a Western interpretation emerges either; that which lies at the foundation of Eastern thought is interpreted in terms of the languages of the West. These languages are in turn interpreted on the basis of Eastern ways of thinking.
> *Nishitani:* Today's youth are finding it increasingly easier to understand English than classical Japanese. This may provide them with an opportunity to examine and understand what lies in the East through the translations now emerging.
> *Soga:* If there were an essential difference between the East and the West, then there would be no basis for mutual understanding. . . .
> *Nishitani:* If Westerners come to understand, then today's Japanese will as well.
> *Soga:* It's true with anything. It must be taken once to the West and then brought back again. Even something as Japanese as Shin Buddhism cannot be understood by the Japanese simply as it stands. . . . It is through the interpretation of Westerners that we will really come to understand ourselves. That's the way the Japanese have been throughout their history, isn't it?
> (Suzuki et al. 1985: 116–17)

This dialogue could also be mapped as an Insider-Outsider binary along with East-West. Interestingly, both Westerners and Japanese youth could be categorized as "other" for these distinguished older Japanese thinkers who are at home reading classical texts. Moreover, from their vantage point atop Mt. Hiei, the four plot a course that predicts better understanding of Japanese religious tradition through the cultural encounter and mutual transformations of those two "others." They chart cross-cultural currents of adaptation, translation, and mutually constitutive understanding in this exchange between—and I would argue beyond—East and West.

The Way Forward, beyond East and West

Perceiving the shifting contemporary landscape of Buddhism worldwide in all its cross-cultural complexity requires a global eye. The terms "East" and "West" arise, but plotting them in a meaningful way requires attention to global influences and mutually transformative networks and recursive recirculations well beyond the simple East-West binary. Observations of contemporary Buddhist dynamics challenge other binaries, such as religious-secular, which McMahan examines in the next chapter. Here, I will sketch a few examples to suggest that by looking beyond East-West the correspondence between map and territory improves. Moreover, an updated map attentive to contemporary dynamics and to enduring entanglements helps one recognize that Buddhist forms, supporters, movements, and techniques have transformed, and may not be captured by old models of Buddhism. The three examples in the following text provide three quite different reflections on Buddhism, religion, secularity, and modernity that participate in a global framework beyond East and West even though the terms continue to be invoked.

The first example comes from a sociological analysis of secularity, religion, and looping influences. In his provocatively titled 2017 book, *Secular Beats Spiritual: The Westernization of the Easternization of the West*, Steve Bruce argues that interest in "Eastern" religions in the "West" since the 1970s does not challenge secular dominance because "while it is the case that eastern religious themes have proved attractive to some in the West, they have often been changed in ways that looks like capitulation to the West's secular culture" (2017: 177). These dynamics, including the role of objectives shaped by secular demands, have been addressed within Buddhist Studies with greater attention to shifting forms of Buddhism and global dimensions that challenge the divisions of East and West. For example, David McMahan analyzes the relationship between Buddhism and various global secularisms in the next chapter of this volume. Moreover, works such as Jeff Wilson's 2014, *Mindful America: The Mutual Transformation of Buddhist Meditation and American Culture*, already provide insightful analysis of fluid adaptation and marketing responsive to shifting needs and contexts.

Moving beyond Bruce's East-West analysis, the studies by both Wilson and McMahan are attuned to global dynamics beyond an East-West binary. Wilson declares that most "significant religious phenomena" are "transnational in some noteworthy way," and he calls attention to dialogical transformations and international dimensions of the mindfulness movement, which is "the product of a global circulation of monks, meditation teachers, books, articles, television programs, Internet websites, and everyday practitioners, Buddhist and otherwise. Its channels run from Asia to the West and back again" (Wilson 2014: 6). Similarly, McMahan describes the global context of Buddhist modernism as a transnational genre that provided a much fuller picture than sketches of traits in isolation that have at times been mistakenly depicted as merely local, adaptations: "Buddhist modernism . . . . Although influenced by the West, it is not simply 'Western Buddhism,' but rather a global network of movements created by both Asians and Westerners that is not the exclusive product of one geographic or cultural setting" (McMahan 2012c: 160).

The confluence of secularism and global movements that adapt insights and techniques rooted in Asian religious traditions can take forms that promote Buddhism as an especially fulfilling religion, that elevate Buddhism above the category of religion, or that remove explicit references to Buddhism from the technique all together. In all of these forms, there remains a multivocal and global discourse beyond East and West promoting Buddhism, or at least some of its teachings or techniques, if unnamed. Similarly, some contemporary sympathizers describe Buddhism as a philosophy or way of life sympathetic to their own "spiritual but not religious" self-description. This position often signals a suspicion of institutional religion. Even this aversion to formal religious doctrines and organizations is a global discourse with advocates from East and West. Elevating Buddhism above critiques directly aimed at religion as a whole is often linked with representing Buddhism as rational, logical, and empirical rather than requiring beliefs that cannot be substantiated or with practices deemed superstitious. Strategies for promoting Buddhism include those that obscure its identity as a religion.

This brings us to the second example, epitomized by a Buddhist pioneer claiming new territory beyond Buddhism. Stephen Batchelor is a contemporary Buddhist practitioner who has trained in several forms of Buddhism and studied the tradition deeply. He delimits his Buddhism to the parts that map with his own orientation of personal and contemporary relevance in his book *Buddhism Without Belief* (1997). One of Batchelor's more recent works, *After Buddhism: Rethinking the Dharma for a Secular Age* (2015), is an even more startling title when juxtaposed with the previous chapter in this *Buddhism in the Global Eye* volume. Victor Hori's chapter surveys how "Buddhism" was born out of the late-nineteenth-century creation of "world religions"—itself a construct built from the confluence of secularism and global encounter. Batchelor implicates our twenty-first-century-secular times in bringing about a post-Buddhist era where core teachings might live on reconfigured in the religion's absence. Despite the contrasting role of the secular relative to the life cycle of Buddhism as a world religion, there is a shared sense of promoting the relevance of Buddhism through a fluid, global discourse beyond East and West.

The flexibility of Buddhism's global popularity even extends to unlikely non-Buddhist sources of support in our own time. The third example relates to the accolades for Buddhism from an atheist critic of religion, who demarcates a rational Buddhism superior to other religious traditions, if not to the category of religion itself. Merging Buddhist and secular confluences shape proclamations by prominent Western atheist Sam Harris. In his 2014 book, *Waking Up: A Guide to Spirituality Without Religion*, Harris claims "there is something to the notion of uniquely Eastern wisdom, and most of it has been concentrated in or derived from the tradition of Buddhism" (2014: 28). Although he cautions the reader about the shortcomings of "Eastern" societies and institutions, and acknowledges the "superstitions that many Buddhists cherish," Harris posits "a practical and logical core" to Buddhist doctrine and a clear preference for Buddhism over primarily faith-based religions because its "central teachings are entirely empirical" (2014: 28). Ideas of East and West remain, but Buddhism is credited here as the primary generator of "Eastern" wisdom and simultaneously perceived as essentially rational and empirical—consistent with science but not with negative connotations of religion nor with previously essentializing characteristics of the non-rational "East."

Conclusion

In the early examples of mapping Buddhist transmissions within premodern Asia, the meanings of East and West were more contextual—as directions of Buddhist movement and symbolic markers of cultural identity. In contrast, the discursive metageographic notions formed in modernist global discourse moved and changed more quickly—floating signifiers shaped by cross-cultural flows. Examples of collaborative mutual influence and global looping recirculations further reveal the inadequacy of the East-West binary to model the much more complex global interaction among nodes of influence and agents beyond East and West. These examples shifted not only beyond the East and the West but also seem on course to travel beyond Buddhism. By following these fluctuating global currents, there is the danger of falling off the map altogether. That is all right. Maps are provisional and need to be brought up to date if they are to meaningfully correspond with their surroundings. To more accurately track Buddhist movements, a global perspective is required in combination with keen insight—able to see through illusions of stability or independence, whether of East and West, or religious and secular.

3

Buddhism and Global Secularisms[1]

David L. McMahan

Buddhism in the modern world offers an example of (1) the porousness of the boundary between secular and religious; (2) the diversity, fluidity, and constructedness of the very categories of religious and secular, since they appear in different ways among different Buddhist cultures in divergent national contexts; and (3) the way these categories nevertheless have very real-world effects and become drivers of substantial change in belief and practice. Although the very concepts of "religious" and "secular" are of European vintage, they have been adapted in different ways in different Buddhist contexts. This adaptation has shaped Buddhism in different places (particularly under different systems of government) in distinctive ways, suggesting multiple secularisms, multiple modernities, and indeed, multiple Buddhisms. Drawing from a few examples of Buddhism in various geographical and political settings, I hope to take a few steps toward illuminating the broad contours of the interlacing of secularism and Buddhism. In doing so, I am synthesizing some of my own and others' research on modern Buddhism, integrating it with some current research I am doing on meditation, and considering its implications for thinking about secularism.

The Religious-Secular Binary

The wave of scholarship on secularism that has arisen in recent decades paints a more nuanced picture than the previous reigning model. For most of the twentieth century, social theorists adhered to a linear narrative of secularism as a global process of religion waning and becoming less relevant to public life. The processes of disenchantment, social differentiation, displacement, and the growing dominance of instrumental reasoning and scientific thinking would gradually come to occupy the spaces once inhabited by religion, and religion would fade away or at least become increasingly a matter of private belief.

The classical secularization narrative parallels a prominent narrative of Buddhism in the modern world. In the nineteenth and twentieth centuries, authors from around the globe began to create a narrative of Buddhism, celebrating the rediscovery of "true" Buddhism, in part by Western scholars: a Buddhism of texts, philosophy, psychology, meditation, and ethics that contrasted starkly with the "degenerate" Buddhism that colonists found on the ground in places they occupied. The latter Buddhism was a matter of "cultural baggage" that had accumulated around the core of the Dharma and was inessential—even corrupting—to its original liberative message (Almond 1988; Lopez 2002; McMahan 2008). Most scholars today are quite skeptical of this narrative and recognize the picture of a pure rational core of Buddhism enveloped by various cultural impurities to be inadequate to account for the complexities of Buddhism in all its varieties today and throughout history. Yet the picture persists in many different contexts of the rescue and renewal of Buddhism from moribund tradition and its (re)emergence into its true ancient form—which turns out to be the most compatible with the modern.

Both of these narratives—that of linear secularization of the world and of the linear modernization (and recovery) of Buddhism—are now, I believe, untenable. Yet there is still sense to be made of secularism, as well as Buddhist modernism, and their mutual intersections. After the Iranian revolution and the rise of resurgent Islam, the flourishing of evangelical Christianity and Pentecostalism in the global south, the "return" of religion in China and the former Soviet Union, we need not rehearse all of the reasons why most social thinkers today have become skeptical of the "classical" secularization thesis (Berger 1999). What has emerged is a more complex picture of the interlacing of secular forces with religious ones, along with the increased appreciation of the interdependence and co-constitution of these categories. Rather than seeing secularization as the inevitable and global fading and privatization of religion in the face of inexorable processes of modernization, we see heterogeneous, geographically differentiated processes in which different societies adopt certain themes that might fall into the category of "secular" and combine or juxtapose them in unique ways with particular understandings of the "religious." Although perhaps governed by an underlying logic rooted in its origins in the European Enlightenment, secularization is not a uniform process of the withering of religion from public life, as many twentieth-century thinkers imagined. The fact that this had happened to a great extent in western Europe makes that area the exception rather than the rule. Nor is the division between secular and religious a stable, incontestable, and impermeable membrane but rather something constantly renegotiated in various national and legal contexts.

The contemporary compulsion to put "religion" and "secularism" in scare-quotes betrays a metareflective stance that has come to recognize the extent to which the very categories of religious and secular are modern, co-constitutive categories that cannot simply refer to natural, unambiguous species of phenomena. What some have begun to call the religious-secular binary is (or is part of) a *discourse*—a particular way of constituting knowledge, subjectivity, meaning, power, and practice that increasingly pervades modern societies. This discourse determines what counts as secular and what counts as religious and what is marginalized as superstition or cult, as well as what counts as a legitimate exercise of religion and what does not.[2] To point out the discursive or constructed character of these categories, however, does not imply that they are of merely academic or taxonomic concern or that they are categories without a referent. Indeed, how these categories are deployed can have profound real-world effects on nations, communities, and individuals, since they are matters not only of rhetoric but also of legitimacy, law, and practice. Whether a practice falls under the category of religious, secular, or superstitious can have high stakes. In the face of such stakes, practices change to accommodate these categories: where "superstition" is discouraged or even outlawed, communities may modify rituals so that they take on a new life within what is considered legitimate religious expression. In other cases (meditation, for example, as we shall see in The Secularization of Meditation), adherents may attempt to move a practice out of the religious category into the secular, availing themselves of the prestige of the dominant construals of science and rationality and the institutional resources available only to secular projects. Secularity, therefore, does not simply displace religion (though in some cases it may); rather, it serves as a driver of change and reconfiguration of religious belief, practice, and interpretation.

The way secularism operates is also a product of its complementary constituting of the realm of religion. "Religion," in the religious-secular binary, is often modeled largely on Christianity (especially in its Protestant forms) and construed as a matter of private belief, experience, and personal choice, while the secular is construed as a kind of neutral space of rational, public discussion and political activity in which sectarian matters and unfalsifiable matters of faith are purportedly set aside. A naturalistic picture of the world lurks in the background. What is often masked, however, is that the secular is not something that is simply *there* as the natural state of things that remains after we strip away the religious. Rather, it is rooted in a complex of tacit assumptions, views, and social practices that make this position seem "natural" even though it is deeply cultural, contingent, and historically constituted, emerging largely from the European Enlightenment and its intellectual and cultural successors. The categories of religious and secular constitute particular ways of carving up and shaping modes of human life. Moreover, the very naturalization of secularism—its presumption of the rational, empirical, natural, and unbiased stance—masks, while at the same time making more effective, its potential ideological functions, which can sometimes be deployed repressively.

We should be cautious, therefore, about taking religious and secular as descriptive categories adequate to the task of discerning social realities. While we might in a general way use these categories to distinguish certain phenomena—a ritual sacrifice versus a democratic election, for example—we would be misguided in thinking that the world naturally and unambiguously cleaves itself into these two categories, as modern secular states often portray it. Rather, the categories are rhetorically deployed for various purposes by groups—religious institutions, state actors, scientific organizations, etc.—to particular ends within particular sociopolitical contexts. The setting up of religious and secular categories in such contexts opens up certain possibilities and closes down others. These categories, when bolstered by force of law, can have the power to help establish or curtail certain forms of life.

Yet not all "secular" or "religious" forms are uniform across cultures. There are, I would suggest, multiple secularisms that draw upon traditional cultural resources and vary with particular national formations of law and governance. The secular and the religious are configured in ways particular to the sociopolitical configurations of particular states. Different national cultures have taken up this set of categories and adapted it to various indigenous cultural ingredients and different purposes, debates, commitments, and projects.

Secularism and Early Buddhist Modernism

Lest we get too lost in generalities, let us turn our attention to some particular examples to illustrate the porousness, constructedness, diversity, and real-world effects of the religious-secular binary. Buddhism provides illustrations in which particular configurations of this binary have been a significant factor in religious change. The case of Buddhism also demonstrates the inadequacy of a purely oppositional understanding of Buddhism as a religion and secularism as simply the lack of religion. Instead, Buddhism has often been transformed and indeed strengthened through interface with secular discourses, not by resisting them but by incorporating them. Indeed, one of the major ways in which Buddhism around the world has modernized is through its rearticulation in the languages of science and secular thought. This began in the colonial period in Asia, when Buddhists who were either colonized, as in Ceylon and Burma, or concerned about the economic and military hegemony of the West, as in China and Japan, began reinterpreting and representing Buddhism as a system of thought and ethics more attuned than the religion of the colonizers to the emerging scientific worldview. Anagārika Dharmapāla (1864–1933) in Ceylon, Shaku Sōen (釈 宗演 1859–1919) in Japan, and Taixu (太虛 1890–1947) in China, all put forward the idea that Buddhism was uniquely compatible with modern science and, further, was itself a kind of scientific endeavor. All three figures developed a similar rhetoric that tapped into Western anxieties about the status of Christianity in the face of an emerging and powerful scientific positivism of the late nineteenth and early twentieth centuries, a rhetoric that in some cases attempted to undermine the power of Christianity and its claims of a God who interfered in the course of natural law, a savior who performed miracles and rose from the dead, and a world that was created in six days. On all of the points upon which modern science was challenging a traditional Christian worldview, these Buddhist reformers claimed that Buddhism was on the side of science (Lopez 2008; McMahan 2004, 2008).

This attempt to ally Buddhism and modern science was an important part of Buddhist reform movements in Asia and of their resistance to colonial powers. All of these early reformers tied karma and rebirth to evolution, and they assimilated the Buddhist doctrine of all things emerging from causes and conditions (*hetupratyaya*) to the modern scientific understanding of causality (Dharmapāla, Shaku Sōen). Attempting to explicitly assimilate Darwin's theory of evolution to the doctrine of rebirth, for example, Taixu described evolution as "an infinite number of souls who have evolved through endless reincarnations" (T'ai hsu 1928: 39–40). He similarly invoked passages from various Buddhist sūtras to suggest that they anticipated modern scientific findings on the infinite vastness of space, the microbial world, and various astronomical phenomena (T'ai hsu 1928: 48–52) and concluded that a "union between science and Buddhism" (T'ai hsu 1928: 49) would not just be of benefit to Buddhism, but even more to science itself. The former, he contended, is actually an extension of the scientific method to the "sphere of supreme and universal perception, in which [Buddhists] can behold the true nature of the Universe, but for this they must have attained the wisdom of Buddha himself, and it is not by the use of science or logic that we can expect to acquire such wisdom. Science therefore is only a stepping stone in such matters" (T'ai hsu 1928: 54).

Taixu was only the most prominent Chinese Buddhist thinker of the early twentieth century to take an active interest in interfusing Buddhism with science. As Erik Hammerstrom shows, other Buddhist thinkers in China similarly promoted parallels between secular science and the Dharma in this period (Hammerstrom 2015). This effort involved navigating the newly established categories of "religion," "science," and "superstition" adopted largely from the West. Especially important in early-twentieth-century China was the rejection of "superstition": science was the road to knowledge, and superstition represented not just a personal weakness on the part of practitioners but also an obstacle to the growth and flourishing of the newly established nation-state. Those articulating a place for Buddhism under the conditions of Chinese modernity were compelled to vigorously differentiate it from superstition and align it with science—science not just as a set of practices or an epistemological approach but also as a "sign of modernity," an "ideological entity, a reified concept referring to an epistemology and a set of cultural values, all of which had political implications" (Hammerstrom 2015: 4). In navigating these categories, many Buddhist thinkers drew upon Buddhist logic, epistemology, and theories of (especially) the Consciousness-only school. Yet they did not only simply attempt to force Buddhist doctrine into a scientific mold but also used it to critique scientism, materialism, and social evolutionism by suggesting that Buddhism offered a sort of higher empiricism and a more humane, nonviolent philosophy of life.

The case of China was one unique component of an emerging discourse of "scientific Buddhism" in which an initial sorting began within Buddhism between the religious and the secular, as well as the perhaps equally potent categories of the superstitious and the spiritual. Many Asian reformers implicitly accepted some colonists' critiques of their own tradition in terms of foreign categories "idolatry" and "superstition" and strove to move Buddhism away from practices that could be interpreted as such and toward an emphasis on philosophy, ethics, and texts. They also made use of interpretations of the "spiritual" emerging in, for example, Transcendentalism, as a transcultural, transreligious reality at once deeply personal and universal, in which all religions participated but to which none could lay exclusive claim. It is no coincidence that this idea of the spiritual mirrored in some respects the notion of the secular as a neutral realm free from sectarian bias.[3] Under colonialism, the threat of colonialism, and European economic hegemony, these Buddhist reformers reformulated their tradition, sorting that which could be interpreted along the lines of scientific rationalism and spirituality away from what the colonists considered superstitious, idolatrous, and primitive. As the emerging categories of religious and secular congealed, therefore, the most prominent Buddhist thinkers of this period drew primarily upon secular discourses like physical science, psychology, and semisecular schools of philosophy like Transcendentalism and Idealism in their reinterpretations of their tradition (McMahan 2012b). And yet it is important to note that most of these reformers were Asians, not Westerners imposing a "Western" worldview on passive Asian Buddhists. Reformers were creatively combining elements of traditional Buddhist doctrine with selected facets of secularity and science for their own purposes—purposes often at odds with those of the European powers.

S. N. Goenka and the De-Religioning of Meditation

This early alliance of Buddhism and secular thought laid the foundations for the conception of Buddhism as uniquely compatible with modern science, an idea that would contribute to the globalization of Buddhism and the secularization of meditation. The recent global prominence of Buddhist and Buddhist-derived forms of meditation and mindfulness practices is rooted in this history of colonialism and the reframing of Buddhism in scientific and secular language. The laicization and secularization of meditation provide a ready example of: (1) how the categories of religious and secular are blurry and co-constitutive and yet have real effects in the world; (2) the transnational, multinodal manner in which certain features of Buddhism have modernized (3); the importance of different societal configurations of religious and secular in shaping Buddhism in particular countries.

The emergence of the Vipassanā movement and its recent secular descendants is one example, and one that also involves a considerable stripping down of Buddhism. As Eric Braun ably chronicles in his recent work, *The Birth of Insight* (2013), mass lay meditation is a recent phenomenon. It began with Ledi Sayadaw (1846–1923) in Burma, who, after the British colonized his country, became convinced that the only way to keep the Dharma from dying out was to begin teaching philosophy and meditation—previously the province of monks—to the laity. In the course of the twentieth century, the lay meditation movement, Vipassanā, spread throughout Southeast Asia and Sri Lanka. The moment in its development that I want to highlight is in the mid-to late twentieth century, when *vipassanā* began to be promoted as a distinctively *nonreligious* practice. Having moved beyond the monastery, it now began to move beyond Buddhist institutional control altogether. While Ledi's approach was firmly embedded in Buddhist doctrine and institutions, the more recent wave of *vipassanā*, represented by the Burmese-Indian teacher S. N. Goenka (1924–2013), shifted focus both rhetorically and practically. Goenka, a lay Buddhist, was the teacher perhaps most responsible for spreading *vipassanā* meditation beyond the boundaries of Buddhism and promoting it as a technique for living in this world and for revealing to the individual the universal human condition.

Practitioners in the Goenka wing of the Vipassanā movement place a great deal of emphasis on *vipassanā* as a *technique* rather than doctrine and on learning the technique from authorized teachers in highly standardized ten-day retreats. This technique, in Goenka's view, was the essence of the Buddha's teaching. This does not mean Goenka eschewed all other Buddhist doctrine, however. Recognizing impermanence, selflessness, and suffering—the three marks of existence in Buddhism—is, he believed, essential to the gaining of insight. Universal compassion, the Five Precepts, and several other basic Buddhist doctrines also figure prominently in his work. Most of the doctrines he emphasized, however, are those that most comfortably fit within a broadly secular framework of knowledge and a naturalistic picture of the world. There is very little ritual or emphasis on the supernatural, and instead, the language he used to describe *vipassanā* combines traditional Buddhist ideas with many drawn from the lexicon of secularity—*vipassanā* is an *art of living, a technique, a science*. It discovers the *law of nature* within. It is *result-oriented*, like physical exercise (Goenka 2002: 15). Goenka insisted that Vipassanā is not tied to any dogma, belief system, institution, or religion. Although he presented the movement as perpetuating a practice developed 2,500 years ago by the Buddha, he displayed an ambivalent relationship to "Buddhism" and indeed all religions. While emphasizing tolerance between religions, he often spoke and wrote dismissively of "gurudom," cultism, dogmatism, and sectarianism. He often took pains to differentiate *vipassanā* from "magic and miracles." "*Vipassanā*," Goenka once insisted in an interview, "is beyond all religion, beyond all sects, beyond all beliefs, beyond all dogmas and cults—it is a pure science of mind and matter." (2002: 14). Goenka not only repeatedly denied that he was teaching a religion but also denied that the Buddha himself taught one. Instead, Gautama taught the *dhamma* (Sanskrit: *dharma*), the natural order of things. Use of the term "*dhamma*" in this sense frees it from simply being "doctrines" of Buddhism as an institutional religion. According to Goenka, the *dhamma* that the Buddha perceived was not "Buddhism"—it was a universal truth. Goenka, therefore, took the term *dhamma* back to at least one of its original meanings—the way things are, the natural order of things—and quite deliberately attempted to disaggregate it from the "religion" of Buddhism.

Also prominent in Goenka's teachings is an insistence on universalism paralleling the purported universalism of secular and scientific epistemic orientations. Indeed, part of the skeptical attitude toward "religion" among this branch of Vipassanā is due to its tendency to fracture humanity into competing factions. When he did speak favorably of religion, it was the "quintessence of religion"—morality, discipline, and love—rather than the "outer shell" of religion—"rites, rituals, ceremonies, etcetera, which are likely to turn into different cults" (2002: 49–50). The truth he invited people to partake in was not the truth of a particular religion, but what he insisted was a universal truth revealed not by dogma or religious authorities but by direct experience of a "law of nature [which] is the same for everybody" (2002: 13).

This framing of *vipassanā* as a scientific, universal, instrumental, and empirically based art of living in this world was a pivotal move in the modern history of meditation, one whose consequences have extended considerably beyond the Vipassanā movement itself. It is in no way a coincidence that this framing makes liberal use of the vocabularies of secular disciplines and forms of knowledge, quite consciously placing *vipassanā* outside the realm of the religious and, especially, the "superstitious." For the first time in history, Buddhist meditation practices were beginning to be taught outside explicitly Buddhist institutional contexts, and to be welcomed into these uncharted territories, it would have to negotiate the boundaries of the religious-secular binary. No doubt this reframing has been an essential factor in the spread of *vipassanā* to, according to the website, over 170 centers in dozens of countries around the world (Dhamma.org n.d.). Perhaps more important to our inquiry than this wide geographical diffusion, however, is that it is also taught in secular institutions like prisons, hospitals, and schools. Goenka advocated the penetration of *vipassanā* into all areas of society and employed the vocabulary of science and universalism over against religion to aid in this effort. "Some people take [*vipassanā*] as a religion, a cult, or a dogma, so naturally there is resentment and opposition. But Vipassanā should only be taken as pure science, the science of mind and matter, and a pure exercise for the mind to keep it healthy. What could be the objection? And it is so result-oriented, because it starts giving results here and now. People will start accepting this" (2002: 31). And, indeed, many have.

Vipassanā, therefore, was fashioned to resemble the kind of neutrality to which the secular gaze aspires: a nonjudgmental, nonreactive, unbiased observation free of sectarian influence. This, I want to suggest, is neither a seamless convergence of ancient and modern modes of inquiry into one technique nor merely the foisting of modern secular epistemology onto Buddhist ones. Rather, it is a selective bringing forward, reinterpretation, and transformation of specific Buddhist practices that can be made to resonate with modern secular ones and function in secular institutional contexts. No doubt, there is some amount of borrowing from the prestige, legitimacy, and authority of scientific and secular discourses. But the stakes here are not merely rhetorical. They involve the place that Goenka and his movement have hoped to gain for *vipassanā* in Indian and many other societies—the hope that it would filter into every facet of modern life, including government, corporate, and educational life.

The Secularization of Meditation

The new meanings and functions of Buddhist-derived meditation practices have spread around the globe taking up residence in different locations and institutional settings. But this—and other forms of modernization—have not been a simple linear process of the Westernization or uniform secularization. To illustrate this point, let's look briefly at a few examples of how different ways of constituting the religious and the secular have shaped Buddhist practice in different countries. When the mass meditation movement began in Burma, use of secular language was not necessary because Burma was a fairly homogeneous Buddhist society. Ledi Sayadaw was not attempting to take meditation beyond the ken of Buddhism but rather to strengthen Buddhism and its institutions, which were threatened and weakened by colonization. It was when the Vipassanā movement was taken to the far more pluralistic environment of postcolonial India that it had to situate itself in relation to various religions, secular institutions, and a secular government. The idea that Hindus, Muslims, Buddhists, Jains, and people of all religious traditions could equally benefit from *vipassanā* practice mirrors the very shape of secularism in India, which is not a separation of church and state but a pluralism in which all religions ostensibly have the same rights and are included in the public sphere. But the success of Vipassanā in India depended on a new gambit: to present it not simply as a movement within one of the world's great religions but as something beyond the fray of the multifarious religions jostling for allegiance; something that was at once the essential element of the Buddha's teaching and yet not bound to Buddhism as a "religion," as well as something that could be practiced by people of any religion because of its universality.

Because of the Indian origins of Buddhism and the particular pluralistic conception of secularism in India, incorporating "religious" practices into public life does not pose the same kind of problem that it does in the United States, where the next significant move in the reframing of meditation as a secular practice would take place. In the United States, practices that might be considered "religious" have a greater hurdle for being promoted in the public sphere. Unlike in India, the US constitution prohibits state establishment or support of any religion. Secularism is interpreted as separation of church and state rather than equal inclusion of all religions in the public sphere. And while it is well known that religious influence (nearly always Christianity) often transgresses the putative boundaries of the secular, there is, in Thomas Jefferson's words, a "wall of separation" between church and state. No state organization is permitted to support, promote, or fund a religious organization.

It is not surprising, therefore, that when *vipassanā* and other Buddhist and Buddhist-derived meditation practices came to the United States, they underwent a more radical secularization process. Perhaps the epitome of this process is Jon Kabat-Zinn's highly successful Mindfulness-Based Stress Reduction program. Kabat-Zinn, who has had extensive training in both *vipassanā* and Zen meditation, combined elements of each into a meditation program that has been quite consciously excised of explicitly religious language in accordance with the particular religious-secular configuration of the United States (Kabat-Zinn 1990).[4] In his books, talks, and articles, he avoids all but the most vague references to the Buddhist origins of these practices and rearticulates them as secular, therapeutic, clinical, and sometimes "spiritual" practices. "Mindfulness" has subsequently taken on a life of its own in the United States, quite outside any Buddhist organizations, and it is rapidly spreading worldwide.

Perhaps the most striking development in this story is that within the last decade or two, the mindfulness movement has established itself firmly in some of the most powerful institutions in the United States and, therefore, the world. Many major corporations, such as Google, Target, and General Mills, offer their employees courses in mindfulness and meditation. It has become a staple of clinical practice in psychologists' offices and hospitals. Most significant for our purposes, it is being taught in many government-funded institutions as well, including many public universities that now have graduate programs in contemplative studies, and in public middle and high schools, which are forbidden to promote religion. Numerous government grants have been awarded to study clinical applications of mindfulness and meditative practices. Health insurance companies are beginning to cover it, and even the US military has experimented with a mindfulness program.

What are the conditions for the possibility of such a shift in the institutional home of meditation practices from (exclusively) Buddhist monasteries to some of the most prominent and powerful secular institutions in the world? Perhaps the most important is the articulation of mindfulness as something that can be studied scientifically and produce empirically verifiable results. The number of scientific studies of meditation in the West has increased exponentially in the last two decades, many focusing on clinical applications of meditation, brain imaging, and neuroplasticity. Popular media in the United States have reported many of these studies and sometimes inflated their claims, causing a storm of enthusiasm among both clinicians and popular readers. A rash of recent mindfulness literature extols the capacity of a practice originally developed by celibate ascetics hoping to transcend *saṃsāra* to increase satisfaction in countless areas of worldly, secular life: career, marriage, parenting, sex, business, sports, money management, business acumen, efficiency at work, playing musical instruments, and knitting. It is widely promoted as a form of stress relief and as a therapeutic technique for the alleviation of various psychological ailments, especially for the professional classes with frenetic work lives.

These radical developments in the history of Buddhist meditation are the result, first, of the Asian reformers' reframing of Buddhism in secular-scientific language beginning over a century ago, and second, of figures such as Goenka and Kabat-Zinn adapting meditative practices to particular configurations of the secular-religious distinction especially in India and in the United States. Thus, the very category of the secular, not just as an abstract conceptual category but as a matter of law, has helped generate a new form of quasi-religious practice tuned to the sensibilities of professionals in the often highly stressful, competitive marketplace of global capitalism and the personalized and tailored demands of consumer society (Wilson 2014). Yet, despite the apparent secularity of the mindfulness movement, it cannot be construed as simply a move from "religion" to the "secular" in some absolute sense. Indeed, this example shows that the line between these two is blurry, ambiguous, and negotiable. Meditation, of course, continues to be practiced in monasteries along with Buddhist soteriological, ethical, and philosophical elements, and a continuum of practice exists between this and the most utilitarian and clinical applications of mindfulness. Many people consider meditation not just a secular, therapeutic practice but as part of "spiritual life," which in its contemporary usage opens up new attitudes, dispositions, beliefs, and practices that fail to conform neatly to the religious-secular binary. There is a sense in many writings on mindfulness that it can re-enchant and sacralize all of everyday life. Through these practices, the literature suggests, the dullness, stressfulness, and meaninglessness of alienated work in a system of utilitarian global capitalism can be reinterpreted as bristling with nuance and hidden meaning, and that it can reinvigorate ethical life and fine-tune one's connections with others. Thus, in many cases it retains concerns that at the very least echo those of religion, inhabiting and helping to constitute an indeterminate zone between religious and secular.

Secularism and the Reconfiguration of Buddhism in China and Tibet

My next example is Mainland China, where Buddhism today is in a state of revival in a country with a very different type of secularism than those of either India or the United States. The uniquely Chinese version of secularism is not just a background of tacit assumptions, nor a political structure that relegates religion to the private sphere, nor a matter of separation of church and state. Nor does the model of religion as private belief derived from Christian nations fit well.[5] While all secular states play some role in defining religion and thereby determining what is and is not a legitimate religion, Chinese secularism functions as a more aggressive instrument of control, definition, legitimation, and marginalization, than many secularisms of European, North American, and Asian states. Communist Party officials must be atheist, and despite the recent resurgence of religion, official policy, while no longer aggressively dedicated to the destruction of religion, by no means encourages it unless it can be wrapped into sanctioned political and social agendas. Current policy adopts a managerial approach in which certain expressions of religion are encouraged and others discouraged or outright repressed, depending on whether they can be employed toward larger Party goals (Goossaert and Palmer 2011; Ji 2011). And in contrast to India, and to a certain extent the United States, where religion has been a valued part of national culture, in modern China it has been seen largely as an obstacle to progress.

Examples of such management with regard to Buddhism include both overt and subtle forms, which often blur the boundaries between secular and religious in ways quite different than those mentioned in this chapter. They include the often aggressive involvement of the government in Tibetan monastic affairs (Cabezón 2008) and the choosing of reincarnate lamas (Barnett 2012). A more subtle shaping of Buddhism in China is illustrated by a current revival of the theme of scientific Buddhism that we've been addressing. The World Buddhist Forums, of which there have now been four, beginning in 2006 with the most recent in 2015, have served as platforms for the presentation of Buddhism as scientific, "cultural," and aligned with larger Communist Party social and political goals.[6] A Xinhua News Agency article entitled "China Encourages Buddhism-Science Dialogue to Promote Building Harmonious Society" illustrates this (Li Jianmin 2009). It reports on a seminar at the Second Forum that brought together Buddhist leaders with scientific thinkers. The article mentions "physics, brain science, and psychology" as productive fields for the meeting of Buddhism and science. Zhu Qingshi, a chemist from the Chinese Academy of Sciences, is quoted saying: "If you think Buddhism only means burning incense and praying, then you are going far away from its real spirit" (Li Jianmin 2009). He thinks of Buddhism, he says, as a system of knowledge and "not a religion." The article quotes participants on the compatibility of Buddhism and science; the humanity, rather than divinity, of the Buddha; the atheism and rationality of Buddhism; and its support of science and technology against "superstition . . . the enemy of science." It also lauds Buddhist monks who use technology, learn science, and are "communicating [with] 'this world' via cell phones and promoting their doctrines via computers and Internet" (Li Jianmin 2009), presumably in contrast to those who attempt to communicate with the "other world" of spirits and ancestors. The piece also quite clearly promotes Buddhism as a potential force for contributing to China's creation of a "harmonious society," a concept that floods official media: "China has been committed to building a harmonious society in the country and pushing for building a harmonious world over recent years, and it has been rallying all positive forces to attain the goal, including seeking wisdom and inspiration from its profound traditional culture" (Li Jianmin 2009). Another Xinhua article on the recent Third Buddhist Forum also repeatedly refers to Buddhism as a "science of mind" and emphasizes its usefulness in building a "harmonious society" and promoting world peace (Li Jianmin 2009).

These conferences are organized by the State Administration for Religious Affairs, which regulates all recognized religions in China, and the Buddhist Association of China, which often serves as a bridge between Chinese Buddhists and the government and is charged with communicating government regulations to Buddhists.[7] The themes at the conferences mirror themes publicly articulated by the Chinese Communist Party in recent years (Ji 2011: 43–44). So here we see articles in the state-sponsored media outlet putting forth not simply a report on a conference but a normative presentation of Buddhism, a sketch of what kind of Buddhism is to be sanctioned and nourished in the building of the harmonious society. This is clearly a rationalized, secularized Buddhism intended to contrast starkly with anything that could be considered "superstitious." Buddhism is construed as a science of mind, a culture, a traditional moral resource—all terms that surface repeatedly in officially sanctioned descriptions of Buddhism.

While claiming this rationalized Buddhism as a part of its own culture, Chinese media often portray Tibetan Buddhism as an exotic, fascinating but primitive other and Tibetans as subject to irrational religious and separatist passions, a "little brother" to be helped along the road to prosperity and material development by its wiser elder brother. In this sense, it adopts features of the religion-secular binary from the West—as well as an exoticization of the other resembling Western Orientalist representations of the East—but deploys them in service of large-scale, secular, and distinctively Chinese social and political projects.

Meanwhile, outside of China, it is precisely Tibetan Buddhism that currently enjoys considerable attention for its engagement with the sciences and is itself sometimes characterized as a "science of mind." The Fourteenth Dalai Lama, especially, has been a dialogue partner with physicists and neuroscientists, has been instrumental in promoting the scientific study of meditation, and has written a book and several articles connecting Buddhism and various aspects of the sciences (Dalai Lama 2005). He is often acclaimed by the Western press for his declared openness to revising Buddhist doctrines in light of scientific truth and is seen as a rational reformer pioneering the fusion of ancient wisdom and modern science. All of this has indirectly helped generate more awareness of Tibetan Buddhism among Europeans and Americans and has brought more people into the fold of sympathy with the cause of Tibetan autonomy. The Dalai Lama has also promoted "secular ethics" on the model of Indian secularism. Other Tibetan teachers outside of China have programs that have explicitly "secular" curricula that require minimal adherence to traditional Buddhist doctrines and values and other programs that are more explicitly based on Mahāyāna and Tantric literature (McMahan 2012b).

Thus, we see two distinct communities employing the Buddhist engagement with science and secular modes of knowledge toward two very different ends. Outside of China, Tibetan Buddhism is transforming itself through its ever-closer interactions with scientific and secular institutions in Europe and the United States. Emory University, for example, has an exchange program that sends American students to Dharamsala, India, to study Tibetan Buddhism while monks in monasteries there go to Emory specifically to augment their monastic curriculum through courses in science. Meanwhile, in China, as Ji Zhe puts it:

> The political use of Buddhism by the government continuously affects Buddhist discourse and performance. The Buddhist institutions have to adapt themselves as closely as possible to politically correct rhetoric and organize Buddhist collective activities according to the demands of the state. . . . Chinese Buddhism as a social field has been reconfigured and continues to be reconfigured during this process,

because the social reputation and influence of a monastery no longer depends only on its traditional religious prestige, but more and more on its leaders' capacities, and the possibilities and choices for managing its relations with outside secular forces. (2011: 45)

In both cases, Buddhist communities become more intertwined with secular institutions and cultural forces, gaining greater legitimacy and prestige, which does not lead necessarily to the decline of Buddhism as a religion but may indeed be an engine of religious change. Such alliances include both costs and benefits. Buddhism in China enjoys a degree of legitimacy and a public stage afforded by reframing itself in terms of science, culture, commercialism, and secular political forces, but it becomes beholden to those forces and loses autonomy and its more explicitly religious aspects in the process. This is not to say that all of Chinese Buddhist intertwining with the secular is a top-down process imposed by the state, with a population passively accepting state-sponsored iterations of the dharma. Popular Buddhist movements that also respond to and incorporate elements of modernity and secularism also have emerged. Gareth Fisher, for example, discusses groups that creatively blend widely diverse elements in modern Chinese "cultural repertoires," that is, inventories of knowledge and practice that contain "cultural building blocks that active agents creatively combine and recombine as part of their making of self and society" (2011: 347). Such creative combinations might include liturgies of sutra chanters as well as narratives of Mao as a bodhisattva (Fisher 2011). Ji Zhe also discusses popular movements in tension with "official Buddhism" and the possibility that "constraints may be transformed into resources" in a secularism that constitutes a "dialectical process for deconstructing and reconstructing religion" (2008: 260).

For Tibetan Buddhists outside of China attempting to preserve their tradition in exile, alliance with secular discourses and institutions is less a matter of necessity and more a matter of highlighting certain elements of the tradition—philosophy, ethics, meditation—that resonate with the cultures in which exiles live. While free from the politically repressive forces within China, Tibetan Buddhists in exile still must navigate social imaginaries quite different from their own and make difficult choices about which seeds of the dharma will likely flourish and which might wither in the West. In the broadest sense, this is not historically unique. Buddhists have always had to negotiate with larger social and political forces. What is unique about this period is that Buddhists of different schools and in widely divergent locales must all position themselves in relation to the same discourse that constitutes the various configurations of the religious-secular binary.

Buddhism, Binaries, and Ironies

These cases of Buddhist communities and individuals navigating the boundaries of religious, secular, spiritual, and superstitious illustrate the intertwining of secular and religious motivations, the co-constituting of the very categories of religious and secular, and the porousness of the boundaries between them. While the secular may have been invented to keep the supposedly irrational realms of religion and superstition at bay, it is also deployed for particular social, political, and indeed *religious* ends. The essential irony of secularism is that its rhetoric paints it as a neutral, authoritative space of nonsectarian rational discussion—a common ground upon which all can stand in order to come to unbiased conclusions—yet the secular itself becomes a realm of contestation, a discourse of power, and in some cases a mode of quasi-religious ideological formation. The search for a common rational framework in which the passions of the religious imagination are set aside remains elusive. Secularizing modes of Buddhism can acquire a similar irony. They can appear as forms of Buddhism that, following the classical narrative of secularism, have simply cast off outdated rituals and beliefs leaving the essentials. Yet if we take into account the more complex narrative of secularism—that it is not simply the "subtraction" of religion; that it is not a neutral space but a family of value-laden discourses with their own histories, cultures, and sociopolitical projects; that it is not simply the opposite of religion but is co-constitutive of the very concept of "religion"—then these new forms of secularizing Buddhism also become more complex and incapable of fitting a narrow model of either "religion" or "secularism."

Yet, despite the limitations of these categories, their deployment in various state contexts has had profound real-world effects on Buddhist traditions. The particular ways in which secularism and religion have been configured in the United States, for example, has provided the background conditions for a radically new chapter in the long history of Buddhist meditation traditions. For the first time in history, these practices have taken on a life outside any Buddhist institutional control and have taken up residence in some of the world's most prominent secular institutions. They are utilized to ends in some cases peripheral or even antithetical to those of "traditional" forms of Buddhism. Buddhist institutions, in turn, draw from the prestige of scientific studies of meditation and in some cases offer explicitly "secular" programs. In the Chinese case, Buddhist institutions have significantly transformed themselves under pressure of the managerial secularism of the Communist Party, having to carve out places within the narrow space of legitimate, state-sanctioned "religion" while avoiding falling into the realms of "superstition." In all of these cases, the categories of religious and secular pose particular problems and provide concrete opportunities and limitations that vary significantly depending on national context. Rather than a singular, monolithic secularization process spreading across the globe uniformly, we find multiple secularisms and multiple configurations of the religious-secular binary— in our examples, in India, the United States, and China—each of which nourishes certain forms of religion, discourages others, fosters new movements, and encourages others to wither. The field of tensions erected by the religious-secular binary drives transformation of religious traditions as they must navigate these tensions and refashion practice in diverse and rapidly changing sociopolitical landscapes.

4

Women and Vietnamese Buddhist Practice in the Shadow of Secularism

Alexander Soucy

In the late 1990s, when I started doing research in Hanoi, Vietnam, most Buddhist practitioners did not conceive of Buddhism as a religion in the Modern sense, and many still do not.[1] When I went to pagodas and joined in chanting sutras, old women—who were the overwhelming majority of practitioners at the time—would ask if I followed the Buddha (*theo Phật*) but would not ask if I was a "Buddhist" (*Phật tử*—literally "child of the Buddha").

The common practices were devotional in nature, and consequently Vietnamese Buddhism has been often inaccurately described in sectarian terms as "Pure Land Buddhism," despite the fact that most practitioners did not make sectarian identity claims. Furthermore, they would not specify that attaining the Pure Land—much less enlightenment—was the goal of their practice. Buddhists in Hanoi in the late twentieth century chanted sutras, made offerings, supplicated members of the Buddhist pantheon, and burned spirit money. They mostly spoke about their Buddhist practice as bringing peace of mind, improving overall disposition, or bringing good luck, health, and material benefit to themselves and their families (Soucy 2012: Ch. 4).

They also held rituals for the dead, aimed at easing their passage through hell, or at (more vaguely) providing a more comfortable afterlife. Spirit mediumship was also a common occurrence in mother goddess shrines that were part of the Buddhist pagoda precincts, sometimes performed by mediums who would be brought in to service the deities in the shrine, but sometimes by resident nuns or monks who doubled as mediums. These rituals, too, were aimed entirely at bringing about positive this-worldly outcomes, like success in business ventures or escaping illnesses (mental or physical) that were attributed to the workings of the supernatural. Conspicuously absent were expressions of soteriological or transcendent goals, which are a central feature of the modern construct of religion as laid out by Peter Beyer (2006: 81), Niklas Luhmann (2013: 56), and Charles Taylor (2011: 32–33).

To a large degree, this engagement with the supernatural world is still the way that Buddhism is practiced today, both throughout Vietnam and in the majority of community-based overseas Vietnamese Buddhist pagodas. However, in Hanoi there has been the beginning of a shift since the new millennium. Groups that express a distinctly Zen identity are becoming more commonplace (e.g., Soucy 2016, 2017: 150–57). In response, I am now seeing a more pronounced counter-assertion of Pure Land sectarian identity made by some monks.

These assertions of sectarian identity are integral to the Modernist discourses that have sought to resituate Buddhism by creating distinctions between an orthodox Buddhist "world religion" (usually framed as being directly transmitted from the historical Buddha) and the regular practices and beliefs that we might call "traditional" as a shorthand. My contention is that these changes have emerged out of the globalization of Buddhism, which was initiated from the colonial encounter, the pressures of Christian missionaries, improvements in communication and transportation, and both spiritual and intellectual interest in Buddhism in the West. David Held et al. (1999) make a strong case that the acceleration caused by the advancement in communication and transportation technologies has brought about a unique kind of globalization that was distinct from the globalization that existed in the premodern period. They characterize the older form of global flows as "thin" globalization, which they contrast with the qualitatively different modern form of "thick" globalization. The latter started in the 1500s, accelerating in the 1800s, until reaching its apogee after 1945. The consequences of "thick" globalization on Buddhism is that it has created and spread a recognition (or construction) of unity between the traditions of different Buddhist cultures in Asia. As interactions between Buddhist practitioners, missionaries, and Western scholars increased, Buddhism was systematically restructured as a singular "world religion" through this process. In doing so, orthodoxies have hardened, and distinctions within the religion, and between other religions, have been accentuated.

The problem that arises, and the one that I will look at here, is that the creations of orthodoxies continue to also be thoroughly wrapped in the exercise of hegemonic power that asserts authority over marginalized groups, particularly women. In the Vietnamese context, labels like "superstition" (*mê tín dị đoan*) are employed to discursively marginalize women's practices and beliefs as lacking legitimacy. Those practices are contrasted with a Buddhist orthodoxy that was constructed only in the recent past. This orthodoxy is, not coincidentally, particularly attractive to men and regulated by the male-dominated Buddhist institution. So, for example, the monk Thích Thanh Ân has written a book called *An Explanation of Orthodoxy and Superstition* (Luận giải Chính tín và Mê tín) in which he contrasts various superstitions (spirit mediumship, burning spirit money, divination, séances, supplications, and so on) with correct beliefs, like causation, karma, and the Three Refuges (Thích Thanh Ân 2012). In making these contrasts, he is perpetuating reformist discourses that can be found in the Buddhist journals in Vietnam starting in the 1930s (e.g., Thích Niệm Châu 1937). The way that the Vietnamese state has been involved in enforcing these distinctions, through the creation of laws that target superstitious practices as detrimental to the modern socialist state, and enforcing them through the instruments of institutionalized violence (particularity the police and the judicial systems) shows the interlacing of hegemonic gender structures that serve to maintain male authority and disempower women (Connell 1987).[2] The restructuring of Buddhism as a religion with specific orthodoxies has, therefore, been entirely codependent with the hegemonic masculine power and its institutional political and economic structures.

This creates an interesting dilemma, which is the central focus of this essay: why have women continued to practice Buddhism in a way that is marginalized, in the face of heavy hegemonic pressure, rather than conforming to the sanctioned orthodoxy? In the past, I have partially dealt with this quandary by showing that the disempowering critiques of women's practice were less important to women than the immediate and more readily perceived benefits attained through Buddhist practice, including building community, identity construction, and building symbolic capital through displays of self-sacrifice and caring in the context of the family (Soucy 2012). I still maintain that these are important considerations. However, here I would like to explore the question by taking into account the way that globalization has restructured Buddhism into a religion with established orthodoxies. I argue that, while orthodoxies were established, the globalization of structures of religion served to create a space that both marginalized and insulated them from critiques emanating from outside the religious field. Meanwhile, the Buddhist institution in Vietnam has always been weak and unable to enforce notions of orthodoxy beyond a small group of elite, male, and mostly urban followers (McHale 2004: 163–64; Woodside 1976: 193–94). Before getting to this central question, I will first outline some theoretical underpinnings of how Buddhism has modernized as a result of globalization. I will then go on to discuss the specific way that this has played out in the Vietnamese context. Finally, I will explore the main issue, of how women's practice often does not conform with the way that Buddhist orthodoxy stipulates, and the reasons for why they persist, despite seemingly compelling pressures to conform to the orthodox discourses.

Buddhism as a Religion

The Buddhist reform movements in the late nineteenth and early twentieth centuries were part of a bigger process of what Peter Beyer has argued was the globalization of religion. Beyer, in *Religions in Global Society* (2006), borrowing from Niklas Luhmann, demonstrates that Western society reorganized itself in the Modern period into self-referential and differentiated "function systems," beginning around the fifteenth century (Beyer 2006: 30). These function systems, according to Luhmann, include the economic system, the political system, the legal system, and so on (Borch 2011: 80–87). Function systems are structured communications that are recursive, in the sense that they have a tendency to be self-referential communications that are directed at, and pertain to, those who are active in the system (Beyer 2006: 41). That is, there are internally established and implicit rules for the way that they work, and while they are understood by participants, they do not necessarily translate into other systems. At the core of function systems are binary codes and programs that serve to give function systems their identities (Beyer 2006: 44; Borch 2011: 71–72). These binary codes serve to define the systems and distinguish them from other function systems and include: healthy/sick for the medical system; true/false for the scientific system; owning/not-owning for the economic system; legal/illegal for the legal system; powerful/powerless for the political system, and so on. Programs put these codes into operation, so that, to give one example, the program for the economic system involves buying and selling.

In the Modern period, religion has also been restructured in this way, which is to say that it has been constructed and recognized as a form of social activity that is distinguished from other nonreligious forms. One effect of this is the differentiation between the religious and the secular, and another is the birth of the academic discipline of Religious Studies. For religion, the overall code relates to salvation (in opposition to damnation, however that is defined within a particular tradition.) Modern societies are characterized by these divisions of human activities, which are both integrated in some way and independent. Thus, religion is seen in distinction to science; medicine should not be contingent on faith; religions are suspect if they are primarily geared toward making money, and so on.

This way of organizing society and structuring behaviors and institutions, including the differentiated religious system, has become globally dominant. For religion, this is seen in the way that all traditions in one way or another feel compelled to position themselves in relation to the structure of religion as a category, even though individual practitioners may not habitually think in this way.[3] The ways that traditions relate to the globalized structure of religion as a function system may include remodeling in such a way that previous beliefs, practices, and institutions take on the particular characteristics of religion as a system (which is the approach that dominated the Buddhist reform movements of the nineteenth and twentieth centuries.) It could also result in self-exclusion through declarations that one's tradition is not "religion" but "spirituality," a "practice," a "way a life," or other similar designation (Beyer 2006: 8).

The result of the globalization of religion as a system has, therefore, been that certain constellations of practices and beliefs have come to be defined as religious (and constituting particular religions), and others have not. The fact that it has been globalized can be seen not in that all traditions have been remade into religions but that religion is universally acknowledged and recognized as a phenomenon—a thing— by which traditions are measured, remade, or contrasted. So, while a particular person would not necessarily claim their tradition as a religion, all but the most isolated would understand what religions are and be willing to attribute the label to other traditions, if not their own.

One of the effects of the structuring of religion as a function system is that it creates differentiations. It does this in three ways (Beyer 2006: 15). Firstly, it creates internal differentiations between what is and is not within the boundaries of a particular religion and establishes internal divisions (e.g., between sects.). In other words, it creates orthodoxies, authority to define them, and strategies for their enforcement. Secondly, it distinguishes between one religion and another, creating and defining unities within a religion and differences from others in new ways. Thirdly, it differentiates religion, overall, as a system that stands apart from other nonreligious (i.e., secular) systems. For us, Beyer's ideas are particularly useful in that they provide the framework to look at how Buddhism has taken on an identity and structure as a discrete religion. While Buddhism has always been somewhat held as distinct, this process of religion becoming a globalized system has meant that Buddhism has been restructured, and the distinctions are understood and experienced in fundamentally new ways. This has given rise to what has been called "global Buddhism" (e.g., Baumann 2001), "Buddhist modernism" (e.g., McMahan 2008), and so on. The Modernist Buddhist discourse has had a number of profound effects, including: reinforcing and spreading some traditional sectarian differences, reorganizing them as types of Buddhism; establishing Buddhism as a world religion and constructing a unified core and set of symbols (e.g., the historical Buddha as founder, Bodhgaya as the geographical center, a Buddhist flag, making Wesak into the main Buddhist celebration, making the Three Refuges as the core statement of faith, and so on); creating an orthodoxy that distinguished Buddhism from other religions; reinforcing the notion of a "true" Buddhism (usually framed as the original teachings of the historical Buddha) from misunderstandings, superstitions, or cultural degenerations; and establishing institutions to reinforce the orthodoxy, communicate with other official bodies (the state, other national associations, and so on) that also may have some power to censure.

While Buddhism, of course, existed before the Modern period, the colonial encounter brought about a drastic restructuring of Buddhism and a shift in the way that it was understood and, to some extent, experienced. This process started in the West, with the conceptualization of a Buddhism that "could be construed as a transhistorical and self-identical essence that had descended on various cultures over the course of history" (Lopez 1995: 7). In fact, as Almond has pointed out, it took a number of centuries before Western missionaries and scholars were able to link together the "various culturally diffuse religious phenomena" and recognize them as having the same source (i.e., as being a single religion) (Almond 1988: 7–10). In this way, Buddhism came to be restructured into a thing with a "stable ontological structure" (Lopez 1995: 7), with a founder and a canon that laid out an orthodoxy.

The Buddhist Reform Movement in Vietnam

The hegemonic nature of foreign domination and colonial rule in the nineteenth century led to deep soul-searching by Vietnamese intellectuals, and a consensus that the reason they had been so easily subjugated was due to their own deficiencies (Dutton, Werner and Whitmore 2012: 336; McHale 2004: 4–7). As Marr points out, by the 1920s Vietnamese intellectuals moved away from an East-versus-West paradigm and started to explore options other than full adoption of French culture or total rejection of it. They paid attention to upheavals in China, the Communist Revolution in Russia, Gandhi's struggles in India and their own culture and history for ways to create a uniquely Vietnamese modernity (Marr 1981: 10). Some Buddhists in Vietnam responded by starting a movement to reform Buddhism, influenced by similar movements elsewhere in Asia (DeVido 2007, 2009). The Buddhist reform movement (*Chấn hưng Phật giáo*) aimed to simultaneously make Buddhism modern, and yet to return it to an imagined original state, free from the superstitions that reformers felt had encrusted the authentic tradition. In essence, Vietnamese Buddhists started participating in a global discourse that was remaking Buddhism. While Buddhism had been in Vietnam since possibly as early as the first century CE (Dutton, Werner and Whitmore 2012: 10), it was not an "ism" until the Modern period, when it was reconstituted as a world religion.

The reformers in Vietnam were somewhat late to the game, as other Buddhist countries had started this process decades earlier. They joined in an exchange of ideas through a global network of reformers. Buddhist journals in Vietnam regularly published translated foreign articles. For example, in 1940 the journal published by the Tonkin Buddhist Association, called Đuốc Tuệ (Torch of Wisdom), published a series of articles written by Bernard L. Broughton, the head of the English Maha Bodhi Society, entitled "Why I Believe in Buddhism" [Vì sao tôi tin Phật Giáo] (Broughton 1940). However, it was the Chinese reformers, particularly Taixu, who had the greatest impact, with his ideas of Humanistic Buddhism (DeVido 2007, 2009).

This creation of an orthodoxy was made through the assertion of distinctions that contrasted Buddhism as it was either taught by the historical Buddha, or in the Vietnamese context against an imagined Zen past. The very name of the movement in Vietnamese (Chấn hưng Phật giáo), and the widely used English translation, Buddhist "Revival," contains with it an implicit critique of the majority contemporary practices. The discourse portrayed a Buddhism in decline that had been encrusted over the centuries by beliefs and practices that were not (in the terms of the discourse) really Buddhist at all, despite the obvious religious effervescence that existed at the time (McHale 2004: 145). Burning spirit money was perhaps the foremost of the targeted practices, as was the supplication of the Buddha(s) for the purpose of seeking worldly benefit. This discourse gave reformers legitimacy, particularly since it synchronized with other Modernist trends. It has persisted in the writings of Buddhist monks like Thích Thanh Từ, who in a booklet called *Superstition and Right Belief* calls burning spirit money an absurd practice (vô lý) (2010: 21) and making wishes to the Buddha nothing but superstition (2010: 26).

The reimagining of Buddhism as a "religion" also involved the creation of unifying symbols. Among the most important was the establishment of the historical Buddha at the symbolic center, as the founder of the religion. Before the modern period, as Snodgrass points out, the Buddha was understood as one of the buddhas rather than being cast as the founder (2009: 22). The concrete results of this process included in the Vietnamese context: remaking Wesak into an internationally celebrated Buddhist holiday (Lễ Phật Đản), which was taken up in Vietnam in the 1930s (Nguyễn-Khoa-Tân 1934: 61); adopting a calendar date based on the birth of the historical Buddha (Phật lịch); adopting the clan name of the Buddha (Śākya, or Thích in Vietnamese) as part of monastic names; adopting an international Buddhist flag in 1950, after participating in the first World Buddhist Congress in Sri Lanka; Bodhgaya displacing more local pilgrimage sites as the epicenter of the religion; transplanting cuttings from the original Bodhi Tree in several locations, including two in Hanoi; and so on.

The new emphasis on a Buddhist orthodoxy required new efforts in public and monastic education. Dharma talks became a common occurrence at the pagodas that were driving this new discourse. Publication also became an important activity in the 1930s. While all kinds of Buddhist publications were emerging, including sutras and devotional texts (McHale 2004: 145), there was an explosion of print material in line with the reformist vision of Buddhism. Another prominent activity was the formation of monastic schools that had a systematized curriculum, to ensure that monks fully understood orthodox Buddhist teachings and did not perpetuate what reformers felt were false understandings and erroneous practices. The educational activities that emerged in the 1930s were precisely because it became necessary to teach and enforce this Buddhist orthodoxy.

Buddhism was also constructed within the framework of Western understandings of religion as distinct from other social activities (or function systems). Religion was seen as taking place at certain times, in certain places, and comprising particular activities that could be recognized as Buddhist. All of this reconstruction of Buddhism stood in stark contrast to the normal ways of practicing. Buddhism was not seen as distinct from other religious expressions in Vietnam. Many saw the natural world interpenetrated with supernatural forces that were potent and could bring great benefit and fortune to oneself, one's family, and one's community. Or, they could be terrible and pernicious, bringing ill-luck, social disharmony, sickness, poverty, drought, accidents, and death. The very categories of natural and supernatural that I use to explain this were, therefore, foreign to this way of thinking. The main focus of Buddhist practice tended to be aimed at interacting with these supernatural forces (buddhas, bodhisattvas, spirits and saints, ghosts, among others) in order to ease one's passage in this life and in the next. However, the forces of Modernity were lining up against this view.

The State and Buddhist Reform

The views that had been propagated by the reformers dovetailed with state intentions and elite discourses and formed a symbiosis that continues to be perpetuated today by the instruments of the state, which in Vietnam include—among others—the media, the Academy, and the Buddhist institution. The state favored the reformist view of Buddhism because it reflected the rationalist, Modernist, discourse that distances religion from superstition and most easily fit with the humanistic ideology of the Communist state. Quán Sứ Pagoda, the headquarters of the state-backed Vietnamese Buddhist Association (*Giáo hội Phật giáo Việt Nam*), continues to reflect this reformed Buddhism in its valorizing of the historical Buddha, in its institution-wide portrayal of a pointedly un-Vietnamese Buddhism, and in the practices and opinions of many in its community (Soucy 2012: 42–51).

From the 1950s until around the turn of the millennium, the predominant discourse in northern Vietnam was staunchly antireligious. After wresting control of Vietnam from France in 1954, the Communist Party started a process of social engineering, which included land distribution and collectivization. They also tried to dismantle institutions that they felt challenged their authority, which represented, in their view, the corrupt feudal society of the past (Malarney 2002: 58–59). This is what Appadurai identifies as an imperative to "subvert and annex the primary loyalties attached to more intimate collectives" (1996: 162), in order to assert the interest of the fragile abstraction of the new nation. Particularly targeted were the institutions of local power. For that reason, communal houses, where the village tutelary deity was worshipped and where the Council of Elders made decisions at the local level, were more quickly and thoroughly dismantled (Endres 2001: 77–80). The family was another institution that was targeted, with attempts made to reform the main life-cycle rituals of weddings and funerals because they were seen as being wasteful and because they were prominent opportunities for conspicuous consumption and the building of status at the level of the village.

Wastefulness and superstition were central arguments aimed against all manifestations of religion. Divination, fortune telling, spirit channeling, geomancy, and possession rituals were particularly targeted and made illegal, and the police heavily enforced this by arresting and harassing anyone who participated, though some officials did it with more vigor than others.

However, the traditions that had been globally restructured as religions were less susceptible to pernicious state oppression. Although allowed to continue (unlike other traditions not classified as religion, like the mother goddess cult), their activities were nonetheless curtailed. The Catholic Church was permitted to exist, but the state undermined the authority of the Vatican (Keith 2012: 248). Buddhism was recognized and allowed to exist on an official level, but Buddhists were harassed in various ways. Some pagodas had properties confiscated. Major rituals were limited. The role they played in performing funerals was, for a while, taken away (Malarney 1996).

While the hard power of the state was exercised against religious practitioners, the negative discourses toward religions were perpetuated in parallel. The media published stories that alternatively criticized and ridiculed religious practice as wasteful, superstitious, and backward remnants of an oppressive feudal past. The Vietnamese Academy, too, participated to some extent, by recognizing certain traditions as being proper religion and others as being less legitimate. For example, an ethnologist who studies in Moscow, named Đặng Nghiêm Vạn, wrote:

> Except for a number of monks, priests and a few of the faithful who declare that they embrace only one religion, such as Buddhism or one of the traditional religious doctrines, the majority of Hanoi believers, although setting up Buddhist altars at home, still go to pagodas for worship, attend medium services, worship their ancestors, consult diviners, and simply, put faith in something friendly whispered in their ear. Since they have faith in a variety of religions, most of them keep up worship practices but few of them are fully committed. In reality, they could be seen as credulous people seeking satisfaction for a momentary spiritual need. (Đặng Nghiêm Vạn 2001: 246)

Membership in the Communist Party was given only to those who were declared atheists. In order to advance in a society where businesses were all state-owned, membership in the Communist Party was effectively mandatory for those who wanted to progress in their careers. Because this concern was more for men than women, men were forced to avoid all religious practices completely, including Buddhism. Buddhist followers for the most part were reduced to a few old women chanting sutras a few times a month (Malarney 1999: 190), which mitigated their threat to the state.

The overwhelming discourse was, therefore, against Buddhist practice. The result was that up until Đổi Mới (the Vietnamese version of Glasnost that began in the late 1980s) most people avoided all religious spaces. Given that the consequences for engaging in religious practice during this period were quite severe, it is not a surprise that involvement with Buddhism was limited to those who were already economically marginalized—particularly old women. After Đổi Mới, this freeze on religious practice continued for a number of years. So, for example, one old man I knew who had been an intelligence officer became interested in Buddhism as he neared retirement, but would only interact with monks away from Hanoi, and did not start taking part in Buddhist rituals until after he retired.

When I started fieldwork in Hanoi in 1997, very few men could be found doing anything at Buddhist pagodas. Young men may have brought their girlfriends to make offerings and supplicate the buddhas for help, but they usually waited outside of the pagoda. Old men, such as the one I just mentioned, sometimes practiced Buddhism, but mostly only if they were involved as ritual experts or leading the chanting sessions (Soucy 2012: Ch. 9). Men who were interested in Buddhism—particularly young ones—were seen as effeminate and were the butt of jokes and caricatures.

The discourse against Buddhism, while losing some of its forcefulness today, has been quite sustained for almost sixty years in northern Vietnam. Under these circumstances, one might think that Buddhism would die out. However, old women, as I have said, continued to go to pagodas and chant sutras through the worst period and continue to do so in large numbers today. So, the question is why, if Buddhist practice was so marginalized by the dominant discourses emanating from the Buddhist institution, the state, the media, and the academy, did women persist in practicing Buddhism? Furthermore, why were they not swayed by the reformers' discourses of orthodoxy pushed by the Buddhist institution and state sanction? Instead, they persisted in practicing a form of Buddhism that did not differentiate between Buddhist and non-Buddhist, between religion and superstition.

Women's Practice in the Face of Power

The construction of gender in Vietnam shapes practice in the Buddhist field. Gender structures and performative expectations have led to men generally avoiding Buddhist spaces and encouraged women to more overtly engage in religious practice. At Vietnamese Buddhist pagodas, both in Vietnam and in the diaspora, the majority of participants are older women. In northern Vietnam, where my research is based, the proportion is as high as 90 percent (Luong 1992: 182; Malarney 1996: 118–20; Soucy 2012: 3), with some exceptions. The men who do participate are mostly older and retired, though this trend is starting to shift.[4] For women, there is a close association between Buddhist practice and constructions of femininity. For younger women, supplication of the buddhas feeds into expectations of emphasized femininity, stressing weakness and dependence as sexually attractive attributes (Soucy 2012: 101–8). For older women, Buddhist practice is usually framed as being done on behalf of the family and is an extension of their expectational role as the primary caregivers (Soucy 2012: 108–17).

In addition to soteriological concerns, Buddhist practice has some clear strategic social benefits for women. Buddhist practice is framed primarily as being done on behalf of the family in order to bring good fortune and harmony and, therefore, has important implications for building identity and accruing symbolic capital within the family and the community. In other words, religious participation and Buddhist identity for women are important for immediate relationship, though this benefit does not transfer to more public economic or political fields.

These concerns of women are in direct conflict with Modernist constructions of Buddhist orthodoxy. Buddhist activity undertaken in the traditional way is usually directed toward this-worldly concerns. By contrast, the idea that Buddhist practice can help with mundane concerns has been systematically marginalized and even ridiculed by reformers, as misunderstandings of Buddhism. The orthodox discourse runs completely counter to the religious practices and aspirations of most female participants by stressing individual salvation through one's own efforts, denying the efficacy of praying to the Buddha for help in the problems of daily life. As the monk Thích Thanh Từ succinctly put it: "Have you ever heard the Buddha praying for liberation of the deceased at any funeral? Never" (Thích Thanh Từ 2000: 33). Furthermore, the distinctions between religions that are characteristic of Modernist orthodoxies also do not agree with the normal views or ways of practicing, which integrate a wide variety of practices to harness an array of supernatural forces for the purposes of bringing benevolence and mitigating the impact of negative supernatural forces. Thus, women supplicate the buddhas and bodhisattvas at pagodas, but they also typically make offerings and supplications at the mother goddess shrines that are also typically included in Buddhist pagoda complexes in the north, leaving money offerings on the various altars of the pagoda precinct in order to be bestowed health, success at work or school, harmony in the family, and so on, rather than for soteriological concerns.

Women's participation in Buddhism is, therefore, being conducted in the face of strong discourses against superstition that discount their efforts as premodern, irrational, wasteful, fruitless, and frankly, silly. These discourses have mostly dissuaded men from practicing Buddhism and presumably should have a cost for women as well. However, I have suggested elsewhere (Soucy 2012) that the pervasive antireligious discourses were not aimed so much at women as they were at men, who were pressured to conform with structural expectations of masculinity by performances of skepticism that built symbolic capital within primarily male fields of contestation. The effect of the Modernist discourse that reshaped Buddhism and established an orthodoxy that focuses on salvation, therefore, is that women's participation in Buddhism reinforces pervasive hegemonic gender structures. This is, I think, true but does not really solve the puzzle of why women have seemingly been impervious to these discourses.

One answer can be found in the way that the Modernist construction of religion, and particularly of Buddhism restructured as a religion, has framed Buddhism as a part of a religious function system. As discussed in this chapter, one of the aspects of modernity has been the construction of function systems, whereby religion is identified and labeled as a system distinct from other systems. Beyer (2006) argues that this modern view of religion is historically a very peculiar social construction but is one that has become globalized. Buddhism, restructured as a religion, was differentiated from other religions, as well as distinctions being drawn between legitimate Buddhism and illegitimate superstition.

More importantly, for our discussion, secularism separates religion, making it fundamentally apart from other function systems (or fields).[5] It is for this reason that Modern democracy separates church and state. This separation means that religion (and Buddhism in this case) operates under its own set of rules, as other function systems similarly follow system-specific rules. It has also created a distinct field in which religion can legitimately take place. This field, like all fields, has its own logic of practice and its own symbolic economy (Bourdieu 1990). Participation in the internal logic of Buddhism as a field self-legitimizes its practices and acts as an insulator that renders discourses that are external to the system as muted, even irrelevant. This has rendered criticisms of religious practice from outside the Buddhist field as irrelevant, since they emanate from those who are not participants of that system and not part of that communication. In a practical sense, it meant that discourses that marginalized Buddhist practice from outside (i.e., in state propaganda, academic discourses that defined Buddhism, or media rhetoric that targeted superstition) had no value for those who were participating within the field.

So, at my main field site at a local pagoda in Hanoi, everyone continued to engage in practices that the state did not condone and the media regularly attacked: spirit medium rituals were held, people burned spirit money and supplicated the buddhas and spirits for worldly benefit, rituals were held for gods outside of the Buddhist pantheon in order to ensure prosperity in business, and so on. However, for those who participated, there was a complete disattachment from the broader discourses that condemned their activities. Instead, they regarded their actions as vital for the well-being of their family and were part of a community that supported this view.

The modern separation of religion as self-contained and distinct (i.e., the religious/secular distinction) helps explain why women have persevered in their practice despite the sometimes heavy secularist, antireligious, humanist, hegemonic discourses over the last century. Going one step further, we notice that women continue to practice Buddhism in a way that defies the Buddhist orthodoxy that was put forward earlier in the twentieth century and has been taken up by the institutions of Buddhist authority. It has been noted by historians like Alexander Woodside that the Reform Movement had limited impact at the time (1976: 193). While reformers sought to delimit the boundaries of the field by distinguishing Buddhism from the non-Buddhist culture or heterodox "superstition," most women continued to perceive the field as being a much wider religious field rather than a delineated Buddhist one. For that reason, most devout Buddhist women do not rely completely on Buddhism, but engage in a full range of religious practices, including Buddhist rituals and sutra chanting, but also fortune telling, geomancy, contacting and assuaging the dead in their various forms, and participating in spirit medium rituals.

If Modernity has insulated Buddhist practitioners from antireligious discourse from powers outside the specific function system, we still need to understand why the Buddhist reformers' discourses—presumably situated within the field—similarly lacked persuasiveness. An explanation for this can be found in the historical weakness of the Buddhist Institution, as a fairly new construction that has not yet fully established itself. Before the twentieth century, there was never any central organization like the Catholic Vatican, nor even the sectarian structures of Buddhism in Japan. By and large, each pagoda was entirely independent, run by the resident monastic without direction from outside. In the last century, as part of the reformist restructuring of Buddhism (and later the state's desire for a central body that could be controlled), various associations were formed in different regions of Vietnam. In the south after the partition of Vietnam (in 1954), the Unified Buddhist Church grew out of the reform associations, as a political force to oppose President Ngô Đình Diệm and then to oppose the war and American intervention (Topmiller 2002). After reunification, the Communist Government formed the Vietnamese Buddhist Association as the central organization to represent and control Buddhism. However, this organization, while important, still does not have much control at the level of individual local pagodas. This weak institution means that at the pagoda level, practitioners have largely been able to continue practicing without interference and rarely pay serious heed to the discourses emanating from the central Buddhist institution.

So, in summary, the separation of the supernatural and the natural continues to impact Buddhism as it is presented at a national level through the Buddhist media, as well as the regular media. Nonetheless, while people draw on the legitimacy that association with this central institution continues to hold, most still practice Buddhism in a way that does not conform with the intentions of the reformers. Neither the state nor the Buddhist institution has had much of an impact on these practices and beliefs, which continue in the face of significant marginalizing discourses.

Conclusion

I have suggested here that the criticism of traditional practices emerged out of the Buddhist reform movement in the first half of the twentieth century, which, in restructuring Buddhism into a religion, created a Buddhist orthodoxy with distinctions between Buddhism and non-Buddhist "superstitions" (*mê tín dị đoan*), "traditions" (*phong tục*), and "culture" (*văn hóa*). While this discourse became dominant in state representations, women especially continued to practice in more holistic ways that did not distinguish between the Buddhist and non-Buddhist but instead saw the world of humans thoroughly infused with supernatural beings and forces. My main argument is that while these distinctions were made, the separation of the religious and the secular turned religion into a function system, or a field, that had its own internal structure. This construction both marginalized and insulated practitioners, who continued to act within the field according to its own logic. The structures of Modernity made the communications of religion internal to the function systems. At the same time, the diffused nature of power, with authority resting at the local (pagoda) level, has meant that efforts to establish central institutions have been slow to establish full authority. Therefore, beyond the central pagoda in Hanoi, practitioners at local pagodas continue to practice in ways that were not sanctioned by discourses of official orthodoxy.

The construction of religion, and of Buddhism as a religion, is fluid and historically contextual. Even in the time I have been doing research in Vietnam, which started in 1997, I have seen a significant shift. Women still continue to engage in traditional practices that were targeted as non-Buddhist by the Buddhist reformers and later by the state-controlled Buddhist institution (embodied in the Vietnamese Buddhist Association) and Buddhist Modernists. Nonetheless, there is a shift by many toward practices that are seen as more orthodox, such as Zen meditation. This shift, I think, is strengthening the Modernist construction of Buddhism as a religion and strengthening the boundaries of a distinctly Buddhist field. The result is that now I am starting to hear more Buddhists create distinctions between Buddhist and non-Buddhist practice in a way that I did not at the beginning of my career and similarly making sectarian identity claims. This suggests that the global spread of the construction of Buddhism as a religion is increasingly influencing the way that Buddhism is practiced and experienced in Vietnam today.

This construction of Buddhism is not inviolable, and while it is gaining increased prominence, there are signs in the twenty-first century that this Modernist construction, while still hegemonically dominant, is starting to crack. Buddhism as a religion that is separated from a secular, nonreligious, world has continued to gain power as a discourse, but there are counter discourses that are starting to emerge. Paradoxically, while Modernist constructions are becoming more prominent, so too is Vietnam also becoming re-enchanted (Taylor 2007). One outcome of this is that the association of structures of masculinity is becoming less entangled with Modernist discourses of secularism, resulting in more men than ever to become participants in a range of Buddhist and other religious practices. Religion in Vietnam is in flux right now, and it is hard to predict what will happen, but I am certain that gender will continue to play an important role in shaping ways in which people are religious.

Part Two

Global Flows

In their attempts to modernize Buddhism, the various Asian reform movements learned from each other. The first formal attempt to modernize Buddhism in Asia was in Siam with King Mongkut's reforms of Buddhism in 1851 (Pearson [2554] 2012). In 1873, in Ceylon, the Panādura debates between a Buddhist monk and a Christian spokesman took place, triggering a Buddhist reform movement that by the end of the 1800s had created "Protestant Buddhism" (Gombrich 1988). In 1868, as Japan entered the Meiji period, the new government organized a persecution of Buddhism that destroyed Buddhist temples, confiscated their land, and forced monks and nuns out of monasteries and back into lay life. This official critical attitude toward Buddhism caused Buddhist adherents to start a *shin bukkyō*, "new Buddhism" movement, whose outlook decades later was much in evidence at the World's Parliament of Religions of 1893 (Ketelaar 1990). In 1885, the British takeover of Burma caused the Theravāda monk Ledi Sayadaw (1846–1923) to reconceive *vipassanā* meditation and make it available for lay people (Braun 2013). By the 1920s, the Chinese reformist monk Taixu (1890–1947) was planning a thorough overhaul of Chinese Buddhist doctrinal teaching, monastic training, and social role (Pittman 2001). Taixu criticized contemporary Buddhist practice as too concerned with ghosts, spirits, deceased ancestors, funerals, and memorial services. To indicate the correct direction, he coined the term *renjian fojiao* (人間佛教), "Buddhism for human life." This evolved into "humanistic Buddhism," the motto of the modern Buddhist movements of Taiwan: Fo Guang Shan (Buddha Light Mountain), Buddhist Compassion and Relief Tzu Chi, and Dharma Drum (Madsen 2007). In Vietnam, the Buddhist Thích Nhất Hạnh translated *renjian fojiao* as "engaged Buddhism," and this evolved into "socially engaged Buddhism" (Hunt-Perry and Fine 2000: 36).

These examples illustrate that the flows of communication and people that propelled the Buddhist reformers were not simply East-West, involving the adoption of European ideas and values into Buddhism. In this part, three chapters address the fact that the Westernization paradigm ignores how Buddhist reformers in Asia were in conversation with each other. The diversity of these encounters and variety of circulations of influence span Ober's survey of Marxist and Buddhist thought connecting Russia to India, Li's examination of the fluctuating relationship between the Japanese Zen proponent D.T. Suzuki and the emergence of modern Chinese Buddhism, and Lau's exploration of the recent case of mainland Chinese interest in non-Chinese forms of Theravāda meditation. These conversations, intra-Asian encounters, and global circulations of influential discourses are crucial to understanding the forms that Buddhism has taken today, around the world. The various agents of Buddhist reform taught and learned from each other to shape new Buddhisms that continue to transform.

5

Socialism, Russia, and India's Revolutionary Dharma

Douglas Ober

In reading the archives of modern Buddhism, most scholars have understood the encounter between Marxism and Buddhism to be a post-1950s phenomenon marked by events such as the Communist invasion of Tibet in 1950, Ne Win's "Burmese Way to Socialism" in the early 1960s, the Cambodian King Sihanouk's Buddhist Socialism of the late 1950s, or the pseudo-Marxist rhetoric of Pol Pot's Khmer Rouge in the 1970s. However, in recent years, a number of scholars have shown how the dialogue between Buddhism and Marxism actually began several decades earlier in places like China, Mongolia, Russia, and Japan.[1] The encounter between Buddhists and Marxists had an equally formative role in colonial India with several of the most influential leaders of Indian Buddhism publicly advocating various strands of Marxist ideology either as close alternatives to Buddhism or in conjunction with it. Most Indian Buddhist interactions with Marxism developed as attempts to resolve the social and political problems of the period. That is, they had shared roots in the reaction against British rule and indigenous systems of exploitation. Like other Indian "leftists"—a term used here to denote those individuals or organizations whose ideologies were oriented toward a socialist worldview, and in which the writings of Marx held the primary place of influence—many operated inside the Indian National Congress led by Gandhi and Nehru or as part of the international Communist movement.

Indian Buddhists may not have been the only progenitors of the Buddhist-Marxist dialogue, but they must be seen as quintessential examples of what the sociologist Roland Robertson (1992: 173–74) famously called the "glocal": local phenomena that are affected by and yet simultaneously shape wider global forces. To illuminate the intersections of these global-local relationships, this chapter examines the lives of two prominent Indian intellectuals, Dharmanand Kosambi (धर्मानंद कोसंबी 1876–1947) and Rahul Sankrityayan (राहुल सांकृत्यायन 1893–1963), who took strongly to the Buddhist-Marxist ecumene. The close reading of their thought in the context of their own travels through India, Russia, America, Tibet, and beyond reveals significant patterns of global commonality and interconnectedness in Buddhism's modern history. It is now commonly acknowledged that globalization and its various facets can lead to different outcomes depending on different socioeconomic, geographical, and cultural factors. For that reason, scholars now often speak of "multiple globalizations" (Axford 2013) just as they speak of "multiple modernities" (Eisenstadt 2000). Thus, the study of Kosambi and Sankrityayan helped provide a *global view* of Buddhism and Marxism in the first half of the twentieth century as well as critical insights into one of the many modernities expressed and imagined by Buddhist intellectuals in the twentieth century.

Marx and Buddha: The Early Indian Manifestations

While Indian discussions of "Buddhist Socialism" only became more pronounced in the early 1930s, there were much earlier strands of thought that may have inspired the language and idioms later used to propagate the view of Buddha as a Marxist-like revolutionary intent on transforming Indian society. Some colonial schoolbooks, like Rājā Śivaprasād's (राजा शिव्रसाद) *Itihās Timiranāśak* (इतिहास तिमिरनाशक *History as the Destroyer of Darkness*), treated Buddha as a liberator of the lower castes, even comparing him to the Russian Tzar and Abraham Lincoln (Śivaprasād [1874] 1880: Pt. III: 49). In no less provocative terms, the Hindu mystic Swami Vivekananda (1863–1902) described the Buddha as Hinduism's "rebel child" (c.f., Joshi 1983) while anticaste intellectuals like Iyothee Thass (1845–1914) and Lakshmi Narasu (1863–1934) portrayed early Buddhism as a religion of the oppressed in an endless struggle against landowning Brahmins (Aloysius 1998). While these arguments provided a subtle layer of continuity to the emerging vision of Buddha as a Marxist, the images, assumptions, and strategies upon which these "Buddhist liberators" were constructed made no explicit reference to Marxist doctrine.

Instead, it was two powerful forces that began to fire the imaginary encounter between Buddha and Marx. The first was the cathartic and bloody events of the Russian Revolution of 1917. Historians of India generally agree that a sustained and widespread engagement with socialist doctrine and organizations did not emerge inside India until after the October Revolution and the making of the Soviet state (Habib 1998: 5; Chowdhuri 2007: 26). From the 1920s onward, the new Soviet government was widely perceived as an anticolonial and anti-imperial force that had "liberated" the Russian peasantry from "the yoke of Tsardom" and was committed to the right of all nations (including India) to self-determination. For these reasons, many Indian revolutionaries began to see Marxism as a potential tool in their own independence movement against the British. They watched eagerly, with both anticipation and admiration, as the Soviet policies of the 1920 to 1930s transformed Russian society, instituting a new era of social equality, rapid industrialization, and low unemployment. At the same time, they expressed both horror and fear toward the bloody events of the Revolution, the draconian turn under Stalin, and the purges of the mid-to-late 1930s. The possibility that these same events could occur in India had a profound impact on the Indian national leadership.

The second transformation responsible for the interaction of Buddhism and Marxism was less a singular flashpoint than it was a generational shift. During the nineteenth century, most of the well-known Indian spokespersons for Buddhism had been affiliated with institutions of Orientalist learning, with government schools, or alternatively, with either of Calcutta's two major Buddhist organizations, the Bengal Buddhist Association and Maha Bodhi Society (Ober 2016). While this earlier generation's contribution to Buddhism was monumental, the social and political terrain that most of its leading lights occupied was in contrast to a new generation longing for revolution and radical social reform. In short, many of India's "new Buddhists" had very different agendas shaped by the moral and political climate of the age. Some, like Bhikkhu Bodhanand (1874-1952) and Dr. Bhimrao Ambedkar (1891-1956), were primarily concerned with the ability of Buddha's teachings to combat Brahmanical discrimination and provide a new cultural anchor for India's subaltern classes. Others, such as Dharmanand Kosambi and Rahul Sankrityayan, whose writings and lives we turn to now, were equally concerned about the suffering of India's impoverished populations, but the political strategies they employed, and ideological conventions on which they depended, were of a radically different nature.

Dharmanand Kosambi and the "Remarkable Revolution"

Dharmanand Kosambi was one of colonial India's most eminent scholars of Buddhism. Having studied at monastic institutes across southern Asia as well as at Harvard University, where he earned a PhD in 1929 for his critical edition of the *Visuddhimagga* (विसुद्धिमग्ग), Kosambi was an anomaly in his time. Much of his life was consumed by modern Buddhist scholarship and ultimately its vernacularization for west Indian audiences. Editing texts, collecting manuscripts, translating scriptures, writing and teaching assignments at universities in India, America, and Russia: this was the basis of Kosambi's career. Yet Kosambi was also very much a product of the anticolonial and Indian nationalist movement as well as the modernist programs of Buddhist social service he learned as a young bhikkhu in Burma and at the Vidyodaya Piriveṇa in Ceylon.[2] These all informed the making of Kosambi's and ultimately, modern India's Buddhism, but it was the discovery of socialism that caused, as he put it, a "remarkable revolution" in his thinking (Kosambi 2010b: 221).

The "remarkable revolution" began when Kosambi's talents in Pāli and Sanskrit languages came to the attention of the Harvard Sanskritist James Woods (1864-1935), who invited Kosambi to Harvard to work on a critical edition of Buddhaghoṣa's *Visuddhimagga*.[3] When Kosambi arrived in Cambridge in 1910, the socialist and progressive movements in America were at the pinnacle of their national influence (c.f., Kipnis [1952] 2004). The Socialist Party of America's and American Federation of Labor's sensitive portrayals of working-class conditions had a profound impact on his thinking. It was not just the solutions that the socialists proposed, however, that Kosambi found so compelling. On the contrary, as he studied them more closely, he became convinced that their ideas paralleled those of the early Buddhist scriptures and living monastic communities he knew so well. In his view, there were two major similarities (Kosambi 2010b: 313-14). First, just as democratic socialists stressed collective-decision making, so did monks within the sangha when reaching decisions about assembly or punishments. Second, the socialist argument for the nationalization of property was akin to those monastic rules forbidding the individual ownership of property (minus the eight items a monk is allowed). Eager to share his "discovery," Kosambi published an essay in the nationalist Marathi-language journal *Kesarī* (केसरी), contending that the idea of democratic-socialist governance was born in the early Buddhist sangha and, therefore, not of modern European origin. Using passages taken from the *Mahāparinibbāṇa Sutta* and *Saṃyutta Nikāya* as evidence, Kosambi declares:

> The structure of the sangha of monks—through which the Buddha conducted the task of uplifting the people—was based upon the principle of collective ownership which is the highest stage of democracy. And in Burma the Buddhist Sangha still observes this principle. Those who propound the principle of collective ownership are known as "socialists" in this country [the USA] and in Europe . . . the chief principle of socialism is "to establish national ownership over privately owned property, and to induce all citizens to work in a manner conducive to the collective good without falling prey to the temptation of personal gain under the guise of trade or anything else." (Kosambi 2010b: 314–15)

Kosambi's idea that early Buddhism operated according to democratic-socialist principles was to become one of the most persuasive and enduring arguments of modern Indian Buddhism. At this time, Kosambi's support for this "democratic Buddhist socialism" was delicately stated, but in the ensuing decades, it was a position he and many others around the globe fervently defended. Placed in a wider context, Kosambi's argument needs to be read alongside similar propositions made by religious modernists and dissident scholars attempting to withstand the colonial and scientific assault on religion. Kosambi's predecessors, like the Hindu reformer Dayananda Saraswati, had long been arguing that all of the discoveries of modernity, such as chemistry, physics, and engineering could be found in the Vedas if only approached with the right eyes (van der Veer 2001). Similarly, Erik Hammerstrom (2015) has shown how numerous Chinese intellectuals in the early twentieth century boldly proclaimed that Buddhism had transcended the discoveries of modern science. Clearly, Kosambi's own argument that Buddhism was a kind of precursor to Marxism shared similar agendas. By showcasing its "modernity," Kosambi was molding Buddhism into a religion of reason, one that could withstand scientific critiques and refute colonial discourses of Asian "backwardness" and "superstition." At the same time, it is important to recognize that unlike some of his colleagues, Kosambi did not idealize the Indic past to the extent of claiming that all knowledge, scientific, spiritual, or otherwise was achieved by Buddha and lay deposited in the Tripiṭaka. He undoubtedly possessed a nostalgic look upon history and accepted the common narrative of Asia's decline from a great cultural past, yet even in his most provocative historical works (to be discussed in the paragraphs that follow), he remained adamant that Buddhism was neither identical to nor superseded Marxism.

Following his return from the United States and during a decade of teaching at Indian universities in the 1920s, Kosambi's belief that "real political strength is concentrated in the union of workers" grew more adamant, and he continued to publicly advocate the Marxist ideology of "equality of status and power" as solutions to India's sociopolitical misfortunes (Kosambi 2010b: 221). While he remained unsure over the universal applicability of the Soviet model and, most importantly, its advocacy of violence and class conflict, there were developments in Soviet Russia that were to have a powerful impact on his thinking.

During the first decade after the Russian Revolution, the Soviets had not only implemented radical social and economic policies but also taken what the historian Vera Tolz (2011: 160) calls a "pragmatic" or "tolerant" position toward its religious minorities. One result of this policy was that many of the most prominent Russian "scientists" (*akademiks*) in Imperial Russia's "Rozen School" of Orientalism had been deemed essential to the new Soviet bureaucracy. Similar to the role of anthropologists and Orientalists in the European colonization of Asia, their knowledge of minority Buddhist regions and neighboring Buddhist nations was praised by Soviet leaders, including Lenin himself (Hirsch 2005: 58–61). Two of the most important of these "scientists," Sergei Oldenburg (1863–1934) and Fyodor Stcherbatsky (1870–1942), were widely known in Russia and abroad for their scholarly contribution to India's Buddhist history. They were the founding editors of the major academic series, *Bibliotheca Buddhica* (est. 1897), and with Aghvan Dorjiev (1853–1938), the Buryatian tutor and ambassador to the thirteenth Dalai Lama, they established the first Buddhist temple in St. Petersburg (est. c. 1909). During the immediate postrevolution period, these *akademiks* set about establishing Buddhist exhibitions, international conferences, and museums, all of which promoted the compatibility of Buddhism and Bolshevism. The idea that Buddhism could help facilitate the spread of Enlightenment values had much older roots, but under the auspices of the Leningrad Academy of Sciences, "Bolshevik Buddhism" took on a new pulse. At events such as the Buddhist exhibition in Petrograd in 1917, Buddhism was argued to be "extraordinarily close to the modern scientific worldview" and a "religion of the oppressed" that had the potential to "advance the brotherhood of nations" (Tolz 2011: 142–47).

It was in the midst of these developments that Kosambi—by now an internationally respected Pāli scholar and freshly minted Harvard PhD—was invited by Stcherbatsky to work at Leningrad's new Institute for the Study of Buddhist Culture (est. 1927). Kosambi's work among the Russian Orientalists from 1929 to 1930 and again in 1932 or 1933 coincided with two distinct moments that would have a long-lasting influence on his later thought. On the one hand, he was working alongside scholars, in particular Stcherbatsky, widely recognized by American and European scholars alike to be one of the greatest scholars of Buddhism at the time (Nakamura [1980] 1999: 301). Thus, it is important to recognize that the statements they made regarding Buddhism's purported affinity to Marxism were not evidence of rogue scholars gone mad but of "scientists" at the vanguard of Buddhist thought. Naturally, the ideas they held about Buddhism as a progressive, liberal force in the modern world only served to strengthen the ideas that Kosambi already held about its compatibility with socialism. On the other hand, Kosambi's travels in Russia overlapped with the beginning of the draconian turn under Stalin, his campaigns against religion and "dispersal" of those communists who did not fall in line with Soviet orthodoxy. These were the precursors to the horrendous purges of the mid-to-late 1930s, events that disillusioned Kosambi as much as the mainstream Indian leadership.

Shortly after Gandhi inaugurated the Civil Disobedience movement in 1930 by picking up a handful of salt on the Dandi seashore in Gujarat, Kosambi returned to India to join the anti-imperialist effort. Despite his interest in the Communist Party of India (CPI) and their steady growth in the subcontinent's urban trade unions, he remained loyal to Gandhi's Congress party, confident that it still provided the best opportunity for eradicating Indian poverty and gaining political freedom. In the period between April and October, he was arrested twice: first, during the Salt March at Shiroda, and a second time in October where he was sentenced to a year of hard labor. Most of his political efforts during this time were focused in Parel (Bombay), a densely populated neighborhood of low-caste and outcaste millworkers and stevedores that formed the metropolitan underbelly of colonial Bombay's workers' movements (Chandavarkar 1998: 266–305).

While Kosambi's own memoirs are particularly silent about these events, daily reports furnished by intelligence officials and the Bombay Presidency Police provide important glimpses of his activities. In the reports and intelligence abstracts furnished by the Bombay police commissioner, Kosambi's name appears more than fifty times for those entries dating between April and October of 1930 (Chaudhari 1990). They report that amid crowds of up to five thousand people, he regularly delivered speeches on the "workers' duty to the country," "the fight for bread," and the "happy and contended [sic]" history of India before British rule (Chaudhari 1990: 186). In handbills and pamphlets written and signed by Kosambi, "white officers with fat salaries" (1990: 55) and their "callous and heartless capitalist" (1990: 314) cronies are ridiculed for protecting the "faithless pledges of a dying Empire" (1990: 403).

After's Kosambi's release from jail, he grew increasingly disillusioned with Gandhi's Congress and their failure to address the grievances and problems of India's peasant and labor movements. Despite never returning to formal politics, his scholarly writings continued to address sociopolitical issues. While teaching in the mid-1930s at Kashi Vidyapeeth (काशी विद्यापीठ), an institution then under the guidance of the socialist ideologue and budding Buddhologist, Acharya Narendra Dev (आचार्य नरेन्द्र देव 1889–1956), Kosambi wrote his most significant work of political theory, *Hindī Sāṃkṛtī āṇī Ahiṃsā* [हिन्दी संस्कृति आणि अहिंसा *Indian Civilization and Non-violence*] ([1935] 2010).[4] *Indian Civilization* is a creative and ambitious work, covering several thousand years of Indian history, from the Vedic era to the rise and fall of śramaṇa cultures up through the present day. It demonstrates Kosambi's mastery over Sanskrit and Prakrit sources, and at the same time, its Marxist undertones are obvious, as the reader is taken on an evolutionary journey following the classical Marxist historiography of primitive communism, slavery, feudalism, capitalism, and finally, communism. While a Marxist focus on private property shapes the text, the thread that pulls the entire narrative together is Kosambi's argument that Buddhist (and Jain) nonviolence (*ahimsa*) is central to the progress of human civilization. In the last chapter of the text, which bears the same name as the title of the book, Kosambi makes explicit his thesis. The premise is simple: as nonviolence advances, so too does civilization; when violence ensues, civilization declines. Yet Gandhian-style nonviolence alone is not enough, as Kosambi makes clear in his assessment of the present state of Indian affairs:

India's Hindu middle class is agitating for independence. It wants independence—whether through non-violence or violence. A sickly man thinks little of whether a medicine (*auṣadhi*) contains the pure essence (*pavitra*) of plants or impure essence (*apavitra*) of meat and such things. He only wants good health (*ārogya*, literally "absence of disease") and the sooner it comes the better. The medicines of the Ārya Samāj, Lokamanya [Tilak's] Ganesh festival, and Mahatma Gandhi's non-violent and constructive project have been tried, but none have brought the cure (*lābh*). If the Bolsheviks have freed the working classes (*mazdūr-varg*) in all of the Russian Empire by destroying the aristocrats (*sardār*) and landowners (*zamindār*) all the while fighting the entire world, then why are we not able to free India of her suffering by taking the same path? (Kosambī [1935] 2010: 168)

In the final chapter, Kosambi outlines his own revolutionary strategy that avoids the unnecessary bloodshed of the Bolsheviks by welding Buddha's doctrine of nonviolence, the Marxist wisdom of socioeconomic reform, and the tactical brilliance of Gandhi's *satyāgraha*. This socialist dharmic remedy should be understood as part of what scholars like David Scott (2004) and Barnard Yack (1986) have described as the modern "longing for total revolution." According to Scott (2004: 64), the modern conception of revolution is based on "distinctive ways of defining the problem to be overcome . . . so as to achieve satisfaction." For Kosambi, the problem is not just Indian independence but also human suffering (*duḥkha*) more widely, and his solution is clearly a blend of Buddhist and Marxist strategies.

Only toward the end of the book when dealing with the contemporary period does Kosambi depart radically from Marxist historiography to begin his own rigorous Buddhist critique. He begins by suggesting that while the Marxist criticisms of capitalism as based upon greed and exploitation are correct, they are better understood through a Buddhist lens. Using a series of passages from the *Tripiṭaka* literature, Kosambi ([1935] 2010: 176) explains how existential suffering (*duḥkha*) is created by the three types of cravings (Pāli, taṇhā; Sanskrit, *tṛṣṇā*): for sensual pleasures (*kām* काम), for experiences (*bhav* भव), and for nonexperiences (*vibhav* विभव). Pursuing these pleasurable, but ultimately temporal experiences, he explains, will lead only to decay and further suffering. Having established this point, he then argues that Marxists conceive of suffering primarily through the lens of servitude and bondage related to the ownership of private property. This too, Kosambi explains, is linked to Buddhist craving. For according to Kosambi, the sangha's eventual demise in India stemmed from its desire for and accumulation of private property—in the form of land (*zamīn* ज़मीन), women (*strī* स्त्री), and slaves (*dāsa* दास) (Kosambī [1935] 2010: 182–83). This leads him to conclude that religion, including Buddhism, has indeed been an opiate for the masses.

The craving of modern-day nations, he adds, however, is no less deadly an addiction. If religion is an opiate, he declares, "nationalism is liquor" (Kosambi 2010b: 354). While the Buddhist scriptures point to collective and personal craving as sources of suffering, here Kosambi envisions a new criterion of suffering in the modern world, a quality he calls "nationalist craving." Echoing Marx, but couched in a uniquely Indic Buddhist idiom, he recounts how the nationalist craving for "profitable trade" among the upper classes of England drove them to conquer the world, from the Americas to Asia to Africa. "The national good, that is, bringing into the country the wealth of other countries, turned every evil deed into a praiseworthy one! . . . instead of feeling disgusted by craving, England developed greater greed. The result was the last world war" (Kosambi 2010b: 339). Warning that Britain's "imperial greed" will lead again to massive violence and exploitation, Kosambi concludes that the foremost solution to "national craving" is the same as suggested for other forms of craving: the doctrine of *aparigraha* (अपरिग्रह) or "avoidance of possessions." Here again, as in his earlier writings, he argues that this parallels the nationalization schemes theorized by democratic socialists. However, this time, Kosambi cleverly equates the revolutionary call to nationalize property with a verse he translates from the *Bodhisattvacaryāvatāra* in which Śāntideva proclaims: "Nirvana is giving up everything, and that is what I wish for. If I have to give up everything, it is best to do so for the welfare of all creatures" (Kosambi 2010b: 353fn12). Commenting on this, Kosambi asks rhetorically: "By abandoning their great and small estates for the good of mankind, would our wealthy people not share in such *unparalleled joy*?" (Kosambi 2010b: 353fn12, emphasis mine)

Having shown that Buddhism and Marxism propounded similar views for the "welfare of mankind," Kosambi prescribes his new tonic: the practice of "true wisdom" (*prajñā*) and nonviolence (*ahimsa*). Marx, in Kosambi's vision, was a dispenser of the former but "suffered from the narrow-mindedness of Europeans" (Kosambi 2010b: 355). That is, while his scientific knowledge of social evolution was instrumental in the advancement of mankind, it has been ultimately destructive because it was not accompanied by nonviolence. Turning Marx's historical sociology on his own head, Kosambi calls Marx a product of his culture, a culture that "demands an adversary" and believes that "civilization will not advance without such competition" (Kosambi 2010b: 356). According to Kosambi, the Marxist solution to nationalism and capitalism was to unite the entire working class and oppose the bourgeoisie with the premise that the hostility between the two would wane after the struggle was over. Yet this, he argues, simply transfers the hostility between nations to a hatred between bourgeoisie and workers (Kosambi 2010b: 356).

The only viable way to free man's cravings from the mundane agonies of daily life, he proposes, is an eclectic blend of *ahimsa*, socialist wisdom, and Gandhian political strategy (*satyāgraha*):

> In our country, Parshwa [the Jain Tirthankara] and the Buddha turned the current of non-violence towards the good of the masses. But it did not get into the political sphere and was, as a result, mired in a puddle of religious sectarianism. Around it grew the forest of the puranas [Hindu myths]. Mahatma Gandhi's attempt to give that further impetus and turn it to the political sphere is truly to be congratulated. But it was obstructed midway and suffered a loss of direction. This was good, in a way, because if it had continued it would have fallen into the ditch of nationalism and proved detrimental. Only if non-violence is accompanied by the wisdom of socialists will this current [the looming threat

of war] turn in the right direction, and lead to the welfare of mankind. (Kosambi 2010b: 357)

Kosambi was no doubt aware that this very kind of political critique had been waged two decades earlier by those communists who went on to found the Third Communist International. What is original in Kosambi's argument, however, is his rather eclectic articulation of this in an indigenous Indic terminology much more likely to precipitate his Marathi-reading audience into action. The spectrum of global voices in Kosambi's philosophy of history—Gandhi, Tolstoy, Marx, Aśvaghoṣa, Voltaire, Śāntideva, Buddha, Lenin—is testament to the ideological conventions intellectuals like Kosambi had to depend on in giving Buddhism a respected place in the modern Indian conscience. The loom upon which Kosambi's philosophy is set is undoubtedly Marxist, but in the final weave, the design is most clearly a modern democratic Buddhist socialism set to clothe the poor, the oppressed, and the left-leaning nonviolent revolutionary. As is clear in *Indian Civilization*, the role of Buddhist nonviolence always took precedence over not just the core Buddhist doctrine of suffering but also the Marxist thrust on exploitation. The First World War, the Soviet purges, and the experience of witnessing bodies "being reduced to corpses" at the Shiroda *satyāgraha* had cemented Kosambi's dedication to Gandhi's nonviolent tactics (Kosambi 2010b: 230).

Indian Civilization was Kosambi's last major written attempt to influence political developments. His later works continued to show the stamp of leftist thought, but it was his son's scholarship during the next decades that would associate the Kosambi name with Marxism, not the father's.[5] At the same time that Kosambi's efforts to explicitly synthesize socialism and Buddhism began to wind down, one of Kosambi's distant colleagues and no less an influential scholar began espousing his own revolutionary dharma.

Rahul Sankrityayan and the Marxist Reform of Buddhism

If Dharmanand Kosambi forged a Maharashtrian Buddhist public, then the radical scholar and intrepid explorer Rahul Sankrityayan did the same for the Hindi-speaking world. Unlike Kosambi, however, Sankrityayan's engagement with Marxism was more forceful, his Buddhist vision couched in the language of Marx rather than Kosambi's socialism couched in the language of the Buddha. Before becoming a globe-trotting bhikkhu in the 1930s and Communist propagandist from the 1940s onward, Sankrityayan had lived the life of a Vaiṣṇava sadhu, an Arya Samaji social reformer, and Congress politician.[6] Yet writing was always his primary domain and source of income. While his roughly 150s published books and seventy-plus published articles (Bhaṭṭācārya 2005: 205–15) speak to the breadth and depth of his intellectual engagements, it was his prolific research as scholar that gained him fame in Buddhist circles.

Sankrityayan's own reading of Buddhism was deeply shaped by those Pāli scriptures, such as the *Kālāma Sutta*, which were widely seen by Buddhist modernists as expressing Buddhism's scientific tendencies (McMahan 2008: 64). In his memoir, *Merī Jivan Yatra* (मेरी जीवन-यात्रा *My Life Journey*), Sankrityayan writes of the first time he encountered the text:

> When in the *Kālāmas*, I discovered the Buddha's teaching—do not accept the teaching of any book, any tradition, out of concern for your elders, always decide for yourself before you take it on principle—my heart suddenly said, listen, here is a man whose unswerving faith in truth [*satya*] understood the strength of man's independent reason [*buddhi*]. (Sāṅkṛtyāyan [1944] 2014: 19)

As his study of the Triple Gem intensified throughout the 1920s and 1930s, it began to fuse with the wider message of social equality and political liberation that he encountered both in India and abroad.

Sankrityayan's first sustained journeys into the lived Buddhist world began when he took full ordination (*upasampadā*) as a bhikṣu at Vidyalankara Piriveṇa in Ceylon in 1930. The Buddhist atmosphere that he encountered there was extremely cosmopolitan, studying alongside Chinese, Sinhalese, Indian, and European monastics. Sankrityayan's memoirs ([1944] 2014: 1–28, 106–10, 124–28) describe a vibrant atmosphere in which a cacophony of multilingual literature from across the globe was circulated among the bhikkhus. Alongside Pāli manuscripts, Sanskrit literature, and Orientalist scholarship, one could find the writings of Marx and American atheist freethinkers like Robert Ingersoll (1833–99).

While the intellectual space of these institutions may disrupt the sanitized visions of Buddhist monasticism imagined by many, this was not just a setting unique to British Ceylon. Elsewhere, Sankrityayan's global encounters with Buddhism were met by individuals acutely aware of, and keen to discuss, the politics of decolonization and the rise of the Marxist paradigm. During his four major research expeditions in central Tibet between 1929 and 1938, rumors of a new "Buddhist dialectic" always hovered in the air. As early as 1929, his Mongolian tutors informed him of the Soviet-instigated "renewal movement" to restore Buddhism to its "primitive form, which has no friction with atheism, communal ownership of property . . . [and] Marxism" (Sankrityayan 1984: 137). The "Buddha and Marx are not antagonistic," he was told, "but complementary to one another" (Sankrityayan 1984: 137). When serving as a missionary (*dharmadūt* धर्मदूत) for the Maha Bodhi Society in London and Paris from 1932 to 1933, these ideas were further confirmed by European Orientalists who all pointed to the Soviet *akademiks* as being at the cutting edge of this new scholarship (Sāṅkṛtyāyan 1957: 195).

By 1935, when Sankrityayan made his first journey to Russia, Buddhism was, in his own view, a teaching based on reason (*buddhi*), human pragmatism (*manuśya māpavād* मनुष्य मापवाद), and atheistic humanism (*nāstik mānaviyatā* नास्तिक मानवियता). These were the same types of qualities, which David Scott has argued in the context of Marxism's global rise in the 1930s, that gave Marxist revolutionaries "a new idea of the rhythm of history, a new conception of historical agency, and a new idea of how to self-consciously wrest the future from the past" (2004: 68). Yet by the time Sankrityayan was finally granted permission to work for a more extended period with

Fyodor Stcherbatsky in Leningrad in 1937–38, the Soviet attitude toward Buddhism had changed, moving from tolerance to outright condemnation and persecution. Stcherbatsky's own works on Buddhist logic were condemned as part of the "ideological struggle against Leninism," a deliberate slandering of "the logic of dialectical materialism," and his well-known series *Bibliotheca Buddhica* was shut down for being "a mouthpiece of the Buddhist-Lamaist religion" (Tolz 2011: 18–19). Stalin himself had even felt it necessary to publicly ridicule "the absurd theory of the identity of the Communist and Buddhist doctrines" (Snelling 1993: 234). Six of Stcherbatsky's closest colleagues at the Institute of Buddhist Culture (where Kosambi had also worked) had been arrested, denounced as "counter-revolutionaries," and one was even executed. In Soviet Mongolia, the Stalinist turn against Buddhism was even more catastrophic when the Soviet state instigated the killing of "approximately eighteen thousand lamas and a similar number of other people and the physical destruction of the monasteries" (Kaplonski 2014: 32–33). In Stalin's Russia, such were the consequences for comparing the Buddha with Marx.

Yet throughout the 1930s, Buddhist intellectuals elsewhere in the globe continued to grapple with the possibly complementary visions of modernity prescribed by Buddhism and Marxism. As China's future became increasingly divided along Guomindang and Communist paths, "progressive Buddhists" like Master Juzan (1908–84) argued that the study of Marxist thought could be of immense help to Chinese Buddhist traditions by removing "superstitions" and "feudal elements" (Yu 2016). Across the sea, the Japanese monk Seno'o Girō (1889–1961) adapted and appropriated the language of Marx in his own struggle to reform Japanese Buddhism. According to James Mark Shields (2012: 343–44), Seno'o felt that the problem with Buddhism was not only "a matter of priestly corruption or institutional generation" but with "the very heart of the way that Buddhism is practiced as a 'religion.'" In Russia, Sankrityayan pondered Buddhism's own downfall in India by approaching the problem from the context of his own training in Indian philosophical traditions and Marxist historiography. There were distinct cultural differences among all of these figures, yet they drew from common pools of thought—in this case, Buddhist and Marxist—to solve the problems that lay before them.

By the time that Sankrityayan left Russia in 1939, his perspective on Buddhism had moved from somewhere between strict Soviet orthodoxy and Kosambi's "Buddhist socialism." Like Juzan in China or Seno'o in Japan, he began to argue that if Buddhism could be "purified" of its links to the landed classes and returned to its "primitive" or "original" state of "atheistic humanism" (*nāstik mānaviyatā*), it could once again act as a dynamic and progressive force in human evolution (Sāṅkṛtyāyan [1942] 1974). However, while he remained supportive of Buddha's atheism, dynamic thought, and call for social equality, he was now convinced that the teachings of Buddha were incapable of doing what Marxism could. Buddhists had learned how to understand the world, to accept change and impermanence (*anitya/anicca*), but they had failed to change situations for their own ends, in accordance with their own desires. In Sankrityayan's view, that had been enunciated only by Marx (Sāṅkṛtyāyan [1944] 2014: 229).

Imbued with a newfound commitment to the forces of international Communism, Sankrityayan renounced his monastic vows, in turn marrying Stcherbatsky's student, a Tibetologist Ellena Narvertovna Kozerovskaya (dates unknown), and in 1939, left Russia to join the peasant movements in Bihar. There is no space to discuss the full scope of Sankrityayan's activities among the Kisān Sabhā (किसान सभा peasant associations) and Communist Party of India (CPI) during the next decade. Along with J.K. Narayan (1902–79) and Swami Sahajanand Saraswati (1889–1950), he quickly emerged as one of the foremost leaders of the organization, working on their behalf to fix the "agrarian problem" through the mobilization of peasants on radical Marxist platforms.[7] Yet while fighting *zamindāri* (ज़मींदारी) or "landlordism" was primary to the movement, so too was the destruction of institutionalized religion or the "illusion of dharma" as Swami Sahajanand (1995: 133) called it. Thus, it is not difficult to see how the early Buddhist impulse against the Vedas and Brahmanical interests could be easily invoked as part of the movement's wider political theology. What was of no less importance was that this ancient Buddhist teaching was rooted in the soil of the Bihari peasants themselves. This, in other words, was construed as a truly autochthonous message. While working for the Kisān Sabhā, Sankrityayan was jailed for a total of twenty-nine months on three separate occasions with his third and final arrest as part of the British government's "exceedingly drastic" measures to "cripple the Communist machinery" during the spring of 1940 (Overstreet and Windmiller 1959: 183–84).

In the two decades after his release from prison in 1942, Sankrityayan's writings took on a much more rigorous Marxist critique. Although much of this literature concerned Buddhism and Marxism independently, it is in his novels and popular books where the relationship between the two is most explicitly addressed. In two of his more popular nonfiction works on the topic, a short English essay, "Buddhism and Marxism" (Sāṅkṛtyāyan 1984) and a Hindi-language biography of the Buddha, *Mahāmānav Buddh* (महामानव बुद्ध) (Sāṅkṛtyāyan [1956] 2011), he provides a clear synopsis of his views. To begin with, the Buddha's critique of caste, teaching of self-dependence or reliance (*ātmāvalamban* आत्मावलम्बन) and intellectual freedom (*buddhisvātantra* बुद्धिस्वातन्त्र) was far ahead of its time, on par with Marxist thought. Echoing Kosambi, he applauds the Buddha for trying to introduce "absolute communism [*pūrṇ sāmyavād* पूर्ण साम्यवाद] inside the sangha" and points to the early Buddhist preference for democratic republics (*gaṇa* गण) (Sāṅkṛtyāyan [1956] 2011: 35, 104–9). The Buddha's rationality, criticism of revealed scriptures and atheism—all qualities shared by Marx, he adds—allowed him to recognize that "the origin of monarchy did not lie in any divine source but . . . was the product of the growth of private property" (Sāṅkṛtyāyan 1984: 4). Furthermore, the Buddha's doctrine of *bahujan hitāya, bahujan sukhāya*, (बहुजन हिताय बहुजन सुखाय) or "the good of many, the happiness of many," he points out, rivals Marxist ethics.

On the economic and social fronts outside the sangha, he paints a more complex picture. Although the Buddha was to be praised for advocating universal brotherhood, preempting the Marxist ideology of humanity, he was to be criticized for failing to abolish caste in society at large. Like most Marxists, Sankrityayan viewed caste from a class perspective: "The caste system originated in economics. The high castes owned property, whereas the low castes were deprived of it. One could only be abolished by abolishing the other" (Sāṅkṛtyāyan [1956] 2011: 103). Had the caste system not been based on wealth (*sampatti* सम्पत्ति) and had the Buddha allowed debtors (*ṛṇī* ऋणी), slaves (*dāsā* दासा), and soldiers (*rājsainik* राजसैनिक) into the sangha, thus undercutting the strength of the landed classes, caste inequalities could have been eradicated. Instead, the Buddha barred these groups from taking ordination for fear of reprisal from the merchants and kings that the sangha relied upon. In Sankrityayan's historiography, this had profound consequences.[8] Although Buddhism possessed the will of the people, this act made it a tool of the status quo, thereby undercutting its ability to revolutionize the masses.[9]

Despite these shortcomings, Sankrityayan believed that Buddhist philosophy continued to shake the foundations of Indian history in ways similar to what Hegel and Marx had done in Europe (Sāṅkṛtyāyan 1984: 12). And just as Marx is said to have turned Hegel's theories on his own head, Sankrityayan saw in the eighth-century Buddhist philosopher, Dharmakīrti, a figure close to Marx. Dharmakīrti argued that reality was defined by "that which is capable of objective action" (*artha-kriyā-samartham* अर्थ क्रिया समर्थम्) and in learning to accept "objects as our guide," Dharmakīrti had touched on the fundamental principle of modern empirical science. Sankrityayan calls this a "big weapon" (1984: 14) but laments that it was "not used," for by Dharmakīrti's lifetime, Buddhism's ties to the status quo had forced it to "soften its sharpness" (Sāṅkṛtyāyan 1942: 105). The failure to utilize Dharmakīrti's knowledge of the conditions necessary to change objective reality with the "rational and heart-stirring" message of the Buddha was in effect the failure of Buddhism as religion (Sāṅkṛtyāyan 1942: 105). In an evocative passage, he outlines his solution to revitalizing the Buddhist revolution through a radical revision of the Buddha's Four Noble Truths:

[1] Suffering is to be found in the world;
[2] it is caused by exploitation;
[3] suffering will cease to exist if exploitation is done away with, that is, [if the] road to communism is followed;
[4] and communism is the way to the cessation of suffering (quoted in Bhattacharya 1994: 119).

What Marxism can provide Buddhism, it seems, is the revolutionary praxis to free Buddhists from the bondage of their own historical failures.

Despite Sankrityayan's commitments to reforming Buddhism via Marxism, his sympathies for Buddhism were at times too much for more hardline colleagues, who often attacked him as a "revisionist" (Chudal 2016: 239–41). Nowhere were these sympathetic gestures more evident than in his fictional writings. Among the seventeen novels Sankrityayan wrote in the last two decades of his life, several of them touch on themes or events connected to the ancient Buddhist world. These works, which need to be read as part of the Progressive Writer's Movement and its theory of "purposive art" (as opposed to "art for art's sake"), largely subscribe to the ideals of socialist realism and were intended as propaganda pieces. As always, Sankrityayan extolled the ancient Indian republics (*gaṇa*) as symbols of democratic equality. In his novel *Jay Yaudheya* (जय यौधेय 1944), for instance, the reader is taken on an imaginary journey to Yaudheya, an ancient Indian state said to embody the absolute communism of the Buddha's sangha and where there are neither masters nor slaves and equal rights are offered to all. Likewise, in his most famous piece of historical fiction, *Volgā se Gaṅgā* (वोल्गा से गंगा *From the Volga to the Ganges*, [1942])—which underwent multiple editions in fourteen different languages—Buddhism rarely comes under severe critique. Through most of the text, the suffering of slaves and working classes is often at the hands of corrupt Brahmin priests, greedy *banias* (बनिया merchants), belligerent mullahs, and Christian capitalists. In stark contrast to these images, the Buddha is described as a man who "wanted a revolution (*kranti* क्रांति), one that would make the world a better place"; his dharma is compared to "a sort of communism," and his sangha as "a kind of model for a world of tomorrow" (Sāṅkṛtyāyan 1942: 138, 174, 142–43). The Buddha, it seems, was indeed the heart of a heartless world.

Conclusion: Reconsidering the Buddha and the Left

When examined more broadly, allowing the Indian Buddhist Marxist milieu to fade from the picture, the pre-1950s Buddhist-Marxist union was typically short-lived, based on an intense but ultimately superficial understanding of one another. In most parts of Asia, Buddhist dialogues with Marxism were typically based on rather simplistic notions of Marxist thinking. As Agehananda Bharati suggested long ago in the case of Sri Lanka, the term Marxism was more a twentieth-century buzzword capable of inciting terror and uniting the masses than a sophisticated appreciation of its competing discourses (1976: 107). Trevor Ling has argued similarly in respect to the collaboration between Buddhists and Marxists in Burma and Cambodia (1979: 91). The early Buddhist appeal to Marxism, Ling suggests, was less the doctrine of historical materialism than its criticism of the materialistic capitalism of the West. In short, in most Asian Buddhist case studies, Marxist doctrines were used strategically as rhetorical tools in the fight against imperialism and colonialism but only in rare occasions formed a central part of a sustained ideological alliance.

Rather than thinking of Marxism's influence on Buddhism as a unilateral diffusion of ideology from the "West" to the "East," it is more accurate to think in terms of linked global networks where conversations and encounters between intellectuals from across the globe produced a number of parallel outcomes, disjointed chains of influence, and creative interpretations. The intensity and speed through which these encounters and conversations occurred were due in large part to the widespread participation of Buddhists and Marxists in the major transformations of the nineteenth and twentieth centuries, namely the expansion of state power, international commercial interests, and the "death of long distance"—the communications and transportation revolutions in printing, telegraphs, steamships, railways, etc. Nor can the connection between Buddhism and Marxism be solely reduced to modern political alliances and/or desperate attempts by Buddhists to survive Communist regimes. In the late 1940s, the French belletrist Andre Migot asked rhetorically whether "the words of Engels might not equally well have been those of the Buddha" (quoted in Ling 1979: 167). A decade later, the famed structural anthropologist, Claude Lévi-Strauss, dedicated an entire chapter of his monumental work, *Tristes Tropique* (1955), to exploring the links between Buddhism and Marxism. The two systems, he proposed, are each "doing the same thing as the other, but on different levels." Buddhism, he concluded "has achieved something that, elsewhere, only Marxism has brought off: it has reconciled the problem of metaphysics with the problem of human behavior" (quoted in Shields 2012: 334–35).

In India, the intersections between Buddhist and leftist ideologies gave rise to animated discussions, new ways of thinking and being. For instance, it is undeniable that the Indian Socialist Party's popular platform of "social humanism" in the 1950s and 1960s was deeply influenced by its founder Acharya Narendra Dev's deep studies of Buddhist philosophy.[10] Similarly, for the "people's poet," Kavi Nagarjun (वैद्यनाथ मिश्र, नागार्जुन 1911–88), who moved to Ceylon to study Pāli and don Buddhist robes before returning home to Bihar to join the peasant movement, one could be both modern and traditional, a progressive thinker and Buddhist *bhūmiputra* (भूमिपुत्र) or "son of the soil" (c.f., Jha 1999). The great Dalit leader and Buddhist convert, B.R. Ambedkar (1891–1956) was no less cognizant of the Buddha's relationship to the left, even delivering a major speech at the World Fellowship of Buddhists in 1956 in which he argued that the two "-ism's" were nearly the same. Like Kosambi and Sankrityayan, he praised the Buddha for his communist-like sangha and equated Buddhist *duḥkha* with the Marxist emphasis on poverty and exploitation. The only fundamental difference between Marxism and Buddhism, he argued, was in their methodology. While the Buddha used persuasion, moral teachings, and love, Marx advocated power and violence. In Ambedkar's logic, this was Marxism's fundamental error. Russia's Communists, he remarked, "forget [that] the wonder of all wonders is that the Buddha established Communism so far as the Sangha was concerned *without dictatorship*" (Ambedkar 1987: 461).

The enduring influence of these idioms and images in South Asia and beyond demonstrates that modern Buddhism was shaped as much by Marxist ideas about property, economic organization, and the sources of political authority as it was by the Orientalists who "discovered" India's "lost" religion. Yet remarkably, the role of Marxism on the sociocognitive conditions of modern-day Buddhists is greatly undertheorized. In two of the most important works on "Buddhist modernism," that of David McMahan (2008) and Donald Lopez (2002), the influence of Marx and/or Marxism on the making of Buddhist modernism is almost completely absent. Part of this may relate to the fact that the history of their encounter has been (understandably) seen through a post-1950s lens in which Communist and/or pseudo-Marxist regimes in Tibet, Russia, Cambodia, and elsewhere led to horrific campaigns to destroy Buddhist institutions and ideologies. With our knowledge of these catastrophic outcomes, it may seem misguided to give serious consideration to the earlier efforts to reconcile Buddhism and Marxism, but studies such as these not only help explain why these circumstances arose but also serve as an important corrective to received histories. The studies of Buddhism contained in this volume reveal wider global patterns and simultaneously probe the assumptions that lie dormant behind the narratives all scholars construct. In the case of this study, the claims of ancient Indian Buddhist communism may be dubious in historical detail, or at the very least, greatly misplaced anachronisms, but they were powerful as modern myth. The importance of these images for understanding modern Buddhism then is not in the historical truth itself but in the way in which they speak to the revolutionary world that modern Buddhists lived.

6

D.T. Suzuki and the Chinese Search for Buddhist Modernism

Jingjing Li

What does it mean to say that Buddhism in China and Japan has been modernized? Scholars have long become accustomed to using the West-impact/East-response narrative model to answer such questions. Through this, the modernization of Buddhism in the East Asian region is construed as a mere reaction to the West. Implicitly equating modernization with Westernization downplays the agency of Buddhist reformers and clerics in East Asia who initiated the revitalization of Buddhism in the early twentieth century. As an alternative to this Western-centric narrative, this chapter will present an account of the interactions between Daisetsu Teitarō Suzuki (鈴木大拙貞太郎 1870–1966), a well-known reformer of Japanese Buddhism, and his Chinese peers, including Ven. Taixu (太虛 1890–1947) and Ven. Yinguang (印光 1862–1940), to demonstrate how China-Japan relations shaped the modernization of Buddhism in the East Asian region throughout the twentieth century.

Daisetsu Teitarō Suzuki, commonly known as D.T. Suzuki, rose to prominence as a proponent of Zen Buddhism in the West during the 1930s (Wang Leiquan 1986: 143; Li Silong 2014: 143). Recent critiques of Suzuki's writings portray him as a supporter, or even a propagandist, of Japanese cultural nationalism (Jaffe 2015: xvi; Sharf 1993: 41; Sueki 2013: 2). Though much has been written about Suzuki's influence in the West, the interactions between Suzuki and Chinese Buddhists have yet to be discussed. Indeed, aside from his communications with Hu Shih (胡適 1891–1962) (Xing 2012: 353; Lou 1987: 62; Jiang 1995: 92), the reception of Suzuki in China has largely escaped scholarly attention. This lacuna, in part, can be explained as a product of the predominance of the popular West-impact/East-response narrative.

The chapter begins with a brief overview of the interactions between China and Japan following the decline of the Sinocentric tribute trade system in the latter half of the nineteenth century, an event that can be seen as the starting point of modernization in East Asia and, I contend, that motivated Suzuki's new expression of Buddhism. It then explores how this event shaped the early interactions between Suzuki and his Chinese contemporaries and thus contributed to the reformation of Buddhism in China in the 1930s. The next section analyzes the polarized receptions of Suzuki's writings inside and outside Mainland China from 1949 to 1976. While Suzuki's journey from preceding decades faded from popular memory in the newly established People's Republic of China (PRC), Suzuki acquired great fame in North America during the 1960s. The chapter concludes with an examination of how Suzuki's name re-emerged in the minds of the Chinese and was incorporated into their popular discourse in the late 1980s when the PRC reformed their religious policy.

Nation-Building and Buddhist Modernism in Japan and China in the 1930s

The following historical survey is centered on what Hamashita Takeshi calls "the region" *qua* East Asia, which represents an "intermediate category between the nation and the world" encompassing both the local and the global (Hamashita 2008: 12). The relationship between China and Japan within this region can be characterized as one of mutual impact/response, such that the interactions between these two nations affect the course of their own nation-building. The China-Japan relationship undermines the predominant and unilateral West-impact/East-response paradigm that construes Eastern modernization as a reaction to Western stimulus. Recognizing the interconnectedness between China and Japan allows us to foreground the agency of East Asian Buddhist reformers who encountered the similar challenge of trying to revitalize Buddhism at a global level while taking into account their country's national interests at the local level.

The concept of Buddhist modernism has been incorporated into the discourse of Buddhist Studies to capture new forms of Buddhism that "emerged out of an engagement with the dominant cultural and intellectual forces of modernity" (McMahan 2008: 7). Drawing on this definition, this chapter understands Buddhist modernism, which can be traced back to the late 1800s, not as a *sui generis* phenomenon but as an integrated dimension of the modernization of Japan and China.

Prior to the 1800s, the Chinese imagined their homeland as the cosmic center of "the realm under heaven" (*Tianxia* 天下) that was surrounded first by its subordinate tribute countries such as Korea and Vietnam and then by "barbaric" trading countries from Europe. Economic relations between these states were sustained by the Sinocentric tribute trade system, otherwise known as the Tianxia System. Chinese traditions, such as Confucianism and Buddhism, dominated the shared culture of this region.

Although they arrived in East Asia as early as the 1600s, European colonizers did not intend to challenge this tribute trade system until the mid-1800s (Hamashita 2008: 21). To gain more control of trading in the region, colonizers propelled East Asian countries to enter the Eurocentric economic order that was based on treaties. With its victory in the First Opium War (1839–42), Britain signed the Nanking Treaty of 1842 with China. Likewise, in 1853, the United States sent its navy to Japan and imposed on Japan the Kanagawa Treaty in 1854. The disintegration of the tribute trade system eroded the Sinocentric worldview, gradually resulting in the collapsing of the previous superior-subordinate relation between China and its "barbaric" trading countries, such as the European nations. Euro-American colonizers disseminated the message that the West was rational and superior to the nonrational inferior East, glorifying their invasion of Asian countries under the guise of helping "the non-rational East" modernize. Consequently, modernization in Asia emerged not as a backlash against the West but as a reaction against the Sinocentric world order or in Hamashita's terms, "against the all-inclusive superior-subordinate relations of the traditional tribute system" (Hamashita 2008: 26). In this sense, the decline of *Tianxia* heralded the modern epoch in Asia.

After the Meiji Restoration (1868–1912), Japan soon became militarily strong and defeated the previous regional superpower, China, in 1895. This victory further reshaped the power dynamics in East Asia insofar as Japan renounced its preceding role as a subordinate tribute country and transformed itself into a new colonial power in the Eurocentric global order. However, Japan soon found itself trapped between the Eurocentric system and the Sinocentric one: to avoid being submerged by the West, Japan strove to demonstrate the distinctness of its culture, yet, since Japanese culture was historically indebted to that of China, Japan equally had to distance itself from the Sinocentric worldview.

Eventually, ultranationalism arose as the state ideology at the end of the 1920s. This was the era when Suzuki began to publish extensively on Zen, and his writings were then incorporated into the ultranationalist discourse. Armed with this new ideology, Japan imagined itself to be the cosmic center, on the periphery of which all other nations ought to find their proper positions (Maruyama 1963: 12). In this idealized worldview, an eternal peace was said to descend when all nations properly positioned themselves (Maruyama 1963: 12). Under the guise of bringing eternal peace upon the world, Japan glorified its expansion in East Asia, envisioning its modernization as the realization of this Japan-centric order.

While the Meiji regime reinvented Shinto and championed it as the state religion, it persecuted Buddhism for being inimical to the advancement of Japan (Sharf 1993: 3). Defending Buddhism against the growing antagonism, several Buddhist apologists initiated the New Buddhism movement (*shinbukkyō* 新佛教)), which sought to demonstrate the usefulness of the tradition for a modern Japan. Suzuki's sensei, Shaku Sōen (釋宗演 1859–1919), was a proponent of New Buddhism. In addition to justifying the harmony between Buddhism and science, Sōen attempted to export this new brand of Buddhism to the world (Sharf 1993: 9). In 1893, Sōen lectured on Buddhism in the World's Parliament of Religions in Chicago. During the same period, numerous Buddhist missionaries journeyed to China and North America to establish *Betsuin* (別院), branch temples of Japanese Buddhism. Ogurusu Kōchō (小栗栖香頂 1831–1905), a contemporary of Sōen, established the first *Betsuin* of Jōdo Shinshū in Shanghai in 1876. Upon arriving in China, Japanese missionaries proclaimed that Buddhism was pivotal to Japan's advancement (Ge 2001: 664). Many Chinese, familiar with the rise of Japan, were convinced that a new form of Buddhism would resolve the crisis of their religion and their state.

Unlike Japan, which transformed into a colonial power after the Meiji Restoration, China embarked on a different search for modernization that in turn shaped the development of Chinese Buddhism. In 1912, the Republic of China replaced the Qing Dynasty (1644–1912), officially ending the imperial regime (221 BCE–1912

CE). Sun Yat-sen (孫中山 1866–1925), the founding father of the Republic of China, put forward the "Three Principles of the People" (*sanminzhuyi* 三民主義), namely, nationalism (*minzu* 民族), democracy (*minquan* 民權), and the welfare of people (*minsheng* 民生), to prescribe the way for China to establish a modern identity. Drawing on the success of the Meiji Restoration, Sun conceived of the formation of a united nation-state as the key to sovereignty (Sun 1924). Nevertheless, witnessing how Japan embraced imperialism, Sun remarked that China should endorse a new global discourse of mutual respect and prosperity after retaining its sovereignty (Sun 1924). This political climate nourished mixed feelings among the Chinese toward Japan. Instead of belittling Japan as a subordinate tribute country that imported culture from China, the Chinese hoped to learn from Japan's efforts at modernization while remaining cautious of Japan's ambitious attempts at expansion.

Mixed feelings likewise arose among Chinese Buddhists. At that time, Buddhism was under great pressure, due to the movements of "Requisitioning Temples for Promoting Education" (*miaochanxingxue* 廟產興學), which began in the 1890s. Local powers manipulated the campaign to confiscate Buddhist properties. For instance, in the Tai County of Shandong in 1929, there were 348 schools in all, 94.25 percent of which were reconstructed from Buddhist and folk religion temples (Huang Yunxi 1991: 298). Chinese monasteries had the option to seek help from Japanese missionaries, on the condition that they would voluntarily become Betsuin, the branch temples of Japanese Buddhist lineages. Nonetheless, many Chinese Buddhists saw Betsuin as a manifestation of the cultural expansion of imperial Japan and perceived this offer as a threat to their religion. The conflict reached its peak in 1904, when Chinese Buddhists and intellectuals protested against the attempt of Itō Kendo (伊藤賢道 dates unknown) to incorporate thirty-six local temples into the lineage of Japanese Shin Buddhism (Huang Yunxi 1991: 300). This conflict was later known as the Hangzhou incident. In the wake of Japan's invasion of China (post-1930s), Chinese Buddhists, who also envisioned their religious reform as a two-pronged project of reviving the religion and rejuvenating the nation, were driven to reconsider their interactions with Japan.

Ambivalent Impressions of One Another: Interactions between Suzuki and Chinese Buddhists (1934)

The Sino-Japanese relations were increasingly tense due to Japan's 1931 and 1932 invasions of Manchuria and Shanghai, respectively. In 1933 after colonizing Manchuria, Japan officially withdrew from the League of Nations to prepare for the Second Sino-Japanese War (1937–45). It was in this context that Suzuki and a group of followers visited China in 1934. Though Buddhist clerics in China welcomed Suzuki, their attitude toward Japanese Buddhism was ambivalent due to the mounting antagonism toward Japan in China. Suzuki, after visiting Buddhist clerics and monasteries in China, also expressed his ambivalent impressions of Chinese Buddhism upon his return to Japan. The apprehension felt by both parties is exemplified in the reports of Suzuki's meetings with Taixu and Yinguang.

The Dual Nature of Suzuki's Buddhist Modernism

Drawing on and developing the argument of his *sensei*, Shaku Sōen, Suzuki contended that Buddhism was not only compatible with, but also indispensable for, global modernity, an idea that was strongly reflected in his articulation of Zen and Jōdo Shinshū (commonly known as Shin Buddhism or Shin). In the 1930s, most Buddhists in Japan still pursued their training, meditation for instance, in monasteries. This traditional representation of Buddhism was not the image that Suzuki desired to export to the rest of the world. From 1927 onward, Suzuki rearticulated the teachings of Zen and Shin in psychological terms. He encouraged students of Zen to shift their focus from monastic training to the direct experience of satori, the awakening of a nondual mental state between the finite self and infinity. He started to speak of satori as the essence, the "sine qua non" of Zen (Suzuki 1933: xxxi). As Suzuki proclaimed, "Zen may lose all its literature, all its monasteries and all its paraphernalia; but as long as there is satori in it, it will survive to eternity" and thus "when there is no satori, there is no Zen" (Suzuki 1927: 216; 1933: xxxi). While Zen enabled practitioners to ascend from their finite self to the infinite Buddha nature, Shin allowed them to descend back to the everyday world where devotees realized the absolute power of Amida Buddha in them (Suzuki 2015: 19). This realization amounted to their rebirth in Amida's Pure Land.

By articulating Buddhism in psychological terms, Suzuki was able to designate Buddhism as the antidote to the existential crisis in the West. According to Suzuki, the European Enlightenment, armed with reason and intellect, set the initial rift between the individual and the rest of the world (Suzuki 1927: 6). This split generated frustration, fear, worry, and uncertainty, thus ushering in an era marked by existential crisis (Suzuki 1970: 73). Against this backdrop, Suzuki proposed that the Buddhist wisdom of nonduality could fuse the divide between human and nature (Suzuki 1927: 24). Expressing deep concern for the psychological needs of Westerners, Suzuki won himself the reputation as the "godfather of Western Zen," the authority of Zen, and the awakened master (Ge 1986: 210).

Elaborating Buddhism's potential for resolving the crisis of rationality, Suzuki, meanwhile, localized this transnational Buddhist wisdom in Japanese culture. Against the depreciatory view of Buddhism in Japan, Suzuki revealed how Zen epitomized the essence of Japanese culture (Suzuki 1934: 318). Due to its exclusive possession of the "priceless treasure" *qua* the Buddhist wisdom of nonduality, Japanese culture became superior to those of the rest of the world (Suzuki 1938: 14; 1987: 1).

It should be noted that most of Suzuki's books on Zen and Shin were published after 1927 when ultranationalism started to arise as the state ideology during the economic recession in Japan. These writings, filled with a sense of cultural superiority, were integrated into the Japanese nationalist discourse. Appropriating the rational-West/nonrational-East dichotomy, Suzuki gave this binary a twist by arguing that the nonrational East in possession of Buddhism was superior to the West (Faure 1993: 89). More importantly, although Japan imported Buddhism from China, the latter no longer preserved the pure form of the Buddha's teaching. Thus, China as well as other East Asian countries should follow the lead of Japan to revive Buddhism and to resist Western culture. Affirming the leadership of Japan in East Asia, Suzuki *ipso facto* facilitated the expansion of Japanese power. His modern conception of Buddhism subtly shaped his lens for observing Chinese Buddhism in 1934.

Suzuki's Brief Exchange with Taixu

Prior to 1934, Suzuki had met Taixu during the 1925 East Asian Buddhist Conference (Taixu 2005, vol. 31: 271). As a prominent Buddhist modernizer, Taixu was known as the founder of *Renjianfojiao* (人間佛教), which literally translates as "Buddhism in the human realm" (Taixu 2005, vol. 25: 354). The salient feature of his expression of Buddhism was humanism (*renbenzhuyi* 人本主義), the doctrine of prioritizing human well-being in this-worldly life (Taixu 2005, vol. 3: 187). The English term "humanistic Buddhism" was thus formulated by later scholars to capture Taixu's Buddhist reform from the institutional level to the doctrinal one.

The common social perception of Buddhism as corrupt and superstitious that arose in the 1890s in China set the stage for the Qing emperor and later the Republican government to launch the movements of Requisitioning Temples for Promoting Education. This bias propelled Taixu to conduct a series of reforms to restore the reputation of Buddhism beginning in 1910 (Taixu 2005, vol. 31: 47–51). While proposing to eliminate corruption inside monasteries by reforming Buddhist institutions, Taixu took the initiative to promote education inside Buddhist communities and established several academies so that local powers would have no reason to confiscate monastic properties. Yearning for communication with the government, Taixu played a leading role in the formation of Buddhist associations in China. Aside from these institutional reforms, Taixu demythologized several Buddhist concepts. Like Suzuki, he depicted the Pure Land as a human society free from evil and turmoil, not as a heavenly realm (Taixu 2005, vol. 25: 348). What obstructed the arrival of this Pure Land was egoism, which empowered imperialists to invade other countries for their own self-interest (Taixu 2005, vol. 24: 138). As such, China's fight against Japanese invaders in the 1930s could be seen not only as a defense of national sovereignty but also as a means to combat egoism (Taixu 2005, vol. 30: 363). Taixu thus encouraged young monks to join the Chinese army during the anti-Japanese wars (Taixu 2005, vol. 27: 276). Stressing how Buddhism could ameliorate the well-being of humans in this-worldly life, Taixu demarcated Buddhism from superstition. His articulation of humanistic Buddhism allowed Taixu to integrate his religious reform into the nation-building of modern China.

In the 1920s, Taixu became involved with the Global Buddhist Movement (*shijiefojiaoyundong* 世界佛教運動) (Taixu 2005, vol. 31: 88). He particularly valued cooperation among Buddhists throughout the world, including those in Japan (Taixu 2005, vol. 31: 88). Nonetheless, seeing how the Buddhists in Japan aligned themselves with Japanese imperialism, Taixu gradually broke away from New Buddhism and embarked on exploring alternative ways of reforming Buddhism (Taixu 2005, vol. 30: 53). This exploration resulted in the emergence of his humanistic Buddhism, which exemplified Taixu's ambivalence toward Japan. On the one hand, Buddhists throughout the world should unite to prevent egoism from prevailing; on the other,

Chinese Buddhists must safeguard the sovereignty of China against imperial Japan. These global and local aspects of humanistic Buddhism explain why Taixu initially agreed to meet with Suzuki in 1934 but then abruptly ended their meeting.

Suzuki and Yinguang, the Disputes between Modernism and Traditionalism

Compared with Taixu, Yinguang was a more traditional reformer. When Yinguang passed away in 1940, he was elevated to the status of thirteenth patriarch of the Chinese Pure Land School. With deep respect, Suzuki visited Yinguang at Baoguo Temple (報國寺) in 1934 where he lived a secluded life known as *biguan* (閉關) (Suzuki 1968: 549).

During their talk, as relayed in Suzuki's essay "Impressions of Chinese Buddhism," Yinguang described the practice of Pure Land Buddhism as the "easy path" for the inferior ignorant beings who were not superior and intelligent enough to realize Buddha nature on their own. Yinguang contended that, in the current time of "final dharma," most humans were ignorant and needed to follow the easy path for salvation relying on Amitābha's compassion (Suzuki 1968: 549–50). To be reborn in Amitābha's Pure Land after death, devotees should collect karmic merits and cultivate their faith in this Buddha. Drawing on Yinguang's description, Suzuki questioned how the inferiors, who were so ignorant, could effectively use their self-power to collect merits. Suzuki, following the teaching of Japanese Shin Buddhism, suggested that devotees, whose attempts through self-power were futile, must depend on the absolute power of Amida for salvation (Suzuki 1968: 550). Yinguang, however, adamantly refused to discuss Japan's Shin tradition, as he considered Japanese Shin Buddhists heretics who consummated marriage and consumed meat (Suzuki 1968: 550). Though enjoying their conversation, Suzuki regretted such misunderstandings and the overall unpopularity of Japanese Shin in China (Suzuki 1968: 550).

When recounting his meeting with Yinguang in 1935, Suzuki construed the inferior and the superior as two psychological types, namely, the devotional type of mind versus the intellectual type of mind (Suzuki 2008: 110). Yinguang, however, never articulated Buddhism in psychological terms. Instead, he strove to revive traditional Pure Land practices. After observing corruption within Chinese monasteries, Yinguang silently distanced himself from monastic life in his refusal to become a resident abbot, ordain disciples, and join any associations or organization (Yinguang 1997b: 1). Meanwhile, he encouraged devotees to practice Buddhism at home to restore their faith in karma, for he believed the loss of faith heralded the time of final dharma (Yinguang 1997b: 1065). Yinguang viewed the loss of faith in karma as the cause of the crises of Buddhism, China, and the entire world, further heralding the time of final dharma (Yinguang 1997b: 1065). No longer afraid of karmic consequences, people audaciously engaged in egoistic actions: local powers encroached on Buddhist properties for benefit; warlords initiated civil wars for power; imperialists participated in global expansion for wealth (Yinguang 1997a: 377, 497). To resolve these crises, people should engage in moral actions to collect karmic merit (Yinguang 1997b: 378). By doing so, they would live in a harmonious society in this life and be assured by Amitābha to be reborn in the Pure Land upon death. Yinguang did not develop the conception of a Pure Land on earth, partly because he believed that a transcendent Pure Land could better motivate people to cultivate their faith in karma and partly also because once everyone complied with moral rules, a harmonious earthly society would appear.

Stemming from this faith in karma, Yinguang's critique of Japanese Shin grew. Considering how meat eating and sexual pleasure stimulated violence and negative karma, Yinguang typecast Japanese Shin Buddhists as heretics (Yinguang 1997b: 1063). This critique also indicated Yinguang's opposition to Japan's cultural expansion. In the 1936 Shanghai Dharma Assembly, Yinguang urged Pure Land devotees to raise funds for the anti-Japanese army as a form of collecting karmic merit (Yinguang 1997b: 1074).

Suzuki's Ambivalent Impressions of Chinese Buddhism

Aside from meeting with Buddhist clerics such as Taixu and Yinguang, Suzuki also visited several Chan ancestral temples in Eastern China, such as Lingyin Temple (靈隱寺) and Xuedou Temple (雪竇寺), many of which had been reconstructed after the Taiping Rebellion (Suzuki 2008: 83). While strolling through these monasteries, Suzuki was struck by their enormous scale (Suzuki 2008: 83). Although he encouraged believers to finance social charity rather than temple construction, he still appreciated the passion of the Chinese to revive Buddhism (Suzuki 1968: 502).

Lay Buddhists fundraised most of these temple renovations. In 1934, Suzuki met with the two foremost leaders of lay Buddhists, Wang Yiting (王一亭 1867–1938) and Han Qingjing (韓清淨 1884–1949). They funded public enterprises in various ways: establishing Buddhist academies, publishing Buddhist texts, and constructing hospitals and orphanages (Suzuki 1968: 512–14). Suzuki complimented the philanthropic activities of the lay leaders, noting how their efforts improved the living condition of the underprivileged (Suzuki 1968: 512–14). These lay Buddhists also engaged in the study of Buddhist philosophy, especially that of Yogācāra. Suzuki remarked that their study of Yogācāra could "harmonize the spirit of Buddhism with the psychology of modern people" (Suzuki 1968: 512). His remark reflected the popular perception embraced by many Chinese Buddhist scholars at the time that Yogācāra was comparable to Western science and philosophy.

Unlike the Chinese who were passionate about Yogācāra, Suzuki was curious about Zen/Chan and Shin, which he depicted as two aspects of awakening. After his conversation with Yinguang, Suzuki confirmed that Japanese Shin Buddhism was not prevalent in China. Further perceiving what he understood as the corruption of Chan, Suzuki became critical toward Chinese Buddhism. He documented his observations of the Kālachakra Dharma Meeting in a Chan temple that was conducted by the ninth Panchen Lama (1883–1937) (Suzuki 1968: 503). The religious syncretism he observed at this meeting prompted Suzuki to proclaim that "[the pure form of] Chan no longer exists. There remains only a mixture with *nianfo* (念佛, chanting Amitābha's name) and several esoteric mantras" (Suzuki 1968: 546). In his later life, Suzuki never revised his opinion of Chinese Chan (Jaffe 2015: xvi). His comments on Chinese Buddhism reveal his underlying sense of Japanese cultural superiority—although Japan imported Buddhism from China, the latter no longer preserved the authentic Buddhist wisdom, and he concluded that China must therefore cooperate with Japan for the revival of Buddhism (Suzuki 2008: 82).

Through these experiences, Suzuki developed an ambivalent impression of Chinese Buddhism. On the one hand, he appreciated the hospitality of his "Chinese brothers" with whom Japanese Buddhists must align for transmitting Buddhist wisdom to the West (Suzuki 2008: 82; 1968: 551); on the other, he depreciated the revived Chinese Buddhism as inauthentic for his cultural nationalism and required Chinese Buddhists to follow the lead of Japan. His Chinese acquaintances demonstrated similar mixed feelings toward Japanese Buddhism. Taixu, when trying to unite Japanese Buddhists, resented the expansion of Japan. Likewise, Yinguang, though extending welcome to Suzuki, criticized Japanese Shin for being heretical. The interactions between Suzuki and Chinese Buddhists in 1934 epitomized the struggles experienced by most Buddhists in East Asia. As followers of the Buddha, they hoped to forge international collaborations to rehabilitate Buddhism at the global level. Yet, as children of warring homelands, they were required to prioritize their own nation's interests. The tension and misgivings between Chinese and Japanese Buddhist reformers thus demonstrate that their religious reforms were not mere reactions to the West.

The Reception of Suzuki Inside and Outside of Mao's China (1949–76)

Three years after Suzuki's visit to China, the Second Sino-Japanese War broke out. Soon after Japan's surrender in 1945, Kuomintang (國民黨 KMT), the ruling party of the Republic of China, initiated the civil war against the Communist Party of China (共產黨 CPC). The war ended with the 1949 victory of the CPC who then founded the People's Republic of China (PRC). The KMT continued its regime by withdrawing to Taiwan. Before moving to Taiwan, Hu Shih traveled in 1949 as the diplomat of the KMT to the United States where he resided in New York City until 1952. During his stay, Hu debated with Suzuki on the proper approach to Zen/Chan. Soon, the Cold War became intense between the communist and capitalist worlds. By the 1960s, China and North America went through their respective cultural revolutions. These events had a lasting impact on Suzuki: while his works fell into obscurity among the intellectuals of Mao's China, his ideas were integrated into popular discourse of North America.

Debates between Suzuki and Hu (the 1950s)

The friendship between Suzuki and Hu can be dated as early as the late 1920s when Suzuki attributed an anonymous review of his Essays in *Zen Buddhism First Series* to Hu. During his 1934 visit to China, Suzuki met with Hu in Beijing. Many scholars claim that Suzuki reunited with Hu during the 1949 East-West Philosophers' Conference in

Hawai'i, after the Second Sino-Japanese War (Yanagida 1975: 19); however, the diary of Hu suggests otherwise. In July of 1949, while the Hawai'i conference was in full swing, Hu was having cocktails in the Metropolitan Pub in New York City where he had taken residence three months prior (Hu 2003, vol. 33: 754). In fact, Hu did not reunite with Suzuki until 1951 (Hu 2003, vol. 34: 90). The two started to have more interactions when Suzuki served as guest professor at Columbia University in 1952 (Hu 2003, vol. 34: 222). Later that year, Hu completed the first draft of his paper "Ch'an (Zen) Buddhism in China Its History and Method" before returning to Taiwan (Hu 2003, vol. 34: 233). This paper was published, together with Suzuki's rejoinder, in 1953. Encapsulated in the debate was their decade-long dispute on the proper approach to Zen/Chan, to modern Buddhism, and to the modernization of their nations.

As previously discussed, Suzuki conceived of Zen as that which was beyond intellectual cognition. Hu, however, found such an interpretation too irrational to be plausible. To demonstrate that Chan could be accessed through intellectual cognition and common sense, Hu positioned Chan in "the general history of Chinese thought" (Hu 1953: 3). For Hu, the introduction of Buddhism impaired the Chinese's indigenous rationality and "a practical and matter-of-fact race was gradually worked up to religious enthusiasm, even to religious fanaticism" (Hu 2003, vol. 36: 48). Nonetheless, since the eighth century, the Chinese had initiated several movements to restore their indigenous mentality that stressed common sense and well-being in this-worldly life (Hu 1953: 13). Inside the Buddhist community, this restoration was epitomized by the rise of the Sudden Enlightenment School. Discovering the fabricated history of the Chan lineage with the help of the newly discovered manuscripts in Dunhuang, Hu concluded that the transition from the Gradual Enlightenment School to the Sudden Enlightenment School was not as smooth as widely assumed but rather demonstrated an "internal revolution within a section of Buddhism" against religious enthusiasm (Hu 1953: 17). Masters in the Sudden Enlightenment School renounced all Indian Chan practices and used "the most profane language in speaking of things sacred in Buddhism" (Hu 1953: 19). As such, the masters developed "a pedagogical method of conveying truth through a great variety of strange and sometimes seemingly crazy gestures, words and acts," for the purpose of encouraging their disciples to travel around the world, whereby these disciples expanded their horizon and increased their common sense until one day they finally came to understand Chan (Hu 1953: 20). Hu therefore remarked that those who construed Zen/Chan as illogical and beyond intellectual understanding *ipso facto* failed to appreciate the educational value of this distinct Chan pedagogy.

In response, Suzuki contended that his adversary confused the show (namely, the historical manifestations of Zen) with the actors (that is, Zen-in-itself) (Suzuki 1953: 25). For Suzuki, even though historians could distinguish between authentic and inauthentic Zen materials, "Zen-in-itself" could only be awakened from within rather than being grasped by intellectual means (Suzuki 1953: 25). It was this underlying anti-intellectualism that Hu "emphatically refuse[d] to accept" (Hu 1953: 3). Indeed, such anti-intellectualism pertained to what Hu viewed as a "religious fervor and fanaticism" from India, a zeal that would impair rationality (Hu 2003, vol. 37: 338). Hu's deep confidence in rationality, exemplified by his depiction of Chan, shaped his conception of modern religions. As Hu expressed in 1926, modern religions should be rational, humanistic, and able to promote a nonegoistic morality (Hu 2003, vol. 3: 12). For Suzuki, however, rationality was not the cure but the cause of the problematic modernity. To remedy this problem, humans needed the direct experience of the Buddhist wisdom of nonduality.

As McRae argued, Hu's studies of Chan, which were an integral part of his project of "reorganization of the national past," were subservient to a dual mission: to understand the history of his own nation and to benefit the modernization of China (2001: 72). This style of historical writing that summons the past to enlighten the present has been widely used in China ever since the Spring-Autumn Period (770 BCE–403 BCE). Through the historiography of Chan, Hu implicitly justified his proposal for modernizing China. He envisaged modernization as the linear process of realizing the principle of reason and depicted this process as such: humans interrogated every hypothesis with reason, exploring nature through modern science, replacing superstition with rational religion, prioritizing this-worldly life over otherworldly concerns, and substituting monarchy with democracy (Hu 2003, vol. 3: 13). Hu was optimistic that the liberation of reason would eventually bring about human emancipation. Turning to world history, Hu remarked that European nations, due to specific sociohistorical conditions, liberated human reason earlier than others (Hu 2003, vol. 2: 253). China, though temporarily falling behind, could easily catch up by rejuvenating its indigenous rationality (Hu 2003, vol. 2: 253). Through this theorization, not only did Hu formulate the modernization of China as a renaissance rather than Westernization, but he also debunked the colonial discourse that typecast the East as nonrational.

This exaltation of rationality nourished Hu's dispute with Suzuki and his critique of the modernization of Japan. As Hu remarked in 1940, though Japan quickly became militarily strong, its modernization artificially preserved medieval culture that could bring grave danger upon Japan (Hu 2003, vol. 37: 58). The Second Sino-Japanese War, as Hu conceptualized, was thus a battle of human reason against a nonrational medieval culture (Hu 2003, vol. 37: 492). From their dispute on the approach to Chan/Zen, there emerged their separate proposals for nation-building. While Hu discerned rationality as the national characteristic of China throughout history, Suzuki built the image of Japan through nonrationality. This underlying divergence determined the impossibility of reconciling their disagreement.

While residing in the United States, Hu noted the growing antagonism toward him in the PRC for being the ally of the KMT (Hu 2003, vol. 34: 49). In 1954, Mao Zedong (毛澤東1893–1976) officially launched the anti-Hu Shih campaign. Ren Jiyu (任繼愈 1916–2009) targeted Hu on his approach to Chan. According to Ren, the so-called principle of reason yielded a bourgeois idealism in opposition to Marxist materialism as it was induced from personal experience rather than material facts (Ren 1955: 80; 1963: 176). Hu's cooperation with Imperial Japanese scholars (probably including Suzuki) confirmed his identity as an antirevolutionary bourgeois, an enemy to the Chinese people (Ren 1963: 182). For Ren, the rise of the Sudden Enlightenment School was not a revolution but an attempt to better assist the ruling class in deluding the working peasants. Like most intellectuals in Mao's China, Ren perceived ideas through the lens of class.

Buddhism in Mao's China and the Absence of Suzuki

The ideology of Mao's China, characterized by the theory of class struggle, indicated the approach taken by the CPC to modernize the nation. According to Marxism, the logic of class struggle linked the philosophical critique of idealism with the political struggle against capitalism. In this sense, idealism became the philosophical worldview of the bourgeoisie or the capitalists who exploited the working class or the proletariat who endorsed materialism. Thus, to create a communist society, the proletariat should struggle against the bourgeoisie as well as their worldview. Depicting Japanese invaders and the KMT as representatives of the bourgeoisie who enslaved workers and peasants for profit, the CPC encouraged Chinese commoners to fight for emancipation (Communist Party of China 1981). Allies of the bourgeoisie, such as Suzuki, Taixu, and Hu, were equally classified as enemies of the Chinese.

After defeating the KMT in 1949, the CPC implemented policies to eradicate feudalism and capitalism, to transform China into a socialist country. In rural areas, People's Communes (人民公社) were founded to operate the collectively owned lands that were obtained from landlords. In urban areas, privately owned companies and industrial plants became public properties (Communist Party of China 1981). Since 1958, the CPC started to commit "Leftist Errors" (*zuoqincuowu* 左傾錯誤). These Leftists Errors culminated during the Cultural Revolution (1966–76). As the leader of the CPC, Mao misperceived opposing opinions expressed among the working class as bourgeoisie sabotage against the Communist regime. He thus unleashed the Cultural Revolution to eliminate bourgeois elements, which would jeopardize the newborn socialist state (Communist Party of China 1981). By the time Suzuki passed away in July of 1966, two months after the launch of the Cultural Revolution, Japan had terminated its diplomatic relations with the PRC for almost two decades.

In the wake of Leftist politics, religion was perceived as "the opium" used by the bourgeoisie to delude the working class into overlooking exploitation (Wang Leiquan 1995: 3). Since religion facilitated bourgeoisie rulership, it should be eradicated from socialist China (Zhao 2007: 416). During the land reform (1950–3), the CPC required landlords to hand over their privately owned property to the country; this included Buddhist monasteries (Xuyue 2009: 207). Red Guards confiscated monastic property during the Cultural Revolution and tortured several clerics to death, including the president of Chinese Buddhist Association, Geshe Sherab Gyatso (喜饒嘉措 1884–1968) (Zhao 2007: 440). Buddhist clerics such as Ven. Xuyun (虛雲 1840–1959), the legendary master who strived to revive all five Chan lineages, barely managed to protect their religion from destruction. In this sociopolitical context, Buddhist reform came to a halt. Monastics and academics barely maintained connections with the outside. Cut off from the capitalist world, they gradually forgot thinkers like Suzuki.

Buddhism in North America and the Suzuki Boom

Unlike in Mao's China, the 1960s was when Buddhism flourished in North America. Prior to this period, Buddhism had little cultural influence and was mostly practiced among Asian immigrant communities. After the 1960s, Buddhism was incorporated into mainstream American culture. This change precipitated the rediscovery of Suzuki's writings.

Scholars usually attribute the flourishing of Buddhism in North America to two factors, the obvious one being the changes to American and Canadian immigration laws in 1965 and 1967, respectively, which increased the number of Asian immigrants to both countries. After removing previous discrimination against Asian immigrants, Canada further implemented the policy of multiculturalism in the 1970s, thus "officially welcoming people of all races and cultures" (Harding, Hori, and Soucy 2010: 4). Newcomers from Taiwan, Korea, and other Asian locales, when arriving in North America, brought with them their own Buddhist traditions (Seager 1999: x).

The second, and more significant, factor that contributed to the flourishing of Buddhism in North America stemmed from the advent of "the age of authenticity" (Taylor 2007: 473). Charles Taylor formulated this term to capture the zeitgeist of the 1960s when North American youth experimented with new ways of expressing their individual identity and revolted against the conservative social culture of the preceding decades. The change of Buddhism from a brand of ethnicity to a carrier of cultural identity soon problematized the distinction between Asian immigrants and Western converts (Hori 2010: 16). The cultural revolution in North America was quite different from the concurrent Chinese "Cultural Revolution," the salient feature of the former being the yearning for authentic identity, whereas the latter was characterized by class struggle.

The revolution against North American mainstream culture spurred the rediscovery of Suzuki's writings. Suzuki's description of Zen as the direct experience of inner awakening fit with the zeitgeist of the 1960s and offered North American youth an alternative way to express their individual identity. This led to a "Suzuki Boom." Pioneers of this beat generation, among them Jack Kerouac (1922–69), hailed Suzuki as their spiritual mentor (Li Silong 2014: 133). Two decades later in the 1980s, a similar "Suzuki Fever" emerged in China, whereby both Suzuki and his friend Hu reclaimed their previous reputation as Buddhist masters.

Suzuki's Inspiration within Contemporary Chinese Buddhism (1976–Present)

After officially terminating the Cultural Revolution in 1976, the PRC restored its communications with the capitalist world, including Japan. Beginning in 1978, the CPC, under the leadership of Deng Xiaoping (鄧小平 1904–97), initiated a public policy known as "Reform and Opening-up." This socioeconomic reform marked the advent of a new era in the 1980s. For the Chinese, the term "the eighties" (*bashiniandai* 八十年代) is shorthand for a time when China reconnected itself with the outside world, the private economy was resuscitated, universities reopened their doors, and poets exalted human dignity and individual happiness. This specific context nourished the "Suzuki Fever" in Mainland China toward the end of the Cold War.

Liberating Ideas and the "Suzuki Fever" (the Late 1980s)

To facilitate economic reforms, the CPC implemented the policy of "liberating ideas" (*jiefangsixiang* 解放思想) (Communist Party of China 1978). Traumatized by the Cultural Revolution, the Chinese refused to let political movements override human dignity. This refusal nourished humanism. After reconnecting with the capitalist world, Chinese intellectuals seized the opportunity to import new thoughts. Gradually, the 1980s became the golden era of liberating ideas.

Though China established diplomatic relations with Japan in 1972, the interactions between the two officially grew after 1978. In this cultural sphere of exchange, Suzuki's Zen writings soon garnered a growing level of attention. According to the Chinese database Duxiu (读秀), in 1987, fifty academic papers were published on Suzuki's ideas. Between 1988 and 1989, ten of Suzuki's books were available in the Chinese language (Huang Xianian 2013: 30). He became the most frequently translated and studied Japanese scholar in Mainland China. Ven. Jinghui (淨慧 1933–2013) even claimed that the Suzuki Fever became the forerunner of the subsequent Chan Fever (Jinghui 2005: 280).

For Chinese intellectuals, Suzuki was an exponent of "Buddhist humanism" (*fojiaorendaozhuyi* 佛教人道主義) (Yuan 1990: 14). Translators particularly stressed the humanistic aspect in Suzuki's writings that depicted traditional Zen wisdom as the cure to existential crises (Feng 1998; Xie 1989; Ge 1989). Chinese intellectuals contended that Suzuki's Buddhist humanism would promote compassion, thus safeguarding human dignity and happiness (Yuan 1990: 18). After the Cultural Revolution, the Chinese yearned for compassion and empathy. Therefore, they endorsed Suzuki's modern articulation of Buddhism. Buddhist clerics such as Jinghui encouraged young scholars to introduce Suzuki's ideas, which he helped circulate in national and provincial journals (He 2013: 70; Weiye 1989: 228).

Suzuki Fever was an integral part of the humanistic movement of the 1980s in China. Nevertheless, it was not as widespread as North America's "Suzuki Boom" in the 1960s. Although Suzuki had articulated Buddhist modernism to justify the superiority of Japanese culture, this nationalistic aspect of his writings almost entirely escaped the attention of his Chinese proponents who appropriated Suzuki's ideas.

Suzuki Fever gradually waned in the 1990s. Its decline was, in one respect, due to the resurgence of a radical nationalism in China after 1989 (Chen Yan 2006); in another, it was an attempt on the part of Chinese academics and monastics to depart from Suzuki and to formulate their own expressions of Buddhist modernism.

The Revival of Taixu's Humanistic Buddhism in Mainland China and Suzuki's Input

Jinghui, the disciple of Master Xuyun, who held all five Chan lineages, was one of the clerics who assisted in the dispersion of Suzuki's writings. Though never directly crediting Suzuki as his source of inspiration, he was very conversant with Suzuki's Buddhist modernism (Jinghui 2005: 280, 415). Impressed by Suzuki's success in the world, Jinghui urged Chinese clergy to learn from Suzuki regarding making Buddhism accessible to people of all cultures (Jinghui 2005: 5). According to Jinghui, this accessibility, together with humanism and social engagement, should characterize any modern form of Buddhism (Jinghui 2005: 6).

Since the 1980s, changes in the CPC's religious policy gave an impetus to the revival of Taixu's idea of "Buddhism in the human realm." The CPC no longer demeaned religion as "opium." Instead, it intended to guide religion to fit socialism (Wang Leiquan 1995: 3). This change offered a ground for clerics to resume their religious reform after the Cultural Revolution. Prior to Jinghui, in 1980, Zhao Puchu (趙樸初 1907–2000), the president of the Chinese Buddhist Association, equated Amitābha's Pure Land with the prosperous socialist China to suggest the compatibility of humanistic Buddhism with Marxism (Zhao 2007: 560). This idea of Buddhism in the human realm continued to flourish when, during the era of liberating ideas, many taboo names reappeared in the public sphere, *inter alia*, Taixu and Hu Shih. Later in 1986, the CPC embarked on a project to reconstruct both the material and spiritual dimensions of Chinese civilization. Buddhist clergy, Jinghui for instance, seized this opportunity to depict their religious reform as the Buddhist way of constructing a spiritual civilization (Jinghui 2005: 119). Buddhism, as part of traditional Chinese culture, could improve spiritual civilization by encouraging the Chinese people to comply with moral rules (Jinghui 2005: 11). Jinghui made a strong case for his expression of humanistic Buddhism known as Life Chan (*shenghuochan* 生活禪) in contemporary China at a time when the CPC launched the policy of reviving traditional culture (Communist Party of China 2017).

In 1993, Jinghui organized the first summer camp in Bailin Temple (柏林寺), which marked the birth of Life Chan. Since public proselytizing outside monasteries is still prohibited in the PRC, Jinghui took the initiative to attract Chinese people, especially the young, to participate in summer camps and winter retreats inside temples where they could learn about Life Chan (Jinghui 2005: 423). Jinghui spoke of Life Chan as the process of living as one with Chan. Instead of conducting a philosophical analysis of Chan, Jinghui formulated Chan as the nondualistic wisdom, which can be awakened in every life moment, such as walking, standing, sitting, and sleeping (Jinghui 2005: 142). This awakening would elicit compassion and motivate followers of Chan to engage in moral actions (Jinghui 2005: 263). Through performing altruistic deeds, Chan practitioners would realize the nonduality between the self and the other and live eventually as one with the awakened wisdom. In his lectures on Life Chan, Jinghui deliberately addressed Hu Shih's Chan historiography. Jinghui recollected how deeply he revered the Sixth Patriarch Huineng (惠能 638–713) and Ven. Hanshan (憨山 1546–1623) when seeing their mummified bodies (Jinghui 2005: 111). He thus believed that if disciples respected and revered their masters to such a degree, they would never have the audacity to fabricate stories about their teachers (Jinghui 2005: 111). By questioning the authenticity of Chan lineage, Hu Shih displayed a "lack of common sense," which led to his failure to understand the essential roles of these masters in Chan history (Jinghui 2005: 112).

Due to its promotion of moral actions, Jinghui presumed that Life Chan could advance the spiritual civilization of China and eventually the entire world (Jinghui 2005: 10, 119). In part, Jinghui inaugurated Life Chan to popularize Chinese Chan, especially after noting how, through Suzuki's efforts, Zen became the symbol of Japanese culture (Jinghui 2008: 155). Nevertheless, he did not proceed to argue for the superiority of Chinese culture. As described earlier in this chapter, the mission of Life Chan was to introduce the world to a Buddhist modernism that was humanistic, socially engaged, and accessible to people of all cultures.

Conclusion

As history unfolds from early Republican China (1912–49), to Mao's China (1949–76), and finally to post-Mao China (1976–present), a pattern within the Chinese reception of Suzuki can be discerned: when national sovereignty became the primary concern of the Chinese, they felt threatened by the cultural expansion expressed by Suzuki and distanced themselves from his ideas. However, when China secured its sovereignty and reopened its doors to globalization, the Chinese expressed a strong affinity for Suzuki's Buddhist humanism. Suzuki was similarly affected by the sociopolitical climate between China and Japan; his perception of Chinese Buddhism was very mixed: on the one hand, he had to recognize Japanese Buddhism's indebtedness to Chinese Buddhism, yet he could not reconcile Chinese Buddhist beliefs and practices with the modern image of Japan that he hoped to realize. Therefore, it is through their attempts to balance the reformation of religion with the building of a modern nation that Buddhists in China and Japan eventually put forward their own proposals for the modernization of Buddhism.

This historical survey of Buddhism inside East Asia problematizes the West-impact/East-response model. By juxtaposing the East against the West, this model fails to recognize and appreciate the diverse values and regional tensions inside East Asia. Consider the exchange between Yinguang and Suzuki: their dispute was not a result of the East-West clash but rather an example of different interpretations of the Buddha's teaching in the East Asian context. Like most clerics and monastics, the two summoned the past to justify their own prospects for the future of the nation and the religion, following the decline of the Sinocentric worldview. This is how Buddhist modernism emerged in East Asia. As this chapter contends, Buddhist modernism was not a reaction to the West; it was an East Asian reform movement that strove to reconcile the need for reviving the religion at the global level with the demand for nation-building at the local level. While the global level served as a ground for the followers of the Buddha to forge transcultural connections, the local level functioned as the baseline for the interactions among citizens of their own nations.

7

Recent Emergence of Theravāda Meditation Communities in Contemporary China

Ngar-sze Lau

On the last morning of the ten-day meditation retreat, the closing session was about to start in the meditation hall of Yun Shan Monastery in Jiangxi in South China.[1] Yellow interlocking foam mats had been placed neatly on the cold stone floor, making a corridor for people with bare feet to walk to their bench seats. About fifty retreat participants took off their shoes at the main entrance before stepping into the meditation hall. Then all put their palms together and knelt down either on a bench or on a foam mat. U Tejaniya Sayadāw, the meditation teacher from Myanmar, dressed in a maroon robe, walked up to the hall stage. Everyone bowed three times, the usual practice in the Theravāda tradition. The abbot then gave a short closing speech encouraging all participants to continue the practice after the retreat. After that, he invited U Tejaniya to lead everyone in taking the Three Refuges and Five Precepts (*sanguiwujie*). U Tejaniya asked all to follow him sentence by sentence in Pāli, *Namo tassa bhagavato arahato samma sambuddhassa* [I pay homage to the Blessed One, the Worthy One, the Fully Enlightened One].

U Tejaniya was not the only traveling guru from the Theravāda traditions visiting Mainland China recently. In the same year, there were six meditation retreats led by monks from Southeast Asia at Yun Shan monastery. Since the turn of the century, there have been an increasing number of Han Chinese monastics and laity joining various kinds of meditation retreats from the Theravāda traditions, highlighting *vipassanā* and foundations of mindfulness (*satipaṭṭhāna*). The growing Theravāda meditation communities in Mainland China have attracted Chinese monks, nuns, educated young people, middle-class professionals, and therapists (Lau 2017). Apart from attending a seven-day or a ten-day meditation retreat at monasteries across the country, some Han Chinese monastics and laity even travel to Southeast Asian countries to practice as yogis or short-term monastics in the Theravāda tradition. Learning Pāli language has become fashionable in meditation communities. However, while Mahāyāna Buddhism has been the mainstream tradition ever since Buddhism spread to China, it is significant and interesting to explore these questions: Why and how do some Chinese Buddhists today accept Theravāda meditation practice? How have various Theravāda meditation practices been introduced and adapted to Chinese Mahāyāna Buddhist communities in China? Is the recent popularity of Theravāda meditation in China an extension of, or a rejection of, traditional Mahāyāna Buddhism?

To answer these questions, in this chapter, I examine changing understandings of Buddhism since the Republican period, based on both a literature review and my ethnographic fieldwork.[2] Firstly, after the encounter with Orientalist Buddhist scholars, Yang Wenhui (楊文會 1837–1911) and Taixu (太虛 1889–1947) started the project of reforming Chinese Buddhism through building transnational networks and modern Buddhist institutes. I argue that all these have facilitated the extension of "Chinese Buddhism" to incorporate Theravāda Buddhism and Tibetan Buddhism in the modern Buddhist institutes. Second, the transnational networks developed by Buddhist reformers have enhanced the recent popularity of Theravāda Buddhism in China. Finally, from my recent fieldwork, I demonstrate how and why the transplantation of various Theravāda meditation communities has intersected with the desire for self-healing in the context of an economic boom, tourism, and cyber technology. Throughout the chapter, I argue that the emerging Theravāda meditation practice has reconstructed Buddhism in the contemporary Chinese context as a supplement to the existing mainstream traditions.

Theravāda as Inferior to Traditional Chinese Mahāyāna Buddhism

Theravāda means literally "Doctrine of the Elders," which refers to the teachings collected by the 500 Arahant elders in the First Council after the death of Gautama Buddha. Gombrich concedes that Theravāda doctrines "have undergone very little change or development since [their] origin in ancient India" (1988: 21). However, along the complex history, Theravāda was only one of the earlier schools that spread from India to Ceylon (now Sri Lanka), about 250 BCE. In the seventh century CE, it spread to Burma (now Myanmar), Thailand, Laos, and Cambodia. Theravāda Buddhism is well supported by the modern state and the majority population nowadays in most Southeast Asian countries, especially Thailand, Myanmar, and Sri Lanka. As Skilling (2009) argues, Theravāda is a constructed identity and by-product of globalization. It has recently spread to some other Asian countries, including Singapore, Malaysia, and Nepal and to Europe, North America, and Australia in the West. The use of Pāli, originally meaning "canonical text," as the main sacred language, and the Pāli scriptures, are the hallmarks of Theravāda Buddhism.[3] The Pāli scriptures are generally referred to as the *Tipiṭaka*, which means "three baskets," comprising the *Sutta Piṭaka*, the *Vinaya Piṭaka*, and the *Abhidhamma Piṭaka*.

Around the Common Era, Mahāyāna Buddhism emerged in India, with new kinds of Buddhist literature, now known as the early Mahāyāna texts. The phrase "Thus I have heard" was added at the beginning of these texts to claim the status of "the word of the Buddha" (Gethin 1998: 56–65). Mahāyānist religious followers consider that the Mahāyāna sūtras were preached by the Buddha (Williams 1989: 4). Over the seven centuries that followed, philosophies and texts of several schools of the Mahāyāna tradition developed in India with great diversity and complexity, for example, the Mādhyamaka school and the school of Yogācāra. In general, the path of Mahāyāna, which means the "great vehicle," is the path of the Bodhisattva leading to full enlightenment (Gethin 1998: 224–25), for example, Avalokiteśvara is a popular Bodhisattva worshipped by the Chinese. In Mahāyāna tradition, it is generally believed that all beings can practice the path of a Bodhisattva. From the general perspectives of Mahāyāna, the path of Hīnayāna, which means "the inferior vehicle" or the "small vehicle," leading to arhatship is not as highly valued as attaining Buddhahood.

Mahāyāna Buddhism flourished exclusively in East Asia, as Gethin (1998: 224–25) notes.[4] Many scriptures were translated from Prakrit and original Sanskrit into Chinese or Tibetan. While Buddhism was declining in India in the eleventh century, Chinese Mahāyāna Buddhism spread to East Asia, including Japan, Korea, and Vietnam. Indian Mahāyāna Buddhism spread to Nepal, Bali, and Bhutan. Buddhists from nearly all countries produced their own kinds of literature and commentaries. Historical evidence has demonstrated interaction between Mahāyāna and Theravāda Buddhists in the premodern period. For example, Faxian (法顯 337–c.422), a Chinese monk, visited Ceylon in the fifth century and returned to China with several Indic texts (Gombrich 1988: 121). Nevertheless, influential exchange between Buddhist traditions may have really started only in the modern period, especially after encounter with the Orientalists.

Orientalism and Theravāda Buddhism in the Nineteenth Century

Examining the scholarship of Orientalism is important for the understanding of the construction of modern Buddhism. Edward Said defines Orientalism as a "Western style for dominating, restructuring, and having authority over the Orient" (Said 1978: 3). In Orientalist discussion, European powers dominated colonized countries not only with military power but also through knowledge. Some scholars have discussed the impact of Orientalism in constructing modern Buddhism and Buddhist scholarship in European-American contexts. During the Victorian era, the British selectively accepted or rejected perspectives of Buddhism based on their cultural values (Almond 1988; Harris 2006). Western Buddhist scholars had demythologized Buddhism and highlighted rational elements, creating an "original" Buddhism with a humanized Buddha and a textual tradition (Lopez 1995: 1–30).

Orientalist scholars considered that Pāli Buddhist texts represent the most original and authentic form of Buddhism, although this interpretation indeed is in contrast to living Buddhist practices in many modern Asian countries. In other words, Orientalist scholars explicitly condemned Mahāyāna Buddhism as degenerate. Theravāda Buddhism from Southeast Asia was accessed through Pāli scriptures during the colonial era. Early British scholars such as T. W. Rhys Davids and Caroline Rhys Davids, who founded the Pāli Text Society in 1922, highly praised the knowledge of ancient languages of Pāli. They translated Pāli texts as pioneers and constructed a rational interpretation of Buddhism. Their understanding has been foundational to many modern Buddhist scholars and Buddhists in the West.[5]

Nevertheless, as Richard King (1999: 148–50) argues, the tendency of Orientalist Buddhist scholarship of presenting "authentic Buddhism," what he calls "nostalgia for origins," is not only a Western interest. Throughout the history of Buddhism, reformers of movements have tried to establish their authority with their connection to the Buddha and the teachings. King suggests that a reflection on the engagement of Asian Buddhists in the construction of Orientalist Buddhism is necessary. For example, from recent research, the current usage of the term "Theravāda" to refer the tradition in Southeast Asia is a "Western coinage." "Theravāda" was used for the first time in the 1830s as an alternative to "Hīnayāna." Yet it became popular in Asian Buddhist communities after the World Fellowship of Buddhists passed a resolution in 1951 in Sri Lanka (Collins 2010: 8).

Crisis and Buddhist Reform in Late Qing

From the late Qing, Buddhism along with other Chinese religions was criticized by Protestant missionaries, Republican elites, and social reformers as superstitious (*mixin*), nonscientific, and backward (Ashiwa and Wank 2009). Without great support received from the state, there was no screening mechanism for those joining the Buddhist community as monks or nuns. In the early twentieth century, it was estimated that there were a half million monks and one thousand nuns in China (Welch 1967: 287). Many tried to escape from their life's misfortunes by becoming monks or nuns at monasteries as a form of asylum. For example, some poor peasants sent their unwanted children to monasteries. Some others went to monasteries after broken marriages, illness, poverty, or even after committing crime (Chen 1964: 452–53). Most of these monastics were not educated and not able to teach Buddhist knowledge. Local gods and ghosts were worshipped in most Buddhist monasteries. Many monks and nuns conducted chanting rituals for funerals to earn income (Welch 1968: 14). The overall social perception of the Buddhist monastic community was that of its members being uneducated, ignorant and corrupt, and generally unappealing to social elites and young reformers (Chan 1953: 54–55). For instance, in 1898 Zhang Zhidong (張之洞 1837–1909), a Qing government officer, launched a movement to convert all temples into schools (Goossaert 2006: 307–36).

Facing the crisis of Chinese Buddhism in the late Qing, Buddhist reformers, with insight from Christians and Orientalists, started new projects to change their practices and communities. Yang Wenhui, the father of the Chinese Buddhist revival, visited Europe and later devoted himself to Buddhist modernization (Welch 1968: 1–22). In 1866, Yang established the famous Jinling Sutra Publishing House (*Jinlingkejingchu* 金凌刻經處) in Nanjing for reprinting Buddhist texts (Chao-Yang 1969: 75–82). As an ambassador of the Qing government in London in 1878, Yang had the chance to explore the Orientalist discovery of early Buddhism (Welch 1968: 4–5).[6] During his stay in Europe, Yang (2000) started historically significant interactions with Nanjō Bunyū (南条文雄 1849–1927), a Japanese scholar who studied Sanskrit under Max Müller, the German Sanskrit scholar. Yang and Nanjō communicated with letters before they first met in London on June 30, 1881, at the residence of Suematsu Kenchō

(末松謙澄 1855–1920), who was working at the Japanese embassy (Chen 2017: 13; Goldfuss 2001: 72–73; Yang 2000: 473). Despite the obstacles of oral communication, Yang and Nanjō had continued to communicate by writing letters discussing Chinese Buddhism and Sanskrit grammar.[7]

Over the past thousand years, Chinese scriptures were spread in China as well as East Asia. Neither Pāli or Sanskrit texts nor their languages were popularly known in late Qing. Also neither Chinese Buddhists nor Japanese Buddhists knew the difference between Pāli and Sanskrit during that time (Chen 2017: 23).[8] With the impact of Meiji Restoration, Japanese scholars started studying Buddhism and Sanskrit in the West in the mid-nineteenth century. Nanjō was one of the key pioneers sent to Europe, in his case to study Sanskrit in Britain. He introduced knowledge of Orientalist Buddhist scholarship and Sanskrit to Japan after his study in Oxford. Yang was the first Chinese who recognized the value of learning Sanskrit and Orientalist Buddhist scholarship. Through contact with Western scholars, Yang knew that there still existed Sanskrit Mahāyāna texts in India and Nepal and also Theravāda Pāli texts in Southeast Asia.

About three years after his first trip to Europe, Yang returned to China with knowledge of sciences and new technologies, including printing skills, the telescope, and the microscope. It is believed that the stay in Europe had inspired Yang in promoting Dharmalaksana (Faxiang 法相) or Yogācāra (Weishi 唯識), as compatible with science. With the great support of Nanjō Bunyū, over 300 lost sutra texts from Japan were imported to China and reprinted. Yang also met Anāgārika Dharmapāla, the Ceylonese Buddhist reformer, in 1893 in Nanjing, to explore cooperation with Chinese Buddhists about reviving Buddhism in India and spreading it throughout the world.[9] Dharmapāla also advised Yang to send missionaries from China to India for translating some Chinese Buddhist texts to Indian language. Inspired by Dharmapāla, in 1908, Yang established the Jetavana Hermitage (*Zhihuan jingshe* 祇洹精舍), the first modern Buddhist Studies institute as an attempt to teach Sanskrit, English, and the Yogācāra school teachings (Welch 1968: 6–8). Yang also founded the Association for Research on the Buddhist Religion (*Fojiao Yanjiuhui* 佛教研究會) before his death, on the eve of the Republican revolution in 1911 (Welch 1968: 23). His first attempts at Buddhist reform were carried forward in the Republican period by several of his remarkable followers, who included both monastics and lay reformers. With inspiration from the Orientalist perspectives, Yang initiated Buddhist reform through education with the support of a globalized network from Japan, Ceylon, and also Europe. As a social reformer, Yang believed that Buddhist thought could contribute to the well-being of the human world (Chao-Yang 1969: 75–82). Yang's disciples, especially Taixu, further succeeded in the goal of reforming Chinese Buddhism as a globalized religion.

Building New Buddhism with "Buddhism for Human Life" in the Republican Era

Over the Republican era, an antisuperstition movement promoting science and a modern state was launched by the Kuomintang (KMT), the Nationalist Party of China.

Several nationalist laws, such as "Rules for Temple Registration," were announced to convert temple properties to public service in the late 1920s (Nedostup 2009: 295–99). Traditional Chinese religions—including Buddhism, Daoism, and local cults—were seen as international embarrassments and became targets for attack by being labeled as "superstition."

Taixu, who had studied under Yang Wenhui, proposed a new Buddhism that would be humanistic, scientific, engaged, and global. Buddhism could be reformed to compete with other world religions, such as Christianity. Taixu proposed the idea of modern Buddhism with the notion of "Buddhism for human life" (*rensheng fojiao* 人生佛教), focusing on the "human life" instead of "ghosts" and "death." In the teaching he promoted, the perfection of human personality is a prerequisite of achieving Buddhahood. Taixu also suggested the idea of "Pure Land on Earth" (*renjian jingtu* 人間淨土) by building Buddhist communities with Buddhist moral practices. Taixu first mentioned the notion "Buddhism for this world" or "Renjian Buddhism" (*renjian fojiao* 人間佛教) in a public speech at Hankou in 1933 (2017: 431).[10]

In 1918, Taixu set up the Bodhi Society in Shanghai to publish articles about his notions of Buddhist reform. He started publishing "The Reorganisation of the Sangha System" in 1915, then put out the journal *Haichaoyin* (海潮音 *Voice of the Sea Tide*) in 1920. Finally, the government reaffirmed the principle of religious freedom and protected temple property (Nedostup 2009). In spite of facing the decline of Chinese Buddhism, Taixu was optimistic about reforming Chinese Buddhism and promoting Buddhism outside of China. He imagined ambitious projects such as the recovery of Buddhism on a scale like the early Tang. He looked forward to support from Japan and the West, visits to Ceylon and Tibet, the study of Pāli and Tibetan texts, and bringing Buddhism to the new global world (Taixu [1930] 2017: 3–21).

The Attempt to Translate the Pāli Canon from Japanese

Neighboring countries, especially Japan, had a great impact on Buddhist reform in China. The modernization of Buddhism in Japan started after the Meiji Restoration in the late nineteenth century. Buddhist reform in Japan began with the establishment of Buddhist universities and Buddhist Studies and sending scholars to study abroad in Europe. In the early twentieth century, Japanese scholars completed new editions and translations of the *Tipiṭaka* (Pāli canon), the Tibetan *Tripiṭaka*, and the Chinese *Tripiṭaka* (Fafang 2013, vol. 1: 433–56). Political reformers, such as Kang Youwei (康有為) and Liang Qichao (梁啟超), were also involved in the Buddhist revival movement (Kiely and Jessup 2016: 1–34).

The Japanese Buddhist scholar Kimura Taiken (1881–1930) in 1924 commented that the development of Buddhist Studies in China lagged behind Japan by about three decades (Fafang 2013, vol. 1: 104–9). Taixu and his disciples were eager to learn from the Japanese Buddhist reformers. With the idea of establishing a global connection, Taixu set up the World Buddhist Association (*Shijie Fojiao Lianhehui* 世界佛教聯合會) in 1922 and organized the World Buddhist Conference (*Shijie Fojiao Dahui*

世界佛教大會) at Dalin Temple at Lushan in 1924. Taixu proposed to unite Buddhists in China, then in East Asia, and then to spread Buddhism from East Asia to Europe and America. A few students of Taixu were sent to Japan to study "original Buddhism." Kimura Taiken's (木村泰賢) *On Original Buddhist Thought* (*Genshi bukkyō shisō* 原始佛教思想) was translated in 1933 into Chinese (Wang Enyang [1940] 2006). Chinese Buddhists had a chance to access the perspective of original Buddhism. Between 1928 and 1929, with the support from the KMT, Taixu spent nine months visiting the United States and some European countries. He was the first Chinese Buddhist monk and started a network with Western Buddhists.

In 1935, representatives from Japan visited Taixu and proposed to organize a Sino-Japanese Buddhist Studies Society (*Zhongri Foxue Huishi* 中日佛學會事) (Yinshun 1950: 380–82). In the meeting, Taixu agreed to invite D. T. Suzuki to give a talk during his coming visit to China. Outstanding monastic disciples of Taixu, including Daxing (大醒 1899-1957), Zhifeng (芝峰 1901-71), and Fafang (法舫 1904-51), visited Japan in the following year. Besides this, Japanese representatives proposed to Taixu a project of translation of the Tipiṭaka (Pāli canon) from Japanese into Chinese.[11] Taixu arranged for Zhifeng to coordinate the Tipiṭaka translation project. The content was published in *Haichaoyin* (Fafang 2013, vol. 1: 141–51). However, after the Japanese invasion of China in 1937, the interaction between Chinese and Japanese Buddhists immediately stopped. Due to the unstable political situation in China, the Japanese *Tipiṭaka* translation project was delayed for fifty years (Yinshun 1993).

Establishing Modern Buddhist Institutions and Teaching Theravāda Buddhism

In the late nineteenth century, Christian missionaries in China started establishing schools offering Western education. Taixu was impressed and inspired by the Western theological seminaries and the system of Christian schools involved in education in the West. In the vision of Taixu, education was the key to upgrading the quality of monastics to reform Buddhism in China. Taixu planned to have ten thousand monks getting academic degrees, eight hundred receiving the doctoral degree, and another twenty-five thousand engaged in all kinds of charitable work, including service for hospitals, orphanages, and meditation (Welch 1968: 52). Reviewing the schools of Buddhism, he proposed that modern Buddhist education institutions be established with three major Buddhist systems. The first schools would study the first stage of Indian Buddhism, based on Pāli and Sanskrit texts in Ceylon, Thailand, and Myanmar. The second schools would study the second stage of Indian Buddhism, based on Chinese texts in China, Japan, and Korea. The last schools would study Mahāyāna Buddhism based on Tibetan, Mongolian, Manchu, Sanskrit, and Nepalese. Taixu foresaw that existing Chinese Buddhist scriptures belonged to the second stage of Indian Buddhism. The knowledge from the Theravāda and Tibetan traditions could complement the insufficiency of theories and practices in Chinese Buddhism (Fafang 2013, vol. 3: 91–110).

From 1922 onward, Taixu established modern Buddhist academies (*foxueyuan* 佛學院) for educating monks, using secular university models from the West. The first and the most influential institute was the Wuchang Buddhist Institute (*Wuchang foxue yuan* 武昌佛學院), established in 1922, with the financial support of a group of businessmen. The institute was managed on the model of a traditional Chan monastery but with curriculum design influenced by that of Bukkyō University in Japan.[12] Taixu established the South Fujian Seminary (*Minnan foxue yuan* 閩南佛學院) in 1925 in Xiamen, specializing in Japanese studies. The institute of Chinese and Tibetan Buddhism (*Hanzang jiaoliyuan* 漢藏教理院), specializing in Tibetan studies, was founded in Chongqing in 1932. Taixu organized the Bailin Monastery Buddhist Studies Society (*Bailinsi foxue yanjiaoshe* 柏林寺佛學研究社) specializing in English language studies at Beijing in 1930. Unfortunately, it was closed down due to the Mukden incident in 1931. The Seminary of Pāli Studies was established as a college of the Pāli Tipiṭaka (*Balisanzangyuan* 巴利三藏院) in Xi'an in 1945.[13] In all, it is estimated that about 7,500 seminarians completed their education in 35 institutes between 1912 and 1950. Courses on modern history, Western philosophy, foreign languages, and mathematics were included in the curriculum (Welch 1968: 285–87).

Most institutes suffered from the interruptions of wars, the Japanese invasion, and political turmoil over the Republican period. However, the impact of modern Buddhist institutes was revolutionary and influential in the history of Chinese Buddhism. The new monastic education system has created not only a new identity of "student-monk" but also an imagined role for Buddhism in engaging in the new nation-state (Lai 2013: 1–24). The approach to studying Buddhism was a breakthrough in that it was not restricted to one sect or one tradition. Both Theravāda and Tibetan traditions were highly regarded and included in modern Buddhism. In the vision of Taixu, the first stage of Buddhist education is to develop Chinese Buddhism with a new methodology and modernized form. The second stage is to spread Buddhism, targeting all human beings in the world. As Fafang highlighted, modernizing Buddhism was about unifying all Buddhist systems to be powerful in saving the world (Hou 2009: 13–107). The purpose of sending students to Japan, Tibet, and Ceylon was to study in order to gather information for the revival of Chinese Buddhism, rather than replace Chinese Buddhism with other traditions. I argue that Taixu's efforts in establishing institutes for the modern study of Buddhism, including Theravāda and Tibetan traditions, and sending monks to learn about other traditions contributed to the expansion of Buddhism rather than rejection of the Chinese Mahāyāna Buddhist tradition.

Sending Chinese Monks to Learn Theravāda Buddhism in Southeast Asia

Taixu was ambitious in building an international Buddhist network to promote Buddhism in the world. He had started collaboration with Japanese Buddhists, until the Japanese invasion of China in the mid-1930s interrupted this plan. Taixu and his disciples then turned their hopes to working with Southeast Asian Buddhists. Bhikkhu Narada, a Buddhist missionary from Ceylon who had stayed in Shanghai for six months to teach Pāli in 1935, also supported the Chinese monastics' efforts to strengthen monastic education and to reform the *saṅgha*. He suggested, for example, replacing the gray monastic robes with yellow (Ritzinger 2016: 155). Narada even suggested that China reimport the ordination lineage from Ceylon as very few Chinese monks lived according to the Vinaya (Taixu [1936] 2017: Ch. 17). After meetings between Narada and Taixu, a monk exchange scheme was then launched by sending five young Chinese monks to Ceylon for a five-year study in 1936 (Ritzinger 2016). They were Huisong (慧松 date unknown), Fazhou (1918–2017), Xiulu (date unknown), Weihuan (1916–97), and Weishi (惟實 date unknown) (Fafang [1936] 2006). One goal of the scheme for Chinese monks was to learn Pāli texts. This stemmed from an insight from the Orientalists that Pāli *suttas* are the key to understanding the original Buddha's teachings. As Fafang, Taixu's close disciple, pointed out, the four *Āgamas* are the core of original Buddhism and the foundation of both Mahāyāna and Theravāda Buddhism (Huang Xianian 2006, vol. 46: 408–9). Another goal was to revitalize the deficient Chinese Buddhist monastic community after the five monks returned to China.

Although all five monks disrobed and left Ceylon within five years (Welch 1968: 55–63), the shocking experiences of the exchange monks about the teachings and monastic practices in Ceylon had an impact on Buddhist modernization in the following decades (Ritzinger 2016: 157). For example, Weihuan returned to Beijing in 1954 to serve in the Buddhist Association of China (*Zhongguo fojiao xiehui* 中國佛教協會) and translated texts into English and Chinese (Ritzinger 2016: 170; *Fayin* 2017). Fazhou, who studied further in India and worked as Professor of Eastern Religions with the name Wang Pachow at University of Iowa, translated some significant Pāli works into Chinese (e.g., the *Milinda Pañha*). One key impact of the exchange program was the breakdown of the image of Mahāyāna superiority and Hīnayāna (or early Buddhist) inferiority, which had persisted in the Chinese Buddhist imagination for many centuries. As Huisong—one of the exchange monks—argued, the *Āgamas*/*Nikāyas* are foundational to all Buddhism and also the essential source of later teachings such as Mahāyāna Mādhyamaka and Yogācāra. He also argued that only the Pāli language could access the true Dharma, because Pāli was the language of the Buddha (Huisong [1938] 2006). Since the import of Mahāyāna texts like the *Lotus Sūtra* to China, early Buddhist texts were categorized as "Hīnayāna" (*Xiaocheng*). The *Āgamas* as counterparts of the Pāli *Nikāyas* had been ignored by Chinese Buddhists for over a thousand years. With the Orientalist view of valuing early texts as the true word of the Buddha, it rendered a change of the status of the *Āgamas* among Chinese Buddhist texts a few decades later, when Pāli *Nikāyas* were translated into Chinese. The negative label "Hīnayāna" has consequently been gradually replaced by "Original Buddhism" (*Yuanshi fojiao* 原始佛教) or Theravāda Buddhism (*Shangzuobu fojiao* 上座部佛教) over the past fifty years.

Establishing Transnational Networks in Ceylon, Myanmar, and Thailand

Besides establishing modern Buddhist institutes and sending monks to learn Theravāda Buddhism, Taixu actively built transnational networks with Southeast Asian countries.

In 1940, Taixu visited several Southeast and South Asian countries to unite Buddhists worldwide for world peace, including Myanmar, Ceylon, India, and Malaysia (Fafang 2013, vol. 5: 83–98). At the meeting with Dr. Gunapala Piyasena Malalasekera, the president of the All Ceylon Buddhist Congress, Taixu discussed initiating a Sino-Ceylon Culture Society (*Zhongshi Fojiao Wenhua Xuehui* 中錫佛教文化學會), setting up monk exchange programs and establishing a world Buddhist organization based in Ceylon (Fafang 2013, vol. 5: 2–3). Malalasekera received financial support from Taixu for publication (Fafang 2013, vol. 1: 153–61). As Malalasekera recalled, Taixu's previous visit had inspired him to successfully establish the World Fellowship of Buddhists (WFB) (*Shijie Fojiao Lianyihui* 世界佛教聯誼會) in 1950 (Pittman 2001: 143).[14] At the meeting of Dharmapāla and Yang Wenhui in 1893, establishing a world Buddhist organization was on the agenda discussed for promoting global Buddhism. The goal was finally reached in Sri Lanka five decades later (Welch 1968: 64).

Fafang had taken a key role in building transnational networks in Southeast Asia and in promoting the notion of peace by uniting Buddhists in the world. He translated articles written by French and Japanese Buddhists and published them in *Haichaoyin*. He helped Taixu reply to letters from Buddhists from all over the world. With a similar vision to Taixu, Fafang thought Buddhism could engage in a powerful world peace movement (Fafang 2013, vol. 5: 99–117). With financial support from the KMT government (Hao 2015: 213–18), Fafang stayed in India in 1942 and then in Ceylon in 1943. As an expert on the *Abhidharmakośa* (*Jushelun* 俱舍論), he gave lectures on Chinese Mahāyāna Buddhism and Chinese Buddhist literature to students in India and Ceylon. Fafang learnt Pāli, Sanskrit, the Tipiṭaka, and the history of Ceylon at *Vidyalankara Pirivena* (*Zhiyan Xueyuan* 智嚴學院) in order to read scriptures. At the same time, he guided Malalasekera to read Chinese *Āgamas* (*Ahanjing* 阿含經) (Liang 2015: 213–18). He also translated texts from Pāli into Chinese, including the *Mangala sutta* (*Jixiang Jing* 吉祥經).

Through publishing articles in *Haichaoyin*, Fafang introduced the main features of Theravāda Buddhism to Chinese Buddhists (2013, vol. 3: 179–83). He contributed to the establishment of the World Fellowship of Buddhists with Malalasekera and had further plans for a monastic exchange scheme between Ceylon and China. After the end of the Second World War, the two Chinese monks Guangzong (光宗 1916–2018) and Liaocan (了參 1916–85) from Wuchang Buddhist Institute were sent to Ceylon in 1946 (Yinshun 2005: 35–40). After Taixu passed away in the spring of 1947, Fafang went back to China for mourning and gave speeches in Hong Kong and Malaysia. With the invitation of Malalasekera, Fafang went to Ceylon University to teach Chinese Buddhism until he died in 1951. After staying in Ceylon for eleven years, Liaocan finished translating scriptures from Pāli into Chinese: the *Dhammapada* (*Fajujing* 法句經) and *Visuddhimagga* (*Qingjingdaolun* 清淨道論) [The Path of Purification], and *Abhidhammatthasaṅgaha* (*She abidamo yilun* 攝阿毘達磨義論) [A Manual of Abhidhamma] (Yinshun 2005: 156). From my ethnographic study, these translated texts have been salient in the wide spread of Theravāda meditation in Chinese societies since the 1980s. In summary, Taixu intended to reform Chinese Buddhism by including Theravāda Buddhism instead of rejecting Chinese Mahāyāna Buddhism, through establishing modern Buddhist institutes, sending monks to Southeast Asian countries, and translating the Pāli canon. All these have contributed to the conditions of the recent popularity of Theravāda meditation in Chinese societies. Next I will examine how Yinshun (1906–2005) has further made efforts to promote the significance of "original Buddhism."

Promoting "Buddhism for This World" and "Original Buddhism"

Yinshun, one of the brightest students of Taixu, has produced massive serious scholarly works on Chinese Buddhism. His thoughts about "Buddhism for this world," which succeeded from Taixu's legacy, have had great impact on Buddhism in Taiwan and other Chinese societies in the diaspora in the late twentieth century (Pittman 2001: 262–70). Influenced by the exchange monks, including Huisong and Fafang, Yinshun (1993) wrote books about early Buddhism, Indian Buddhism, and the *Āgamas*, the collection of early Buddhist texts. Although he is fond of the thought of Mahāyāna schools, especially the Mādhyamaka, he rejected sectarianism by arguing that "doctrinal differences are only different rivers flowing toward the same ocean of enlightenment" (Pittman 2001: 268).

Yinshun succeeded to Taixu's teachings on promoting "the Dharma common to the five vehicles" (*wucheng gongfa* 五乘共法) (Taixu [1937] 2017: 72–73). Taixu suggested that the beings of the five vehicles—human beings, deva (deities), *sāvaka* (hearer), *pacceka*, and bodhisattva—are all on the same path of enlightenment. In other words, there is no urgent need to abandon the world for the Pure Land. Seeking rebirth as a human being and perfecting human personality in the mundane world can be a foundation for full enlightenment. More importantly, Yinshun reminded Chinese Buddhists that Gautama Buddha was enlightened in the human world and not in the heavens. Thus, Buddhists should put more focus and effort into spiritual practice in the human world rather than in the world after death. This notion of "Buddhism for this world" not only has succeeded Taixu's idea but also moved further by rejecting the worship of gods and ghosts (Hou 2009). This notion has become progressively more influential to the next-generation Buddhist communities during the Buddhist reform movement in Taiwan since the 1980s. The three most successful Taiwanese Buddhist organizations, such as Buddha's Light Mountain (*Fo Guang Shan*), Dharma Drum Mountain (*Fa Gu Shan*), and Tzu Chi, have rigorously promoted "Buddhism for this world" via establishing modern Buddhist academies, hospitals, schools, environmental work, social services, Buddhist weddings, and relief work. Madsen (2007) even argues that these modern Buddhist organizations have contributed to the development of democracy and civil society in Taiwan.

The KMT took over Taiwan as the Republic of China (ROC) and controlled Buddhism through the Buddhist Association of the Republic of China (BAROC) over the Martial Law period, beginning in 1949. After the abolition of Martial Law in 1987, the institution of political democracy, economic growth, civil society, and religious freedom has facilitated not only the rapid change of Buddhist organizations but also the emergence of various new religious sects, such as Theravāda Buddhism and Tibetan Buddhism (Kan 2004).

Recent Flourishing of Theravāda Buddhism and the Āgamas

Theravāda Buddhist meditation started flourishing in the 1980s in Taiwan after Chinese translated books on Theravāda Buddhism were published. For example, *What the Buddha Taught*, which introduces the key ideas of Theravāda Buddhism from Pāli texts by Ceylon scholar monk Walpola Rahula, was first translated into Chinese and published as *Fotuo deqishi* (佛陀的啟示) in 1968 (Chen Chialuen 2012). This book has been reprinted thousands of times and is freely distributed in Taiwan, Hong Kong, and more recently in Mainland China. *The Path of Purification* (*Visuddhimagga*) and *Verses of the Truth* (*Dhammapada*), two important Pāli texts about Theravāda meditation, were translated into Chinese by Liaocan. The two texts were freely distributed in Taiwan in 1987 and 1988, respectively, then later in Hong Kong and Mainland China. In 1987 Yuan Heng Monastery at Kaohsiung, Taiwan, started the project of translating the Japanese translations of Pāli scriptures into Chinese, a project that was completed in 1990. The Chinese texts have been included as a collection of the Chinese Buddhist Electronic Text Association (CBETA) database, the most popular free digital online Chinese Buddhist database.

Vipassanā, or "insight meditation," is a contemporary form of meditation developed from the recent lay meditation movement in Myanmar since the nineteenth century. The model of lay meditation originated from the era of Ledi Sayadaw (1846–1923), a Buddhist scholar and meditation teacher (Braun 2013). The transnational lay meditation movement that started in Myanmar then spread to other Southeast Asian countries, the West, and then Chinese societies. Books of a few world-renowned Theravāda meditation teachers who visited Europe and North America were published in English in Taiwan in the 1980s. Many were then translated from English into Chinese by Taiwanese monastics or lay people since the 1990s. For example, *Our Real Refuge*, collected Dhamma talks by Thai meditation teacher Ajahn Chah, was in 1992 translated into Chinese as the book *Women Zhenzheng Diguisu* [我們真正的歸宿]. The book was reprinted in over 50,000 copies in Taiwan (Ziyan 2009). Until now, there have been over ten charitable or commercial publishers producing books of the teachings of recent significant Theravāda meditation teachers, including Buddhadasa Bhikkhu from Thailand, Mahāsi Sayadaw, U Pandita Sayadaw, and Pa-Auk Sayadaw from Myanmar.

Most Theravāda Buddhist meditation practices were generally introduced first into Taiwan in the 1990s, then into Hong Kong and later Mainland China. For example, Lin Chung-on first invited Thai meditation teacher Luangpor Thong to teach meditation in Taiwan in 1992 and then invited S.N. Goenka in 1995. The Mahasati Association and a permanent Vipassanā Meditation center were set up in 2002 and 1997, respectively, to promote meditation practice (Dharma Light Monthly 2000). The transmission of Goenka's *vipassanā* meditation to Hong Kong and China has been influenced directly by Taiwanese meditators (Lau 2014). In summary, Theravāda meditation has become influential to Chinese Buddhists in Taiwan and Hong Kong since the late 1990s.

Buddhist Revival in Contemporary China with Transnational Support

The development of Buddhism in China since the 1950s was seriously interrupted by a series of political movements, including the Land Reform and the Cultural Revolution. Monasteries of the Han, Theravāda, and Tibetan traditions were seriously damaged or destroyed. All monks were forced to return to their lay life of farming or working in industry. However, since the 1980s, formerly demolished Buddhist monasteries and local temples in China, particularly historical ones, have been reconstructed with the support of local governments and overseas funding. For example, Nanputuo Monastery was restored with support from Southeast Asia and North America (Ashiwa and Wank 2005). Bailin Monastery was reconstructed by Jinghui (淨慧 1933–2013), a disciple of eminent Chan Master Xuyun (虛雲 c. 1864–1959),[15] with overseas funds.

Traditional ritual activities in Han Buddhist monasteries have been revived, such as the regular daily practice of the one-hour morning chanting and one-hour evening chanting at the main shrine hall (Birnbaum 2003). Normally breakfast and lunch at the dining hall are eaten according to the *guotang* (過堂) ritual. Regular Chan retreats were organized at historical Chan monasteries, such as Nanhua Chan Monastery, Yunmen Dajue Chan Monastery in Guangdong, and Gaomin Monastery at Nanjing. Some Chan monasteries have revived traditional practices such as daily chores, menial work, farming, carrying woodblocks, and cooking, emulating the large public monasteries (*shifang conglin* 十方叢林) of ancient times. Buddhist institutes for monastic education have been re-established throughout the country. Fully ordained monks and nuns are given ordination certificates (*jiedie* 戒牒) to identify themselves when they stay at other monasteries.

The Buddhist Association of China (BAC) has been active in rebuilding transnational networks with Buddhist organizations in Asia and the West since the 1980s. Academic exchanges and cultural events with Buddhists all over the world have been organized. For example, five young monks, who had graduated from the Buddhist Academy of China (*Zhongguo foxueyuan* 中國佛學院), were selected to study at the University of Kelaniya in Sri Lanka in 1986. These five monks, namely Bhikṣu Jingyin (淨因), Guangxing (廣興), Xueyu (學愚 1964–), Jianhua (建華 1964–), and Yuanci (圓慈), were the first batch sent to Sri Lanka officially by the Buddhist Association of China (BAC) after the establishment of the People's Republic of China (PRC) (Buddhist Association of China 2003: 255). After completing certificates and Master's degrees in Buddhist Studies, most of them continued to study further in the West and then worked as academics in Buddhist Studies.[16] BAC also sent monks to study in Myanmar, Thailand, South Korea, and Japan. Moreover, BAC has organized four World Buddhist Forums in China, Taiwan, and Hong Kong by inviting Buddhist leaders from Asian and Western countries. The Theravāda and Tibetan traditions have been recognized in both academic exchange and Buddhist sangha.

Chan "Fever," Mind-Body Practices and Theravāda Meditation in Contemporary China

Various kinds of religious and mind-body practices have been reinvented and redeveloped in Mainland China. For example, a modernized form of *qigong* was reinvented as simple gymnastic methods by a group of Communist cadres in Hebei in the 1950s. The *qigong* "fever," which swept post-Mao China in the 1980s, provoked the popularity of body technology for healing, intersecting with ancient culture, religion, and science. Millions of Chinese practiced various kinds of *qigong* to cultivate "*qi*" in public areas, such as parks and squares in cities, every morning (Palmer 2007: 1–5). Martial arts films, such as Shaolin *gongfu* in the 1980s, started the "Chan fever" (*chanxuere* 禪學熱), which aroused popular interest in Buddhist tourism, Buddhist practices, and notions of well-being (Ji 2011: 32–52). Following that was the "psycho-boom" (*xinli re* 心理熱) (Pritzker 2016) and health cultivation (*yangsheng* 養生) culture (Dear 2012), covering bodily exercises, lifestyle, nutrition, and Chinese medicine.

Chan fever attracted people to explore Chan practice, but it has not been easy to revive traditional Chan practice due to a lack of prominent Chan meditation teachers, resulting from the generation gap in monastic lineages. After eminent Chan monks, such as Laiguo (來果 1881–1953) and Xuyun, passed away, the monastic lives of the next generation of disciples, such as Foyuan (佛源 1923–2009) Laiguo, Jinghui, and Delin (德林 1914–2015), were disrupted by political turmoil. Although there was interest in reviving Chan practice, many monks could not understand the traditional Chan practices and rituals, such as *canhuatou* (參話頭).[17] Lay people also found it difficult to understand the classical language of traditional Chan practices. Until now, Chan has been practiced by monks mainly at monasteries in Mainland China, as only males have access to the Chan hall. Most nuns and female laity are not allowed to practice traditional Chan in monasteries.[18]

Jinghui worried that Buddhist rituals or ceremonies, seen as superstitious and old-fashioned, would not attract young people in the twentieth century (2005). To save the Chan lineage, Jinghui, the abbot of Bailin Monastery, started organizing "life Chan summer camp" in 1993, to suit the needs of modern life, targeting the young educated generation. By using Chan wisdom, he promoted "Buddhism for this world" to young people. The camp, which could attract about 200 university students every year, provided lectures by young monks and scholars, discussions on ethical issues, meditation sessions, performances, and candle lighting nights. Similar camps have been organized by monasteries throughout the country.

With the popular atmosphere of learning meditation, various kinds of Theravāda Buddhist meditation started to spread in contemporary China in the late 1990s. The first ten-day *vipassanā* meditation retreat in China was held at Bailin Monastery in 1999. The ten-day retreat followed the teachings of Goenka, a lay meditation teacher with Burmese lineage, who offers one of the most popular *vipassanā* retreats in the world. This retreat was pioneering and inspiring in the Chinese Buddhist communities in China. After that, similar meditation retreats have been organized at different monasteries or secular venues led by invited teachers from Taiwan and Southeast Asia.

Since the regulations were relaxed in the 1980s, some Taiwanese have started industries and businesses in China. Cultural interflow and academic exchange between Taiwan and China have also been developed. For example, the books of Nan Huaijin (南懷瑾 1918–2012), a famous lay teacher who preached traditional Chinese thought and spiritual practices including Confucianism, Daoism and Buddhism, were printed in simplified characters and published in China. Buddhist monastics following the masters of "Buddhism for this world" also started visiting China and sharing their teachings. About the end of the 1980s, some printed copies of Theravāda meditation texts translated by Taiwanese Buddhists were distributed from two Buddhist monasteries in China, Wenshuyuan at Chengdu and Guanghua Monastery at Putian. Later these printed copies were distributed as electronic copies on websites in China (Lau 2018). Some Taiwanese monastics, such as Bhikṣu Konghai (空海 1955–) and Bhikṣu Tifang (體方), started traveling to China to teach early Buddhism, *Āgama*, *satipaṭṭhāna*, and to guide meditation retreats in China. The number of Chinese Buddhists exploring Theravāda Buddhism and meditation has been increasing.

From my ethnographic research, the Chinese who traveled to Southeast Asia to practice meditation included monks, nuns, laymen, and laywomen. Many of them were experienced Buddhists who were interested in Chan but not in esoteric practices and rituals. As Ji argues, the recent popularity of "Chan fever" and Buddhist pilgrimage has aroused a lot of interest in Buddhist revival, but it has also commercialized Buddhism (2011: 50–54). Informants told me that the materialistic orientation of Chinese monasteries and the lack of Chan masters have disappointed some devout Chinese Buddhists. With the party-state relaxing tourist policy, educated Chinese yogis have been attracted to the modernized Theravāda meditation practices, experienced meditation teachers, and the ideal meditation environment available at the international meditation centers in Southeast Asia. My research indicates that the motivation for learning meditation practices abroad is diverse. Some monastics found that Theravāda meditation could complement and enrich their understanding of Dhamma. Chinese nuns and lay women could enjoy their right to meditate in Theravāda tradition. Many lay practitioners practiced Theravāda meditation as a way of relaxation and settling daily life issues. Some psychotherapists and new-age healers learned Theravāda meditation in order to consolidate their professional knowledge and skills (Lau 2017).

As I observe, individualized spiritual experience has become the key motivation for Chinese practitioners who travel again and again to Southeast Asian countries to explore the ideal *Dhamma*. The living conditions at traditional Chinese monasteries, with a big room shared with many people, are not regarded as satisfactory by these young educated urban middle-class Chinese practitioners. My informants, such as Yaozhen and Zhou Fu, said that a single room is an ideal meditation accommodation, and they said they could find their "paradise" in Myanmar but not in China (Lau 2017). Overall, the trend of Chinese practicing Theravāda meditation is similar to those of international yogis. I find that the popularity of Theravāda Buddhist meditation in contemporary China follows a similar path to that found in the West—privatization and self-reflexivity of spiritual experiences.

After returning to China, many Chinese yogis, including monastics and lay people, share their experiences with friends in their meditation communities. In the past decade, these practitioners have "transplanted" the Theravāda meditation experience from Myanmar or Thailand into their community in China and created an imagined sacred space spreading their favorite teachings, through networking, organizing *gongxiudian* (regular practice group), fund raising, and even establishing new meditation centers in Mainland China. The existing Theravāda meditation activities in contemporary China can be categorized into four main models: a) retreats in one tradition held at Chinese Mahāyāna Buddhist monasteries, b) retreats in various traditions held at Han Buddhist monasteries, c) Theravāda Buddhist community, and d) retreats in secular spaces (Lau 2018).

Conclusion

In this chapter, I have examined the underlying historical and social conditions producing the changing notions of "Buddhism" in modern China and the popularity of Theravāda meditation. This has led to a deconstruction and reconstruction of the meaning of religion and Buddhism in contemporary China. Since Buddhism was brought to China in the first century, Mahāyāna Buddhism has been the exclusive tradition. Along with the historical development of Chinese Buddhism, Mahāyāna doctrines and practices have been seen as superior to early Buddhism. The doctrines of early texts, such as the *Āgamas*, and practices of Theravāda Buddhism in Southeast Asia have been marginalized as inferior "Hīnayāna" (*xiaocheng* 小乘) in the Chinese context until recent decades. The encounter of the Chinese Buddhist reformers and the Orientalist Buddhist scholars in the early twentieth century led to the start of revolutionary change concerning the concept and imaginaries of "Buddhism" in China. It has alarmed the Chinese Mahāyāna Buddhists to face questions such as those posed by anthropologist David Gellner: Is Mahāyāna Buddhism authentic? What kind of religion is Buddhism (1990: 100–4)?

With the crises of Buddhism, the leading Buddhist reformers were enthusiastic in modernizing Chinese Buddhism by interacting with the Orientalists. Taixu proposed the notion of "Buddhism for human life" and was ambitious in promoting Buddhism to the modern world by establishing transnational networks. Chinese monastic students were sent to Ceylon to learn and translate Pāli scriptures. The established transnational networks have not only facilitated Chinese translation of some important Pāli texts, such as the *Visuddhimagga*, but also inspired Yinshun, to promote "Buddhism for this world." By re-examining Buddhist scriptures, he has suggested a reconstructed model of Chinese Buddhism—practicing the path of humans and deities as a foundation path for *arahants* and *bodhisattvas*. Through his writings, Yinshun has also discussed the *Āgamas* and appreciated the early Indian Buddhist traditions. But he concedes that Mahāyāna still holds the highest goal. Overall, the effort of Yinshun in reinterpreting early Buddhist texts, the discovery of "original Buddhism," and renewed understanding of Buddhist practices has been a revolutionary influence in contemporary Chinese society. I argue that the reconstruction of modern Buddhism and Buddhist scholarship in the modern Chinese context is a process of "intercultural mimesis," as suggested by Charles Hallisey (1995: 32). Chinese Buddhist reformers, including Taixu and Yinshun, tried to create their own way to reform Chinese Buddhism rather than fully accept the Western constructed "Orient." All these actors have rendered the texts and practices of Theravāda Buddhism accepted in the contemporary Chinese Buddhist context.

Moreover, in the rapidly changing Chinese society, spiritual seekers in urban areas search for the meaning in life by finding spaces of religious practice through privatized religions and spirituality. I argue that the social suffering caused by political movements in the past few decades and the recent social problems brought by the economic boom have created a great demand for healing (Lau 2017). The mind-body healing practices, including *qigong* fever, *yangsheng* culture, psycho-boom, and *vipassanā* from Theravāda tradition, have filled the gap in the demand for healing in contemporary Chinese societies, a gap that has not been met by the medical support system. From the social perspective, Theravāda meditation practices have taken the role of mind-body healing.

With the restriction of the party-state policy, most Theravāda meditation activities are held in Chinese Mahāyāna monasteries. It has encouraged the constitution of hybrid religious forms and modern reinterpretations of Buddhism. In summary, this chapter has explored the changing understanding of Buddhism in Chinese societies with the global forces and transnational networks since the nineteenth century and how it has rendered the rise of the Theravāda meditation communities and a new landscape of Buddhism in China today.[19]

Part Three

Asian Agencies

A corollary to the awareness that global flows have not only been between East and West, but are much more nuanced, sometimes involving exchanges within Asia, is the recognition that the interchange between Buddhism and Modernity has not been passive. Buddhists in Asia were not simply transformed by modernity and by encounters with Western colonial hegemonic power. They grappled with the pressures and ideas that they encountered and then set about responding in unique ways.

This can be seen in all of the examples from the previous part, where Indian intellectuals drew from Western Marxist sources, but also from Buddhism, to formulate modern responses to societal changes, where Chinese reformers looked to the writings of D.T. Suzuki from Japan or looked to sources like Theravāda Buddhism as inspiration for modernizing Chinese Buddhism. They made active choices, strategic decisions about how they wanted to represent Buddhism to the West and how they felt it needed to change at home. Stortini shows that when Nanjō Bunyū studied under Max Müller, he was selective in the ideas that he chose to adopt and how he decided to implement them.

The view of Asians as passive even colors critiques of Orientalism. Deneckere amply demonstrates in this section, that while we show many examples of Asian agency, even in critiquing Orientalism we sometimes presume that all transformations have been somehow in response to Western colonialism. In fact, some of the transformations we attribute to modernity are not rooted in Western ideas at all but are domestic developments inspired by elements that pre-existed within Asian traditions.

Even in the context of North America, Asians are not passive observers in the transformation of Buddhism. Verchery analyzes how Hsuan Hua and his followers are active in reconceiving what "East" and "West" mean, in a way that shapes their identity as both "traditional" and "American." It is important to note that the power imbalance that was part of the colonial experience has changed. The example that Ellsworth explores, of the Taiwan-based Fu Chih organization, shows that Asian Buddhists are, in some ways, now colonizing the West. It is no longer Western ideas reshaping Buddhism but Buddhist ideas reshaping Canada.

8

Shin Buddhism in Chōshū and Early Meiji Notions of Religion-State Relations

Mick Deneckere

Within the study of the modernization of Buddhism, the "Westernization" paradigm assumes that in the modernizing process, Western culture imposes its cultural characteristics on a passive Buddhist tradition. By contrast, this paper focuses on how local conditions triggered the modernization of Buddhism in Japan, well before the opening of the country in the mid-nineteenth century, and on how this process links in with the country's modernization. It will do so by focusing on the evolution of the relationship between True Pure Land or Shin Buddhism and the political authorities in Chōshū, one of the domains that was instrumental in bringing about the Meiji Restoration in 1868 and widely considered as the starting point of Japan's modernity.

Indeed, the mid-nineteenth century was a period of great upheaval for Japan.[1] From the outside, the country experienced pressure from Western powers, who urged Japan to open its borders. While China's fate in the First Opium War (1840–2) had clearly shown that this Western threat should not be taken lightly, the idea of opening the borders was squarely opposed to the 250-year-long Tokugawa policy of keeping the country secluded. When the American Commodore Matthew C. Perry (1794–1858) appeared in the bay of Edo in 1853 with his black ships to force the opening of Japan to Western trade, the weakened state of the Tokugawa military government (*Bakufu* 幕府) soon became apparent: it was no longer capable of defending Japan and keeping Westerners out. The Bakufu's willingness to negotiate with the Americans was seen as a sign of its diminished power and led to a rise in antiforeign sentiment in domains like Chōshū, which were traditionally opposed to the Tokugawa.[2] They gave the slogan *sonnō jōi* (尊王攘夷 "revere the emperor and expel the foreigners")—which originally pointed at the Bakufu's loyalty to the emperor and the proscription of Christianity—its new meaning of overthrowing the Bakufu and replacing it with a government that would truly show its loyalty to the emperor, that is, that was capable of executing the emperor's will of keeping the foreigners out.

As an outer coastal domain, located in the south-west of Japan's main island Honshū, Chōshū experienced the foreign threat first-line and was determined to maintain Japan closed. In 1863, Chōshū forces started to fire without warning on all foreign ships that traversed the Strait of Shimonoseki. Seeking retaliation for the attacks, in 1864 British,

Dutch, French, and US ships joined forces to bombard Shimonoseki, thus destroying Chōshū's ability to wage war on Western powers. Chōshū was also embroiled in wars against Tokugawa forces, wars that eventually led to the domain's rise in national politics. Also in 1864, the Bakufu undertook the First Chōshū Expedition, a punitive campaign against Chōshū for its responsibility in the Kinmon Incident (禁門の変), a rebellion against the Tokugawa Shogunate earlier that year, at the Imperial Palace in Kyoto. Through mediation from Satsuma (薩摩) Domain, the conflict ended without a fight but with the imprisonment of the rebellion's leaders and a nominal victory for the Bakufu. Meanwhile, Chōshū experienced within the domain a power struggle between loyalists, who called for radical change, and conservatives, who preferred espousing allegiance to the Bakufu. In the twelfth month of 1864,[3] representing the loyalist faction, Takasugi Shinsaku (高杉晋作 1839–67), a Chōshū samurai credited with conceiving of the idea of auxiliary militia (*shotai* 諸隊) that recruited both samurai and commoners, started a war against the conservatives. Takasugi's mixed military units proved superior to the conservatives' old-fashioned samurai forces and achieved victory two months later.

Tokugawa forces undertook a second expedition against Chōshū in 1866, in hopes of nipping in the bud Chōshū's rearmament. Having meanwhile concluded a secret alliance with Chōshū, this time Satsuma refused to provide the Bakufu forces with troops. Its military force being better equipped and more efficiently organized than the Tokugawa troops, Chōshū now defeated the Bakufu army and won the conflict. No longer capable of imposing its will on the domains, the fate of the Shogunate was sealed, and in 1867, shōgun Tokugawa Yoshinobu (徳川慶喜 1837–1913) proposed to return power to the Imperial Court. Consequently, Emperor Meiji was restored to the throne on the ninth day of the twelfth month of 1867. However, when Yoshinobu also showed willingness to abdicate as shōgun and to surrender his domains to the Court, this was not to the liking of his retainers, who continued to advocate war. This led to the Boshin (戊辰) War (1868–69) during which the Satsuma and Chōshū armies, who now called themselves the Imperial Troops, decisively brought the Tokugawa forces down in the Battle of Toba-Fushimi (鳥羽・伏見) in the first month of 1868. Thus, it was a combination of such great external and internal forces of history playing out in Japan that led to the momentous historical events entailing the fall of the Tokugawa regime, the restoration of the emperor, and the ensuing modernization of Japan.[4]

This study is to be understood in light of this historical background. It will first introduce the particular relationship that existed between the Mōri (毛利), the clan that ruled Chōshū during the Tokugawa period (1603–1868), and Shin temples and clergy. Next, it will highlight how this relationship enabled Shin clergy to play an active role in the domain's plans to overthrow the Tokugawa regime. In turn, it will focus on how such activities constituted fertile ground for a generation of educated Shin priests from Chōshū who, as a result of their shared domain background, were well connected with the political class that came into power after the Meiji Restoration.

In 1872–3, in the wake of the diplomatic Iwakura Embassy that toured America and Europe to obtain a revision of the unequal treaties that Japan had been forced to conclude with several Western nations from the mid-1850s onward, a delegation of these priests undertook a mission to Europe to observe the religious situation abroad. One of the mission's members was Shimaji Mokurai (島地黙雷 1838–1911), a Shin priest well-known for his notion of separation of state and religion that he famously expressed in a memorial addressed to the Meiji government in 1872. Since he wrote this memorial while in Paris, one might be left with the impression that the origins of his thought are to be found in his experiences in Europe. The separation that Mokurai advocated was, however, of a different nature to, for example, the model of France. Moving away from the "Westernization" paradigm, this study aims to locate the origin of Mokurai's views not in some European example but in the particular relationship between Shin Buddhism and the Chōshū authorities. This will lead to questioning the validity of secularism as a universal marker of modernity, by taking into account not only Mokurai's views but also the issue of Meiji government officials' cooperation with Shin Buddhists in their search for a viable state-religion relationship for a modern Japan, two elements the origins of which can be traced back to the state of affairs in pre-Meiji Chōshū.

Chōshū and Shin Buddhism

In his study *Chōshū in the Meiji Restoration* (1961), Albert Craig discusses the political, social, and economic factors that enabled Chōshū to perform its historical role in the overthrow of the Bakufu. However, there was yet another, lesser-known aspect of Chōshū that was instrumental in preparing the domain for this historical task, namely its religious landscape, in which Shin Buddhism occupied a crucial place: throughout the Tokugawa period, the Shin sect had retained a strong influence among the populace, and Shin priests acted as active political agents.[5]

From the early sixteenth century onward, the daimyō family that had ruled Chōshū were the Mōri. The Mōri were Zen Buddhists, but they were careful in their dealings with Shin followers. Shin Buddhism had spread to the Chōshū area relatively late compared to other regions of Japan, and the Mōri managed to avoid the mistake of other domains to adopt oppressive measures against Shin believers after their participation in the so-called *ikkō ikki* (一向一揆) uprisings, rebellions by "leagues of the single-minded" against daimyō rule. Instead, they embraced a policy of turning Shin Buddhists into allies and coopting them into their own forces, the rationale being that protecting Shin temples, which had an overwhelming majority of the population as their base, was the most effective way of avoiding friction.

As part of their policy, the Mōri encouraged intermarriage between their family and Shin priests and sought to strengthen their ties with the Seikōji (清光寺) and Kōshōji (興正寺) temples in Hagi, the domain capital. Kōshōji had been particularly active in spreading Shin Buddhism in the western provinces, whereas Seikōji had been built by Lord Mōri Terumoto (毛利輝元 1553–1625) at his wife's death and had been made into the administrative temple (*sōroku* 惣録) in charge of liaising between the authorities and the Shin temples of Chōshū. Such rapprochement with Shin temples illustrates how Shin Buddhism represented a power in the domain that could not be ignored.

Although the different Japanese Buddhist sects and schools lost much of their economic and military power under warlords Oda Nobunaga (織田信長 1534–1582), Toyotomi Hideyoshi (豊臣秀吉 1536–1598), and Tokugawa Ieyasu (徳川家康 1542–1616), they regained a prominent position in society as important cogs in the Tokugawa machine. As a way to enforce the ban on Christianity, issued by Ieyasu in 1614, Buddhist temples started to issue "temple guarantees" (*terauke* 寺請), stating that the holder of the certificate and his household were faithful Buddhists. Gradually this procedure became institutionalized, and by the latter half of the seventeenth century, it had evolved into a requirement for every Japanese to register as a parishioner (*danka* 檀家) of a temple. This was a double-edged sword for Japanese Buddhism: Buddhist temples served the state and saw their freedom reduced but also benefited from the system, which required a vast expansion of the Buddhist institution (DuBois 2011: 108–9).

Despite its defeat in *ikkō ikki* uprisings against Nobunaga in 1576, Shin Buddhism survived the transition into the Tokugawa period well, favored by the circumstance that Ieyasu was a devout Pure Land Buddhist and had close relations with True Pure Land Buddhism (Amstutz 1997: 21; DuBois 2011: 109). After Hideyoshi's sword hunt of 1588, which had disarmed commoners and priests and only allowed samurai henceforth to carry swords, Shin Buddhists no longer constituted a military threat. However, the large number of Shin followers in all layers of society, particularly at the grassroots level, functioned independently from any form of centralized control and still constituted a considerable force. Although Shin Buddhism was further disempowered by Ieyasu's decision to divide its main temple Honganji (本願寺) into a West (Nishi 西) and an East (Higashi 東) branch in 1602, its actual strength at the end of the Tokugawa period is exemplified by the fact that, in 1850, the two branches together could claim 25 to 30 percent of the entire Japanese population (Amstutz 1997: 21–23). Whereas the Tokugawa regime's strict control and restrictions on the content of priests' sermons led many Buddhist sects to increasingly alienate themselves from society, Shin priests maintained a proximity to their followers, regularly violating the ban on preaching in laymen's houses. In regions with a strong Shin Buddhist presence such as Chōshū, practices other than "repeating Amida Buddha's name" (*nenbutsu* 念仏) were rejected, hence enabling Shin Buddhism to preserve its characteristic religious style and customs throughout the Tokugawa.

Ieyasu's division of Honganji led to a careful re-examination of the affiliation of all Shin temples in the country. In Chōshū, the Mōri ordered that all Shin temples be henceforth subordinate to either Kōshōji or Seikōji. In turn, since Kōshōji and Seikōji were to become affiliated with Nishi Honganji, by necessity all Shin temples in Chōshū became associated with Nishi Honganji. As *sōroku*, Seikōji was in charge not only of transmitting orders from the domain authorities but also of liaising between temple authorities and affiliated temples. If priests from affiliated temples wished to visit Nishi Honganji in the capital, they needed approval both from Seikōji and Kōshōji. Through their strong ties with these two temples, the Mōri could thus keep track of the business of all Shin temples and their priests in Chōshū.

Three Important Chōshū Figures

Toward the end of the Tokugawa period, the ground for the pursuits of educated priests like Shimaji Mokurai was prepared by important figures of a variety of backgrounds in Chōshū, three of whom will be introduced here. Their activities exemplify how the mutually supportive relationship between Shin Buddhism and the Chōshū authorities had persisted under Tokugawa rule.

Murata Seifū (村田清風 1783–1855) was a high official who initiated the Tenpō economic reforms in his domain in 1838. Initially, Seifū was on his guard against the potentially destructive influence of Shin Buddhism, which confirms the power the sect retained in Chōshū in the nineteenth century. Realizing that Shin Buddhist power could be transformed into an asset, instead of suppressing the group, Seifū followed the Mōri tactics of skillfully channeling its energy: a strong Shin Buddhism could help protect Chōshū against an invasion by Western powers and the Christian teachings they brought with them.

Seifū was a strong advocate of the *sonnō jōi* movement, and it was here that a connection with Shin Buddhism could be found. As for *sonnō*, throughout the Tokugawa period, the house of Mōri, originally of the Kyoto official class, had managed to maintain its long-standing, unique relationship with the Imperial Court (Craig 1961: 24–25). Shin Buddhism also had a close relationship to the Court, dating back to the sixteenth century, when Honganji had enabled the accessions of emperors through financial support. In the Tokugawa period, this tie had been further supported by marriage, as well as by the fact that the highest Honganji leadership had remained aristocratic (Amstutz 1997: 19, 36). Concerning the expulsion of foreigners, as a coastal domain, Chōshū was acutely aware of possible invasions, but it also recognized that Japan needed to learn from Western countries if it was to offer resistance. Therefore, "expelling foreigners" did not mean the rejection of Western practical knowledge or technology but was aimed at keeping at bay the beliefs and notions, often influenced by Christianity, that were simultaneously imported. In Seifū's view, only Shin Buddhism would be able to offer resistance to this type of enemy, given its strong base among the common people and its doctrine that preached endurance and endeavor. In 1854, one year after the Americans had arrived in Japan to force the opening of the country, Seifū sent a letter to the Chōshū Shin priest Gesshō (月性 1817–58), in which he expressed his wish for cooperation between Shin Buddhism and the Chōshū administration.

Gesshō himself was a well-known, charismatic figure. In his sermons, which usually attracted large crowds, he was highly critical of Christianity. For him, the duty of all Buddhist priests consisted in "protecting the state" (*gokoku* 護国) from Christianity by means of the Dharma. Gesshō emphasized that Shin followers should solely rely on Amida Buddha's power to protect themselves from the delusions caused by Christianity. But he also encouraged his audience to fight without sparing their lives if Japan's coasts needed defending, as a way of repaying their debt to the country as a whole. Thus, in Gesshō's discourse, *gohō* (護法 protecting the Dharma) and *gokoku* were inseparable notions. This connection between Buddhism and the state was no novel idea, since the Dharma (*buppō* 仏法) had entered Japan in the sixth century as a teaching that would protect the state (*ōbō* 王法 the Kingly Law). The doctrine of mutual dependence of the two Laws emerged in Japan in the eleventh century, when Buddhist temples started to form a political force as powerful landholders. In this capacity, they sometimes criticized the authority of those in power—be it the emperor, the court, or leading warrior houses—then again cooperated with them in a system of shared rule. In the Tokugawa period, this "mutual dependence" came to an end as Buddhism found itself dominated by the Bakufu (Kuroda [1983] 1996: 271, 284). Gesshō's call for "mutual protection of the Dharma and the state" was no doubt an attempt to reverse the fortunes of Buddhism and return it to a position where it would be, once again, on a par with secular power. In his writings, Gesshō spoke of the importance of mobilizing peasants, an idea also advocated by Murata Seifū.

Documents that are preserved at Myōenji (妙円寺) (a temple where Gesshō served as abbot) show that he had close contacts with many figures active in the *sonnō jōi* movement and the overthrow of the Tokugawa (Kodama 1976: 285–86).[6] After Gesshō's death, many of the peasant brigades that formed in Chōshū were led by his disciples. Through his connections with the domain authorities, Gesshō paved the way for Shimaji Mokurai's generation of priests to play an active part in politics, firstly in their domain and later on the national scene. They were to establish close connections with figures like Takasugi Shinsaku and Kido Takayoshi (木戸孝允 1833–77), whose roles in the Meiji Restoration and the Meiji Government are widely recognized.

A third important figure is Yoshida Shōin (吉田松陰 1830–59), the most famous Chōshū samurai of the *sonnō jōi* movement. Many of the young men who studied at Shōin's school, Shōka Sonjuku (松下村塾), played important roles in bringing about the Meiji Restoration and took up key positions in the Meiji government. Shōin considered Murata Seifū as "the most important figure in Chōshū" at the time and seems to have had similar expectations of Gesshō and Shin Buddhism as Seifū had (Kodama 1976: 281). Although it is unclear whether Shōin himself was a Shin believer, members of his family certainly were, and he was close to a number of prominent Shin priests. Shōin admired Gesshō for the power and impact of his sermons, so much so that when Gesshō was in the neighborhood, Shōin would cancel classes so his disciples could listen to the charismatic priest instead.

It was in the domain's military campaigns that the connection between Seifū, Gesshō, and Shōin became apparent. Shin temples and their priests participated in coastal defense from 1863, when Chōshū attacked foreign ships in Shimonoseki. Soon after, an official priest regiment, the Kongōtai (金剛隊 "the thunderbolt regiment" or "the indestructible regiment"),[7] was organized in Hagi, to give priests proper military training. It consisted of approximately three hundred priests from all over Chōshū and was based at Seikōji. Furthermore, notes by the Shin priest Akutagawa Giten (芥川義天 1847–1915), who had studied under Gesshō, clarify the active role that Shin priests played in winning over popular sentiment for Takasugi Shinsaku's loyalist faction, which eventually succeeded in overthrowing the Tokugawa regime.

The Shin Buddhist participation in the military can partly be understood in the context of growing anti-Buddhist sentiment. While the term *haibutsu kishaku* (廃仏毀釈 "abolish Buddhism and destroy Shakyamuni") mostly refers to anti-Buddhist movements of the early Meiji period, in several domains, including Chōshū, similar campaigns had already emerged before the Restoration. Local anti-Buddhist measures went hand in hand with increased support for "Shinto" elements, a tendency also seen in Chōshū. In such a climate, Shin priests saw their participation in military matters as an opportunity to receive the military training that might prove necessary to fend for themselves: as members of the militia, they were allowed to arm themselves again (Craig 1961: 278; Hackett 1971: 27).

These are the circumstances in which Mokurai grew up and developed his activities as an adult priest. In 1853, at the age of 16, he attended his first annual summer retreat in Hagi. This is around the time that Murata Seifū approached Shin clergy. Yoshida Shōin's school formed the center of intellectual activity in Hagi, and given Shōin's proximity to Shin priests, it is quite possible that Mokurai was exposed to Shōin's ideas.[8] In late 1863, Mokurai preached at the Shinkōji temple (信光寺) on the occasion of the 600th yearly memorial for Shinran (親鸞 1173–1263), the founder of Shin Buddhism. At the time, Shinkōji had become a base for the Shūgitai (集義隊 "the staunch regiment") that had formed to fight the Bakufu. After Chōshū's attempt to restore the emperor to power in the Kinmon Incident of 1864, Mokurai experienced the return of the defeated Chōshū troops and the ensuing punitive expedition against his domain.

While the political and social restructuring of what was to become the modern Japanese nation was at hand, anti-Buddhist sentiment culminated to the point where young Shin priests in Chōshū became convinced that internal sectarian reform was needed if their sect was to survive such turbulent times. Mokurai became actively involved in this reformation that led to the opening of a Reform Bureau in Seikōji. Petitions for reform included the demand that the education of the future clergy be improved and in 1866 resulted in the opening of a school in the same temple, where instruction in the literary arts as well as French-style military training was provided (Honpa Honganji 1927: 93). Mokurai became one of its instructors.

In sum, the history of Shin Buddhism in Chōshū illustrates the need to revisit the narrative that Japanese Buddhism as a whole was weakened by the end of the Tokugawa period.[9] Shin priests' agency and their connections with the domain authorities indicate that, far from being on the decline, Buddhism (and in particular Shin Buddhism) was a vibrant institution in a historically important domain as Chōshū in the mid-nineteenth century. This continued to be the case at the time of the Meiji Restoration and beyond.

Nishi Honganji and the Transition from Tokugawa to Meiji

Under Tokugawa rule, Japanese inhabitants identified themselves as subjects of their domain under their lord, rather than as Japanese nationals, ruled by one shōgun or symbolized by an emperor. As a result, one of the major challenges that Meiji officials faced in the construction of a modern state apparatus was the unification of the people. The young Meiji government, which counted many nativists (*kokugaku* 国学 "scholars of National Learning") and Shinto supporters in its ranks, constructed a Shinto-based ideology around the figure of the emperor to achieve this goal. This ideology was referred to as "the Great Teaching"(*taikyō* 大教), the state doctrine that later came to be known as State Shintō.

That Confucian and nativist scholars had increasingly depicted Buddhist priests as profiteers and Buddhism as a useless social institution throughout the Tokugawa period had among other reasons to do with the perception that Buddhist temples and their priests sought to enrich themselves through the lucrative temple registration and parishioner systems, as well as funeral services (DuBois 2011: 109). By the mid-nineteenth century, the decline of the Tokugawa, whose power was strongly linked to the Buddhist institution, was accompanied by an intensification of anti-Buddhist views. The Meiji government's decision to make use of a newly constructed form of Shinto rather than Buddhism to unify the country can therefore be understood as an expression of its wish to break with the past. On the 28th of the third month of 1868, two weeks after the Emperor had promulgated the Charter Oath (*Gokajō no goseimon* 五箇条の御誓文), the government issued the first of a series of orders to clarify the relationship between Buddhism and Shinto and to end the centuries-long practice of amalgamating Buddhist and Shinto deities. Although it was not the government's intention for these orders to be carried out with violence, those in power passively watched as anti-Buddhist groups interpreted them as imperial consent to attack and persecute Buddhism. This led to a short but violent *haibutsu kishaku* movement in the early years of Meiji (Ketelaar 1990: 65), this time aimed at the whole of Japan.

Shin Buddhism survived the tribulations of early Meiji anti-Buddhist policies fairly well and recovered relatively quickly in comparison to some other Buddhist sects. Several factors played a role in this quick recovery. First, the independent character of the religious life of Shin followers and temples resulted in tenacious actions and resistance against persecution (Yasumaru [1979] 2003: 196–99). Next, Nishi Honganji did not suffer from separation and land confiscation edicts the way other Buddhist sects did, because of the absence of linkage with shrines and of its relatively little landed wealth (Breen 2000: 243). Indeed, the emphasis in Shin Buddhism on faith and reliance on Amida Buddha alone made some followers disparage *kami* worship, a stance that had discouraged the amalgamation of Buddhist and *kami* in this particular sect. In the case of Nishi Honganji, one more reason should be taken into consideration. The pre-Meiji Shin Buddhist reform movement in Chōshū and Chōshū priests' zeal to reform their head temple (*honzan* 本山) Nishi Honganji in Kyoto had enabled Shin Buddhism to start modernizing in parallel with Japan's political and social modernization process and thus to adapt itself well to the changes brought about by the Meiji Restoration (Kodama 1994: 207–11).

Furthermore, the role that Nishi Honganji played in bringing about the Meiji Restoration explains, at least partially, why the early Meiji *haibutsu kishaku* movement was as short-lived as it was. In the early 1860s, whereas Higashi Honganji chose to further deepen its ties with the Tokugawa, Nishi Honganji strengthened its adherence to the Imperial Court (Naramoto 1987: 96–7). Nishi Honganji's position should come as no surprise given that all Shin temples in Chōshū, a domain with strong pro-emperor sentiment, were affiliated with it. In 1863, Nishi Honganji abbot Kōnyo (広如 1798–1871) distributed a letter based on Gesshō's writings, which explained how priests should behave in this time of national crisis: "When thinking about our debt to the country, this is not a time when we should simply be watching from the sidelines. Our temples have the duty to exert themselves in serving the emperor and the country" (Naramoto 1987: 98). He also opened a dojo inside Nishi Honganji to provide the temple's retainers and priests with military training.[10] Moreover, he dispatched people to explain to branch temples the purpose of *sonnō jōi*. As a confirmation of his loyalty to the emperor, Kōnyo offered the Imperial Court 10,000 gold ryō, despite his temple's own dire financial situation (Ōtani 1973: 165; Honpa Honganji 1927: 30). The Court on its side showed its appreciation for such support by bestowing honorary titles upon its abbots (Naramoto 1987: 98–99).

By 1863, the *sonnō jōi* movement had gained momentum, and supporters from different parts of the country gathered in Kyoto, the imperial capital. In these circumstances, Chōshū samurai clashed with samurai from Aizu (会津) Domain, whose lord was in charge of keeping the peace in the capital on behalf of the Bakufu. This Aizu resistance further enflamed the Chōshū men's *sonnō jōi* convictions, and extremists did not hesitate to kill those who expressed opposition, calling their acts "Heavenly punishment" (Naramoto 1987: 98–101). In 1864, Chōshū's clash with the *kōbu gattai* (公武合体) faction (composed of members of both the Imperial Court and the Shogunate), formed by Satsuma and Aizu, resulted in the Kinmon Incident, which forced Chōshū men to flee Kyoto. Nishi Honganji and its branch temple Kōshōji—which had meanwhile been relocated from Chōshū—sheltered Chōshū fugitives (Shirasu 2002: 46; Naramoto 1987: 124–28).

After the rebellion, the *sonnō jōi* extremists disappeared from the capital, but peace did not return, since Chōshū's "Heavenly punishment" faction made way for the violent actions of militias that supported the Tokugawa shōgun. When the involvement of Nishi Honganji and Kōshōji in the Kinmon Incident came to light, Hitotsubashi Yoshinobu (一橋慶喜 1837–1913), the commander of the imperial palace's defense, searched both temples. The military post of one of these new militias was moved inside Nishi Honganji temple grounds to increase the pressure (Shirasu 2002: 46). If Chōshū was held responsible for the Incident, it was not least because of its share in causing the inferno that ravaged important parts of the capital after Chōshū samurai had deliberately set the Chōshū residence in Kyoto on fire (Naramoto 1987: 102, 124–28).

Notwithstanding the Bakufu's ensuing punitive expedition against Chōshū, the domain did not respond to any of the Bakufu's demands. In the second expedition that was organized as a result, Chōshū managed to defeat the Bakufu forces, owing to its secret alliance with Satsuma. After shōgun Yoshinobu proposed to return power to the emperor, the newly installed Meiji government usurped Yoshinobu's post of Inner Minister at the Court and pressed the Bakufu to return its lands to the emperor, so as to not only strip it of its political authority but also undermine its economic base. Rejecting this arrangement, the Bakufu brought together an army to fight the new government's army at Toba-Fushimi. On the day of the battle, an important meeting took place at the Hiunkaku (飛雲閣) pavilion of Nishi Honganji, during which soon-to-become Meiji statesmen Saionji Kinmochi (西園寺公望 1849–1940) and Iwakura Tomomi (岩倉具視 1825–1883) discussed the government's order to dispatch an army. When the roar of artillery could be heard in Nishi Honganji, the temple sent the abbot's successor Tokunyo (徳如 1827–68) with one hundred men to the palace, where he was ordered to protect the Sarugatsuji (猿が辻) Gate. When Emperor Meiji went to Osaka later that year, abbot Kōnyo was put in charge of guarding the Nishi Honganji branch temple Tsumura Betsuin (津村別院) in Osaka that served as the emperor's temporary palace.

These circumstances indicate that in the critical events surrounding the Meiji Restoration, Nishi Honganji was never far away from the center of action, thereby bringing to fruition the vision to protect the state by means of the Dharma. The entire Nishi Honganji organizational structure served to promote support for the new government among the people, and the temple mobilized more than 37,000 men to serve in the new government army, until the surrender of Edo Castle (and of the Bakufu) in the fourth month of 1868. Moreover, the Meiji government's finances extensively relied on contributions from Nishi Honganji (Shirasu 2002: 47–49; Ketelaar 1990: 73). Given its allegiance to the emperor and the government, the "clarification edicts" issued with the purpose of promoting "Shinto" elements and discarding Buddhism must have come as an unpleasant surprise: governmental policies attacked the very institution that played a vital role for the success and acceptance of the new state structure. Such a situation was untenable in the long run.

Back in Chōshū, in the spring of 1868, Mokurai discussed with like-minded colleagues the reform of the *honzan* in Kyoto, following the reforms they had carried out in their domain. It seemed to them that the uncertainty and upheaval caused by the events of the late 1860s created the ideal climate for proposing a reorganization of temple structures and customs. After arriving in Kyoto, Mokurai submitted in the seventh month of 1868 a *Proposal for Reform of the Honzan* (*Kengen: honzan kaikaku* 建言・本山改革 [Futaba and Fukushima 1973, vol. I: 97–98]), written by him and signed by five Chōshū priests (Futaba and Fukushima 1973, Suppl.: 14–15).

The proposal's main purpose was the abolition of the traditional system that appointed retainers who held actual power at the *honzan*, while the priesthood remained excluded from organizational matters (Shirasu 2002: 50). It also asked for a transparent accounting system based on proper budgeting and requested that the management of the *honzan* be entrusted to capable priests from branch temples. Furthermore, it advocated a revival of Shin teachings within and a loyal attitude in serving the emperor and the state without (Futaba and Fukushima 1973, vol. I: 98). These improvements, which were to take place simultaneously, clearly reflected Gesshō's *buppō gokokuron*, while also showing signs of an evolution in meaning toward "the mutual protection of the Dharma and the state" (*gohō gokoku* 護法護国). In the midst of the turmoil surrounding the Restoration, the abbot accepted the proposal. This meant that lower ranked priests from branch temples had been successful in carrying out the reform of the *honzan*, something previously unthinkable. The reforms caused the majority of Nishi Honganji's four hundred retainers to leave and made the abbot the true head of the temple.

Having gained the abbot's trust, Mokurai would, in the following years, continue to write, on behalf of his temple, petitions and memorials to the Meiji government requesting changes in its religious policies. Against the backdrop of an increasingly uncertain future for Buddhism in Japan, caused by the construction of and support for a Shinto-based ideology and the *haibutsu kishaku* movement, not to mention the arrival of Christians in Japan after the opening of Japan's borders, Mokurai would growingly emphasize the importance of the mutual support of the Dharma and the state to ensure a bright future for the Japan that was under construction. This notion came particularly to expression while he was in Paris as a member of the Nishi Honganji Mission to Europe.

The First Japanese Buddhist Mission to Europe

In the fall of 1871, Kido Takayoshi, former pupil of Yoshida Shōin in Chōshū, sent a letter to Myōnyo (明如 1850–1903), the new abbot of Nishi Honganji, inviting him and a number of government officials and noblemen on a trip abroad. This trip is now known as the diplomatic Iwakura Embassy, in which Kido served as a vice-ambassador. In his letter, Kido explained that Mokurai had shared with him the view that it would be beneficial for the future of Buddhism if the abbot saw the situation abroad with his own eyes (Yoshida 1959: 103–4).

Why did a government official ask a Buddhist abbot, upon the recommendation of a Buddhist priest, to join the Iwakura Embassy in the midst of governmental efforts to develop a state ideology based on "Shinto" elements to the detriment of Buddhism? A first reason can be found in the domestic and foreign pressures that Japan was facing in the field of "religion." Doubts were arising as to whether *kami* worship had what it took to function as the doctrine that could keep the newly founded Japanese nation together. Moreover, now that Japan's borders were opened to international trade, the removal of any ban on Christianity would be an important condition for a revision of the unequal treaties. Since priests like Mokurai were well acquainted with Christian thought, Kido may have preferred asking "specialists in the field," rather than entrusting the observation of the religious situation abroad to insufficiently informed officials or Shinto priests.

Secondly, there was the personal factor that Kido was a Shin Buddhist himself.[11] As such, despite the inclination of important pressure groups within the Meiji government toward a Shinto-based ideology, Kido may have considered Shin Buddhism the better choice to support the regime. In his home domain of Chōshū, Shin Buddhism had successfully coexisted in a form of mutual dependence with the authorities for many centuries, and this provided a prototype of a viable religion-state relationship for a modernizing Japan. This assumption is confirmed by the fact that, while in Europe, Kido was quickly convinced by Mokurai's argument that a modern Japan needed (Shin) Buddhism and not Shinto. Mokurai was convinced that, in Japan, only Shin Buddhism was close to the idea of the Western concept of religion. A civilized religion had to be monotheistic and, fortunately for Japan, it had Shin Buddhism, which honored Amida alone, thereby being on an equal footing with monotheistic Christianity, the civilized religion of the West. In Mokurai's opinion, no other Japanese religious practice, Buddhist or otherwise, deserved consideration for the position of "religion of Japan." Shinto, with its worship of myriads of *kami*, was a clear example of a primitive religion and thus not fit for a modernizing Japan (Yasumaru [1979] 2003: 200–1). Moreover, since *kami* worship had no foundation such as a founder or a scripture, it would always remain inferior to Christianity, thus opening the floodgates for the spread of the Western religion in Japan (Futaba and Fukushima 1973, vol. I: 17).

Mokurai's travel diaries reveal that, while in London (August 18–September 3, 1872), he visited Kido Takayoshi on four, possibly five, occasions, at one of which he "ended up sleeping at Kido's place," a diary note indeed suggesting a friendly relationship between the two men. Furthermore, Mokurai met Aoki Shūzō (青木周蔵 1844–1914) on at least two occasions. Sponsored by Kido Takayoshi, Aoki, also from

Chōshū, had traveled to Berlin in 1868 to study medicine but had ended up becoming first secretary at the Berlin consulate. If Aoki was in London in August 1872, it was to welcome his benefactor (Breen 1998: 157).

In his autobiography, Aoki speaks of a meeting "late August," in which all Chōshū men resident in London were present (Breen 1998: 157). Meanwhile, for August 31 we find in Mokurai's diary: "I visited Kido in the evening." Since Mokurai mentions neither Aoki nor Itō Hirobumi (伊藤博文 1841–1909)—another vice-ambassador to the Iwakura Embassy who was also present at the meeting that Aoki speaks of—it remains somewhat unclear whether Mokurai indeed participated in this particular meeting. Nevertheless, there are similarities between Aoki's position in the meeting and the opinions expressed in a report entitled *Observations on Politics and Religion in Europe* (*ōshū seikyō kenbun* 欧州政教見聞, hereafter *Observations* [Futaba and Fukushima 1973, vol. I: 198–204]) that Mokurai produced around the time and discussed with Kido before submitting it to Ambassador Iwakura (Breen 1998: 158).

What then was said or written on "religion"? The discussion between Kido, Itō, and Aoki seems to have started off with Kido's question of "why Westerners were so passionate about religion." To this, Aoki replied that "it was to do with the fact that Christianity was the source of European civilization and enlightenment." However, this did not mean that Japan was to convert to Christianity but that all people needed religion to remain disciplined and that the government needed religion to keep its people in order. In response to Kido's remark that certain members of the Embassy thought the emperor and the government should convert to Christianity if Japan was to be regarded as an equal by Western powers, Aoki replied that it would be a folly "to replace a people's religion with another" and that the strategic conversion of all the Japanese to Christianity would cause civil war (Breen 1998: 158).

In *Observations*, Mokurai started his analysis with a similar idea to Aoki's, namely that "a modern state is sustained by religion." To this fundamental idea, he added that "although politics and religion must occupy distinct realms, [they were to play] mutually supportive roles." Mokurai's second point was that if Japan needed a religion, it was to be Shin Buddhism. This was implicitly in accordance with Aoki's idea that it would be madness to replace a people's religion with another. As the largest Japanese Buddhist sect, Shin Buddhism was certainly a good candidate to take on this role. However, Mokurai took it a step further by arguing that "Christianity, in both its Catholic and Protestant forms, [was] extremely dangerous and should be banned."[12] This was totally in line with Kido's vision when, in 1868, he had told a British diplomat in Nagasaki that "he would do all in his power to thwart the progress of Christianity." The Constitution that Kido ordered Aoki to draft and that was finalized by the end of 1872 with amendments by Kido himself also reflects the ideas proposed by Aoki and Mokurai. Article 12 banned Christianity and all creeds other than Buddhism, and Article 13 established Buddhism as Japan's state creed (Breen 1998: 158–59). When Aoki's idea that there was no need for the entire nation to convert to Christianity, combined with his own view that Christianity should be banned and (Shin) Buddhism was to serve as Japan's main religion, came into expression in a draft Constitution, Mokurai must have felt as if he had reached an important milestone in securing the future of Buddhism in Japan.[13]

When asking Aoki about Westerners' involvement with religion, Kido would have added that he only knew Buddhism "and little more than that it encouraged good and chastised bad" (Breen 1998: 157). Be that as it may, as a Chōshū man he knew that religion was useful for governance and that Buddhism had proven for many centuries that it could fulfill the role of uniting and mobilizing the people for the cause of the domain, thus distinguishing between Buddhism as faith and the social or political role that Buddhism could play. This insight may have influenced the ideas expressed in the draft Constitution of 1872. Unlike the view that "it was in London that Kido became convinced of the real importance of religion to the modern state and, more specifically, of Honganji Buddhism to the modern Japanese state" (Breen 1998: 162), I would therefore suggest that it was Kido's Chōshū background and earlier convictions that had led to the discussions with Mokurai and Aoki in the first place.

It was in the winter of the same year that Mokurai famously wrote that "state and religion are different and should never be confused" in his memorial *A Critique of the Three Doctrinal Standards* (*Sanjō kyōsoku hihan kenpakusho* 三条教則批判建白書) addressed to the Meiji government in criticism of its religious policies.[14] A thorough separation of these two spheres is reminiscent of the situation in France, where Mokurai spent most of his time in Europe. His observations there no doubt inspired him to give expression to this notion. However, further down the memorial, Mokurai suggests that this separation is not absolute in nature:

> Religion improves the people, while the state causes them to thrive. If they maintain flexibility and are applied in a balanced manner, then we get what they call "state and religion as interdependent, the outer show and the inner material in equilibrium." (Futaba and Fukushima 1973, vol. I: 16)

While reflecting the traditional doctrine of the mutual dependence of the Buddhist and the Kingly Laws, this view that, while existing autonomously, the cooperation and interdependence of the two spheres would eventually lead to the fulfillment of their respective essence, is also to be understood as an extrapolation of the situation in Chōshū where Shin Buddhism and the authorities had long coexisted in a structure of mutual support. In order to appreciate this layer of meaning, there is a need to look beyond Mokurai's impressions of Europe and to take into account the Shin Buddhist vision "to reconnect the Imperial Law and the Dharma," which had been burgeoning for more than two centuries in Chōshū. This nuance is important because it highlights Buddhist agency. That is to say, the idea that early Meiji Buddhist intellectuals were driven by an ideological framework of their own stands in sharp contrast with the view that it was the confrontation with the Western concept of religion that led Buddhists to structure Buddhism into a modern religion.[15]

Linked to the newly emerging theories of evolution, in the nineteenth century, "modernizing" came to be seen as an inevitable stage in a state's progression toward civilization. In light of the beneficial effects of the Industrial Revolution and Western nations' imperialistic projects, "the modern" became a notion used to compare not only the Western present with the Western past but also, and more importantly, the Western present with the current state of non-Western countries' progress toward civilization. The attributes of "the modern" in the West, which cover "a wide range of historical phenomena including science, technology, industry, secular government [and] bureaucracy," came to be seen as universal norms of modernity (Morris and Sakai 2009: 219–22). Even within Europe, for example, in Britain where the monarch was (and remains) head of the Church of England, it may be clear that secular government in the sense of a well-defined separation between matters of religion and matters of state was (and is) the exception rather than the norm. Although the modernization of Japan involved the adoption—sometimes even the copying—of many Western attributes of "the modern," in this chapter I have shown that the development of a modern notion of the religion-state relationship was certainly no matter of merely replicating a Western example. In the case of Japan, reflections on the relationship between state and religion originated in the religious sphere and were solicited by the state from within that sphere, as Japan was reinventing itself as a modern nation. The modernization of Buddhism in Japan and, as part of it, the history of Japan's modern religion-state relations thus invite us to contemplate on the questions of what "modernity" and "modernization" stand for and whether so-called norms of modernity, all products of Western modernization processes, can indeed be deemed universal.

9

Nanjō Bunyū's Sanskritization of Buddhist Studies in Modern Japan

Paride Stortini

In his autobiographical *Record of Reminiscences* (*Kaikyūroku*), Nanjō Bunyū (南条文雄 1849–1927), a scholar-priest of the Higashi Honganji sect of Japanese Buddhism, recalls a particular moment of his period of study at Oxford. In the last days of December 1879, he received from his German mentor, Friedrich Max Müller, the Sanskrit version of the *Infinite Life Sutra* (*Sukhāvatīvyūha Sūtra*). Nanjō, at that time a young Buddhist priest, had started to study Indology at the prestigious university only a few months earlier, and he could not contain his excitement at the idea of finally reading in the supposedly original language one of the foundational sutras of Pure Land Buddhism, to which his own sect belonged (Nanjio 1979: 127–28).[1]

It is while reading this sutra that Nanjō first encountered significant and confounding discrepancies between the Sanskrit texts, which Müller had taught him to consider as the original sources of Buddhism, and the Chinese translations in use in Japan. He discovered that whereas the Chinese version of the *Infinite Life Sutra* contained forty-eight vows of Amida, the Sanskrit had only forty-six and that the difference concerned exactly the central and most important vows, from the eighteenth to the twenty-first. Upon such a discovery, he spent the following several days painstakingly working on the sutra.

The mastering of modern philological approaches and Sanskrit played an essential role in Nanjō Bunyū's scholarship, and today he is remembered as one of the pioneers of Buddhist Studies in modern Japan. This chapter focuses on Nanjō's reception and reconception of nineteenth-century Western philology, with particular reference to the ideas of his mentor Max Müller about language and religion. It distances itself from explaining the Indological turn in modern Japanese Buddhist scholarship as the result of a unidirectional importation of scientific knowledge from the West favored by mediators such as Nanjō. My aim is to complicate such views, by stressing the agency and active role the Japanese scholar-priest had in rearticulating the relation between Japanese Buddhism and Western scholarship on religion. After a brief introduction to Nanjō's mission and achievements in Europe, I will focus on the central role that the rediscovery of Sanskrit and of the Indian roots of Japanese Buddhism had in responding to the Western orientalist biases against East Asian Buddhist traditions.

Lost in Translation: Nanjō Bunyū's Mission at Oxford

Nanjō Bunyū was born in 1849 in the village of Ōgaki in central Honshū.[2] He was the third son of the abbot of the Seiunji temple, a local branch of the Higashi Honganji sect of Jōdo Shinshū Buddhism. He received a traditional education focused on the knowledge of the Chinese Classics. His skills in classical Chinese paved the way for his career within his sect, after he was adopted in the more influential family of the abbot of Okunenji temple in Echizen (today Fukui prefecture).

In his youth, he experienced the turbulences of the Meiji Restoration (1868) and was particularly affected by the early Meiji religious policy of Buddhist-Shinto separation (*shinbutsu bunri* 神仏分離) and of the subsequent wave of anti-Buddhist violence (*haibutsu kishaku* 廃仏毀釈). The determinant event in his life, though, was when he was chosen by the future head of his sect, Ōtani Kōei (1852–1923), to travel to Europe to study Sanskrit. This mission was part of the response of the sect to the threats of Western culture and Christian proselytism to traditional Buddhist institutions in Japan.

During his previous journey to Europe in 1872, Ōtani had realized the advanced knowledge that European scholars of Buddhism had of South Asian traditions, and he had found Sanskrit texts with no apparent correspondence with Chinese translations known to Japanese Buddhists. This is why he decided to send two young Jōdo Shinshū priests, Nanjō Bunyū and his colleague Kasahara Kenju (1852–1883), to study Sanskrit and collect texts in Europe (Kashiwahara 1995: 190). The two arrived in London in 1876 and after a few years spent in the capital to study English, Nanjō and Kasahara were accepted at Oxford University to study under the academic celebrity Friedrich Max Müller.

It was as early as his first few months at Oxford that Nanjō realized the discrepancies between the Chinese and the Sanskrit texts. How did Nanjō react to such a discovery that challenged the way in which his Buddhist faith had been built? The answer Nanjō gave himself can be found in a poem he composed precisely while working on the Pure Land sutras:

> I feel the need to learn the origins of the ancient teaching
> There is a profusion of so many sutras transmitted
> Even though texts are sufficient evidence
> There are mistakes in the translations that have been transmitted
> China has no more places with translations
> Japan is of no different profit
> We only follow what we have
> Why is Japan inactive in the monsoon retreat?
> I should have died at sea
> Aimlessly as a wandering monk
> I came here, a foreign land thousands of miles far from my country
> I accomplished the copy of texts that are thousand year old
> The translation has lost the original meaning
> The original texts are worthless too

Idleness, when will I achieve you?
A thirty-year-old man, I will dedicate my time to this work.³

Philology was his answer, and Max Müller was Nanjō's fellow traveler on this journey to the original meaning.

The Role of Language in Max Müller and Nanjō Bunyū

In a miscellanea of lectures and essays published in 1914 with the title *On Uplifting* (*Kōjōron* 向上論), Nanjō reveals his awareness of the historical process in which he became involved by becoming disciple of Müller (Nanjō 1914: 526–49). He traces a long history of the contact between India and the West, whose turning point was the discovery of the common origins of Sanskrit and European languages.

The combination of Enlightenment scientific approaches to language with the romantic quest for the beginning of nations produced what Raymond Schwab defined as the "Oriental Renaissance": the effort to collect and translate Sanskrit texts accompanied by a reimagination of an Indo-European mythical golden age (Schwab 1950). Max Müller's approach to religion as based on the science of language is the legacy of such a process.

He argued for a scientific basis to the study of language, in an era dominated by natural sciences as the model for the production of reliable knowledge.⁴ In the same way that fossils were useful to the geologist to give a chronology to Earth strata, Müller claimed that the analysis of words would lead back to their original meaning, perfectly expressed in their roots, and in this way to understand the origins of religion expressed in the most ancient texts of every civilization. In his quest for the original meaning, he chose Sanskrit not only because it was the language of the oldest written religious documents, the Vedas, but also because it was so close to ancient Greek and Latin and because it was believed to have been preserved in a state of formal perfection, due to a long tradition of grammatical analysis (Müller 1892: 22–30).

It is within the context of Max Müller's theory of the science of language and his search for Sanskrit manuscripts that his initial relation with Nanjō Bunyū and Kasahara Kenju must be understood. The arrival of the two young Japanese priests at Oxford in 1879 represented for the German scholar an opportunity to build a bridge to their homeland and explore monastic libraries in search for Sanskrit manuscripts lost in India or China.

Despite Nanjō's pride for his country's contribution to Buddhist Studies by sending Sanskrit texts found in Japanese monasteries to Oxford, it must be stressed that the knowledge of Japanese Buddhism was not Müller's aim: at this stage, Japan was only a means to get to Sanskrit manuscripts. The Pure Land to which his two Japanese disciples belonged represented for Müller one of the many forms in which the original teaching of Buddhism was corrupted in its spread across East Asia.

The problem with East Asian Buddhist traditions according to Müller did not simply lie in the degeneration of the original message due to popular needs and devotional attitudes but also in the linguistic transmission of the founder's teaching itself. Sanskrit and Chinese being understood as deeply different languages, the translation of the original texts was inevitably compromised. Nanjō acknowledged the fact that Japan had only but a few scattered Sanskrit texts, and this meant that the entire Buddhist tradition in the country was based on Chinese translations of the originals. This is why the acquisition of Sanskrit became for him a means not only to get to the roots of the Buddhist teaching but also to understand its development in its spread to East Asia.

English, having the inflectional grammar in common with Sanskrit, came to play an essential mediating role between the modern Japanese reader and the ancient Sanskrit text, revealing the mistakes made by the early Chinese interpreters. In the series of lectures referred to in this chapter, Nanjō gives an example of how knowing English had been helpful for him in making sense of inconsistencies between Sanskrit original and Chinese translation (Nanjio 1914: 536–37). Both in English and in Sanskrit, the words for the numbers "13" and "30" begin with the root that indicates the number three (thirteen–*trayodaśa*; thirty–*triṃśat*), whereas in Chinese as well as in Japanese, the ideographic kanji system inverts the place for the units and the tens to distinguish thirteen from thirty (十三 for thirteen and 三十 for thirty). The difference explains why in translating Sanskrit sources sometimes the Chinese interpreters misunderstood a thirteen for thirty and vice versa.

The study of Sanskrit through the medium of European scholarship was a necessary premise in Nanjō's attempt to rethink his approach to Buddhism. This would not have been possible using only the Chinese canonical tradition and its language. If we analyze the development of Indology and Sanskrit study as a major turning point in the birth of modern Buddhist Studies in Japan as an example of transfer of scientific knowledge, the role played by language is essential. As noted by the German historian Jürgen Osterhammel, modern science as the authoritative form of knowledge production in the nineteenth century necessarily relied on a system of symbols that made it transmittable, and this made language an indispensable means for the mobility of scientific knowledge (2014: 779–81). Such a process of knowledge transfer between cultures happened in a context of unequal power relations, which forced scholars of colonized countries to learn European languages and favored the one-way transmission of scientific knowledge from the West to the colonized world (Osterhammel 2014: 784–812). Nanjō's travel to learn Sanskrit at Oxford can be interpreted under this model, as a result of colonial aggression toward Japan and as part of a broader reaction by which Meiji political, religious, and cultural elite began learning Western languages in order to appropriate modern scientific knowledge and to redeploy it for the modernization of the country.

The exportation of the modern Western approach to the study of Buddhism could have supplanted local forms of knowledge, such as the Japanese traditional study of Buddhism. Western colonizers claimed that the inherent superiority of their modern scientific production of knowledge was the reason why it was rapidly adopted in other cultures, becoming the universal model against local and particular forms. A global and multiperspectival approach to history, as Osterhammel argues, entails a reconsideration of such a claim: systems of knowledge are always local, and their success in being adopted in other contexts depends on asymmetric power relations, as well as on specific local reasons, such as the practical utility of adopting a foreign system of knowledge. The sociologist of science David Turnbull also explains what is the source of such power: "the source of the power of science lies not in the nature of scientific knowledge but in its greater ability to move and apply the knowledge it produces beyond the site of its production" (Turnbull 2000: 38). Mobility is a key feature that makes a particular system of knowledge universal, and it is reached through technical and social strategies that allow that specific science to connect other local systems and make them commensurate (Turnbull 2000: 19–32).

There was certainly an element of power asymmetry in the decision to send Nanjō Bunyū to study Sanskrit at Oxford, as the British Empire was a major colonizing force in Asia in the nineteenth century and Japan was struggling to get international recognition and to end the unequal treaties with Western countries. What role did Max Müller's Indology, based on the science of language, play in this process? I argue that the role played by Sanskrit was that of the connective language, and as such, it assured the role of universal for the Western approach to Buddhism. Sanskrit and Pāli were the languages in which the ancient Indian sutras were written, and within the discourse of the search for the origins that informed nineteenth-century philology, that gave them a prominent role.

Nanjō's efforts were aimed at linking the particularity of Japanese Buddhism to the universal model of Buddhism, which was defined in Western Buddhist Studies as essentially written in Sanskrit.[5] Since the early-nineteenth-century development of modern Buddhist Studies, Sanskrit had a central role in the formation of the concept of Buddhism as a world religion.[6] This is the reason why it became the universal language in which to translate the particular varieties of Japanese Buddhism. This process is symbolically represented by the change in terminology in Meiji period Buddhist Studies: from the traditional definition of Sanskrit as *bongo* (梵語), especially used in Japanese esoteric sects, to the neologism coined using the transliteration from English *sansukurittogo* (サンスクリット語).

The mediating role of Western Buddhist Studies, as well as Müller's approach to Sanskrit, undeniably shaped the Indological turn in the development of modern Buddhist Studies in Japan, and Nanjō was integral to this process. But the eastward transfer of knowledge did not imply, in Osterhammel's terms, a total suppression of local knowledge. Sanskrit and the sutras written in this language did not replace the Chinese canonical tradition or *kanbun* (classical Chinese) as the dominant language for Buddhism in Japan. If learning English was central for Nanjō in mastering Sanskrit grammar, at the same time his knowledge of the Chinese canon and of the language used in it played an essential role in the appropriation of Max Müller's Indology and provided Nanjō with an active role in the master-disciple relation. Nanjō Bunyū did not simply import Indology from England and apply it to the study of Japanese Buddhism. He also used his "indigenous knowledge"—classical Chinese and the Chinese canon— to correct and supplement those same Sanskrit sutras that constituted the basis of the modern and universal Buddhist Studies developed in Europe.

Very soon, Nanjō and Kasahara's knowledge of classical Chinese, as well as their familiarity with the Chinese canonical tradition, turned out to be helpful in Max Müller's effort to reconstruct both the text and the meaning of Sanskrit sutras. The complexity of Buddhist Sanskrit at times required comparison with their Chinese translations, and Müller could access the Chinese only through the mediation of his two Japanese pupils (Nanjio 1979: 150).

Of particular significance is the collaboration of Nanjō and Kasahara in collecting, editing, and translating the Sanskrit manuscripts published under the title *Buddhist Texts from Japan* (Müller 1881). In the translation of the *Sukhāvatīvyūha Sūtra* contained in this publication, Müller recognizes the difficulty of working with its very irregular form of Sanskrit, but at the same time associates such irregularity with the fact that this language was not simply a literary creation, but carried the vitality of actually spoken expressions (Müller 1881: xvii). Considering his privileged focus on origins, it is particularly intriguing that Max Müller expresses interest for a language that was less grammatically refined than classical Sanskrit, but that could testify of its actual use by Buddhist communities in ancient India.

Nanjō's contribution to this publication was particularly relevant. First, in the Sanskrit edited text Müller makes reference to a Chinese version in order to establish the meaning of unclear terms, which implies the necessary mediation of his Japanese disciples. In addition, the two editors included a series of *gāthas* translated from the Chinese version, again Nanjō's work. Finally, in order to familiarize the Western reader with a Buddhist tradition that was not very well known at that time, Nanjō was charged with writing a short history of Pure Land Buddhism that significantly ends with a chart of the 1880 census of Japanese temples, preachers, and students, which clearly showed that the Jōdo Shinshū sects—Pure Land—counted the largest number of preachers and students in the country (Müller 1881: xviii–xxiv).

In addition to these early collaborations with Müller, Nanjō gave an internationally recognized contribution to the field of Buddhist Studies with his *Catalogue of the Chinese Translation of the Buddhist Tripitaka* (Nanjio 1883).[7] This work was meant to correct a previous one realized by the British sinologist Samuel Beal (1825–89), considered flawed also because of the author's lack of understanding of the Chinese order of sutras.

The real contribution that the *Catalogue* gave to the study of Buddhism must be found in the indices: by linking Sanskrit sutra titles with their Chinese translations, Nanjō could claim to give a chronology to a vast number of Indian sources that previously were not clearly placed in time, a claim also recognized by Müller (Müller 1884: 187). Through the mediation of the Chinese and Japanese reception of Buddhism, it was possible for the modern Buddhist scholars to give a more accurate chronology of the vast amount of Sanskrit Buddhist literature, answering to one of the very sticky problems facing Indian literary scholarship in the nineteenth century.[8]

These examples show that the "Sanskritization" of Buddhist Studies in Japan, associated with Nanjō's scholarship, was not a one-way transfer of knowledge from the West. The knowledge of *kanbun* and the access to the Chinese canonical tradition became essential to the reconstruction of Sanskrit sutras. Using his skills, Nanjō actively intervened in the comparative philological efforts of his mentor Max Müller and later became a leading Buddhist scholar who not only collaborated with some of the most prominent European Buddhologists but also played a role in the introduction of modern Buddhist scholarship to China.[9]

It is possible to interpret Sanskrit as the language that allowed mobility to European Indology, and Nanjō's appropriation of it allowed the placement of Japanese Buddhism within the context of Western-dominated modern Buddhist Studies. The transfer of scientific knowledge, though, did not bring about the dismissal of local knowledge, because the particularity of *kanbun* and of the East Asian Buddhist tradition gained a new role in the construction of a universal image of Buddhism. The Sanskritization of modern Buddhist scholarship in Japan can be seen thus as an attempt to appropriate the discourse on the universality of the Western scientific approach to the study of Buddhism, while preparing to give a global resonance to another particular, Japanese Buddhism, and to the local knowledge of it.

In the next section, we are going to see how the same process of appropriation of the discourse of a universal in order to universalize a particular was in Nanjō's scholarship not limited to language (Sanskrit and *kanbun*) but extended also to religion—namely, Japanese Buddhism.

Competing Universalizations: Religion, Christianity, and Buddhism

In an 1896 letter to his later Japanese disciple Takakusu Junjirō (1866–1945), Max Müller compliments him for the publication of his English translation of the travel records of Yijing (635–713), a Chinese monk of the Tang period. The German scholar also adds:

> If I have gladly given my time and help to you [Takakusu], as formerly to Kasawara [Kasahara] and Bunyiu Nanjio [Nanjō Bunyū], it was not only for the sake of our University, to which you had come to study Buddhist Sanskrit and Pâli, but in the hope that a truly scholarlike study of Buddhism might be revived in Japan, and that your countrymen might in time be enabled to form a more intelligent and historical conception of the great reformer of the ancient religion of India. Religions, like everything else, require reform from time to time. A reformed Buddhism, such as I look forward to, would very considerably reduce the distance which now separates you from other religions, and would help in the distant future to bring about a mutual understanding and kindly feeling between those great religions of the world, in place of the antagonism and the hatred that have hitherto prevailed among the believers in Christ, in Buddha, and Mohammed—a disgrace to humanity, an insult to religion, and a lasting affront to those who came to preach peace on earth, and goodwill towards men. (Müller 1902: 357)

In this passage, Müller makes explicit the reason why he has put so much effort and hope in his Japanese disciples' acquisition of Indology: in order to reform the status of religion in their own country and prepare it for dialogue with Christianity and other world religions.

Was Müller successful in ushering a reform of Buddhism in Japan inspired by the academic rediscovery of its ancient Indian roots? His first Japanese disciple, Nanjō Bunyū, eventually pioneered the development of modern Buddhist Studies in Japan basing them on Indology and Sanskrit. But did he also spread in his country Müller's view of East Asian Buddhism as a late and corrupted version of the original teaching of Śākyamuni?

Nanjō did not simply redeploy Sanskrit in order to place Japanese Buddhism within the framework of Buddhism as a world religion but also followed the example of Müller's scholarship on religion. Nanjō agreed with his mentor in theorizing the universalization of religion as an essential component of human nature, but at the same time he replaced Christianity with Buddhism as the model for another universal religion in competition with Müller's view of Christianity. After briefly presenting the way in which Müller's project of the science of religion was meant to fuel the subsuming of world religions within a modern, universal Christianity, I will dedicate this section to Nanjō's response to his Oxford mentor's model, focusing on his ideas on religion and Buddhism.

Max Müller based his "science of religion" on a comparative and historical approach that focused on the anthropological sources of religion and rejected the metaphysical and theological ones. He described his method as analytical and *a posteriori*, proceeding by comparing and classifying religions based on their textual sources, and in doing so, he modeled it on the same work that he had done with languages in his effort to turn comparative philology into a natural "science of language" (Müller 2002).

Despite the claims of being historically and scientifically based, Müller's approach to comparative religion held the theological assumption that all historical religions represented developments of a more fundamental experience of the infinite defined in natural and universal terms.[10] Romanticism, particularly the idea of a universal perception of the infinite as common basis for all religions, combined in Müller's project with the search for an empirical basis necessary to define his approach to religion in scientific terms.[11]

The ultimate purpose of Müller's comparative study of religion was not strictly scientific but instead reflected its theological premise: It was aimed at fostering a dialogue among world religions, a dialogue that would reveal their common basis in the religious experience of the Infinite. This approach would not only prevent violence and fighting between different religious groups, but it would also promote a new form of religion, suitable to the modern times dominated by progress, science, and industrialization.

The idea that the longing for the Infinite is the common root of all historical religions allowed Müller to give a special role to Christianity in the history of humanity. Christ revealed in the most direct way the divine nature of all human beings: this is, according to the German scholar, the real meaning of his being the "son of God." The comparative study of religion, in Müller's view of a universal unified religion, becomes the means to purify the degenerate forms of current world religions and to make all religious groups aware of the simple, original message of the founders of their faiths: the divine nature of human beings.

How did Müller's view of religion and Christianity affect his relation with Nanjō Bunyū? A Christian missionary that met both the scholars wished that the ultimate aim of Müller was to convert his disciple to Christianity (Thelle 1987: 80–81), but was this actually the case? The idea of the two Japanese priests' possible conversion to Christianity was more likely a hope of those Protestant missionaries than Müller's hidden purpose. Max Müller's intentions in accepting Japanese students, in addition to getting access to texts preserved in their country, cannot be considered merely one of Christian proselytism. His wish was that, by learning Sanskrit and Indology, Nanjō and Kasahara would recognize the falsity of Amidism and prompt a return of Japan, "the England of the East," to the true Buddhism (Müller 1880: 175). Müller planned a restoration of Buddhism, rather than its eradication in favor of Christianity.

The hope of the German scholar was only partially realized by his Japanese disciples. Nanjō Bunyū truly dedicated his academic efforts to establish the study of Sanskrit and Indology as the foundation of modern Buddhist Studies in Japan. But he did not preach the inconsistency of the Pure Land faith with that of original Buddhism. Nor did he proclaim the equality of the Buddha and Christ's teaching. In a similar way as Müller, he sustained the universality of religion as an intimate component of human nature and called for a religious renewal to face the challenges of modernity. In Nanjō's work, however, the model for the new universal religion was not Christianity, but Buddhism, particularly in its Japanese forms.

Nanjō Bunyū's reconceptualization of religion and Buddhism in Japan happened in a period in which these two terms were at the center of a debate that was not limited to religious or academic environments, but that also involved the political discourse of defining Japan as a modern nation. The contact with Western colonial powers and the unequal treaties imposed upon Japan in the 1850s, as well as the increasing presence and influence of Christian missionary activities, prompted a rethinking of the Meiji government policy on religion. This involved a whole host of factors, including the definition of Shinto nationalism and modern Buddhism within the context of the debate on religious freedom, questions and concerns over the separation of state and religion and secularization, and other issues, all of which converged in the 1889 drafting of the Meiji Constitution.[12]

Nanjō participated in this debate from his authoritative position within the academic world, not only because he was one of the earliest pioneers of the modern study of Buddhism but also because, after his return from England, he was put in charge of important Buddhist and academic institutions.[13] His work in the translation of Sanskrit texts, though, touched a very sensitive issue within the Japanese Buddhist world: the debate on the nature of the Mahāyāna teachings as not directly derived from the historical Buddha Śākyamuni (*daijō hibussetsuron* 大乗非仏説論). Such a long-lasting debate had gained new life through the intervention of a generation of scholars who applied historical-critical methods to the study of Buddhism, the most prominent example being Murakami Senshō (1851–1929) (Tamura 2005: 100–12).[14]

Nanjō's contribution to this debate provided these historians with the textual and linguistic evidence, and this evidence was backed with the authority of Max Müller's comparative philology and the authenticity of the rediscovered Sanskrit texts. In 1908 he published a Japanese translation of the Sanskrit *Infinite Life Sutra* (*Sukhāvatīvyūha Sūtra*), based also on the comparison with Chinese versions (Izumi 1928: 164). Such work was not initially welcomed by the elder priests of his Higashi Honganji sect, who feared that the differences between the Chinese canonical version used in Japan and the new one derived from Sanskrit would ignite controversies.

The philological effort is for Nanjō an essential component of the scientific approach to Buddhism, and it is a necessary condition for Japanese Buddhism to undergo the same renewal process that he perceived in other aspects of the Japanese society during the Meiji period (Nanjio 1979: 133–34). The critical attitude of doubting is an integral component of the Buddhist enlightenment, as Nanjō states in the series of lectures, *A Buddhist View of Life*: "From a great doubt a great enlightenment, from a little doubt a little enlightenment" (Nanjio 1917: 386–87). The Buddha nature hidden in each human being makes everybody naturally inclined to thinking, discrimination, and doubt. This attitude has the advantage of including the scientific method that the West considered its own modern creation, but that Nanjō identifies within a Buddhist worldview based on the cause and effect relation (Nanjio 1917: 389–93).

In the previously mentioned *On Uplifting*, Nanjō includes Buddhism in his discussion of science, and he does this within an expanded definition of religion. He translates the debate on religion developed in Western academia and appropriates it to answer the question of whether Buddhism can be defined as a religion (Nanjio 1914: 508–17). He argues that, if we stick to the narrow definition of religion focused on a divine creator, it is difficult to include Buddhism within this category. The Japanese scholar, however, stresses that a categorization based solely on the Judeo-Christian-dominated European context does not make sense and that such an approach simply reflects the tendency of all religious believers to worship one's own tradition. While Müller used the same argument to support the value of comparative religion, his Japanese disciple turned it into a revaluation of Buddhism.

Nanjō agrees with Müller's view of the unity of mankind and the essential religious nature of the human being. If for Müller what separates men and animals is language, Nanjō states it is religion itself: animals may have forms of knowledge linked to the materiality of their brain, but only men have the "religious mind" (*shūkyōshin* 宗教心), which gives them power over nature and other creatures (Nanjio 1917: 382–84). Using the language of natural sciences, Nanjō defines the human being as the "religious animal" (*shūkyōteki dōbutsu* 宗教的動物) and stresses religion as an innate human characteristic.

This universalization of religion is used in response to the position of some Western scholars, who contrariwise argued that religion developed only among certain civilizations. This view, according to Nanjō, was based on the incorrect observation of missionaries that some languages do not have a word for religion. The Japanese priest explains such absence through an evolutionary interpretation: all human groups have religious terms, but they are found at different stages of development, and this fact sometimes makes it more difficult to identify "primitive religion" for the more advanced observers. Following this viewpoint, Nanjō argues that, even before the arrival of Buddhism to the archipelago, Japan has always had a form of religion. Nanjō's theory is here in line with Müller's criticism of racial theories of language, which would deny the universal nature of religion (Masuzawa 2005: 236–38).

Nanjō Bunyū shows his reception and reconception of Western *Religionswissenschaft* also in discussing the purpose of religion. This stands opposite to Müller's approach, where the scientific production of knowledge offers a complementary rather than competitive category. For Nanjō, religion exists in the space of what is inexplicable in natural-scientific terms (Nanjio 1917: 422-25). The progress of science, though, reduces these spaces, and this means that even what was previously interpreted in superstitious or religious terms acquires in modern times a rational explanation. Nevertheless, such knowledge will always be limited, and the way in which humans can make sense of what is beyond nature can only be found in religion.

In addition to the epistemological purpose, religion, according to Nanjō, responds to the emotional needs of humankind and at the same time it offers a basis for morality. This explains why, for example, human beings feel the need to properly bury their deceased peers, a behavior not dictated by rationality (Nanjio 1917: 425-30). In addition, the spiritual power that humans can attain through religion enables them to control their bodies and their desires and to build a society on moral values.

The domain of religion is therefore defined, by Nanjō, as that area of the human existence over which humanity cannot have direct control, be it in knowledge, emotions, or behavior. Buddhism, being a particular form of religion as a universal human category, shows a uniquely harmonious combination of knowledge and morality, from the standpoint of both science and faith. Buddhist scholarship has always thought of the world in terms of cause and effect, defining it as the law of karma, and this view peculiarly matches with the approach of modern science (Nanjio 1917: 385-98). At the same time, though, the academic-scientific (*gakumon* 学問) view of Buddhism represents only one of its two sides, the other being that of religion-belief (*shinjin* 信心). Instead of using a complicated speculative view of the universal law of cause and effect, the religious approach achieves the same result by teaching common Buddhist believers the simple rule of returning favors (*hōon* 報恩).

The universal nature of Buddhism is supported by Nanjō also through its historical development. Here the role played by the Japanese priest's deployment of his Indological knowledge is essential. Sketching the history of Buddhism starting from ancient India, he stresses the egalitarian nature that the Buddha's teaching had since its origins, setting this in contrast with the caste-centered view of Brahmanism (Nanjio 1917: 369-72). In addition, he quotes the example of king Aśoka, not only as the leader who turned Buddhism into a world religion through his political and military action but also as the real first proposer of terms such as religious freedom and tolerance, something that is usually attributed to Christ's message or to modern European Enlightenment.

And yet, the stress on the Indian origins of Buddhism, which the modern, academic approach provided through the translation of Sanskrit texts, posed a problem for Nanjō Bunyū's own Japanese Buddhism. How can a religion born egalitarian and universal, such as the one contained in the original message of the Buddha, respond to the needs of a modern nation such as Japan, one that is focused on the definition of its own individual identity within the Asian context and in opposition to the West? How can a "world religion," such as Buddhism, become a "national one," such as Japanese Buddhism?

Nanjō finds the key to this problem in the historical encounter between Buddhism and Japanese culture: Buddhism is the world religion marked since its origin by tolerance, and this quality matched perfectly with the unique ability of Japanese culture to assimilate and make its own foreign elements that otherwise would be "poisonous" (Nanjio 1917: 371-72). The active process of receiving and reinventing Buddhism explains for Nanjō why this religion is still alive in Japan, in contrast to its fate in India, where it passively "flowed away" (Nanjio 1917: 372).

In addition, Nanjō also uses philosophical concepts to describe the special harmonization of universality and particularity in Japanese Buddhism. The law of karma and the belief in rebirth allow Nanjō to explain why humanity, despite being essentially the same in nature, is also characterized by a variety of statuses and conditions at birth (Nanjio 1917: 376–77). The Japanese school of Tendai distinguishes between, on the one side, hidden skills and possibilities that are the same in all sentient beings at birth, and, on the other, their development in practice and manifestation, which is the basis for the differences we observe in everyday life (Nanjio 1917: 378–79). The philosophical worldview of Buddhism contains, at the same time, universality and particularity, egalitarianism and differentiation.

Finally, the moral consequences that stem from such a worldview distinguish Buddhists from non-Buddhists and agree with the national project of modern Japan. The belief in karmic law and in rebirth inevitably implies for the Buddhist to cultivate the virtue of filial piety toward one's own predecessors and, at the national level, loyalty to the emperor. Nanjō gives a Buddhist interpretation of these traditionally Confucian values and stresses how their presence in the Imperial Rescript on Education (*kyōiku chokugo* 教育勅語, 1890) confirms the perfect matching between Buddhism, as a universal religion, and the particularity of the *kokutai* (国体), the national ideology that the Meiji government fostered (Nanjio 1917: 394–98).

In the section of the lecture dedicated to the more traditionally Jōdo Shinshū concepts of *jiriki* and *tariki* (自力, 他力, the self-power of faith and the other-power of the Amida vow to save all sentient beings by letting them be reborn in the Pure Land), Nanjō offers a simplified definition of religion as "the relation between us [human beings] and god [he uses here the word *kami* (神)]" (Nanjio 1917: 412). If that is the definition of religion, the essential teaching of *jiriki* and *tariki* in Pure Land Buddhism can be interpreted simply as the Japanese Buddhist way of expressing human-god relation, which means that Amida faith is nothing but the Japanese religion. After summarizing the basic teaching of Mahāyāna Buddhism, he concludes by claiming how all the different sects of Japanese Buddhism are essentially based on the same fundamental relation to the Buddha that can be adequately described through the *jiriki-tariki* concept. In this way, Jōdo Shinshū doctrine reflects the essential, universal definition of religion at the same time as it condenses the Japanese particular way of conceiving it through Buddhism.

Finally, the interpretation of Mahāyāna Buddhism that Nanjō gives in another section of the same work becomes the key element to the universalization of the moral element of Japanese Buddhism. This universalization also implies a proselytizing effort toward other countries, especially toward the West (Nanjio 1917: 241–48). The Mahāyāna view of human existence implies a shift of focus from the individual to interpersonal relations based on the principle of "cultivation of loving-kindness" (*jihi* 慈悲), which expands from the family (filial piety) to the nation (loyalty) and finally to the whole world.

Nanjō sees in the Mahāyāna moral values, as developed in Japan, the highest level that civilization can achieve. His use of the term civilization (*bunmei* 文明) has a particularly relevant connotation in this context because, in the early Meiji and the years when Nanjō was studying in England, civilization was very often seen as that which modern Japan needed to import from the West. In these lectures, significantly given during World War I, Nanjō opposes the model of Western civilization with the model of civilization expressed by the harmonious values of compassion and benevolence that guide Japan. The wartime devastation of Europe is interpreted as the ultimate result of a misled scientific and technological development that progressed without religion, instead favoring the excesses produced by liberalism and individualism.

Nanjō also expresses concern with the atheist drift of Europe, which has lost its Christian roots, and he proposes Buddhism not only because of its worldview's compatibility with modern science but also as an alternative to socialism and communism. Such ideologies lose, in their call for egalitarianism, the necessary discrimination that allows one to make sense of the diversity of reality, and in addition, they do not have the conceptual tools like the theory of karma and rebirth that would allow them to explain the existence of inequality and injustice (Nanjio 1917: 375, 377).

The fundamental value of compassion that characterizes the Japanese Mahāyāna view of life implicitly gestures toward the spreading of the same value among other nations. In expressing such need for proselytism, Nanjō interestingly combines Buddhist words with terms coming from the ideology of Shinto nationalism. He describes the Japanese people as the "chosen people of god [or of the *kami*]" (*kami no senmin* 神の選民) or the "messengers of the *tathāgata*" (*nyorai no tsukai* 如来の使い) (Nanjio 1917: 243). The ultimate mission of Japan is to "unify the world in the Mahāyāna" (Nanjio 1917: 244).

Conclusion

Nanjō Bunyū appropriated some of the terminology he learned from the comparative study of religion and from Indology in order to rethink Japanese Buddhism in both universal and particular terms. Like his European mentor, Müller, Nanjō combined a philological approach claiming scientific validity with a rethinking of categories of religion that strengthened the position of his own tradition. His effort to link East Asian scriptural traditions with the Sanskrit sources allowed him to place Japanese Buddhism within Buddhism as a world religion, while at the same time, the positive revaluation of the Chinese canon granted the preservation of the Pure Land and Japanese sects.

The application of the modern concept of religion, duly expanded after the contribution of Asian traditions, to the case of Buddhism, becomes in Nanjō's thought the premise to rethink Japanese Buddhism in a way that harmonizes its universality with its distinctively Japanese nature. Following his reinterpretation, the peculiar form developed through Buddhist contact with Japanese culture fulfills the philosophical premises of the Indian Buddhist worldview and reaches the highest level of morality needed for the true modern civilization. It is through this process that Japanese Buddhism becomes the model for the rest of the world. Instead of realizing Max Müller's project of religious reform for "the England of the East," the Sanskritization of modern Japanese Buddhist Studies pioneered by Nanjō implied the recuperation of Mahāyāna and Pure Land Buddhism and their universalization.

10

An Alternative to the "Westernization" Paradigm and Buddhist Global Imaginaires

Lina Verchery

The *Fajie Fojiao Zonghui* (法界佛教總會 Dharma Realm Buddhist Association, henceforth DRBA) is a global Chinese Buddhist monastic organization founded by the eminent Chinese Chan monk, the late Master Hsuan Hua (宣化上人 1918–95). One of Hsuan Hua's life missions was to bring the "Orthodox Dharma" (正法 *zheng fa*) to the West. Although the DRBA has been headquartered at Wanfo Sheng Cheng (萬佛聖城 the "Sagely City of Ten Thousand Buddhas") in Talmage, California, since the 1970s, curiously its North American and worldwide branch temples remain markedly Chinese in their demographics and institutional culture.[1] Although the DRBA boasts over a dozen branch temples in North America, the group remains largely unknown in the West outside immigrant and Chinese-American Buddhist communities. Despite this, the DRBA unequivocally celebrates Hsuan Hua as the first to introduce orthodox Buddhism to the "West."[2] This apparent contradiction begs the question that lies at the heart of this chapter: What precisely is the "West" in the DRBA imaginaire?

Recent work in the study of religion, modernity, and globalization has deconstructed notions of "East" and "West," rightly noting these are not static geographical or cultural entities but ideological constructs with shifting referents. In the spirit of Said's (1978) famous study of the "Orient" in the Western colonial imagination, or of Kieschnick's and Shahar's (2014) study of "India" in that of the medieval Chinese, this chapter explores the idea of the "West" in the Chinese Buddhist imaginaire of the DRBA. In so doing, we reverse the gaze of much post-Orientalist Buddhist Studies scholarship, which has been primarily concerned with rectifying Western misperceptions of the "East." While this has been a vital intervention in the field, it has also kept Western agency at the center of the scholarly conversation, overlooking the ways in which Chinese agents—like Hsuan Hua and his followers—have also been appropriating, redefining, and inventing new discursive categories for thinking of cultural difference.

By situating this imaginaire of the "West" within the DRBA's global vision, this chapter also explores how the conditions of globalization, transnationalism, and diaspora shape religious identity. In contrast to conventional ways of conceptualizing globalization—in which a binary that implicitly values "connectivity" over "particularity," "isolationism," or "nationalism" is often projected onto the categories of "global" versus "local"—I show that isolation actually plays as vital a part in the DRBA's global identity as does any sense of widespread connectivity. In other words, globalization, as experienced in the DRBA, is not synonymous with connectivity; rather, it is an overarching condition that involves both connection and isolation. This claim, in turn, is part of the chapter's larger structural argument that aims to undercut several binary frameworks through which we model global encounter and religious change. It urges a rethinking of both our uncritical adoption and hasty rejection of facile binaries like "East" and "West," arguing that such oppositional models (East-West, Imagined-Real, Tradition-Modernity, Global-Local), even when used heuristically, obfuscate processes that must be understood together if we are to understand how globalization, transnationalism, and diaspora are shaping Chinese Buddhist identity around the world.

Post Post-Orientalism

One can hardly overstate the impact of Said's *Orientalism* in transforming how scholars everywhere think about "the Other." Following in these footsteps, a wave of Buddhist Studies scholarship began to disabuse the field of many of its long-held assumptions about Buddhists and Buddhism.[3] This critical spirit extended into the study of Buddhism's global developments. Whereas previous scholarship classified global Buddhism under various binary categories—"Asian" vs. "Western," "Ethnic" vs. "Convert," "Traditionalist" vs. "Modernist"—recent work has persuasively shown these binaries to rest on an insidious "West and the rest" discourse in which "Westernization" is assumed to be the driving force behind Buddhism's developments in the modern world.[4] In addition to their problematic ideological bias, these categories are inaccurate: they conflate "groups of people" with "styles of practice" (Hori 2010: 16) and exclude large swaths of those very populations they attempt to describe.[5] The "Ethnic" vs. "Convert" binary also implicitly valorizes active conversion over passive inheritance, as Hori powerfully argues.[6] The label "traditional" is equally fraught—as are its myriad antonyms: "new," "modern," "innovative"—for any careful study reveals that, in both historical and modern contexts, Buddhism has always been in a process of recovering, reforming, and reinventing its "tradition." Although Buddhism has, of course, been present in Asia for longer than it has been in Europe, Africa, or the Americas, it does not follow that Asian Buddhist practices—even, or perhaps especially, when they appeal to a rhetoric of traditionalism—are any less of a response to the conditions of modernity than Buddhist innovations elsewhere in the world.

It comes as no surprise, then, that Buddhist Studies has been gradually moving away from these problematic labels and, in so doing, gaining a clearer awareness of both the historical situatedness of Buddhism as an object of study and the historicity of the scholarly categories through which that study has been undertaken. Rejecting the labels, however, does not necessarily ensure that the underlying structural paradigm has changed. Although there has been widespread critique of the hypostatization of difference that underlies the Orientalist paradigm—essentializing "East" and "West," "Orient" and "Occident"—we must be cautious that in our reactionary zeal we do not simply replace one problem with another. As Hallisey (1995) and others have warned, in rejecting the Orientalist assumptions of our forebears, we run the risk of unwittingly reproducing the very dynamics we sought to dismantle.[7] We may have toppled the Orientalist idea of Buddhism as the romantic projection of naive Westerners only to erect a new *anti*-Orientalist projection in its place. As has been noted, this ironically keeps discursive authority firmly in the hands of those issuing the critique—thereby perpetuating the very imbalance of discursive power that was problematic in the first place—while ignoring the influence of Buddhist agents in their own self-presentation.

A further complication arises when considering the implications of dismantling terms like "Asian Buddhism" and "Western Buddhism" when, despite the problematic historical and ideological paradigms from which they arose, such terms have already been appropriated by Buddhist communities themselves. As Shaw and Stewart note:

> Just as colonial power entailed the categorizing of people into essentialized "tribal" entities with fixed boundaries ("you are the Igbo"), anthropological hegemony now entails taking apart practices and identities which are phenomenological realities for those who use them ("your tradition is invented"). In our enthusiasm for deconstruction ... we may have invented another kind of intellectual imperialism. (Shaw and Stewart 1994: 23)

In other words, scholarly categories are often appropriated by those under study and, alongside other factors, transform that which is studied.[8] We cannot, therefore, brazenly reject categories now deemed problematic in the academy, lest we deny the significance of categories that have since become meaningful within Buddhism itself, once again silencing the voices of Buddhists with the noise of scholarly debate.

Where, then, do we go from here? Rather than reject the categories of "East" and "West" outright—and thereby risk falling into the same kinds of reactionary patterns described earlier in this chapter—I propose we instead consider how these categories have functioned not as historical descriptors but as salient imaginaires for one particular Buddhist community. In so doing, we reverse the gaze of much post-Orientalist Buddhist Studies scholarship that, as discussed, has kept discursive authority in the hands of those issuing the critique while marginalizing the agency of Asian Buddhist actors. By instead looking at the idea of the "West" in the imaginaire of Hsuan Hua and the DRBA, we find it is not only the "Orient" that has been subject to the fantasies of the Western imagination but that the "West," too, has been a canvas for the projections of others. This case study also offers an alternative to, and ultimately a critique of, the "Westernization paradigm." The DRBA's aspiration is decidedly not one of becoming *like* the West but is instead characterized by ambivalence. This observation lays the groundwork for a larger critique in the final part of the chapter, arguing the hypostatization of difference so problematic for the Orientalist/post-Orientalist paradigms has also crept into many current theories of globalization and religious modernity.

Imaginaires of East and West

In an essay entitled *Things We Think We Know*, Chuck Klosterman recalls his experience as a tourist in Germany, reflecting on the misguided stereotypes he formulated about Germans, as well as those he noticed Germans held about Americans—in particular, their overestimation of the importance of cowboy culture. He writes,

> While they had not necessarily misunderstood the historical relationship between Americans and cowboy iconography, they totally misinterpreted its magnitude. With the possible exception of Jon Bon Jovi, I can't think of any modern American who gives a shit about cowboys, even metaphorically.... But European intellectuals use cowboy culture to understand American sociology, and that's a specious relationship.... As it turns out, Germans care about cowboys way more than we do. (Klosterman 2007)

Klosterman argues that the cowboy archetype is not, in fact, how Americans see themselves; it is how non-Americans *imagine* Americans see themselves. As Klosterman reminds us, intercultural encounter is never simply a matter of seeing and being seen but a complex interplay of seeing through the eyes of others and imagining how oneself is seen.[9] Precisely because perceptions of how we are perceived inform the personas we present, these perceptions—even when they are *mis*perceptions—impact reality. The "imagined" and the "real" are not opposing ends of a spectrum but, like the other binary models to be discussed shortly, are mutually determinative. With this in mind, let us now turn to an exploration of Hsuan Hua's and the DRBA's imaginaire of the "West."

Prophecy and Ambivalence

Hsuan Hua was born in 1918 in the town of Lalin (拉林鎮) in Shuang Cheng County (雙城縣), modern-day Wu Chang County (五常縣), in Northeastern China. His biography follows the hagiographic pattern of many eminent monks. The youngest of eight children, he was born to a devout vegetarian mother who, before his birth, is said to have dreamt of Amitābha Buddha radiating light. The occasion of the birth itself was accompanied by miraculous events, including a sweet permeating fragrance. Throughout the DRBA, stories circulate recounting Hsuan Hua's exceptional talents, even early in life: as an infant, he was the champion of a crawling contest among the village babies; he was a strict vegetarian; he had a photographic memory and memorized the Confucian classics; he was a gifted healer and could exorcise nefarious spirits of all kinds. A turning point came when he was eleven; he came across the corpse of a dead baby. Deeply shaken, at that moment he resolved to become a monk. At fifteen, he took refuge with the Elder Chang Zhi (常智老和尚) of San Yuan Si (三緣寺 Three Conditions Monastery), near Harbin.

In his late teens, Hsuan Hua fell gravely ill and sank into a weeklong coma, during which he had a vision. He flew throughout China, stopping at many of its sacred mountains, and also "visited foreign lands and saw people who had blond hair and blue eyes" (Buddhist Text Translation Society 1973: 13). Upon recovery, he was said to have "died, yet not died" and began to call himself a "living dead person" (Buddhist Text Translation Society 1973: 13). Meanwhile, his elderly mother became ill, and he returned home to care for her until her death. Shortly thereafter, he took novice ordination and began a three-year period of ritual mourning at his mother's graveside. During this time, he began the austere practices for which he and the DRBA are now famous, including eating only one meal a day and never lying down to sleep. One day, Venerable Hui Neng (惠能禪師), the illustrious Sixth Patriarch of Chan Buddhism, appeared to him and delivered a prophecy:

> In the future you will go to America. . . . You will teach and transform everyone you meet, innumerable and limitless living beings, countless like the sands of the Ganges river. This will be the genuine beginning of Buddhism in the West. (My translation, Buddhist Text Translation Society 1995: 59)

Here we see a first facet of the "West" in the DRBA imaginaire: namely, the idea of "going West" began as a vision and a prophecy, not a deliberate choice but a supernaturally imposed mandate. And, as in all archetypal hero stories, at first Hsuan Hua was reluctant to accept his mission. Unlike many of his contemporaries—Buddhist reformers in China who sought to strategically align themselves with Western values and ideas—Hsuan Hua was decidedly ambivalent. When, later in life, an interviewer asked what prompted his decision to go West, he responded (in Chinese), "I have always been the one to take what others have abandoned and to go where others don't want to go" (Hsuan Hua 2008). This is a far cry from the Westernization paradigm's vision of the West as a dazzling cradle of modernity and innovation. To the contrary, for Hsuan Hua and the DRBA, the "West" was, and in many ways still is, seen as something more like the *wild, wild West*: a kind of unruly, lawless place, inhabited by not bad people per se but people who never benefited from exposure to the traditional values of Chinese culture and moral education. In this imaginaire, the aspiration is not to become *like* the West but, rather, to reform and reeducate it.

Not an American Dream

It was not until nearly twenty-five years after Hsuan Hua received his prophetic mandate that he first journeyed to America. In the interim, the Communist Party came to power, and like many monastics, Hsuan Hua fled south, passing through Mount Pu Tuo in Zhejiang, where he received full ordination at Fayu Monastery (法雨禪寺). He continued his travels until he reached Nanhua Monastery (南華寺) in Guangdong province, where he trained with the illustrious Chan Master, Venerable Hsu Yun (虛雲老和尚, "Empty Cloud" c.1840–1959). It was from Hsu Yun that he received the name Hsuan Hua—meaning "to proclaim and transform," an appropriate appellation, say DRBA members, for one "destined to transmit the proper Dharma to new soil" (Buddhist Text Translation Society 1973: xxi). Hsu Yun appointed Hsuan Hua Dean of Academic Affairs at the Nanhua Vinaya Academy (南華寺戒律學院) and later gave him Dharma transmission as the Ninth Patriarch of the Chan Guiyang lineage (潙仰宗).[10] He eventually fled to Hong Kong in 1949, where he founded three monasteries: Xi Le Yuan (西樂園), which no longer exists, Fojiao Jiangtang (佛教講堂), an urban temple in a high-rise overlooking the horse racing track at Pao ma di (跑馬地, aka Happy Valley), and Ci Xing Si (慈興寺), a sprawling complex atop one of the forested peaks of Lantau Island (大嶼山 Dayu Shan). After an unsuccessful attempt to garner a following in Australia, in 1962, he finally left for the United States at the invitation of two Hong Kong disciples studying in San Francisco, where they had set up a branch of the *Fojiao jiangtang* in Chinatown.

Hsuan Hua's first years in California were far from an American dream. Although he would later found many branch temples around the world as well as Wanfo Sheng Cheng (萬佛聖城)—which shares the title of largest Buddhist monastery in the Western hemisphere with Fo Guang Shan's Hsi Lai Temple (佛光山西來寺)—the sixties were a time of struggle. Though he had secured a core group of devotees in Chinatown, Hsuan Hua did not immediately gain the support of the Chinese community. Stories still circulate of rivalries with other religious leaders, dangerous encounters with street gangs, and mistreatment at hands of suspicious members of the local community. Indeed, in 1963, Hsuan Hua left Chinatown and began what is now known as his "monk in the grave period."[11] With little money or support, he moved into San Francisco's Fillmore District and spent the next four years living in near solitude, meditating, fasting, and lecturing on the sutras in Chinese. As one of Hsuan Hua's oldest American disciples recalls, some days three or four people would show up for the lecture; other days, he would be the only one. Occasionally, a few attendees could translate between Chinese and English; other days, no one present could understand what Hsuan Hua was saying. Today, DRBA members describe—with a mix of horror, delight, and sheer disbelief—the many faux pas of the curious young Americans who wandered into Hsuan Hua's lectures in those early days. They were students, hippies, hobos, and truth-seekers of all kinds; some were high on drugs, would put their feet up on the furniture, or lie down and fall asleep on the floor. One of the most senior nuns in the DRBA organization recalled one of her first visits with Hsuan Hua; not knowing it was customary to bring offerings of food, she and her companions arrived empty-handed, and it was Hsuan Hua who cooked for *them*![12] This dramatic reversal of the ritual prescription of laypeople making offerings to the sangha is inconceivable to DRBA members today. But rather than rouse judgment, such stories are cherished by the community as proof of their Master's consummate humility and generosity.

Taming the Wild, Wild West(erners)

Today, a casual visitor to the DRBA might have no idea these non-Chinese Americans were ever part of the organization, given how strongly Chinese the DRBA is in its customs and demographics. Even in North American branches, English is relatively rarely spoken, with members typically communicating between themselves in Mandarin, Cantonese, or Vietnamese.[13] But if one wandered into Fuji lou (福居樓 the Tower of Blessings)—the residence for elderly monastics at Wanfo Sheng Cheng—one might bump into a handful of non-Chinese nuns who were among Hsuan Hua's very first American disciples, a group affectionately known as the lao dizi (老弟子, literally, "old disciples"). The few non-Chinese monks and nuns still able to take on heavy work duties are dispersed throughout the DRBA's many branches, serving as liaisons between the Chinese-speaking temple community and the outside world, especially in countries where Chinese is not widely spoken (like Canada, the United States, and Australia.) The remaining lao dizi, however, are quite elderly, and since the late 1980s, the vast majority of new ordinands come from Asia, especially Malaysia and Taiwan. This caused a major demographic shift in the organization; non-Chinese disciples are now, at least numerically, a nearly invisible minority. Even if the participation of these American disciples had been central to helping Hsuan Hua's nascent community take root during its early days in San Francisco, all appearances suggest that the DRBA's "Western moment" has passed.

Despite these dwindling numbers of non-Chinese disciples, however, we find that the idea of the DRBA's engagement with "Western culture" remains a powerful part of the organization's identity and public image, especially in Asia. Should one pick up one of the DRBA's many publications—which are mostly printed in Taiwan, then distributed worldwide—one would see a subtle but significant difference between the Chinese-language publications and their English translations. While the latter are branded with the name of either the DRBA or its headquarters, in Chinese two important characters are added: *Meiguo* (美國), making the phrase "Meiguo de Wanfo Sheng Cheng (美國的萬佛聖城 The American Sagely City of Ten Thousand Buddhas)." This holds true for much of the organization's branding and signage throughout Asia; the placard leading to the DRBA nunnery in the mountains of Hualien, Taiwan, for instance, identifies it as a branch of the American Sagely City of Ten Thousand Buddhas. Indeed, Hsuan Hua's activities in America are far better known among Buddhists in Asia than Buddhists in the West; one routinely sees the Chinese captions below his portraits reading, "美國萬佛聖城開山祖師" (*Meiguo Wanfo Sheng Cheng Kaishan Zu Shi* "Founding Patriarch of the American Sagely City of Ten Thousand Buddhas"), even though most Americans, even in Buddhist circles, have never heard of him. In other words, being perceived as American is a major part of the DRBA's identity and of Hsuan Hua's cachet around the world, particularly in Asia. Ironically, it is in North America that the organization is perceived as least "American" and most "traditionally Chinese" ("it's like stepping into China," an American college student told me about attending classes at Wanfo Sheng Cheng), whereas elsewhere in the world—including throughout Mainland China—Hsuan Hua is famous as the first "American Patriarch" of Chinese Buddhism. This claim carries a great deal of cultural capital, but perhaps not for the reasons one might expect.

As we have seen earlier in this chapter, the "West" in the DRBA imaginaire was and, in some respects, still is seen as an uncivilized, morally lawless place. Westerners, of course, are not bad people; they simply did not have the benefit of traditional Chinese moral education to protect them from the traps of materialism, individualism, and immoral activity. In light of this, note that the cultural capital carried by Hsuan Hua as the first "American Patriarch" is not—as proponents of the "Westernization paradigm" might assume—that he aligned himself with something great and thus shares in its greatness. Quite the opposite: he is lauded for having courageously ventured into "uncivilized" lands (indeed, the rampant violence in 1960s San Francisco plays directly into this imaginaire of the West as a wild and dangerous place), where he successfully converted the locals and triumphantly remolded their "unpromising American clay," as a DRBA member phrased it (Rounds 2008: xiv). One senior monastic wrote, "that the Master, a strictly orthodox exemplar of the ideal of all five schools of Buddhism, has been able to profoundly influence and change the lives of headstrong young Americans gives one a small idea of the perfection of his own practice and strength of his vows" (*Records* 1973: iii). Like in the rodeo—where the wilder the bull, the higher the score—the fact that Hsuan Hua overcame such trials is a testament to his extraordinary abilities; the wilder the students, the more extraordinary the teacher.

Strategic Occidentalism or Complementary Imaginaires

The rhetoric of the "rescue of the modern West" (McMahan 2008: 5) is not unique to the DRBA. Several scholars have identified this as a response to the threat of Western cultural hegemony. McMahan notes "the rise of identity politics in Asia" that has led Asian nations to be "newly emboldened to assert their distinctiveness and unique value, even—and perhaps especially—if they do not conform wholly to the cultures of the modern West" (2008: 5). Even more boldly, some have highlighted how such trends have historically been tied to larger nationalist movements that sometimes included violent or xenophobic elements.[14] Perhaps the best moniker for this is what James Ketelaar (1991) calls "strategic Occidentalism" in his study of the Japanese Buddhist delegation at the 1893 Parliament of World Religions. While many have shown how certain factions used the Parliament as a vehicle to assert Christian superiority under the guise of "religious pluralism" (e.g., Ziolkowski 1993; Seager 1995; Masuzawa 2005), Ketelaar looks at the reverse side of the coin, showing how Japanese responded to the situation by "appropriating" the categories of Orientalist discourse and using them "to defeat the Occident at its own game" (Ketelaar 1991: 38). They celebrated the spiritual and cultural superiority of Asia, reappropriating the very elements of Orientalist discourse used to justify Asia's subordination to the West. In so doing, Ketelaar explains, the Occident "was itself constituted as an object"—just as Orientalism had made an object of the Orient—to be discursively deployed for political ends in Japan (Ketelaar 1991: 39). Might the DRBA imaginaire of the "West" also be a kind of "strategic Occidentalism"?

Although the aforementioned studies have filled lacunae in our scholarship on the globalization of Buddhism—especially by highlighting the agency of Asian Buddhist actors in challenging, appropriating, and ultimately shaping nascent discourses of global Buddhist modernity—we should be careful to heed Hallisey's earlier warning about reproducing the mistakes of our forebears. Though the trope of "Occidentalism" indeed helps rebalance a story in which previously only "Orientalists" had a voice, this paradigm still assumes that the primary framework through which to understand intercultural encounter can be reduced to competition and confrontation.[15] Although such forces are undoubtedly at work, they only represent *part* of the picture—a part that, if mistaken for the whole, simply perpetuates a hypostatization of cultural difference. Both the "Orientalism" and "Occidentalism" models—when taken as comprehensive explanations—are more akin to ideal types than categories adequate for describing the complex motivations of historical agents. A more accurate picture could arise, I suggest, if rather than imagining intercultural exchange on a spectrum ranging from the hypostatization of difference (as in both the "Orientalism" and "Occidentalism" models) to total assimilation (as in the "Westernization paradigm"), we might instead develop a theoretical outlook that sees both difference and similarity as coextensive and mutually dependent. We might examine a final series of examples from the DRBA case study to illustrate what such a model could look like.

If we consider present-day retellings of Hsuan Hua's early days in San Francisco, we find that both he and his early American followers are remembered as fulfilling each other's idea of the exotic "other" while also showing tremendous adaptability in developing common ground. On one hand, Hsuan Hua famously embodied—then and now—the ideal of an enlightened Zen Master.[16] Meanwhile, the early American disciples are remembered as wild hippies who were miraculously tamed and transformed. On this level, we see imaginaires of difference: each is seen by the other as foreign, unknown, exotic. Yet, at the same time—and this is what models like "Orientalism" and "Occidentalism" are wont to miss—each is also lauded for their adaptability in drawing closer to the other. Not only did the Westerners give up, as one disciple put it, the "proclivities of the popular culture for drug experience and sexual promiscuity" (Buddhist Text Translation Society 1995: 61), but they so excelled in monastic etiquette, asceticism, and Chinese language that, to this day, many Chinese consider these Americans more accomplished in traditional Chinese Buddhism than monastics in present-day China, a topic to which we will turn shortly. Similarly, though Hsuan Hua remains the archetypal Chan Master in the minds of DRBA members, he is also remembered as almost *more* wild and free than the freedom-loving hippies. Though he was strict regarding precepts and monastic decorum, he was also totally unpredictable, often shocking his disciples in order to disrupt their mental attachments. One disciple recalled when Hsuan Hua interrupted one of the DRBA's infamously intense meditation retreats with a case of colas, ordering everyone to stop meditating immediately and drink a Coke. Another day, Hsuan Hua showed up with a celebrity yoga instructor from Hong Kong, clad in skin-tight spandex, to test the male novices' concentration. *Did your mind move when you saw her?*, he would taunt them. As hippies, the *lao dizi* thought they were wild and free; yet when face-to-face with Hsuan Hua—though foreign, exotic, and so different from themselves—they realized he was far freer than they were.

Such an encounter—which, like all oral history, blends fact and hagiography—cannot be reduced to either difference or similarity. Rather, this situation involves the working of complementary imaginaires that simultaneously hold difference and similarity in balance. Indeed, it is only because of an assumption of fundamental difference—whereby the Chinese sometimes think that Westerners are incapable of mastering the abstruse profundity of Chinese language, customs, and religious practice—that the *lao dizi* garner such admiration. Similarly, were there not an assumption of fundamental difference between Eastern and Western cultures, it would be far less remarkable that Hsuan Hua—without ever mastering spoken English—would be able to flourish in and even convert the locals of a foreign country. Striking this balance—where intimacy preserves difference and difference allows for common ground—is key to the enduring salience of this imaginaire and its central place in the DRBA's sense of identity. And, as we will see, structurally this concurrence of opposites also yields insights for theorizing experiences of globalization in general.

Imaginaires in Exile

More Chinese than China

Today, the DRBA's global identity is characterized by paradox. As we have seen, the group—especially in Asia—labels itself "American," yet both its Asian and North American branch temples are overwhelmingly Chinese. Indeed, interviews with both lay and monastic visitors from Mainland China revealed that many consider the DRBA a more authentic bastion of "traditional," "orthodox" Chinese Buddhism than can be found today in China proper. Hsuan Hua himself expressed this sentiment, famously claiming that true Buddhism had already disappeared in China and framing his mission in the West as a means "to counteract the declining standards of Buddhist practice in the East" (*Records* 1973: 1) and "sav[e] the Dharma from its impending death in Asia" (Buddhist Text Translation Society 1973: 11). Recall, of course, Hsuan Hua was part of an entire generation of Buddhist clergy who fled the communists and found refuge in the Chinese diaspora. Yet, even though the DRBA operates exclusively outside Mainland China, it still places major emphasis on Hsuan Hua's direct continuity with the authoritative lineages of Chinese Buddhism, especially his transmission from Hsu Yun, one of the most celebrated Chinese Buddhists of the twentieth century.[17] These apparent contradictions bring us to conclude this chapter with the reverse question to that with which it began: namely, what is "China," or, more properly, what does it mean to be "Chinese," in the diasporic DRBA imaginaire?

Like the idea of the "West," the DRBA idea of "Chineseness" is also an imaginaire, one that in this case is intrinsically connected to the DRBA's diasporic situation. As scholars have noted, it is not unusual for diasporic communities to see themselves as custodians of an authentic tradition since lost in the motherland.[18] The DRBA fits this paradigm, which illuminates an important aspect of "Chinese" identity in diaspora: namely, that its sense of authenticity *depends* on its uprootedness. Abstractly, we might say an idea depends on its own negation—as Ketelaar poetically put it, "we name death that we may live" (Ketelaar 1991: 42). Like the idea of "tradition"—meaningful only alongside a notion of "modernity" that serves as its foil—the notion of "Chineseness"—with its connotations of "authenticity," "tradition," and "orthodoxy"—here emerges in a context where China itself is seen to have lost that very authenticity. The distance created by diaspora makes this imaginaire possible, allowing the DRBA to critique China while also developing its own Chinese religious identity from afar. Metaphorically stated, utopias are not opposed to distopias; in fact, they need each other.

Alienation and Assimilation

Scholars have bemoaned theories of globalization and transnationalism that default to a facile global vs. local binary, equating the "global" with connectivity and the "local" with isolation (or nationalism, particularism, xenophobia, etc.).[19] Oakes and Schein, for instance, describe globalization in terms of "connectedness, flows, networks, rhizomes, decenteredness and deterriortiozaliation" (2006: 1), while Shuang Liu describes it as an "interconnectivity [that] breaks down boundaries between us and them, the different and the same, here and there, and indeed between the Eastern and the Western" (Liu 2015: 1). In contrast to these models that implicitly or explicitly equate globalization with connectivity, I argue that connectivity is merely one facet of the experience of globalization. For the DRBA, isolation, particularism, and a sense of alienation run parallel to any sense of connectivity and play at least as important a role in its self-understanding as a globalized organization.

Despite being smaller than other major transnational Chinese Buddhist organizations—like Fo Guang Shan (佛光山 Buddha's Light Mountain), Tzu Chi (佛教慈濟慈善事業基金會 The Buddhist Compassion Relief Tzu Chi Foundation), and Fa Gu Shan (法鼓山 Dharma Drum Mountain)—the DRBA is a closely knit global network, through which DRBA members are constantly traveling. For monastics, travel is always for a practical purpose: a nun may be a skilled cantor (*weinuo* 維那) who specializes in a particular repentance liturgy, traveling around the branches—staying for a month or two in each country—to lead the assembly. While there, she is called upon to formally address the assembly several times to report the latest news from the temples she has recently visited. The same holds for laypeople, who continually travel between temples—some crossing the Pacific three or four times a year—to participate in events at different branches.[20] These lay visitors are also asked to report on the latest news from other branches, and they rarely leave empty-handed; they depart loaded up with boxes of sutras, print materials, audio recordings, and various other kinds of media they then courier to DRBA members at their home temple.[21] In this way, DRBA members the world over share information and develop close bonds despite their geographic distance, resulting in a remarkably intimate global community.[22]

Focusing on this DRBA cosmopolitanism, however, will yield only a partial picture unless we also consider the ways in which DRBA temples relate to their immediate local environment. Unlike other major Chinese transnational Buddhist organizations that do considerable local outreach, the DRBA is ambivalent regarding the extent to which it should localize. While the DRBA upholds Hsuan Hua's mission to spread the Dharma internationally, the organization is acutely aware that popularization can come at the cost of integrity. "When I see the tour buses from China arrive," one nun joked with me at Wanfo Sheng Cheng, "I want to run away!" Both monastics and laypeople in the DRBA maintain a very strict standard of practice, which makes it difficult to participate in most outside activities without violating precepts. In predominantly non-Chinese-speaking countries—like Canada, Australia, or the

United States—cultural difference and language barriers compound this isolation; while, even in countries where Chinese is commonly spoken, strict precept adherence radically limits the types of secular activities in which both lay and monastic DRBA members can engage. Although upholding Hsuan Hua's mandate to spread the Dharma forces a certain engagement with the outside world, there remains an acute sense of the risks such engagement can bring. As lay DRBA members in Taiwan told me, they would sooner travel to another country to attend a Dharma Assembly at a DRBA branch than walk down the street to attend one at the Fo Guang Shan temple near their home.

This feeling of being both locally isolated and globally connected is a hallmark of the DRBA's global identity. Just as estrangement from China opens possibilities for a new, diasporic "Chinese" identity, isolation from the immediate environment strengthens global identity. Ironically, the stronger these global ties, the more acute the separation from the immediate local world.

Conclusion

This chapter argues that the DRBA is best understood through its own contradictions. It identifies as "American" while remaining, in a sense, quite unconnected to America; it identifies as "Chinese" while remaining quite critical of China; it is "globally connected" while remaining guarded and, at times, even insular. Such contradictions, I contend, are not problems to be reconciled but, rather, must be held in tension to understand the complex dynamics that animate this case study; a case study in which it is commonplace to find a Buddhist in rural Taiwan reading Hsuan Hua's San Francisco lectures to learn "traditional Buddhism" or traveling from Shanghai to California to experience "real Chinese Buddhism." Such seeming contradictions are not anomalies in the world of modern globalized Buddhism; they are already the new normal.

In this chapter, I have suggested we attend to such contradictions and develop theoretical models that reflect rather than erase them. Indeed, in true Chan style, Hsuan Hua himself embraced contradiction; though the mission of "introducing Orthodox Buddhism to West" was his life's motto, in his oral teachings, he railed against the imagined distinctions of East and West. In his commentary to the *Shurangama Sutra* (*Lengyan Jing* 楞嚴經), he elaborated:

> The ten directions do not exist. You might say that something is south of you, but if you go south of it, it becomes north. You could then say it is north, but if you go north of that north, it becomes south again. (Hsuan Hua 2003)

Hsuan Hua did not only denounce the mental discriminations that result in *ideas* of East, West, North, and South, he also denounced the politics involved in such discriminations. Though he made his fame as the first "American Patriarch" of Orthodox Buddhism, he would warn his disciples:

> Don't try to promote your teacher by saying things like "My master has come from China with the Orthodox Treasury, the true and proper *Buddhadharma*." Tell

them instead that what your teacher says is empty and false.... Don't be like the disciples of Hui Neng and Shen Hsiu. (Buddhist Text Translation Society 1973: 9)

This reference to the legendary rivalry between Hui Neng, the Sixth Patriarch of Chinese Chan and founder of the "Southern School" and his supposed nemesis, Shen Hsiu of the "Northern School," is remarkable. Though Hsuan Hua received his prophetic mission to go westward from Hui Neng himself, he still denounced the sectarian rivalry between "North" and "South" that eventually built up around Hui Neng's name. Indeed, perhaps the legacies of Hsuan Hua and Hui Neng are not so dissimilar. Both masters are celebrated for having inaugurated a new era in the history of Buddhism—for Hui Neng, it was in the "South"; for Hsuan Hua, it was in the "West"—and yet Hsuan Hua did not want to hypostatize divisions between East, West, North, and South. Hui Neng's legacy is shrouded as much in imaginaires of sectarian difference as it is in the perpetuation of an unbroken, unmediated, atemporal transmission of truth, and perhaps Hsuan Hua is the same: a founder-figure in whom the opposites of East and West, history and hagiography, difference and similarity can rest, both in tension and in balance.

11

Glocalization in Buddhist Food Ventures on a Small Canadian Island

Jason W. M. Ellsworth

In the spring of 2016, I witnessed the official opening of Leezen (里仁), a Buddhist-inspired Taiwanese organic and vegetarian grocery store, in Charlottetown, Prince Edward Island (P.E.I.), Canada. Company representatives stood next to local politicians as they cut the ceremonial red ribbon, and sample tables of organic vegetarian food from both P.E.I. and Taiwan offered the public a taste of the store's products. The opening of the 121st store of the franchise, and the first one overseas, was a significant occasion for the retail chain. The ceremony exhibited the international growth of the chain internationally and the partnerships forged with local P.E.I. farmers and producers, who were on hand. At the same time, the celebration of local and global elements, with a focus on environmental stewardship and animal welfare, displayed how a relatively new transnational Buddhist movement is situating itself within Canada's foodscapes. This chapter explores the global growth of a socially just and economically active Buddhist movement, the establishment of its monastic and lay communities in Canada, and how they are influencing agricultural and food ventures on P.E.I. In this case, the globalization of Buddhism is driven by a Taiwanese group that claims to be influenced by both Tibetan and Chinese Buddhist texts and traditions. This example reverses the hegemonic direction of Buddhist modernism that is characterized by the spreading of a "Western" interpretation of Buddhism globally.

The small province of P.E.I., with a population of 152,000, is now home to a thriving Buddhist community centered around two monastic organizations, called the Great Enlightenment Buddhist Institute Society (GEBIS) for the monks and the Great Wisdom Buddhist Institute (GWBI) for the nuns. From lay charitable organizations, social enterprises, a vegetarian restaurant, a grocery store, organic agricultural enterprises, animal sanctuaries, and a strong lay following it is a fast-growing network of people and separate, but associated, organizations with access to considerable social and economic capital. Buddhist values of environmental stewardship and animal protection inspire many of these ventures and projects on P.E.I. that are connected to the GEBIS and GWBI communities. Originally it was largely a Taiwanese movement associated with the Bliss and Wisdom Foundation (Fu-Chih 福智) in Taiwan that was founded by their late Master Jih-Chang (日常老和尚 1929–2004). The successor to

Master Jih-Chang and the current spiritual teacher is Master Zhen-Ru (真如 birth date unknown), who oversees a Buddhist movement of people and organizations that is now global in character, with followers and associated centers in many countries such as the United States, China, Singapore, Australia, and Canada. On P.E.I., the separate but interconnected monasteries and organizations are also under the guidance of Master Zhen-Ru.

The GEBIS and GWBI communities on P.E.I. are addressing food shortage issues for some of the most vulnerable, protecting animals that are viewed as commodities and developing social enterprises within the food industry that supports local farmers. Many of these projects are gaining this new Buddhist community on P.E.I. favor with locals. Yet, the rapid development and migration to an island with a small Buddhist population create barriers for integration, similar to other diasporic Buddhist communities in Canada where the "come from away" (a common expression for a person not born on the Island) is treated as an "other." There has been little academic research into how P.E.I. is affected socially and economically by the localization processes of this transnational movement (i.e., ongoing exchanges of migration, capital, commodities, and Buddhist practices).

The case study here is one example that moves beyond the traditional roles, narratives, and stereotypes that a simple East and West dichotomy portrays. Under colonialism, Western countries went to Asia to extract commodities and exploit local Asian populations, leaving parts of it impoverished. The orientalist narrative often places the Westerner as the active agent and Asians as more passive. Further, the trope of a mystical East contributes to the construction of a stereotype that emphasizes Buddhism as a separate practice from economics (Anderson 2013). There has been a recent increase in work countering some of this, by examining how Buddhists position themselves within economies (Bao 2015; Bronx and Williams-Oerberg 2016). In this chapter, I build on this, showing how Buddhist values and economics enter Canada. For example, agriculture products are purchased by members of the lay community, shipped to Taiwan, and now commodities are being shipped in both directions. This specific form of economics developed within the context of Taiwanese capitalism may best be understood as an alternative model or countermovement that in some instances is described by the Buddhists as "social enterprises" or charitable projects. In *The Great Transformation*, Karl Polanyi (1975) argued that the process of free-market capitalism both impedes society and at the same time produces countermovements that re-embed markets in social relations. This Buddhist economics can be a countermovement meant to benefit the local population on P.E.I., adding value to the province rather than exploiting it, while at the same time remaining entrenched in the prevailing economy. The transnational frame I use here also helps to move beyond the dichotomies of East and West, to focus on the agency of a global Buddhist movement involved in both charitable and economic affairs. This transnational lens also helps move beyond the constraints of nation-state rhetoric to more properly depict a movement that is not located in any one place or country.

In the broader spectrum of the study of "religious" movement, it is argued that "religions" have a long history associated with global migration (and also elements of transnationalism) (Levitt 2001, 2003, 2007; Vertovec 2009). What makes globalization today different from the past is the intensified nature within capitalist (including neoliberal) systems, where globalization is an increased form of a space-time compression of capitalist accumulation (Giddens 1990; Harvey 1989). Thus, in our global context today, a study of transnational movements and commodities needs to address the myriad ongoing exchanges within these new situations. Transnational frameworks can help focus on the multiple ongoing exchanges of people, commodities, and "religious" practices to understand how identity, community, and ritual practices are both created and sustained in the process, without being contained within one national identity (Basch, Schiller, and Blanc 1994; Levitt 2001; Schiller 1997; Tweed 2006; Vertovec 2009).

Focusing on globalization as a process of movements (both economic and social) elevates the discussion beyond the nation-state to a transnational sphere that explores the modernization of Buddhism as something that has been taking place for decades in multiple geographic contexts (see Harding, Hori, and Soucy 2010, 2014). It should be no surprise that temples are involved in global networks and conversations or that Buddhism's adaptability gives it the ability to flourish globally in an array of situations. While the term "global Buddhism" is used to emphasize that Buddhism at a local level needs to be placed within a global context, at the same time, to fully understand the global, it needs to be placed within the context of the local. Or, as noted by Harding, Hori, and Soucy, the local level becomes the "creative bricolage" of the local and global (2014: 15).

While this chapter in part addresses the migration of Buddhists and Buddhist values, it serves to show how the globalization of Buddhism is also tied to commodification, the movement of goods, and global economic flows. For this, I propose that Buddhist globalism needs to be examined in a dialectical sense, in order to capture the ongoing complex and evolving discourses. I follow a similar methodology described by Alexander Soucy, that moves beyond a focus on "categories or types of Buddhists," to the "process of transformation and the forces that interact in different ways with different groups and individuals" (Soucy 2014: 28). With this in mind, I use an approach that decenters state-based and national categorizations of Buddhism, opting for a transnational lens that explores how social relations are involved in the flows of peoples, capital, goods, and ideas. It is a framework where the distinctions between the global and local become blurred—in what Robertson terms glocalization (1995). Based on my ongoing fieldwork, which began in 2010, the following case study endeavors to add to the ongoing research on global Buddhism within the Canadian context, by creating a snapshot of a number of global interactions taking place in one locale.

Taiwanese Buddhist NGOs

In Taiwan, Buddhist NGOs continue to address local and global issues of social inequality, environmental degradation, and dispossession that stem from processes of capital accumulation. It has been noted that from 1945 to 1965, the Buddhist Association of the Republic of China monopolized the field of Buddhist organizations across Taiwan (Jones 1999: 178–80). From the 1950s to 1970s, the seeds for a challenge to this monopolization took root, paving the way for other legitimately recognized Buddhist organizations in Taiwan to increase their presence in the public sphere (Ip 2009: 167; Jones 1999: 179–80). It was from the 1970s to 1989 that there was a growth in the number of Buddhist organizations in a period known as pluralization, and with policy changes in 1989, the government began recognizing other civil Buddhist organizations.

While many organizations are registered as Buddhist organizations (NGOs) in Taiwan, six groups are claimed to be in some fashion "socially engaged," with global focuses addressing social justice issues such as health, rights, education, and the environment (Huang, C. J. 2003; Jie 2001; Schak and Hsaio 2005). While Taiwanese Buddhist NGOs continue to enter Canada, Canadian scholarship has focused mainly on Tzu Chi and Fo Guang Shan (Laliberté and Litalien 2010; Verchery 2010). This chapter adds to this scholarship by introducing a new Buddhist movement within Canada that is associated with the Bliss and Wisdom community of Taiwan, guided and inspired by their late Master Jih-Chang and their current Master Zhen-Ru.

In the early 1990s in Taiwan, Venerable Jih-Chang established the Bliss and Wisdom Foundation, which is described as one of the six major socially engaged Buddhist groups in Taiwan (Schak and Hsaio 2005). Venerable Chang was born in 1929 on Cong Ming Island, Jiangsu Province of China. In 1947, during the civil war between the Kuomintang and the Communist Party, he moved to Taiwan and would eventually graduate with a degree in Civil Engineering from Tainan Technical Institute. He was ordained in 1965 at Yuan Guang Monastery at Lion's Head Mountain in Taiwan.

Traveling to the United States in the 1970s to spread Buddhism to overseas Chinese, Venerable Chang began studying the *Lam Rim Chen Mo* (Great Treatise on the Stage of the Path to Enlightenment) by fourteenth-century Tibetan reformer Tsong-kha-pa. The *Lam Rim Chen Mo* became the central Buddhist text for teaching the core beliefs to his followers. Followers of Chang form groups to study the *Lam Rim* and commentary materials, such as audio recordings of their teachers. These discussion-based *Lam Rim* classes are emphasized by the members as essential to their Buddhist practice and the defining characteristic that differentiates them from other groups in Taiwan. The overall teachings are associated with the Gelug lineage of Tibetan Buddhism, though are also influenced by Chang's experience and education in Confucianism, and the Lu Tsung lineage of Chinese Buddhism (Nan-Shan Disciplines School).

In Taiwan, community outreach focuses on education, health, and teaching the dharma (Schak and Hsiao 2005: 60). They own a bookstore in Taipei, own a franchise of Leezen grocery stores, run an organic testing foundation that is recognized by the government, educate the public on Buddhism, and place a high importance on organic foods—to protect both the earth and the body from chemical agriculture (2005: 60). Schak and Hsiao note that in Taiwan, they eschew media publicity (Schak and Hsiao 2005: 60), though this may be different from associated groups on P.E.I. today. Upon their arrival on P.E.I., the Buddhist community was quiet about their activities on the Island; however, as of late, a number of Facebook groups continually provide stories of the monks' and nuns' activities. Articles about the monks, nuns, Leezen, or the charitable foundations can also often be found in the local newspaper and online. While some of this may simply be promotional and the media's own interest, much of the publicity is also for the benefit of the curiosity of locals. Schak and Hsiao note that Bliss and Wisdom "literature states that as it globalizes, the organization desires to blend into local cultures, to understand the needs of the local people and society and give them what is suitable" (2005: 60). This mandate displays their directed effort to create an intertwined global-local model for growth. However, the movement and organizations (and component organizations associated and inspired by Jih-Chang) are not solely Taiwanese. Jih-Chang founded one of his first organizations, The Great Enlightenment Lotus Society, in the early 1980s in California. The movement continues to spread internationally with followers and organizations in countries such as the United States, China, Singapore, Australia, and Canada where localized models are implemented.

In interviews with monks, nuns, and lay members of the GEBIS and GWBI communities, I have been told that prior to Master Jih-Chang's passing in 2004, he appointed current Master Zhen-Ru as his successor. On P.E.I. she is sometimes referred to as the Spiritual Lay Master, as well as the Founder and Honorary Chairperson for many of the organizations on the Island. Zhen-Ru is listed as the Master for both GEBIS and GWBI on their respective websites. At times Zhen-Ru's gender and lay status have come into question—particularly regarding whether a female spiritual teacher and lay person can mentor a sangha. It is felt by some that a female leader may disrupt the male patriarchal system that many are accustomed to within monastic communities. At the same time, others claim that Zhen-Ru has been involved in sexual abuses, financial misconduct, and forging political alliances with the Chinese Communist Party on Mainland China. During a leadership change, allegations such as these may destabilize a group and delegitimize a leader. Addressing the question of laity and female leadership in one news article online, Bliss and Wisdom states:

> Whether a spiritual teacher is qualified to give teachings and guide the sangha is not determined by the monastic or lay status, nor by the gender. The sangha is made up of renunciates, each of who has the right to decide the spiritual teacher whom they want to follow. They can observe for themselves whether this individual has the full qualifications of a spiritual teacher. If so, they can choose that person as their spiritual teacher. If not, they can choose otherwise. Also, from the overall viewpoint of the sangha, individuals are not required to abide by a specific spiritual teacher. This is each practitioner's personal choice. (Choesang 2017)

These claims establish individual choice as the reason for monks, nuns, and laity to follow Zhen-Ru. This negates the need to address gender or lay status directly; thus, Zhen-Ru's qualifications for leadership is based on the merits deemed fit by the personal choice of followers. However, in the above-mentioned article and elsewhere, specific historical and contemporary examples are used to show that it is not uncommon to find both female and lay leadership throughout Buddhist history. Mahāyāna scriptures and a number of Buddhist figures are pointed to as examples, displaying a precedence that supports the argument that female laity can become spiritual teachers of Buddhist sanghas (e.g., Bliss and Wisdom Sangha 2017). While Master Zhen-Ru's position has become a contentious issue for some, a loyal following see her as capable of teaching and guiding students in the Gelug tradition. Thus, while claims about gender and laity status can be one avenue for trying to destabilize both a group and its leadership, that very challenge can become the opportunity to further legitimize a leader via claims to Buddhist history and texts.

Establishing Roots on P.E.I.

Originally, Master Zhen-Ru and her followers began to settle in Vancouver, registering as a charitable organization in British Columbia in 2006. They later relocated to P.E.I. and registered a charitable organization in 2008 under the name Great Enlightenment Buddhist Institute Society (GEBIS). Shortly after, the Great Wisdom Buddhist Institute (GWBI) was also established on the Island as a separately registered entity and is the central organization for the Buddhist nuns.

While GEBIS and GWBI's central purpose is to provide a place of solitude for the monks and nuns living on P.E.I., they also promote Buddhist education to lay practitioners. Canada's values of diversity, equality, and religious freedom are some of the stated reasons for the choice to build the new monasteries in Canada. P.E.I.'s quiet and serene landscape away from busy cities compared to the high population density of such places as Taiwan also presented a unique place for monastic education according to their Master Zhen-Ru. While other followers of the late Master Jih-Chang and Master Zhen-Ru have registered organizations with similar names in Canada, such as GEBIS, Toronto, P.E.I. is the larger retreat and home for the monks, nuns, and Master Zhen-Ru. While many of the monks and nuns are from Taiwan, some hail from China, Canada, Malaysia, New Zealand, Singapore, and the United States.

As of 2018, there are three monasteries (campuses) and another in the planning stages. The two GEBIS monasteries on P.E.I. house roughly 200–300 monks. In 2018, GEBIS, as one entity, was listed as having over $37 million in assets, property, and agricultural land on P.E.I. and continues to expand their operations (Government of Canada 2018). One campus in Little Sands, P.E.I., includes prayer halls, dormitories, educational buildings, and is where public gatherings most often take place. Their Montague campus in Heatherdale is expanding to be the new educational hub for the monastic community. It will be able to accommodate up to 3,000 people in an auditorium and house up to 900 people in the dormitories. Initiated in 2015, this project is expected to take seven to ten years to complete (GEBIS 2018; Stewart 2017).

The GWBI monastery houses roughly 130 Buddhist nuns in Uigg, P.E.I. GWBI purchased a new property and in the near future plans to move to a new monastery in Brudenell, P.E.I. The 300-acre monastery with gardens, a green house, walking trails, residences, lecture halls, and spaces of worship will potentially house up to 1,400 nuns.

Both GEBIS and GWBI are said to be funded by donations from followers all over the world. The social enterprises and commercial aspects associated with them are said to be run by lay Buddhists that support the monks and nuns. While many still live in Taiwan or other home countries, there are followers that chose to move to P.E.I. because of GEBIS, GWBI, and Master Zhen-Ru (who I am told spends much of her time on the Island now). The Moonlight International Academy, part of the Little Sands monastery, is an education school that brings in students from Taiwan, Singapore, Malaysia, and China. As reported by Canadian news magazine *MacLean's*, "the provincial government, eager for immigration, changed its education laws last year to allow children to train as monks, as well as Amish families to homeschool their children" (Campbell 2017). The now amended P.E.I. Private School Act allows for the new school to operate with a mixed curriculum.

By 2013, GEBIS reported that over 850 monastics and 3,800 lay practitioners had attended various retreats and programs on P.E.I., a number that has continued to increase since that time (GEBIS 2014). In 2016, on the anniversary of the death of their late Master, the group estimated that 1,200 people attended a day of remembrance at the monastery. This included members of GEBIS and GWBI, roughly 75 locals, and the rest being lay international followers (either on retreat or now residing on the Island). Retreats of lay members from countries internationally, particularly Taiwan, continue to grow and are a central aspect to the community's goals of Buddhist education. As of 2018, GEBIS reports that 1,500 lay Buddhist practitioners from around the world come to participate in retreats and meditation workshops each year.

The Buddhist community as a whole is open to interaction with those that are not already members, and less (at least stated publicly) focused on missionizing—though they are trying to get more local "Islanders" (locals that were born on the Island) to take classes, volunteer, or attend events. There are now dedicated locals from the area attending the *Lam Rim* Study Classes, where they read and discuss the *Lam Rim Chen Mo*. Some Islanders are now teaching at these lay study groups as facilitators, and I know of at least one Islander who is living as a monk at the monastery. Early on, I was told it was tough to attract a wider audience to the Buddhist classes and courses. The six-week Happy Courses, which offer an introduction to Buddhism for the general public, attract upward of sixty to eighty local non-Buddhists to the classes.

In interactions during my fieldwork, the community and organization describe their focus on vegetarianism and organics as inspired by Buddhist ethics of compassion for all sentient beings. The choice to avoid eating meat is a defining characteristic of the community on P.E.I. Up until recently, members of their Buddhist community owned the only vegetarian restaurant on P.E.I.

While at times the curiosity of those unfamiliar with the community seems natural, it should be noted that the community is making a concerted effort to interact with locals. Some of the main events promoted by GEBIS to the general public are to express their gratitude, and information sessions held at the monastery. These open-house-style events started when the organization first arrived on the Island (*Guardian* 2012; Sharratt 2009). They opened the doors at their first location, an old Lobster Shanty restaurant, where they welcomed Islanders with food, tea, and information sessions that discussed their Buddhist practices. They continue these outreach programs in varying ways, and in the spring of 2016, they opened the doors of one of their newer, much larger monasteries to over 3,000 visitors who wished to tour the property in Little Sands, P.E.I. They had to shut down registration, as logistically they did not know how they could handle more cars for parking. The continued open-house model displays the importance that the organization places on including Islanders and building community support. However, it may be the scope of their food initiatives on P.E.I. that is cementing their local presence building local trust and acceptance.

Poverty Relief, Gratitude, Protecting Sentient Life, and Agricultural Food Projects

The GEBIS and GWBI communities' central vision on P.E.I. is to construct an environment for the monks and nuns to study and teach Buddhist philosophy. GEBIS and GWBI's purpose is also to educate and nurture Buddhist practitioners, extending beyond monastery walls and the classroom, including a focus on environmental protection, charity, and relief work. This vision is most evident in the agricultural, food, and animal welfare projects on the Island. Following Master Zhen-Ru's call to address food scarcity issues, both ordained and lay community members developed several food relief programs. In order to thank Islanders for their hospitality, and at the same time help alleviate hunger issues on the Island, GEBIS and associated lay organizations conduct a number of food projects.

Poverty Relief and Gratitude

In October 2015, GEBIS donated 1,000 ears of pesticide-free corn from their fields to the Salvation Army (CBC News 2015a). Two weeks after the initial donation the fields were opened once again, as the community still had an abundance of corn. This second time, corn was made available to the entire general public across the Island. GEBIS stated they wanted to repay the kindness that they, as a new community, felt on the Island, and this was their way of saying thank you. While many did come to pick corn for their own home, many also arrived to help pick more corn for other food banks on the Island. This included help from volunteers from the P.E.I. Food Exchange. Giving thanks and donating to the food banks from the Buddhist-owned farmland is quickly becoming an annual tradition. In addition to helping food banks with food shortages, the monks are also known for selling their agriculture, such as strawberries, to raise funds when there are donation shortfalls at the food banks (CBC News 2015a; McEachern 2016).

The aforementioned examples include three themes that are particularly evident in the Buddhist practices of the entire community. First, the protection of sentient life is of high importance. Farming focuses on plant-based agriculture, as animals are not consumed and are to be protected from suffering. Vegetarianism and sustainable agricultural practices are prioritized as ways to protect the entire ecosystem. Second, charity and poverty relief are used to reduce human suffering. Many of the charitable food projects look to address food scarcity issues. Third, the community is continually looking for ways to express their gratitude to those who helped them settle on the Island.

Another ongoing project garnering much media attention is GEBIS's "Rolls of Love" campaign. After hearing stories that there were many Island children going to school hungry, the monks at the monastery began baking bread rolls. The group bakes an average of 2,000 bread rolls weekly for donation to such groups as the Salvation Army, the P.E.I. Food Share, Island Mothers Helping Mothers, and school breakfast programs. In the spring of 2016 during the wild fires taking place in Alberta, GEBIS increased their roll production to an additional 2,000 rolls a week to raise funds to help the relief effort in Fort McMurray. Rolls were sold for $1 each, and GEBIS made a matching gift of $1 for each sold. GEBIS donated $11,000 through the Canadian Red Cross toward the Fort McMurray Fire Appeal. In addition to helping deal with food scarcity issues and disaster relief, the Buddhists view the practice as a form of merit making that is helpful to their own karma—or, as they were quoted in one recent article, "what goes around comes around" (Stewart 2016a). It also garners media attention that helps with community public relations.

The Moonlight International Foundation, an associated lay-run nonprofit, incorporated on P.E.I. in 2010. It focuses on poverty relief, animal welfare and protection, agricultural and natural lands reservation, and promotion of cultural understanding and diversity (MIF 2014). This includes animal sanctuaries, a vegetarian restaurant, education classes, partnerships with local farmers for buying produce, tree-planting initiatives, winter clothing drives (*Warm Coat, Warm Heart*), healthy eating programs, and food initiatives to help relieve poverty. They also organize many of the Chinese-language classes and cooking classes and participate in festivals across the Island. Many of these activities are highlighted in the local newspaper (Stewart 2012) and are supplemented by pictures being uploaded to Facebook. The Foundation displays an awareness for public relations that is reflected through stories in the local news.

One program of significance, run by Moonlight Charities Inc. (a separately registered charity), includes purchasing unmarketable fresh vegetables and excess produce (largely organic) from local farmers. By buying this produce, they help to relieve pressure on farmers from what would be lost revenue. The purchased produce is then donated to a number of food banks, helping those who face food scarcity. Produce donated includes squash, potatoes, carrots, tomatoes, turnip, romaine lettuce, cabbage, beans, cucumber, broccoli, eggs, and cauliflower. The purchased and donated amount of produce varies greatly, and it is not uncommon to see multiple donations take place within a month, with 500 lbs. to 1500 lbs. donated at a time. The partnership with farmers and food banks represents one example of their poverty relief efforts to help relieve the suffering of fellow human beings (MIF 2014). This has the trifold effect of reducing food waste, supporting small-scale farmers who would normally lose funds, and helping to reduce hunger across the Island.

The focus on poverty relief in the form of food is particularly important. Food Banks Canada's latest Hunger Count Report states that food insecurity continues to rise across Canada and there continues to be an increase in those accessing food banks (2016). Some of the most vulnerable parts of the population are also some of the most affected by the ongoing crisis, including children, immigrants, and refugees. Even on P.E.I., where almost half of all land acreage is cleared for agricultural use (Prince Edward Island, Department of Agriculture and Fisheries 2015), food scarcity remains an issue where local food banks and food security programs cannot keep up with growing need. Since 2008, food bank usage on P.E.I. increased by 23.4 percent, with

35.5 percent of those accessing food banks being children (Food Banks Canada 2016). The Buddhist food sharing projects such as the corn, rolls, and organic food donations are directly helping locals who have few other places to turn.

Animal Welfare and Sanctuaries

Animal welfare and protection is key to this Buddhist community's mission, which matches the ethical concerns that grow from the Buddhist tenets that influence vegetarian and organic food initiatives. The animal sanctuaries are particularly important in carrying out this work. In the spring of 2013, the provincially owned Buffaloland Provincial Park was sold to the lay organized Moonlight International Foundation. According to the reports, the 1,000-acre property that is home to the Buffalo (originally gifted from the Alberta government) was sold to the Foundation on terms that the park be kept free of charge for visitors and that the upkeep would be the responsibility of the Buddhist corporation (*Guardian* 2013a, b; Sharratt 2013). However, I have been told that Moonlight itself does not own the land and that at any time deemed appropriate by either party, the agreement could be ended, with operations being given back to the government. The central notion to privatize the park was to save the government the operating costs and keep the buffalos located in the park. A public forum following the transaction raised questions as to why Moonlight International was chosen. Politicians were on hand to answer questions, yet representatives from the Buddhist community were not (Sharratt 2013). This is not surprising, as the group makes an effort to stay out of political affairs. In addition to feeding and providing the veterinary care of the thirty-eight bison, Moonlight continues to update the facility by fixing animal chutes, fences, and the bison's living quarters. In 2016, a documentary crew from National Geographic TV filmed at the park.

Off the beaten path in Eastern P.E.I., one will also find an animal farm sanctuary for horses, cattle, emu, and chickens, and they continue to add more animals each year. Upon seeing a transport of cows being sent to market, Master Zhen-Ru was inspired to save animals that are often the discarded commodities of the agricultural industry or horses that are the by-products of a racing industry that does not see a use for them anymore. The sanctuary is now a home for these horses and many other animals to live out their lives on large acreages of land in the Eastern region of P.E.I.

Perhaps the most notable aspect of their acquisition of Buffaloland is the ability of a relatively new-to-the-Island NGO to be able to earn the trust of the government. The overall movement's social and economic capital is notable for a new community, something that not all Buddhist migrant communities possess (McLellan 1999, 2009). The economic capital also gives the group an added benefit over many other local community groups on P.E.I. who do not have the economic ability to take over such projects. The ability to draw on both external and internal economic resources is particularly advantageous and helps build further social capital. Thus, social capital and economic capital are closely intertwined in this case. These resources are helpful for integrating into a new country. However, as will be shown in a later section, having access to economic capital can also draw skepticism at the local level.

Agriculture Business

In 1997, Venerable Jih-Chang established the Tse-Xin Organic Agriculture Foundation in Taiwan (TOAF, also referred to as the Compassion Organic Agriculture Foundation) to promote organic products in an effort to "protect the earth and those life forms killed by the use of agricultural chemicals, and to protect human health, both that of the farmers growing the crops and that of consumers" (Schak and Hsiao 2005: 59). The project started by renting 160 hectares of land to grow organic crops and spread education on what the community views as ethically based farming practices, derived from Buddhist teachings (Chang, Wei and Shih 2011: 3). The endeavor grew into an education system including workshops, seminars, camps, field trips, and publications. Part and parcel of this project was an accreditation testing system for organic farming recognized across Taiwan by the Farmers Association (Schak and Hsiao 2005: 59). In 2010, there was estimated to be 433 accredited farmers with 810 hectares of land (Chang, Wei, and Shih 2011: 3).

Another initiative on P.E.I. includes purchasing Island-grown organic soybeans from local farmers and shipping them to Taiwan for the production of soymilk, before being sold in their grocery stores. Grain Essence Incorporated, another lay-run Buddhist entity made up of followers of GEBIS and GWBI and lists Mengrong Jin (Master Zhen-Ru) as a Chairperson, acts as a retailer, distributer, and exporter working with local farmers. The investment and interest are timely, given the current state of agricultural affairs on P.E.I., where overall agricultural sales have decreased, but soybean crop production has increased at an unprecedented rate (Statistics Canada 2012). The overall decrease in agricultural produce sales may continue with the current closing of major local industry processing plants and decrease in the hog farming industry (CBC News 2014). Other organizations are also shipping GMO soy off Island for production, possibly contributing to the growth of another dominant agricultural product across P.E.I.

However, soybeans are not the only agricultural product being bought by the lay Buddhist organization. In 2015, the *Guardian* newspaper reported that in conjunction with 60 tons of organic soybeans, 200 tons of non-GMO soybeans, 25 tons of frozen wild blueberries, 34 tons of frozen cranberries, 4,800 bottles of wild blueberry juice, 5,300 bottles of puree, 6,500 bottles of cranberry juice, and 3,700 jars of jam had been shipped to Taiwan (Stewart 2016b). Some of these products are also derived and produced in the surrounding provinces, such as is the case of the cranberry juice from Nova Scotia. The effects of the lay Buddhist followers' agricultural practices are, thus, impacting the larger Atlantic region.

In Taiwan, and now on P.E.I., the Bliss and Wisdom-associated Leezen grocery stores are one outlet founded in part by the late Master Jih-Chang to distribute many of these agricultural products. Jih-Chang guided lay practitioners to establish Leezen. Starting as a single store, the franchise is now estimated to have 130 stores across Taiwan and 29 overseas service locations (Leezen 2018). While the stores bring in revenue, their main purpose is said not to raise profits but to reduce suffering through Buddhist ideals. As noted it "promotes a culture of religion and praise through songs ... full time logistics and supply chain workers learn and practice Buddhism" (Chang, Wei, and Shih

2011: 4). It also develops many chemical additive-free food products, which are sold throughout Taiwan in its Leezen Shops. For these reasons, they often describe these and many of their other lay-run organizations as "social enterprises"—organizations that use commercial strategies to address human and social problems. Thus, revenue is viewed as secondary, though it should not be minimized, as it is central to the growth of the group. As stated on the Taiwanese Leezen website, "as a social enterprise, Leezen donates all profits to Tse-Xin Organic Agriculture Foundation and Bliss and Wisdom Cultural Foundation" (Leezen 2018). However, as explained to me, the Leezen outlet on P.E.I. is a part of the separate corporation Grain Essence and thus the owners direct this business at their discretion.

The "Come from Away"

In 2015, GEBIS was the focus of a short documentary on the Canadian Broadcasting Channel's Land and Sea, titled "Come From Away" (CBC Land and Sea 2015). The episode title alone offers a glimpse of an othering process that persists in the Atlantic Provinces that directly labels those not born in the area. As noted by Godfrey Baldacchino "while hyperdiversity may be what brands Canada as a whole, mono-culturalism rules largely undisturbed in Atlantic Canada, still marked by a relative lack of diversity" (CBC Land and Sea 2015: 206). Communities on P.E.I. consist of close-knit groups of the same social cohorts (friends and family) and are often noted as having an insular nature as a result. In 2006, the proportion of visible minorities in Atlantic Canada was a mean of only 2.6 percent of the total resident population (Baldacchino 2015: 206). And while provincial immigration programs (such as the Provincial Nomination Program) helped increase the number of landed immigrants, there are large retention issues, especially on P.E.I. Programs that are meant to bring people directly to the Island and keep them there are not always successful. P.E.I. has seen the largest increase in the number of landed immigrants in Atlantic Canada and yet has also seen its retention rate decrease. Many immigrants are using P.E.I. as a stepping-stone to move to other provinces. While there are a number of reasons that a "come from away" may have for leaving (economics, jobs, education, social class, gender, race, etc.), there is a continued and documented discrimination of the other (Baldacchino 2015: 209).

As noted earlier, lay members associated with GEBIS and GWBI have stated that integrating local non-Buddhists into the Buddhist courses and community events has been more difficult than anticipated at times. Several reasons may account for this. First, the Island consists mostly of Christians. Second, while this is changing, Buddhism on P.E.I. has traditionally been practiced by a small number of people in their homes or small meditation groups.[1] Second, the focus on animal welfare and vegetarianism connects with a smaller percentage of people than it would in other parts of the world (compare Canada's overall 4 percent of vegetarians that are centered mainly in Ontario, Quebec, and British Columbia, to Taiwan's 13 percent). Third, visible minorities represent less than 2 percent of P.E.I.'s population (Statistics Canada 2006). Fourth, it has been stated that Islanders lack bridging social capital (Baldacchino 2015: 210). Some of these barriers are slowly breaking down as there has been a recent upsurge in course attendance. This may be due in part to the ongoing efforts of course facilitators to address the wants of the local population in classes. For example, meditation-based activities and classes are now common on P.E.I.; this is different from how the group organizes classes in other countries where meditation is not a common practice for lay practitioners. The familiarity that people now have with the Buddhists may also be part of the reason more people are willing to take classes with the group now.

As a new community on the Island, GEBIS, GWBI, and its lay followers are subjected to skepticism at times from the previously existing local population. Some news articles question the monks' motives, as can be seen in one online magazine article that states the community is mysterious and that "the monks and their followers are friendly—until you start asking too many questions" (Mann 2013). The author calls them secretive, yet as an individual with no previous connections to GEBIS, he is given access for interviews and observations. Similarly, I have been asked many times by other locals on the Island a version of the question "so what are these monks really doing here?" or "what's their agenda?" Curiosity likely plays a part, as there was no visible Buddhist community prior to their arrival on the Island. Seeing monks and nuns dressed in robes is a new sight, and hearing that they have millions of dollars, and the evident ability to build multiple monasteries while buying large amounts of land, is enough to pique many people's interest.

Locals continue to ask questions about the intentions of Zhen-Ru and her followers on P.E.I. For example, questions have been asked about why so much land has been purchased by her followers, the type of Buddhism they are following, the involvement of youth, Zhen-Ru's connections with political parties, and the long-term plans for the associated organizations. Representatives of GEBIS released statements to try and address the ongoing questioning.

Land, as a finite resource on the Island, continues to be a concern for the local population, and the amount of land acquired by GEBIS, GWBI, associated organizations, and lay followers is being questioned. While the law is apparently being followed and no wrong-doing has taken place, many argue that the "spirit" of the Land Protection Act is being abused through "loopholes." The act limits the amount of land that can be owned by any one party or individual on P.E.I. As noted in a local newspaper that covered a symposium on the issue, "a major concern brought up was around loopholes that some say allow corporations to circumvent the spirit of the Land Protections Act, which currently allows individuals to own up to 1,000 acres and corporations to own up to 3,000 acres, while still technically following the law" (MacDonald 2018). Corporations such as Vanco and Cavendish Farms have also been under the microscope. In the case of GEBIS, GWBI, associated followers and organizations, they are often lumped together as one entity—viewed overall by some as one large "Buddhist Corporation." Another person I interviewed asked me why people are not looking into how much land is owned by all the Catholics or Protestants on the Island as well. This person was trying to point out that discrimination may be involved in how people are categorized together simply because they are Asian or Buddhist. Other locals have also indicated to me how lucky P.E.I. is to have new land owners that care so much about the environment and see the Buddhists moving to the Island as a positive step forward, especially for organic farming.

The aforementioned short documentary from CBC offers another perspective, describing how a "come from away" community is breathing new life into struggling rural communities (CBC 2015). The construction industry is noted as seeing an upswing in the Eastern part of the Island due to the large number of buildings and land holdings the Buddhists are developing. This explanation fits with my own research, which points to the food projects previously discussed, as another example of how the community continues to both integrate and support particular aspects of P.E.I. communities.

Conclusion

NGOs, activists, interest groups, and in this case, a number of Buddhist organizations now promote transnational or globalized mandates. The Buddhist and ethically centered projects presented in this chapter operate within the bounds of the economic conditions of globalization, capitalism, and neoliberalism. Rather than approach these as purely alternative networks or countermovements, it is important to note that people must still navigate the existing economic systems. There may also be a shift to "developmentalism" taking place, where these Buddhists offer a counter structure of "social enterprises" that place the environment, people, and nonhuman animals before conventional profits. Their support of organic farmers, poverty relief, and animal welfare initiatives that are not solely economically driven are examples of the possibility of alternative pathways built on a set of Buddhist ethically motivated practices. And while these various groups are under the duress of structural or state-based policies in their movements globally, they are active agents in the process. In this case, this movement and associated organizations take a global approach via local strategies that are implemented on P.E.I. These examples reverse some of the stereotypes and narratives often associated with the notion of the "East" and "West." In part, this is a reversal of Western imperialism that took place in Asia. The Easterner or Asian is no longer viewed as just a subject. Instead, the transnational lens helps recognize this power reversal and explore their agency within the local projects associated with poverty relief and gratitude, animal welfare and sanctuaries, and agricultural businesses.

On the one hand, becoming localized via projects and programs similar to the ones described in this chapter helps migrants gain favor with the preexisting population of Islanders. On the other hand, the "come from away" is seen as "taking over" parts of the Island. There are, thus, both favorable and unfavorable consequences of localization. However, this is not only a moment of tension but also another moment where the global and local are entwined in the constant movement of social relations. Transnational theoretical and methodological approaches that address the global and local forces as processes in a dialectal sense help bring to light the agency of Asian migrants and organizations. This helps explore particular moments and specific communities in an interconnected *glocalized* sense that can be hindered at times by metanational narratives.

Notes

Chapter 1

1 See Peters (2018).
2 Maxey says "Christianity, especially its pietistic Protestant forms ... played a dominant role in shaping conceptions of religion among Japanese elites. Private, doctrinal belief compatible with the universal progress of rational civilization provided the benchmark for gauging authentic religion. Whatever failed to reach that benchmark could be, and frequently was, deemed superstition or simply primitive" (Maxey 2014: 56).
3 See also Cohen (2006: 5).
4 See, for example, Maps of India (2014); Vivekananda Vedanta Society of Chicago (2018); and Wikipedia (2019).

Chapter 2

1 This references Jonathan Z. Smith's 1978 work *Map Is Not Territory: Studies in the History of Religion*, the title of which paraphrases Alfred Korzybski's "The map is not the territory"—a fundamental concept in his founding of the field of general semantics. J. Z. Smith's thought from *Map Is Not Territory*, and from his 1982 *Imagining Religion*, among others, is useful for thinking through what is involved in the act of comparison and for analogies between the scholar's imaginative creation of the category of religion and the construction of East and West.

Chapter 3

1 This chapter is an adaptation of an article entitled, "Buddhism, Meditation, and Global Secularisms," (McMahan 2017). It is adapted with the kind permission of the editors of the journal.
2 For a sampling of recent work reflecting these new articulations of secularism, see Asad (2003); Bender and Taves (2012); Butler et al. (2011); Bubandt and von Beek (2012); Taylor (2007); Warner, VanAntwerpen and Calhoun (2010).
3 Regarding the emerging use of "spiritual" among Buddhist reformers of this period, see McMahan (2012a).
4 For Kabat-Zinn's own account of how he adapted Buddhist meditation techniques to clinical practice, see Kabat-Zinn (2011).
5 For a thoughtful analysis of uniquely Chinese processes of secularization, see Ji (2008).
6 My discussion of these conferences recapitulates and updates my treatment of them in McMahan (2016).

7   Ji Zhe suggests that the co-organizer, China Religious Culture Communication Association, is a front for the RAB (Religious Affairs Bureau) (Ji 2011: 43) and that the conferences are essentially a matter of the Communist Party of China's use of Buddhism for political purposes. Nevertheless, he argues, Buddhists do get some benefit from it as well in that it allows them a public forum otherwise unavailable (Ji 2011: 43–44).

Chapter 4

1   Throughout this essay, I use "Modern" and "Modernist" to specifically refer to the institutions and modes of behavior that developed in postfeudal Europe and have been subsequently globalized (Giddens 1991: 14–15). I use upper case on these words to denote their specificity and to distinguish my usage in these instances from a more vague and general reference to the "modern" as something up to date.
2   For an example in state attempts to restructure "wasteful" funerary practices, see Malarney (1996), and for state attempts at repressing spirit mediumship, see Endres (2006).
3   By "tradition" I mean undifferentiated beliefs and practices, or protoreligions—what existed before "religions" were restructured to fit the Modernist category of "religion."
4   The exceptions are mostly Modernist Zen groups, which have been somewhat successful in attracting young men.
5   I see an overlap between this idea of religion being a function system and Bourdieu's idea of fields in social practice, though they refer to different processes. The former is referring specifically to the construction of society in the Modern period and argues that this construction has become globalized, rather than individual religions becoming homogenized. Bourdieu's field (1990), on the other hand, is used to discuss arenas of power in social practice, with its own specific rules and its own "currencies." Drawing these two ideas together, I think, does not diminish from the strength or purpose of either one but historicizes the field and shows the global discourses around which the Buddhist field has been constructed in locations like Vietnam in the last one-hundred years or so.

Chapter 5

1   See the bibliography for a select list of scholarship on twentieth-century Buddhist-Marxist encounters.
2   On Vidyodaya, see Seneviratne (1999). An introduction to Kosambi's life is available in Kosambi (2010b: 1–52) and in Ober (2013).
3   In total, Kosambi spent nearly eight years on four different trips at Harvard (1910-2, 1919–22, 1926–29, 1933–34) earning a PhD in 1929.
4   My reading of *Indian Civilization and Non-violence* stems from Pandit Viśvanāth Dāmodar Śolāpurkar's Hindi translation of the entire text (Kosambī [1935] 2010) and Meera Kosambi's English translation of the final chapter (Kosambi 2010b: 327–57). When quoting passages from the last chapter, I use Meera Kosambi's English translation for the sake of ease and reference. All other translations refer to the Hindi edition.

5 Kosambi's son, D.D. Kosambi, is typically seen as the "father" of India's Marxist historiography.
6 On Sankrityayan, see Chudal (2016). For a study of his life as it relates to the global Buddhist context, see Ober (2013).
7 As the Kisān Sabhā saw it, the "agrarian problem" referred primarily to issues of bonded labor, population pressures, overtaxation, rural debt, farming techniques, and land ownership.
8 According to Sankrityayan, there were other features also responsible for Buddhism's downfall, but the sangha's material wealth is at the center of his thesis.
9 This idea is remarkably similar to Engels' history of early Christianity (c.f., Boer 2014).
10 During the peak of his political career, from the 1940s until his death in 1956, Dev published a number of influential works on Buddhist history and philosophy. These included a four-volume Hindi translation of Vasubandhu's *Abhidharmakośa* (अभिधर्मकोश based on Poussin's French translation from the Chinese) and a seven-hundred-page tome on Buddhist philosophy (*Bauddhadharma-darśan* बौद्धधर्मदर्शन) that won India's most distinguished literary award from the *Sahitya Akademi* in 1956.

Chapter 7

1 The name of the monastery is a pseudonym.
2 For my PhD study, I did my fieldwork in China, Taiwan, Myanmar, and Thailand between 2013 and 2017 (Lau 2018).
3 Gombrich (1988: 4) notes that Pāli is an ancient derivative of Sanskrit and close to it. Some literature in late medieval Ceylon was composed in Sanskrit.
4 Some historical evidence shows that Mahāyāna Buddhism also spread to some Southeast Asian countries, such as Indonesia and Thailand (Gethin 1998: 224–25).
5 For example, Gombrich (2009: 5–6) argues that the Pāli *suttas* are the key to understanding the Buddha's teachings.
6 Welch (1968) mentioned that Yang Wenhui met Max Müller in the United Kingdom, yet there was no evidence about the meeting, as Chen Jidong confirmed.
7 Yang could not speak Japanese, and Nanjō could not speak Chinese. Yet they could communicate with each other by written Chinese. Most letters between them were published (Yang 2000: 472–507).
8 Nanjō wrote an article on this, see Notes 17, Chen (2017).
9 Ceylon became Sri Lanka after independence in 1948.
10 *Renjian fojiao* is also translated as "Humanistic Buddhism," "This-Worldly Buddhism," or "Buddhism in this world" (Ji 2013).
11 The Japanese *Tipiṭaka* was translated by Takakusu Junjirō (1866–1945). He also contributed to the editing work of *Taishō Shinshū Daizōkyō* (大正新修大藏經).
12 Some learning materials were adapted from Japanese texts, for example, *Shina bukkyōshi no kenkyū* [支那仏教史研究 The Study of Chinese Buddhist History] (Dongchu 1970: 276).
13 Welch mentioned that the college was run from 1939 to 1945 (1968: 286). Yet Yinshun recorded that it was established in 1945 (1950: 516).
14 The twenty-seventh WFB was organized in China in 2014.
15 See Campo (2017) about the birth date of Xuyun.

16 From my fieldwork, Jingyin and Guangxing received their PhD degrees at SOAS University of London. Xueyu received his PhD from the University of Iowa. Jingyin, Guangxing, and Xueyu have been teaching Buddhism at tertiary institutes in Hong Kong. Among the five monks, Jianhua, Xueyu, and Guangxing have disrobed.
17 *Canhautou* is similar to Japanese koan practice but not precisely the same.
18 The only exception I know is Gaomin Monastery at Yangzhou. Delin, the previous abbot, allowed nuns and lay women practicing Chan into the Chan hall.
19 I am grateful for the critical comments from Dr. Douglas M. Gildow and the editors, especially Professor Victor Hori. I thank the kind help from Dr. Chen Jidong and Dr. William Pawlett for providing information.

Chapter 8

1 For this overview of historical events in mid-nineteenth-century Japan, I have drawn on Beasley (1972), Craig (1961), and Jansen (2000).
2 Chōshū had stood against Tokugawa Ieyasu in the Battle of Sekigahara (1600), which led to the Tokugawa's rise to power.
3 Until the third of the twelfth month of 1872—corresponding to January 1, 1873—the lunisolar calendar was in use in Japan. Dates before the change of calendar follow the counting of the months (e.g., "first month").
4 The Meiji Restoration is traditionally equated with Japan's transition from the early modern to the modern period. In reality, however, Japan was already well underway to becoming a "modern" state before the change of regime (Goto-Jones 2009: 24–36).
5 For the history of Shin Buddhism in Chōshū, I have drawn on Kodama (1976), unless otherwise referenced.
6 The documents include such items as an address book.
7 *Kongō* is the Japanese rendering of the Sanskrit term *vajra*, the weapon of the Vedic deity Indra who was absorbed in East Asian Buddhism.
8 Mokurai's adoptive son Shimaji Daitō (島地大等 1875-1927) claimed that this was indeed the case and that Mokurai often referred to Yoshida Shōin in his writings (Yoshida 1967: 352).
9 Traditional narratives hold that the surveillance and protection from the Tokugawa authorities led Buddhism into a state of "general lethargy and uncreativeness" (e.g., Bellah [1957] 1985: 51).
10 Like a domain, Nishi Honganji employed its own retainers.
11 Kido was the first Japanese dignitary to have a Buddhist funeral in 1877 after the ban on cremation (an anti-Buddhist measure) was lifted in 1875. The organization of his funeral was entrusted to Nishi Honganji, and Mokurai assisted the abbot in conducting the service (Futaba and Fukushima 1973, vol. V: 859; Koretsune 2001: 31).
12 Translations and quotes in this section are from Breen (1998).
13 While this draft Constitution was never to be implemented, the Iwakura Embassy "served the Buddhist cause extremely well" (Breen 1998: 162), enabling Buddhism to renegotiate its relationship with the state.
14 The three doctrinal standards were the basic principles of "the Great Teaching": (1) comply with the principle of honoring the *kami* and loving the nation; (2) clarify the Principle of Heaven and the Way of Man; (3) serve the emperor and obey the will of the Court (Futaba and Fukushima 1973, vol. I: 15–26).

15 For example, Hardacre argues that Buddhist reformers "tried to rebuild Buddhism, in line with the new government, by 'modernizing' themselves through foreign study, and by encouraging the religion to take on new social roles," bringing Buddhism "into line with secularists' ideas of the proper sort of religion for modern Japan" (2011: 7).

Chapter 9

1 I would like to express my gratitude to the participants of the conference *Buddhism in the Global Eye: Beyond East and West*, for their attention and comments to my presentation, and the organizers, John Harding, Victor Hori, Jessica Main, and Alexander Soucy. I particularly want to thank James Ketelaar, Wendy Doniger, Bruce Lincoln, Christian Wedemeyer, and Micah Auerback for their feedback during the work on this project, as well as the students of the Problems in the History of Religions seminar at the University of Chicago. Part of it was presented at the Japanese Studies Interdisciplinary Colloquium at the University of Michigan and at the Seminar for the Study of Japanese Religion and Culture 2016, at the Center for Information on Religion, Tokyo. The comments and responses of the participants to both conferences have been precious. Last, I want to express my thankfulness to Adam Miller and Kyle Peters for their help in copyediting the paper and to Kyōhei Mikawa, Bruce Winkelman, and Hiroyoshi Nōtō for their suggestions on the translation of Nanjō's poem, for whose final result and possible errors I take full responsibility. In most sources, Nanjō Bunyū's name is spelled with an older Romanization: Nanjio Bunyiu.
2 In addition to Nanjō's autobiography, information for this biographical sketch has been taken from M. Zumoto (2004) and F. Max Müller (1884: 178–203).
3 "*Kodō hajime wo shiran to yōsu / Ikyō gosha ni afuru / Bunken shirushi tareri to iedomo / Denyaku rogyo ooshi / Uiki yaku ba tae / Fusō icho nashi / Ware ware sudeni koto ni shitagai / Kokoku ani ango sen ya / Gyofuku mi hōmuru subekaraku / Hyōzen unsui no gotoshi / Tazunekitaru banri no soto / Utsushietari sennen no sho / Honyaku jinmi nashi / Genbun mo mata dayo / Mui nan no hi ni ka tassen / Sanjussai kyosho wo tsuiyasu*"
古道要知初。遺經溢五車。文獻雖足徵。傳譯多魯魚。禹域譯場絕。
扶桑無異儲。吾儕已從事。故國豈安居。魚腹身須葬。飄然雲水如。
尋來萬里外。寫得千年書。翻譯真味無。原文亦唾餘。無爲何日達。
卅歲費居諸。
    (Nanjio 1979: 130–31).
4 On the issue of the scientific value of the study of language according to Müller, see van den Bosch (2002: esp. 185–278).
5 For the interpretation of discourses of universality opposed to particularity within modern Japanese intellectual history, I am particularly indebted to James Ketelaar and Naoki Sakai. See in particular: Ketelaar (2006; 1990: esp. Chapter 5) and Sakai (1997: esp. 153–76).
6 On the formation of the model of world religions, see Masuzawa (2005).
7 For a list of Nanjō's works, see also Izumi Hōkei (1928).
8 It must be noted though, as Michael Pye does, that Nanjō's catalogue rendering of sutra titles in Sanskrit was problematic, and his catalogue has been superseded. See Pye (2003: 16).
9 On the influence of Nanjō Bunyū's scholarship in the development of modern Buddhist Studies in China, see Goldfuss (2001) and Wilkinson (2015).

10 On the theological basis of Müller's science of religion: Olender (1992: 90–92) and Kippenberg (2002: 43–49).
11 See van den Bosch (2002: 326–59). See also Turner (2014).
12 On the definition of religion in the Meiji period, see: Maxey (2014); Josephson (2012); Isomae (2003). An English translation of this work is also available: Isomae (2014). On the debate on secularization, see Krämer (2015); Deneckere (2014).
13 Nanjō was among the first receivers of the newly created doctorate in literature by the Japanese Ministry of Education in 1888 and was appointed lecturer and director of different leading academic institutions. See Tsunemitsu (1968: 251–53).
14 See also Sueki (2004: 86–109).

Chapter 10

1 As we will see, the meaning of "Chinese" here is remarkably complex. Because this case study is situated in a diasporic context, our working definition of "Chinese" cannot be limited to the narrow sense of people from Mainland China. Rather, this chapter adopts an expansive use of the term that aims to reflect the usage of DRBA members themselves: namely, including anyone of Chinese ethnic heritage, even if born outside China, sometimes referred to as "Chinese of Different Nationalities (CDN)," see Tan (2007). Thus, here it includes Vietnamese of Chinese ancestry, Malaysian Chinese, Taiwanese, Australian-, European-, or American-born Chinese, in addition to Chinese from Mainland China.
2 Although, historically, we know Buddhism was practiced in North America long before the arrival of Hsuan Hua, our current interest is to explore a historical *imaginaire*. Our goal, in other words, is to attend to how the DRBA tells its own story—both historically and hagiographically—in order to glean how DRBA members themselves see their place in the world.
3 Seminal works in this spirit include those of Robert Sharf (1995a, c), who critiqued romantic and psychologistic assumptions undergirding Zen Studies in the West; Bernard Faure (1993), Alan Cole (2009), Wendi Adamek (2007), and John McRae (2003), who, among other contributions, applied a hermeneutic of suspicion to Buddhist historiography; Tomoko Masuzawa (2005), Philip C. Almond (1988), and others who exposed the Eurocentric biases in the creation and use of the categories "Religion" and "Buddhism" themselves (though, for a salient counterpoint, see Barrett and Tarocco [2012]). As we will see, however, this wave is but one side of a larger debate.
4 See David McMahan (2008) and Victor Hori (2010).
5 Elsewhere (Verchery 2015), I discuss the populations excluded by these models, which include the children of non-Asian Buddhist converts as well as many Asians—including large contingents of the DRBA—who convert to Buddhism, *contra* the "baggage Buddhism" (Nattier 1998) or "traditionalist" (Sugunasiri 2006) models that assume Buddhism in Asia to be a passive cultural inheritance.
6 Hori writes, "in a culture which reveres the autonomy of the self and individual choice, Western/convert Buddhism, just because it is the personal choice of an individual, fits the notion of real religion. By contrast, Asian/ethnic Buddhism is depicted as if it were not authentic religion" (Hori 2010: 21). To further complicate

this picture, the privileging of individual choice is no longer confined to the "American understanding"—as Hori, quoting Bellah et al. (1985), puts it—but is now shared by Asians as well, including Chinese DRBA members, for whom issues of individual choice and sincerity are central for differentiating genuine commitment to Buddhist practice from casual, mainstream Buddhism.

7   Hallisey calls this "latent Orientalism," wherein even the critique of Western fantasies of the "Orient" perpetuates the idea that an "account of Buddhism [can] be made without any reference to the people and places from which it is imagined to emanate," ironically "denying any voice to 'Orientals' in the Western apprehension of what they are about . . . paradoxically leav[ing] the West-Orient divide in place as a paradigm instead of problematizing it or removing it altogether" (Hallisey 1995: 31–32).

8   To mention but two of many examples, see Gombrich and Obeyesekere's (1988) famous study of "Protestant Buddhism" or how the Chinese state appropriated the discursive paradigms of "religion" and "superstition" for purposes of religious reform and political control (Goossaert and Palmer 2011; Nedostup 2009; Poon 2011).

9   The notion of "culture"—and, by extension, that of the "intercultural"—is of course not unproblematic. While we must attend to the manifold critiques of "culture" as an essentialized, bounded, totalizing, or static category, recall that our concern here is to investigate the ways in which categories—even those inadequate for scholarly or historical analysis—have been appropriated, transformed, and made meaningful by the communities under study.

10 Although Hsuan Hua holds transmission in the Guiyang lineage (潙仰宗 *Guiyang zong*)—the oldest of the traditional five "houses" of Chinese *Chan* Buddhism (禪宗五家 *Chanzong wujia*)—he was nonsectarian in his teachings and emphasized the integration of all "Five Schools" of Buddhism (禪教律密淨, *chan, jiao, lu, mi, jing*, the *Chan* school, the Teaching school, the *Vinaya* school, the Esoteric school, and the Pure Land school).

11 Saliently, upon emerging from this period of isolation, Hsuan Hua once again began calling himself a "living dead person," a return to the motif of his near-death experience as a teenager.

12 Hsuan Hua's first generation of monastic disciples in San Francisco—the famous "first five" who ordained at Haihui Monastery near Keelung, Taiwan, in 1969—include Venerable Heng Chi (恆持法師), likely the first American woman to have ever received full monastic ordination in the Chinese Buddhist tradition.

13 Note that in some DRBA temples—most notably *Wanfo Sheng Cheng*—liturgies are occasionally performed in English (though most Asian branches only use Chinese). Even in North America, however, only a minority of monastics are fluent in English, and many simply memorize the English liturgy (which, we might add, is also not uncommon for Chinese speakers who do not read literary Chinese; many Buddhists throughout Asia recite sutras without the ability to "read" them.) Another fascinating aspect of the DRBA's history, which lies beyond the scope of this chapter, is its long-standing connection with the Vietnamese-Chinese Buddhist community, including its resettlement program for Vietnamese and Indo-Chinese refugees (the "Boat People") fleeing to the United States following the fall of Saigon in 1975.

14 For example, Ketelaar (1991); Sharf (1995a, b, c); Heisig and Maraldo 1995; Faure (1993, 1995); Victoria (2006); Ives (2001a, b, 2002, 2009).

15 We might situate this view within a larger scholarly bias that understands the *political*—issues of power, authority, and struggles for legitimation and influence—as implicitly more *real* or *true* than other kinds of human motivation. As Hori succinctly observes, "when a scholar explains the behavior of a religious community, for example, as implicit political protest, or as an attempt by a marginal group to gain social identity, or as the compensatory act of people with weak self-esteem creating a substitute family for themselves, the scholar thereby *de facto* implies that the political, or sociological, or psychological explanation is the real explanation and that the practitioner's own explanation is not" (Hori 1996: 247).

16 During fieldwork, a long-time lay devotee described the first time she laid eyes on the Master. She had wandered into the San Francisco temple, and although Hsuan Hua was not there, she caught sight of his photograph. It gave her chills, she said. The image so embodied her idea of a perfect Buddhist sage, she recalled, that she assumed he must have lived "a long, long time ago." Similarly, a DRBA nun recalled that although born and raised in southern China before the religious iconoclasm of the Cultural Revolution—where she had no shortage of exposure to Buddhist monastics—it wasn't until she met Master Hua that she realized "what a real monk looks like."

17 Venerable Hsu Yun's portraits are hung throughout DRBA temples and members prostrate to him daily during morning ceremony (*zaoke* 早課). The DRBA also holds Hsu Yun's *sarira* relics (*sheli* 舍利) and regularly displays them along with the official lineage transmission certificate Hsu Yun bestowed to Hsuan Hua (copies of the certificate are also typically framed and hung in branch temples.)

18 See Ong and Nonini (1997), Dean (2010), Sharf (1995a). As Dean also notes, those in the motherland, in turn, often look to diasporic enclaves in an effort to recover their own traditions, a phenomenon that is common in the DRBA.

19 Here I build on the insights of scholars who have critiqued this persistent opposition of the global and local (e.g., McKeown 2001; Braun 2009).

20 Excellent work in Daoist studies has explored how tourism has transformed religious identity, creating what Ken Dean calls a new "cosmopolitanism" among Daoist ritual specialists who travel so much between temples that they have become "global citizens" (2012). We find a similar situation in the DRBA: during my fieldwork travels between DRBA temples in Taiwan, Malaysia, California, and Hong Kong, I regularly bumped into monastics and laypeople I had met at temples in other countries.

21 This is so common that as DRBA members learned more about my research itinerary, which had me doing fieldwork in California and several branch temples throughout Asia, I was loaded up with several hundred Buddha-shaped pieces of consecrated cloth, destined for DRBA members in Asia to use for the meritorious activity of sutra copying. Along with the cloths, I carried instructions for the precepts to be observed while copying, which I was also tasked with explaining in person—unwittingly becoming an active agent in this worldwide network.

22 Indeed, many members are on a first-name basis with those in other countries, and they maintain these relationships through both travel and online activities, such as chat rooms, watching DRBA events streamed from around the world, and participating in online Sutra translation workshops. These activities are especially important for Hsuan Hua's followers in countries that do not have official DRBA branch temples, and many specific online groups are set up with the intention of including DRBA members in such places, including South America, Europe, Singapore, Vietnam, and Mainland China.

Chapter 11

1. There is a Shambhala meditation group on the Island. There are now also about ninety Sri Lankans living on P.E.I, who participate in Buddhist practice mainly in their homes and have been working to create a community space for practicing together. See CBC News (2015b).

Bibliography

Adamek, W. L. (2007), *The Mystique of Transmission: On an Early Chan History and Its Contexts*, New York: Columbia University Press.

Almond, P. C. (1988), *The British Discovery of Buddhism*, Cambridge: Cambridge University Press.

Aloysius, G. (1998), *Religion as Emancipatory Identity: A Buddhist Movement Among the Tamils under Colonialism*, New Delhi: New Age International Publishers.

Ambedkar, B. (1987), *Dr. Babasaheb Ambedkar Writings and Speeches*, vol. 3, Mumbai: Education Department, Government of Maharashtra.

Amstutz, G. D. (1997), *Interpreting Amida: History and Orientalism in the Study of Pure Land Buddhism*, Albany: State University of New York Press.

Anderson, C. S. (2013), "The Possibility of a Postcolonial Buddhist Ethic of Wealth," *Buddhist Christian Studies*, 33: 139–52.

App, U. (2010), *The Birth of Orientalism*, Philadelphia and Oxford: University of Pennsylvania Press.

App, U. (2014), *The Cult of Emptiness: The Western Discovery of Buddhist Thought and the Invention of Oriental Philosophy*, Rorschach, Switzerland: University Media.

Appadurai, A. (1996), *Modernity at Large: Cultural Dimensions of Globalization*, Minneapolis: University of Minnesota Press.

Asad, T. (2003), *Formations of the Secular: Christianity, Islam, Modernity*, Stanford: Stanford University Press.

Ashiwa, Y. and D. L. Wank (2005), "The Globalization of Chinese Buddhism: Clergy and Devotee Networks in the Twentieth Century," *International Journal of Asian Studies*, 2 (2): 217–37.

Ashiwa, Y. and D. L. Wank, eds. (2009), *Making Religion, Making the State: The Politics of Religion in Modern China*, California: Stanford University Press.

Axford, B. (2013), *Theories of Globalization*, London: Polity Press.

Baldacchino, G. (2015), "A 'Stopover Place' at Best? Recent Trends in Immigrant Attraction and Retention on Prince Edward Island," in E. Tastsoglou, A. Dobrowolsky and B. Cottrell (eds.), *The Warmth of the Welcome: Is Atlantic Canada a Home Away from Home for Immigrants?*, 206–30, Sydney, Nova Scotia: Cape Breton University Press.

Bao, J. (2015), *Creating a Buddhist Community: A Thai Temple in Silicon Valley*, Philadelphia: Temple University Press.

Barnett, R. (2012), "Mimetic Re-enchantment: The Contemporary Chinese State and Tibetan Religious Leadership," in N. Bubandt and M. von Beek (eds.), *Varieties of Secularism in Asia: Anthropological Explorations of Religion, Politics and the Spiritual*, 29–54, New York: Routledge.

Barrett, T. H. and F. Tarocco (2012), "Terminology and Religious Identity: Buddhism and the Genealogy of the Term Zongjiao," in V. Krech and M. Steinicke (eds.), *Dynamics in the History of Religions between Asia and Europe: Encounters, Notions, and Comparative Perspectives*, 307–19, Leiden: Brill.

Barrows, J. H., ed. (1893), *The World's Parliament of Religions*, 2 vols., Toronto: Hunter Rose and Co.

Basch, L., N. Glick Schiller and C. Szanton Blanc (1994), *Nations Unbound: Transnational Projects, Postcolonial Predicaments, and Deterritorialized Nation-states*, London: Gordon and Breach.

Batchelor, S. (1997), *Buddhism Without Belief: A Contemporary Guide to Awakening*, New York: Riverhead Books.

Batchelor, S. (2015), *After Buddhism: Rethinking the Dharma for a Secular Age*, New Haven: Yale University Press.

Baumann, M. (2001), "Global Buddhism: Developmental Periods, Regional Histories, and a New Analytical Perspective," *Journal of Global Buddhism*, 2: 1–43.

Beasley, W. G. (1972), *The Meiji Restoration*, Stanford: Stanford University Press.

Bellah, R. N., R. Madsen, W. M. Sullivan, A. Swiller and S. M. Tipton (1985), *Habits of the Heart: Individualism and Commitment in American Life*, Berkeley: University of California Press.

Bellah, R. N. ([1957] 1985), *Tokugawa Religion: The Values of Pre-industrial Japan*, Glencoe: The Free Press.

Bender, C. and A. Taves (2012), *What Matters? Ethnographies of Value in a Not So Secular Age*, New York: Columbia University Press.

Berger, P. L., ed. (1999), *The Desecularization of the World: Resurgent Religion and World Politics*, Grand Rapids: Wm. B. Eerdmans Publishing Company.

Beyer, P. (2006), *Religions in Global Society*, Abingdon: Routledge.

Bharati, A. (1976), "Monastic and Lay Buddhism in the 1971 Sri Lanka Insurgency," in B. L. Smith (ed.), *Religion and Social Conflict in South Asia*, 101–12, Leiden: Brill.

Bhaṭṭācārya, Ā. (2005), *Mahāpaṇḍit Rāhul Sāṅkrityāyān ke Vyaktitvāntaraṇ kī prakriyā* [महापंडित राहुल सांकृत्यायन के व्यक्तित्वांतरण की प्रक्रिया Mahapandit Rahul Sankrityayan's Science of Transcending the Individual], Kolkātā: Ānand Prakāśan.

Bhattacharya, R. (1994), "From Buddha to Marx," in A. Chattopadhyaya (ed.), *Essays on Indology: Birth Centenary Tribute to Mahapandita Rahula Sankrityayan*, 118–21, Calcutta: Manisha Granthalaya.

Bhushan, N., J. L. Garfield and A. Zablocki (2009), *TransBuddhism: Transmission, Translation, Transformation*, Amherst: University of Massachusetts Press.

Birnbaum, R. (2003), "Buddhist China at the Century's Turn," *China Quarterly*, 174: 428–50.

Bliss and Wisdom Sangha (2017), "More about Bliss and Wisdom," September 20. Available online: http://bwsangha.org/eng/credence/a/788-1019 (accessed April 23, 2019).

Boer, R. (2014), "Revolutionary Christianity: Friedrich Engels and the Aufhebung of Religion," *Political Theology Today*, June 18. Available online: http://www.politicaltheology.com/blog/revolutionary-christianity-friedrich-engels-and-the-aufhebung-of-religion/ (accessed May 16, 2017).

Borch, C. (2011), *Niklas Luhmann*, London and New York: Routledge.

Bourdieu, P. (1990), *The Logic of Practice*, Stanford: Stanford University Press.

Braun, E. (2009), "Local and Translocal in the Study of Theravada Buddhism and Modernity," *Religion Compass*, 3: 1–16.

Braun, E. (2013), *The Birth of Insight: Meditation, Modern Buddhism, and the Burmese Monk Ledi Sayadaw*, Chicago: The University of Chicago Press.

Breen, J. (1998), "'Earnest Desires': The Iwakura Embassy and Japanese Religious Policy," *Japan Forum*, 10 (2): 151–65.

Breen, J. (2000), "Ideologues, Bureaucrats and Priests: On 'Shinto' and 'Buddhism' in Early Meiji Japan," in J. N. Breen and M. Teeuwen (eds.), *Shinto in History: Ways of the Kami*, 230–51, Richmond, Surrey: Curzon.

Bronx, T. and E. Williams-Oerberg (2016), "Buddhism, Business, and Economics," in M. Jerryson (ed.), *The Oxford Handbook of Contemporary Buddhism*, 504–17, New York: Oxford University Press.

Broughton, B. L. (1940), "Vì sao Tôi Tin Phật giáo" [Why I believe in Buddhism], *Đuốc Tuệ*, 142–43 (15 October and 1 November): 3–22.

Bruce, S. (2017), *Secular Beats Spiritual: The Westernization of the Easternization of the West*, Oxford: Oxford University Press.

Bubandt, N. and M. von Beek (2012), *Varieties of Secularism in Asia: Anthropological Explorations of Religion, Politics and the Spiritual*, Abingdon: Routledge.

Buddhist Association of China, The [中國佛協], ed. (2003), *Zhongguo fojiao xiehui wushinian* [中國佛協五十年 Fifty Years of The Buddhist Association of China], Beijing: The Buddhist Association of China.

Buddhist Text Translation Society [Fojing fanyi wenyuanhui 佛經翻譯委員會] (1973), *Xuan Hua Chanshi Shiji* [宣化禪師事蹟 Records of the Life of the Venerable Master Hsuan Hua], Talmage: Buddhist Text Translation Society.

Buddhist Text Translation Society [Fojing fanyi wenyuanhui 佛經翻譯委員會] (1995), *Zhuisi Jinian Zhuanji, Xuan Hua Lao Heshang, Di Yi Ce* [追思紀念專集, 宣化老和尚, 第一冊 In Memory of the Venerable Master Hsuan Hua, Volume 1], Talmage: Buddhist Text Translation Society.

Butler, J., J. Habermas, C. Taylor and C. West (2011), *The Power of Religion in the Public Sphere*, New York: Columbia University Press.

Cabezón, J. I. (2008), "State Control of Tibetan Buddhist Monasticism in the People's Republic of China," in M. Mei-Hui Yang (ed.), *Chinese Religiosities: Afflictions of Modernity and State Formation*, 261–91, Berkeley and London: University of California Press.

Calhoun, C., M. Juergensmeyer and J. VanAntwerpen (2011), "Introduction," in C. Calhoun, M. Juergensmeyer and J. VanAntwerpen (eds.), *Rethinking Secularism*, 3–30, New York: Oxford University Press.

Campbell, M. (2017), "The Little Monks of Little Sands," *MacLean's*, July 18. Available online: https://www.macleans.ca/news/canada/the-little-monks-of-little-sands/ (accessed September 1, 2017).

Campo, D. (2017), "Chan Master Xuyun: The Embodiment of an Ideal, the Transmission of a Model," in D. Ownby, V. Goossaert and J. Zhe (eds.), *Making Saints in Modern China*, 99–136, New York: Oxford University Press.

CBC Land and Sea (2015), "Come From Away," January 4. Available online: http://www.cbc.ca/player/play/2645847254 (accessed April 23, 2019).

CBC News (2014), "McCain Foods Closing Borden-Carleton French Fry Plant," August 7. Available online: http://www.cbc.ca/news/canada/prince-edward-island/mccain-foods-closing-borden-carleton-french-fry-plant-1.2730051 (accessed September 1, 2017).

CBC News (2015a), "Buddhist Monks Share Corn Crop with Islanders," October 18. Available online: http://www.cbc.ca/news/canada/prince-edward-island/buddhist-monks-share-corn-crop-with-islanders-1.3277055 (accessed April 23, 2019).

CBC News (2015b), "Sri Lankans Hope to Build Buddhist Temple in P.E.I," January 13. Available online: http://www.cbc.ca/news/canada/prince-edward-island/sri-lankans-hope-to-build-buddhist-temple-in-p-e-i-1.2899192 (accessed April 23, 2019).

Chan, W. T. (1953), *Religious Trends in Modern China*, Columbia: Columbia University Press.

Chandavarkar, R. (1998), *Imperial Power and Popular Politics: Class, Resistance and the State in India, c. 1850–1950*, Cambridge: Cambridge University Press.

Chang, L. H., F. H. Wei and C. C. Shih (2011), "Sustainable Business Model for Organic Agriculture—Lee Zen Organic Corporation in Taiwan," *Acta Horticulturae, (ISHS)*, 895: 85–90.

Chao-Yang Buwei [趙楊步偉] (1969), *Yige nuren dizichuan* [一個女人的自傳 An Autobiography of a Lady], Taipei: Chuanji wenxue chubanshe.

Chaudhari, K. K., ed. (1990), *Source Material for a History of the Freedom Movement in India. Vol. XI, Civil Disobedience Movement, April – September 1930*, Bombay: Gazetteers Department, Government of Maharashtra.

Chen Chialuen [陳家倫] (2012), "Nanchuan fojiao zaitaiwan difazhan yuyingxiang" [南傳佛教在臺灣的發展與影響 The Development and Influences of Southern Buddhism in Taiwan], *Taiwanese Sociology*, 24: 155–206.

Chen, J. (2017), "The Dawn of Modern Buddhism: Contacts Between Chinese and Japanese Buddhism in the Late Nineteenth Century," *Studies in Chinese Religions*, 3 (1): 1–25.

Chen, K. (1964), *Buddhism in China: A Historical Survey*, Princeton: Princeton University Press.

Ch'en, K. S. (1973), *The Chinese Transformation of Buddhism*, Princeton: Princeton University Press.

Chen Yan [陈彦] (2006), "Minzuzhuyi Youhuo Yu Rentongweiji" [民族主义诱惑与认同危机 The Temptation of Nationalism and The Crisis of Identity], *Modern China Studies*, 1. Available online: http://www.modernchinastudies.org/us/issues/past-issues/91-mcs-2006-issue-1/941-2012-01-05-15-35-10.html (accessed March 5, 2018).

Choesang, Y. (2017), "We've Never Had any Ties to Chinese Communist Party: Bliss and Wisdom," *Tibet Post International*, October 22. Available online: http://www.thetibetpost.com/en/outlook/interviews-and-recap/5741-weve-never-had-any-ties-to-chinese-communist-party-bliss-a-wisdom (accessed April 23, 2017).

Chowdhuri, S. R. (2007), *Leftism in India, 1917–1947*, New York: Palgrave Macmillan.

Chudal, A. A. (2016), *A Freethinking Cultural Nationalist: A Life History of Rahul Sankrityayan*, New Delhi: Oxford University Press.

Cohen, R. (2006), *Beyond Enlightenment: Buddhism, Religion, Modernity*, London and New York: Routledge.

Cole, A. (2009), *Fathering Your Father: The Zen of Fabrication in Tang Buddhism*, Berkeley: University of California Press.

Coleman, J. W. (2001), *The New Buddhism: The Western Transformation of an Ancient Tradition*, New York: Oxford University Press.

Collins, S. (2010), *Nirvana: Concept, Imagery, Narrative*, Cambridge: Cambridge University Press.

Communist Party of China [中国共产党] (1978), "Jiefangsixiang, Shishiqiushi, Tuanjiuyizhi Xiangqiankan" [解放思想，实事求是，团结一切向前看 Emancipate the Mind, Seek Truth from Facts and Unite as One in Looking to the Future]. Available online: http://cpc.people.com.cn/GB/64184/64186/66677/4493867.html (accessed March 5, 2018).

Communist Party of China [中国共产党] (1981), "Guanyu Jianguoyilai Dangde Ruogan Lishijueyi" [关于建国以来党的若干历史问题的决议 Resolution on Certain Questions in the History of Our Party since the Founding of the People's Republic of China]. Available online: http://cpc.people.com.cn/GB/64162/64168/64563/65374/4526452.html (accessed March 5, 2018).

Communist Party of China [中国共产党] (2017), "Guanyu Shishi Zhonghua Youxu Chuantonwenhua Chuanchengfazhan Gongcheng de Yijian" [关于实施中华优秀传统文化传承发展工程的意见 On the Views of the Implementation of Projects to Promote and Development of Chinese Excellent Traditional Culture]. Available online: http://cpc.people.com.cn/n1/2017/0125/c64094-29049531.html (accessed March 5, 2018).

Connell, R. (1987), *Gender and Power: Society, the Person and Sexual Politics*, Stanford: Stanford University Press.

Craig, A. M. (1961), *Chōshū in the Meiji Restoration*, Cambridge: Harvard University Press.

Dalai Lama, His Holiness the Fourteenth [Bstan-'dzin-rgyat-mtsho] (2005), *The Universe in a Single Atom: The Convergence of Science and Spirituality*, New York: Morgan Road Books.

Đặng Nghiêm Vạn (2001), *Ethnological and Religious Problems in Vietnam*, Hanoi: Social Sciences Publishing House.

De Bary, Wm T., D. Keene, G. Tanabe and P. Varley, eds. ([1958] 2001), *Sources of Japanese Tradition, Volume one: From Earliest Times to 1600*, 2nd ed., New York: Columbia University Press.

Dean, K. (2010), "The Return Visits of Overseas Chinese to Ancestral Villages in Putian, Fujian," in T. Oakes and D. Sutton (eds.), *Faiths on Display: Tourism and Religion in Contemporary China*, 254–75, London: Routledge.

Dean, K. (2012), "Daoism, Local Religious Movements, and Transnational Chinese Society: The Circulation of Daoist Priests, Three-in-one Self-Cultivators, and Spirit Mediums between Fujian and Southeast Asia," in D. A. Palmer and X. Liu (eds.), *Daoism in the Twentieth Century: Between Eternity and Modernity*, 251–73, Berkeley: University of California Press.

Dear, D. (2012), "Chinese Yangsheng: Self-help and Self-image," *Asian Medicine: Tradition and Modernity*, 7 (1): 1–33.

Deneckere, M. (2014), "Shin Buddhist Contributions to the Japanese Enlightenment Movement of the Early 1870s," in M. Hayashi, E. Ōtani and P. Swanson (eds.), *Modern Buddhism in Japan*, 17–51, Nagoya: Nanzan Institute for Religion and Culture.

DeVido, E. (2007), "Buddhism for This World: The Buddhist Revival in Vietnam, 1920–51 and Its Legacy," in Philip Taylor (ed.), *Modernity and Re-enchantment: Religion in Post-Revolutionary Vietnam*, 250–96, Singapore: Institute of Southeast Asian Studies.

DeVido, E. (2009), "The Influence of Chinese Master Taixu on Buddhism in Vietnam," *Journal of Global Buddhism*, 10: 413–58.

Dhamma.org. (n.d.), "Vipassana Meditation as Taught by S.N. Goenka in the Tradition of Sayagyi U Ba Khin," Available online: http://www.dhamma.org/en-US/locations/directory (accessed June 23, 2017).

Dharma Light Monthly (2000), "Fangwen Lin Chung-on jiaoshou tanxuelicheng" [訪問林崇安教授談學佛歷程 An interview with Professor Lin Chung-on about the Journey of Learning Buddhism], *Dharma Light Monthly*, 12: 1–6. Available online: http://www.ss.ncu.edu.tw/~calin/article2008/00.pdf (accessed January 23, 2017).

Dongchu [東初] (1970), *Zhongri Fojiao Jiaotongshi* [中日佛教交通史 A history of Transportation Sino-Japan Buddhism], Taipei: Dongchu Publishing.

DuBois, T. D. (2011), *Religion and the Making of Modern East Asia*, Cambridge: Cambridge University Press.

Dutton, G., J. S. Werner and J. K. Whitmore (2012), *Sources of Vietnamese Tradition*, New York: Columbia University Press.

Eisenstadt, S. N. (2000), "Multiple Modernities," *Daedalus*, 129 (1): 1–29.
Endres, K. (2001), "Local Dynamics of Renegotiating Ritual Space in Northern Vietnam: The Case of the *Dinh*," *Sojourn*, 16 (1): 70–101.
Endres, K. (2006), "Spirit Performances and the Ritual Construction of Personal Identity in Modern Vietnam," in K. Fjelstad and Nguyễn Thị Hiền (eds.), *Possessed by the Spirits: Mediumship in Contemporary Vietnamese Communities*, 77–93, Ithaca: Southeast Asia Program Publications, Cornell University.
Fafang [法舫] ([1936] 2006), "Du Xialuo Xilan liang liuxuetuan baogaoshu" [讀暹邏錫蘭兩留學團報告書 Reading the report of two visiting study tours in Siam and Ceylon], in Huang Xianian [黃夏年] (ed.), *Minguo Fojiao Qikan wenxian jicheng* [民國佛教期刊文獻集 Collected Literature of Buddhist Journals in Republican Era], vol. 195: 271, Beijing: Quanguo tushuguan.
Fafang [法舫] (2013), *Fafangdashiwenji* [法舫大師文集 Collected Works of Master Fafang], 6 vols., Kaohsiung: Buddha's Light Publishing.
Faure, B. (1993), *Chan Insights and Oversights: An Epistemological Critique of the Chan Tradition*, Princeton: Princeton University Press.
Faure, B. (1995), "The Kyoto School and Reverse Orientalism," in C. Wei-hsun Fu and S. Heine (eds.), *Japan in Traditional and Postmodern Perspectives*, 245–82, Albany: State University of New York Press.
Fayin [法音] (2017), "Zhongguo foxie fu huizhang Li Rongxi jushi zaijingshishi" [中國佛協副會長李榮熙居士在京逝世 The passing away of layman Mr Li Rongxi the Vice President of The Buddhist Association of China in Beijing]. Available online: http://www.yxjs.org/big5/fayin.htm (accessed October 7, 2017).
Feng Chuan [冯川] (1998), "Bianzhe de Hua" [编者的话 Translator's Prologue], in E. Fromm, D. T. Suzuki and R. de Martino, trans. Feng Chuan [冯川] and Huang Leiquan [黄雷泉], *Chanzong yu Jingshenfenxi* [禅宗与精神分析 Chan Buddhism and Psychoanalysis], 1–6, Guizhou: Guizhou People"s Press.
Fields, R. (1987), "The Future of American Buddhism," *Vajradhatu Sun*, 9 (1): 1, 22, 24–6.
Fisher, G. (2011), "Religion as Repertoire: Resourcing the Past in a Beijing Buddhist Temple," *Modern China*, 38 (3): 346–76.
Food Banks Canada (2016), *Hunger Count. Food Banks Canada*. Available online: https://www.foodbankscanada.ca/ (accessed April 23, 2017).
Futaba Kenkō and Fukushima Kanryū, eds. (1973), *Shimaji Mokurai Zenshū* [島地黙雷全集 Collected Works of Shimaji Mokurai], 5 vols. and 1 supplement, Kyoto: Honganji Shuppan Kyōkai; Nihon Bukkyō Fukyūkai (hatsubai).
Ge Zhaoguang [葛兆光] (1986), *Chanzong yu Zhongguowenhua* [禅宗与中国文化 Chan Buddhism and Chinese Culture], Shanghai: Shanghai People Press.
Ge Zhaoguang [葛兆光] (1989), "Yizhe Xu" [译者序 Translator's Preface], in D. T. Suzuki, trans. Ge Zhaoguang [葛兆光], *Tongxiang Chanxue Zhilu* [通向禅学之路 The Path towards Chan Buddhism], 1–32, Shanghai: Shanghai Guji Press.
Ge Zhaoguang [葛兆光] (2001), *Zhongguo Sixiangshi* [中国思想史 The Intellectual History of China], Shanghai: Fudan University Press.
GEBIS (2014), "Great Enlightenment Buddhist Institute Society," Available online: http://gebisociety.org (accessed 2014).
GEBIS (2018), "Great Enlightenment Buddhist Institute Society," Available online: http://gebisociety.org (accessed July 26, 2018).
Gellner, D. N. (1990), "Introduction: What is the Anthropology of Buddhism About?," *Journal of Anthropological Society of Oxford*, 21 (2): 100–4.
Gethin, R. (1998), *The Foundations of Buddhism*, Oxford: Oxford University Press.

Giddens, A. (1990), *The Consequence of Modernity*, Stanford: Stanford University.
Giddens, A. (1991), *Modernity and Self-Identity: Self and Society in the Late Modern Age*, Stanford: Stanford University Press.
Goenka, S. N. (2002), *Meditation Now: Inner Peace Through Inner Wisdom*, Onalaska: Vipassana Research Institute.
Goldfuss, G. (2001), *Vers un bouddhisme du XXe siècle: Yang Wenhui (1837–1911), réformateur laïque et imprimeur*, Paris: Collège de France, Institut des Hautes Études Chinoises.
Gombrich, R. F. (1988), *Theravāda Buddhism: A Social History from Ancient Benares to Modern Colombo*, London and New York: Routledge.
Gombrich, R. and G. Obeyesekere (1988), *Buddhism Transformed: Religious Change in Sri Lanka*, Princeton: Princeton University Press.
Gombrich, R. F. (2009), *What the Buddha Thought*, London: Equinox.
Goossaert, V. (2006), "1898: The Beginning of the end for Chinese Religion?" *Journal of Asian Studies*, 65: 307–36.
Goossaert, V. and D. A. Palmer (2011), *The Religious Question in Modern China*, Chicago: University of Chicago Press.
Goto-Jones, C. (2009), *Modern Japan: A Very Short Introduction*, Oxford: Oxford University Press.
Government of Canada (2018), "Schedule 6: Detailed Financial Information—Great Enlightenment Buddhist Institute Society," Available online: https://apps.cra-arc.gc.ca/ebci/haip/srch/t3010form23sched6-eng.action?b=837671320RR0001andfpe=2016-12-31andn=Great+Enlightenment+Buddhist+Institute+Society (accessed January 3, 2018).
The Guardian (2012), "Buddhists Host Neighbourhood Tea," January 10. Available online: http://www.theguardian.pe.ca/Living/2012-01-10/article-2859277/Buddhists-host-neighbourhood-tea/1 (accessed September 1, 2018).
The Guardian (2013a), "Province Finalizes Deal with Moonlight International Foundation to Take Over Buffaloland Provincial Park," June 4. Available online: http://www.theguardian.pe.ca/News/Local/2013-06-04/article-3269170/Province-finalizes-deal-with-Moonlight-International-Foundation-to-take-over-Buffaloland-Provincial-Park/1 (accessed September 1, 2017).
The Guardian (2013b), "Buddhist Monks Look to Take Over Buffaloland Park," May 30. Available online: https://www.theguardian.pe.ca/news/local/buddhist-monks-look-to-take-over-buffaloland-park-95718/ (accessed April 27, 2019).
Habib, I. (1998), "The Left and the National Movement," *Social Scientist*, 26 (5 and 6): 3–33.
Hackett, R. F. (1971), *Yamagata Aritomo in the Rise of Modern Japan*, 1838–1922, Cambridge: Harvard University Press.
Hallisey, C. (1995), "Roads Not Taken in the Study of Theravada Buddhism," in D. S. Lopez (ed.), *Curators of the Buddha: The Study of Buddhism Under Colonialism*, 31–62, Chicago: University of Chicago Press.
Hamashita, T. (2008), *China, East Asia and Global Economy*, L. Grove and M. Selden (eds.), New York: Routledge.
Hammerstrom, E. (2015), *The Science of Chinese Buddhism: Early Twentieth-Century Engagements*, New York: Columbia University Press.
Hao Weimin [郝唯民] (2015), "Fafangfashi yu ZhongShi fojiaoyinyuan" [法舫法師與中斯佛教因緣 Venerable Fafang and the Relation of Sino-Ceylon Buddhism], in Jianlou Liang [梁建樓] (ed.), *Juehaifafang* [覺海法舫 Dharma Boat (Fafang) in the Awakening Ocean], 213–18, Beijing: Tuanjie Publishing.

Hardacre, H. (2011), "The Formation of Secularity in Japan," paper presented at *Secularism Beyond the West*, Onati, Spain: 1–19.
Harding, J. S. (2008), *Mahāyāna Phoenix: Japan's Buddhists at the 1893 World's Parliament of Religions*, New York: Peter Lang.
Harding, J. S. (2016), "Trailblazers of Global Buddhist Networks," *Journal of Contemporary Buddhism*, 17 (2): 393–404.
Harding, J. S., V. S. Hori and A. Soucy, eds. (2010), *Wild Geese: Buddhism in Canada*, Montreal: McGill-Queen's University Press.
Harding, J. S., V. S. Hori and A. Soucy, eds. (2014), *Flowers on the Rock: Global and Local Buddhisms in Canada*, Montreal: McGill-Queen's University Press.
Harris, E. (2006), *Theravāda Buddhism and the British Encounter: Religious, Missionary and Colonial Experience in Nineteenth-Century Sri Lanka*, London and New York: Routledge.
Harris, S. (2014), *Waking Up: A Guide to Spirituality Without Religion*, New York: Simon & Schuster.
Harrison, P. (1990), *"Religion" and the Religions in the English Enlightenment*, Cambridge: Cambridge University Press.
Harvey, D. (1989), *The Condition of Postmodernity*, London: Basil Blackwell.
He Yansheng [何燕生] (2013), "Huiyi Wenge Zhongde Jinghui Zhanglao" [回忆文革中的净慧长老 Recalling Master Jinghui in the Time of Cultural Revolution], *Huangmei Chan* [黄梅禅], 6: 66–70.
Heisig, J. W. and J. C. Maraldo (1995), *Rude Awakenings: Zen, the Kyoto School, and the Question of Nationalism*, Honolulu: University of Hawai'i Press.
Held, D., A. G. McGrew, D. Goldblatt and J. Perraton (1999), *Global Transformations: Politics, Economics, and Culture*, Stanford: Stanford University.
Hirsch, F. (2005), *Empire of Nations: Ethnography and the Making of the Soviet Union*, Ithaca: Cornell University Press.
Hobson, J. M. (2005), "The Eastern Origins of the Rise of the West and the 'Return' of Asia," *East Asia*, 32 (3): 239–55.
Honpa Honganji Hōyō Sōmubu, ed. (1927), *Myōnyo Shōnin* [明如上人], Kyoto: Honpa Honganji.
Hori, V. S. (1996), "The Study of Buddhist Monastic Practice: Reflections on Robert Buswell's 'The Zen Monastic Experience,'" *The Eastern Buddhist*, 29 (2): 239–64.
Hori, V. S. (2010), "How Do We Study Buddhism in Canada?," in J. S. Harding, V. S. Hori and A. Soucy (eds.), *Wild Geese: Buddhism in Canada*, 12–38, Montreal and Kingston: McGill-Queen's University Press.
Hou Kunhung [侯坤宏] (2009), *Zhengshiyufongbian: Yinshunsixiangyanjiao* [真實與方便：印順思想研究 Satyá and Upāya: The Study of Yinshun's Thoughts], Taipei: DharmaDhatu Publications.
Hsuan Hua (2003), *Shurangama Sutra with Commentary* [大佛頂首楞嚴經 *Da fo ding shou leng yan jing*], vol. 5., trans. Buddhist Text Translation Society. Talmage: Buddhist Text Translation Society.
Hsuan Hua (2008), "Shr Fu Questions and Answers," *Insights: The Wisdom and Compassion of a Buddhist Master: Q and A for Every Day*. Talmage: Buddhist Text Translation Society.
Hu Shih (1953), "Ch'an (Zen) Buddhism in China Its History and Method," *Philosophy East and West*, 3: 3–24.
Hu Shih [胡适] (2003), *Hushi Quanji* [胡适全集 The Collected Writings of Hu Shih], 44 vols, Hefei: Anhui Education Press.

Huang, C. J. (2003), "Sacred or Profane? The Compassion Relief Movement's Transnationalism in Taiwan, Japan, Malaysia, and the United States," *European Journal of East Asian Studies*, 2 (2): 217–41.

Huang Xianian [黃夏年], ed. (2006), *Minguo Fojiao Qikan wenxian jicheng* [民國佛教期刊文獻集 Collected Literature of Buddhist Journals in Republican Era], 209 vols., Beijing: Quanguo tushuguan.

Huang Xianian [黃夏年] (2013), "Zhongguofojiao Chubanshiye de Huigu yu Zhanwang" [中国佛教出版事业的回顾与展望 Retrospection and Anticipation of the Publication Industry of Chinese Buddhist Studies], in *Dangdaifojiao lunji* [当代佛教论集 Essays on Contemporary Buddhism], 24–32, Beijing: Religious Culture Press.

Huang Yunxi [黃運喜] (1991), "Qingmominchu Miaochanxingxue yundong dui Jindaifojiao de Yingxiang" [清末民初廟產興學運動對近代佛教的影響 The Impact of the Requisitioning Monastic Properties for Education Movement on Modern Buddhism in Late Qing and Early Republican China], *International Buddhist Studies* [國際佛學研究], 1: 293–303.

Huisong 慧松 [Wabo 哖博 pseud.] ([1938] 2006), "Cong midu Bali Zhuanlunwang Jing shuo qi" [從覓讀巴利轉論王經說起 Speak from Reading the Pāki Cakkavatti Sutta], in Huang Xianian [黃夏年] (ed.), *Minguo Fojiao Qikan wenxian jicheng* [民國佛教期刊文獻集 Collected Literature of Buddhist Journals in Republican Era], vol. 198: 121, Beijing: Quanguo tushuguan.

Hunt, L., M. C. Jacob and W. Mijnhardt (2010), *The Book That Changed Europe: Picart and Bernard's Religious Ceremonies of the World*, Cambridge: Harvard University Press.

Hunt-Perry, P. and L. Fine (2000), "All Buddhism is Engaged: Thich Nhat Hanh and the Order of Interbeing," in Queen, C. (ed.), *Engaged Buddhism in the West*, 35–66, Boston: Wisdom Publications.

Ip, Hung-yok (2009), "Buddhist Activism and Chinese Modernity," *Journal of Global Buddhism*, 10: 145–92.

Isomae, Jun'ichi [磯前順一] (2003), *Kindai Nihon no shūkyō gensetsu to sono keifu: shūkyō, kokka, shintō* [近代日本の宗教言説とその系譜—宗教·国家·神道 Religious Discourse in Modern Japan: Religion, State, and Shinto], Tōkyō: Iwanami Shoten.

Isomae, Jun'ichi (2014), *Religious Discourse in Modern Japan: Religion, State, and Shinto*, Leiden: Brill.

Itō, Miyoji (trans) ([2003] 2004), *The Constitution of the Empire of Japan*, National Diet Library. Available online: https://www.ndl.go.jp/constitution/e/etc/c02.html (accessed May 16, 2019).

Ives, C. (2001a) "Wartime Nationalism and Peaceful Representation: Issues Surrounding the Multiple Zens of Modern Japan," *Japan Studies* Review, 5: 37–45.

Ives, C. (2001b), "Protect the Dharma, Protect the Country: The Continuing Question of Buddhist War Responsibility," *The Eastern Buddhist*, 33 (2): 15–34.

Ives, C. (2002), "Dharma and Destruction: Buddhist Institutions and Violence," *Contagion: Journal of Violence, Mimesis, and Culture* 9: 151–74.

Ives, C. (2009), *Imperial-Way Zen: Ichikawa Hakugen's Critique and Lingering Questions for Buddhist Ethics*, Honolulu: University of Hawai'i Press.

Izumi Hōkei [泉芳璟] (1928), "Nanjō sensei no chosho kaisetsu [南条先生の著書解説" A Commented List of Professor Nanjō's works], *Ōtani Gakuhō* 9 (1): 159–61.

Jaffe, R. (2015), "Introduction," in R. Jaffe (ed.), *Selected Works of D. T. Suzuki, Vol I*, xi–lvi, Oakland: University of California Press.

Jansen, M. B. (2000), *The Making of Modern Japan*, Cambridge and London: Belknap Press of Harvard University Press.

Jha, A. (1999), "Compile All My Poems [and] it Would Be My Autobiography: Nagarjun," *Indian Literature*, 43 (6): 196–206.

Ji Zhe (2008), "Secularization as Religious Restructuring: Statist Institutionalization of Chinese Buddhism and Its Paradoxes," in M. Mei-hui Yang (ed.), *Chinese Religiosities: Afflictions of Modernity and State Formation*, 233–60, Berkeley: University of California Press.

Ji Zhe (2011), "Buddhism in Reform-Era China: A Secularised Revival?," in A. Y. Chau (ed.), *Religion in Contemporary China: Revitalization and Innovation*, 32–52, London: Routledge.

Ji Zhe (2013), "Zhao Puchu and his Renjian Buddhism," *The Eastern Buddhist*, 44 (2): 35–58.

Jiang Canteng [江燦騰] (1995), "Hushi de Zaoqi Chanzongshi Yanjiu yu Huhuagukuaitian" [胡適的早期禪宗史研究與忽滑谷快天 Hu Shih's Early Studies on Chan History and Nukariya Kaiten], *Studies in World Religions* [世界宗教研究], 1: 91–95.

Jie Chen (2001), "Burgeoning Transnationalism of Taiwan's Social Movement NGOs," *Journal of Contemporary China*, 10 (29): 613–44.

Jinghui [净慧] (2005), *Zhongguofojiao yu Shenghuochan* [中国佛教与生活禅 Chinese Buddhism and Life Chan], Beijing: Religious Culture Press.

Jinghui [净慧] (2008), *Shenghuochanyao* [生活禅钥 The Key of Life Chan], Beijing: Sanlian Press.

Jones, C. B. (1999), *Buddhism in Taiwan Religion and the State, 1660–1990*, Honolulu: University of Hawai'i Press.

Jones, D. M. (2001), "East Asia in the Early Modern European Imagination" in D. M. Jones (ed.), *The Image of China in Western Social and Political Thought*, 14–36, UK: Palgrave Macmillan.

Josephson, J. Ā. (2012), *The Invention of Religion in Japan*, Chicago: University of Chicago Press.

Joshi, L. M. (1983), *Discerning the Buddha: A Study of Buddhism and of the Brahmanical Hindu Attitude Toward It*, New Delhi: Motilal Banarsidass.

Kabat-Zinn, J. (1990), *Full Catastrophe Living: Using the Wisdom of Your Body and Mind to Face Stress, Pain, and Illness*, New York: Bantam Books.

Kabat-Zinn, J. (2011), "Some Reflections on the Origins of MBSR, Skillful Means, and the Trouble with Maps," *Contemporary Buddhism: An Interdisciplinary Journal*, 12 (1): 281–306.

Kan Zhangzhong [闞正宗] (2004), *Zhongdu taiwanfojiao: zhanhou Taiwan fojiao* [重讀台灣佛教: 戰後台灣佛教(正編) Re-reading Taiwan Buddhism: Taiwan Buddhism After the War (first edition)], Taipei: Darchen.

Kaplonski, C. (2014), *The Lama Question: Violence, Sovereignty, and Exception in Early Socialist Mongolia*, Honolulu: University of Hawai'i Press.

Kashiwahara Yūsen [柏原祐泉] (1995), *Shinshūshi bukkyōshi no kenkyū* [真宗史仏教史の研究 Research on Buddhist History and History of Jōdo Shinshū], Kyoto: Heirakuji Shoten.

Keith, C. (2012), *Catholic Vietnam: A Church from Empire to Nation*, Berkeley: University of California Press.

Ketelaar, J. E. (1990), *Of Heretics and Martyrs in Meiji Japan: Buddhism and Its Persecution*, Princeton: Princeton University Press.

Ketelaar, J. E. (1991), "Strategic Occidentalism: Meiji Buddhists at the World's Parliament of Religions," *Buddhist-Christian Studies*, 11: 37–56.

Ketelaar, J. E. (2006), "The Non-Modern Confronts the Modern: Dating the Buddha in Japan," *History and Theory*, 45 (4): 62–79.

Kiely, J. N. and B. Jessup (2016), "Introduction," in J. N. Kiely and B. Jessup (eds.), *Recovering Buddhism in Modern China*, 1–33, Columbia: Columbia University Press.

Kieschnick, J. and M. Shahar, eds. (2014), *India in the Chinese Imagination*, Philadelphia: University of Pennsylvania Press.

King, R. (1999), *Orientalism and Religion: Post-colonial Theory, India and "The Mystic East,"* London and New York: Routledge.

Kipnis, I. ([1952] 2004), *The American Socialist Movement, 1897–1912*, Chicago: Haymarket Books.

Kippenberg, H. G. (2002), *Discovering Religious History in the Modern Age*, Princeton: Princeton University Press.

Klosterman, C. (2007), "Things We Think We Know," *Esquire*, February 27. Available online: https://www.esquire.com/news-politics/news/a2133/esq0307klosterman (accessed March 15, 2018).

Kodama Shiki (1976), *Kinsei Shinshū no tenkai katei—nishi Nihon wo chūshin to shite* [近世真宗の展開過程：西日本を中心として The Development of True Pure Land Buddhism in Early Modern Japan: With a focus on Western Japan], Tokyo: Yoshikawa Kōbunkan.

Kodama Shiki (1994), "Shimaji Mokurai," in Kashiwahara Yūsen and Sonoda Kōyū (eds.), trans. G. Sekimori, *Shapers of Japanese Buddhism*, 207–18, Tokyo: Kōsei Publishing Co.

Koretsune Keisuke (2001), *Meijijin no osōshiki, Gendai Shokan* [明治人のお葬式 The Funerals of Outstanding Meiji Figures], Tokyo: Hirakawa Kōgyōsha.

Kosambī, D. [धर्मानंद कोसंबी] ([1935] 2010), *Bhāratīya saṃskṛti aur ahiṃsā* [भारतीय संस्कृति और अहिंसा Indian Civilization and Non-Violence], trans. from the Marathi into Hindi by Pandit Viśvanāth Dāmodar Sholāpurakar, Nayī Dillī: Samyak Prakāśan.

Kosambi, D. (2010b), *Dharmanand Kosambi: The Essential Writings*, ed. M. Kosambi, trans. M. Kosambi, Ranikhet: Permanent Black.

Kowner, R. and W. Demel, eds. (2013), *Race and Racism in Modern East Asia: Western and Eastern Constructions*, Leiden, Boston: Brill.

Krämer, H. M. (2013), "Japanese Discoveries of Secularization Abroad and At Home 1870–1945," in M. Eggert and L. Hölscher (eds.), *Religion and Secularity: Transformations and Transfers of Religious Discourses in Europe and Asia*, 193–215, Leiden Boston: Brill.

Krämer, H. M. (2015), *Shimaji Mokurai and the Reconception of Religion and the Secular in Modern Japan*, Honolulu: University of Hawai'i Press.

Kuroda Toshio ([1983] 1996), "The Imperial Law and the Buddhist Law," trans. J. I. Stone, *Japanese Journal of Religious Studies*, 23 (3–4): 271–85.

Lach, D. F. (1945), "Leibniz and China," *Journal of the History of Ideas*, 6 (4): 436–55.

LaFleur, W. R. (1988), *Buddhism: A Cultural Perspective*, Englewood Cliffs: Prentice Hall.

Lai, L. K. R. (2013), "Praying for the Republic: Buddhist Education, Student-monks, and Citizenship in Modern China (1911–1979)," PhD diss., McGill University, Montreal.

Laliberté, A. and M. Litalien (2010), "The Tzu Chi Merit Society from Taiwan to Canada," in J. S. Harding, V. S. Hori and A. Soucy, *Wild Geese; Buddhism in Canada*, 295–320, Montreal: McGill-Queen's University Press.

Lama Surya Das (1997), "Emergent Trends in Western Dharma," in A. Rapaport and B. D. Hotchkiss (eds.), *Buddhism in America*, 543–54, Rutland: Charles E. Tuttle Co.

Lau, Ngar-sze (2014), "Changing Buddhism in Contemporary Chinese Societies, with Special Reference to Meditation and Secular Mindfulness Practices in Hong Kong and Taiwan," MPhil diss., University of Oxford, Oxford.

Lau, Ngar-Sze (2017), "Desire for Self-healing: Lay Practice of *Satipaṭṭhāna* in Contemporary China," *Asian Medicine: Tradition and Modernity*, 12 (1–2): 317–35.

Lau, Ngar-sze (2018), "Modernising Buddhism: Emergence of Theravāda Meditation Communities in Contemporary China," PhD diss., Lancaster University.

Leezen (2018), "About Leezen," July 23. Available online: https://www.leezen.com.tw/en/about.php (accessed July 23, 2018).

Lévi-Strauss, Claude. (1955), *Tristes Tropiques*. Paris: Blon.

Levitt, P. (2001), "Between God, Ethnicity, and Country: An Approach to the Study of Transnational Religion," Oxford University, Transnational Communities Programme Working Paper Series. Available online: http://www.transcomm.ox.ac.uk/working%20papers/Levitt.pdf (accessed April 23, 2017).

Levitt, P. (2003), "You know, Abraham Was Really the First Immigrant: Religion and Transnational Migration," *International Migration Review*, 37 (3): 847–73.

Levitt, P. (2007), *God Needs No Passport: Immigrants and the Changing American Religious Landscape*, New York: New Press.

Lewis, M. W. and K. Wigen (1997), *The Myth of Continents: A Critique of Metageography*, Berkeley: University of California Press.

Li Jianmin (2009), "China Encourages Buddhism-science Dialogue to Promote Harmonious Society," Available online: http://news.xinhuanet.com/english/china/2012-04/26/c_131552981.htm (accessed April 29, 2014).

Li Silong [李四龙] (2014), *Meiguo Fojiao* [美国佛教 Buddhism in the United States], Beijing: People's Press.

Liang Jianlou [梁建樓] (2015), *Juehaifafang* [覺海法舫 Dharma Boat (Fafang) in the Awakening Ocean], Beijing: Tuanjie Publishing.

Ling, T. (1979), *Buddha, Marx and God: Some Aspects of Religion in the Modern World*, Ann Arbor: University of Michigan Press.

Liu, S. (2015), *Identity, Hybridity and Cultural Home: Chinese Migrants and Diaspora in Multicultural Societies*, London: Rowman and Littlefield International.

Lopez, D. S., Jr., (1995), "Introduction," in D. S. Lopez (ed.), *Curators of the Buddha: The Study of Buddhism under Colonialism*, 1–30, Chicago: University of Chicago Press.

Lopez, D. S., Jr., ed. (2002), "Introduction," in D. S. Lopez, Jr., (ed.), *A Modern Buddhist Bible: Essential Readings from East and West*, vii–xlii, Boston: Beacon Press.

Lopez, D. S., Jr. (2008), *Buddhism and Science: A Guide for the Perplexed*, Chicago: University of Chicago Press.

Lorimer, J. (1893), *The Institutes of the Law of Nations: A Treatise of the Jural Relations of Separate Political Communities*, Edinburgh: Blackwood.

Lou Yulie [楼宇烈] (1987), "Hushi Chanzongshi Yanjiu Pingyi" [胡适禅宗史研究评议 On Hu Shih's Study of Chan Buddhist History], *Academic Journal of Peking University*, 3: 59–67.

Luhmann, N. (2013), *A Systems Theory of Religion*, trans. D. A. Brenner and A. Hermann, Stanford: Stanford University Press.

Lundbaek, K. (1983), "The Image of Neo-Confucianism in *Confucius Sinarum Philosophus*," *Journal of the History of Ideas*, 44 (1): 19–30.

Luong, H. V. (1992), *Revolution in the Village: Tradition and Transformation in North Vietnam, 1925–1988*, Honolulu: University of Hawai'i Press.

MacDonald, M. (2018), "Group Says P.E.I.'s Land Protection Act is Being Abused and Loopholes Must be Closed," *The Guardian*, March 4. Available online: http://www.theguardian.pe.ca/news/group-says-peis-lands-protection-act-is-being-abused-and-loopholes-must-be-closed-190689/ (accessed April 23, 2019).

Madsen, R. (2007), *Democracy's Dharma: Religious Renaissance and Political Development in Taiwan*, Berkeley: University of California Press.

Malarney, S. K. (1996), "The Limits of 'State Functionalism' and the Reconstruction of Funerary Ritual in Contemporary Vietnam," *American Ethnologist*, 23 (3): 540–60.

Malarney, S. K. (1999), "Buddhist Practices in Rural Northern Vietnam," in P. Papin and J. Kleinen (eds.), *Liber Amicorum: Mélanges offerts au Professeur Phan Huy Lê*, 183–200, Hanoi: Nhà xuất bản Thanh niên.

Malarney, S. K. (2002), *Culture, Ritual and Revolution in Vietnam*, Hanoi: University of Hawai'i Press.

Mann, M. (2013), "When the Monks Come to Town," *Maisonneuve*, June 18. Available online: https://maisonneuve.org/article/2013/06/18/when-monks-come-town/ (accessed April 23, 2019).

Maps of India (2014), "11th September 1893: Swami Vivekananda Delivers His First Speech in the Parliament of the World's Religions in Chicago," Available online: https://www.mapsofindia.com/on-this-day/11th-september-1893-swami-vivekananda-delivers-his-first-speech-in-the-parliament-of-the-worlds-religions-in-chicago (accessed June 6, 2019).

Marr, D. (1981), *Vietnamese Tradition on Trial, 1920–1945*, Berkeley: University of California Press.

Maruyama, M. (1963), *Thought and Behavior in Modern Japanese Politics*, trans. I. Morris, London: Oxford University Press.

Masuzawa, T. (2005), *The Invention of World Religions, or, How European Universalism Was Preserved in the Language of Pluralism*, Chicago: University of Chicago Press.

Maxey, T. E. (2014), *The "Greatest Problem": Religion and State Formation in Meiji Japan*, Cambridge: Harvard University Asia Center.

McEachern, T. (2016), "P.E.I. Monks Helping with Montague Food Bank Shortfall," *CBC News*. Available online: http://www.cbc.ca/news/canada/prince-edward-island/pei-food-bank-1.3691380 (accessed April 23, 2019).

McHale, S. F. (2004), *Print and Power: Confucianism, Communism, and Buddhism in the Making of Modern Vietnam*, Honolulu: University of Hawai'i Press.

McKeown, A. (2001), *Chinese Migrant Networks and Cultural Change: Peru, Chicago, Hawaii, 1900–1936*, Chicago: University of Chicago Press.

McLellan, J. (1999), *Many Petals of the Lotus: Five Asian Buddhist Communities in Toronto*, Toronto: University of Toronto Press.

McLellan, J. (2009), *Cambodian Refugees in Ontario Resettlement, Religion, and Identity*, Toronto: University of Toronto Press.

McMahan, D. L. (2004), "Modernity and the Discourse of Scientific Buddhism," *Journal of the American Academy of Religion*, 72 (4): 897–933.

McMahan, D. L. (2008), *The Making of Buddhist Modernism*, New York: Oxford University Press.

McMahan, D. L. (2012a), "The Enchanted Secular: Buddhism and the Emergence of Transtraditional 'Spirituality,'" *The Eastern Buddhist*, 43 (1–2): 205–23.

McMahan, D. L. (2012b), "Intersections of Buddhism and Secularity," in C. Cornille and S. Corigliano (eds.), *Interreligious Dialogue and Cultural Change*, 137–58, Eugene: Wipf and Stock.

McMahan, D. L., ed (2012c), *Buddhism in the Modern World*, London and New York: Routledge.
McMahan, D. L. (2016), "Buddhist Modernism and Multiple Modernities," in S. Mitchell and N. Quli (eds.), *Buddhism Beyond Borders*, 181–95, Albany: State University of New York Press.
McMahan, D. L. (2017), "Buddhism, Meditation, and Global Secularisms," *The Journal of Global Buddhism*, 18: 112–28.
McRae, J. R. (2001), "Religion as Revolution in Chinese Historiography: Hu Shih (1891–1962) on Shen-hui (684–758)," *Cahiers d'Extrême-Asie*, 12: 59–102.
McRae, J. R. (2003), *Seeing Through Zen: Encounter, Transformation, and Genealogy in Chinese Chan Buddhism*, Berkeley: University of California Press.
MIF. (2014), "About Moonlight Foundation," *Welcome to Moonlight International Foundation*. Available online: http://www.moonlightfoundation.org (accessed September 1, 2017).
Morris, M. and Sakai, S. (2009), "Modern," in T. Bennett, L. Grossberg and M. Morris (eds.), *New Keywords: A Revised Vocabulary of Culture and Society*, 219–24, Malden, Oxford and Victoria: Blackwell Publishing.
Müller, F. M. (1872), *Lectures on the Science of Religion*, New York: Charles Scribner and Co.
Müller, F. M. (1880), "On Sanskrit Texts Discovered in Japan," *Journal of the Royal Asiatic Society of Great Britain and Ireland*, 12 (2): 153–88.
Müller, F. M. (1881), *Buddhist Texts from Japan*, Bunyiu Nanjio and G. Bühler (eds.), Anecdota Oxoniensia, Aryan Series., Oxford: Clarendon Press.
Müller, F. M. (1884), *Biographical Essays*, London: Longmans, Green.
Müller, F. M. (1892), *India, What Can It Teach Us? A Course of Lectures Delivered Before the University of Cambridge*, London: Longmans, Green & Co.
Müller, F. M. (1902), *The Life and Letters of the Right Honourable Friedrich Max Müller*, London: Longmans, Green.
Müller, F. M. (2002), "Forgotten Bibles," in J. R. Stone (ed.), *The Essential Max Müller*, 249–64, New York: Palgrave MacMillan.
Mungello, D. E. (2005), *The Great Encounter of China and the West, 1500–1800*, 2nd ed., New York: Rowman & Littlefield.
Nakamura, H. ([1980] 1999), *Indian Buddhism: A Survey with Bibliographic Notes*, New Delhi: Motilal Banarsidass.
Nanjio, Bunyiu (1883), *A Catalogue of the Chinese Translation of the Buddhist Tripitaka, the Sacred Canon of the Buddhists in China and Japan*, Oxford: Clarendon Press.
Nanjio Bunyiu [南条文雄] (1914), *Kōjōron* [向上論 Debate on Uplifting], Tokyo: Tōadō Shobō.
Nanjio Bunyiu [南条文雄] (1917), *Bukkyō jinseikan* [佛教人生観 A Buddhist View of Life], Tokyo: Chūō Shuppansha.
Nanjio Bunyiu [南条文雄] (1979), *Kaikyūroku: Sansukuritto Kotohajime* [懐旧録—サンスクリット事始め Records of Reminiscences. The Origins of Sanskrit], Tokyo: Heibonsha.
Naramoto T. (1987), *Meiji ishin no Higashi Honganji: Nihon saidai no minshū shūkyō wa ikani gekidō no jidai wo ikinuitaka. Arashi no naka no hōjō monogatari* [明治維新の東本願寺：日本最大の民衆宗教はいかに激動の時代を生きぬいたか。嵐のなかの法城物語 Higashi Honganji Temple and the Meiji Restoration: How Japan's Largest Popular Religion Overcame a Turbulent Period. A Tale of the Dharma Citadel in the Midst of a Storm], Tokyo: Kawade Shobō Shinsha.

Nattier, J. (1998), "Who Is a Buddhist? Charting the Landscape of Buddhist America," in C. S. Prebish and K. K. Tanaka (eds.), *The Faces of Buddhism in America*, 183–95, Berkeley: University of California Press.

Nedostup, R. (2009), *Superstitious Regimes: Religion and the Politics of Chinese Modernity*, Cambridge: Harvard University Asia Center.

Nguyễn-Khoa-Tân (1934), "Supplément en Française: Traduction française du discours de S.E. Nguyễn-Khoa-Tân" [French Supplement: French Translation of the Speech Given by Nguyễn-Khoa-Tân], *Viên Âm*, 12 (November and December): 60–64.

Nish, I., ed (1998), *The Iwakura Mission in America and Europe: A New Assessment*, Richmond, Surrey: Japan Library.

Oakes, T. and L. Schein, eds. (2006), *Translocal China: Linkages, Identities and the Reimagining of Space*, London and New York: Routledge.

Ober, D. (2013), "'Like Embers Hidden in Ashes, or Jewels Encrusted in Stone': Rāhul Sāṅkṛtyāyan, Dharmānand Kosambī and Buddhist Activity in Late British India," *Contemporary Buddhism*, 14 (1): 134–48.

Ober, D. (2016), *Reinventing Buddhism: Conversations and Encounters in Modern India, 1839–1956*. PhD diss., University of British Columbia, Vancouver.

Olender, M. (1992), *The Languages of Paradise: Race, Religion, and Philology in the Nineteenth Century*, Cambridge: Harvard University Press.

Ong, A. and D. M. Nonini, eds. (1997), *Ungrounded Empires: The Cultural Politics of Modern Chinese Transnationalism*, New York and London: Routledge.

Osterhammel, J. (2014), *The Transformation of the World. A Global History of the Nineteenth Century*, Princeton: Princeton University Press.

Ōtani Daigaku, ed. (1973), *Shinshū nenpyō* [真宗年表 Chronology of True Pure Land Buddhism], Kyoto: Hōzōkan.

Overstreet, G. and M. Windmiller (1959), *Communism in India*, Berkeley: University of California Press.

Ozeray, M. J. F. (2017), *The First Western Book on Buddhism and Buddha: Ozeray's Recherches Sur Buddou of 1817*, trans. U. App, Paris: UniversityMedia.

Palmer, D. (2007), *Qigong Fever. Body, Science and Utopia in China*, New York: Columbia University Press.

Pearson, Q. ([Buddhist Year 2554] 2012), "Buddhism in Thailand," in O. Abenayaka and A. Tilakaratne (eds.), *2600 Years of Sambuddhatva: Global Journey of Awakening*, 173–86, Colombo: Ministry of Buddhasasana and Religious Affairs, Government of Sri Lanka.

Peters, A. (2018), "Treaties, Unequal," February. Available online: https://opil.ouplaw.com/view/10.1093/law:epil/9780199231690/law-9780199231690-e1495 (accessed June 12, 2019).

Pittman, D. A. (2001), *Toward a Modern Chinese Buddhism: Taixu's Reforms*, Hawai'i: University of Hawai'i Press.

Polanyi, K. (1975), *The Great Transformation*, New York: Octagon.

Poon, S. (2011), *Negotiating Religion in Modern China: State and Common People in Guangzhou, 1900–1937*, Hong Kong: Chinese University of Hong Kong.

Prince Edward Island, Department of Agriculture and Fisheries (2015), *Agriculture on Prince Edward Island*. Available online: http://www.gov.pe.ca/agriculture/AgonPEI (accessed September 8, 2016).

Pritzker, S. E. (2016), "New Age with Chinese Characteristics? Translating Inner Child Emotion Pedagogies in Contemporary China," *Ethos*, 44 (2): 150–70.

Pye, M. (2003), "Modern Japan and the Science of Religions," *Method and Theory in the Study of Religion*, 15 (1): 1–27.

Ren Jiyu [任继愈] (1955), "Hushi de Shiyanzhuyi Sixiangfangfa pipang" [胡适的实验主义思想方法批判 The Critique of Hu Shih's Experimentalist Methodology], in *Hushi Sixiangpipang* [胡适思想批判 The Critique of Hu Shih's Ideas], 8 vols, 77–92, Beijing: Sanlian Press.

Ren Jiyu [任继愈] (1963), *Hantang Fojiaosixiang Lunji* [汉唐佛教思想论集 Essays on Buddhism in Han and Tang Dynasties], Beijing: People Press.

Rhys Davids, T. W. (1907), *Buddhism: Its History and Literature*, New York and London: G. P. Putnam's Sons.

Ritzinger, Justin R. (2016), "Original Buddhism and its Discontents: The Chinese Buddhist Exchange Monks and the Search for the Pure Dharma in Ceylon," *Journal of Chinese Religions*, 44 (2): 149–73.

Ritzinger, J. (2017), *Anarchy in the Pure Land: Reinventing the Cult of Maitreya in Modern Chinese Buddhism*, New York and Oxford: Oxford University Press.

Robertson, R. (1992), *Globalization: Social Theory and Global Culture*, London: Sage.

Roberston, R. (1995), "Glocalization: Time-Space and Homogeneity-Heterogeneity," in M. Featherstone, S. Lash and R. Robertson (eds.), *Global Modernities*, 25–44, London: Sage Publications.

Roetz, H. (2013), "The Influence of Foreign Knowledge on Eighteenth Century European Secularism," in M. Eggert and L. Hölscher (eds.), *Religion and Secularity: Transformations and Transfers of Religious Discourses in Europe and Asia*, 9–33, Leiden, Boston: Brill.

Rounds, D. (2008), "Preface," in Hsuan Hua (Author), ed. D. Rounds, trans. Heng Hsien, *Timely Teachings. Gold Mountain Monastery in the Early 1970s*, xiv–xv, Burlingame: Buddhist Text Translation Society.

Rowbotham, A. (1945), "The Impact of Confucianism on Seventeenth Century Europe," *The Far Eastern Quarterly*, 4 (3): 224–42.

Sahajanand, S. (1995), *Swami Sahajanand and the Peasants of Jharkhand: A View from 1941*, W. Hauser (ed. and trans.), New Delhi: Manohar.

Said, E. W. (1978), *Orientalism*, New York: Pantheon.

Sakai, N. (1997), *Translation and Subjectivity: On Japan and Cultural Nationalism*, Minneapolis: University of Minnesota Press.

Sankrityayan, R. (1984), *Selected Essays of Rahul Sankrityayan*, New Delhi: People's Publishing House.

Sāṅkṛtyāyan, R. (1942), *Volgā se Gaṅgā* [वोल्गा से गंगा From the Volga to the Ganges], Ilāhābād: Kitāb Mahal.

Sāṅkṛtyāyan, R. ([1942] 1974), *Vaijñānika Bhautikavāda* [वैज्ञानिक भौतिकवाद Scientific Materialism], Ilāhābād: Lokabhārtī Prakāśan.

Sāṅkṛtyāyan, R. ([1944] 2014), *Merī Jīvan Yātrā* [मेरी जीवन-यात्रा My Life Journey], Vol. II. Nayī Dillī: Rādhākṛṣṇa Prakāśan.

Sāṅkṛtyāyan, R. ([1956] 2011), *Mahāmānav Buddh* [महामानव बुद्ध The Great Buddha], Nayī Dillī: Samyak Prakāśan.

Sāṅkṛtyāyan, R. (1957), *Jinkā main kṛtagya* [जिनका मैं कृतज्ञ To Those Whom I am Indebted], Ilāhābād: Kitāb Mahal.

Schak, D. and H.-H. Michael Hsiao (2005), "Taiwan's Socially Engaged Buddhist Groups," *China Perspectives*, 59: 1–18.

Schiller, N. G. (1997), "The Situation of Transnational Studies," *Identities*, 4 (2): 155–66.

Schwab, R. (1950), *La Renaissance Orientale*, Paris: Payot.

Scott, D. (2004), *Conscripts of Modernity: The Tragedy of Colonial Enlightenment*, Durham: Duke University Press.
Seager, R. H. (1989), "Pluralism and the American Mainstream: The View From the World's Parliament of Religions," *Harvard Theological Review*, 82 (3): 301–24.
Seager, R. H. (1995), *The World's Parliament of Religions: The East/West Encounter, Chicago, 1893*, Bloomington: Indiana University Press.
Seager, R. H. (1999), *Buddhism in America*, New York: Columbia University Press.
Seneviratne, H. L. (1999), *The Work of Kings: The New Buddhism in Sri Lanka*, Chicago: University of Chicago Press.
Sharf, R. H. (1993), "The Zen of Japanese Nationalism," *History of Religions*, 33: 1–43.
Sharf, R. H. (1995a), "The Zen of Japanese Nationalism," in D. S. Lopez and C. Hallisey (eds.), *Curators of the Buddha: The Study of Buddhism Under Colonialism*, 107–60, Chicago: University of Chicago Press.
Sharf, R. H. (1995b), "Zen and the Way of the New Religions," *Japanese Journal of Religious Studies*, 22 (3–4): 417–58.
Sharf, R. H. (1995c), "Buddhist Modernism and the Rhetoric of Meditative Experience," *Numen*, 42 (3): 228–83.
Sharf, R. H. (2001), *Coming to Terms with Chinese Buddhism: A Reading of the Treasure Store Treatise*, Honolulu : University of Hawai'i Press.
Sharratt, S. (2009), "Buddhist Academy Opens Doors to Overwhelming Crowd at Open House," *The Guardian Newspaper*, November 23. Available online: http://www.theguardian.pe.ca/People/2009-11-23/article-1372960/Buddhist-Academy-opens-doors-to-overwhelming-crowd-at-open-house/1 (accessed April 23, 2019).
Sharratt, S. (2013), "Residents Upset Province Handing Buffalo Park to Buddhist Group for $1," *The Guardian Newspaper*, June 5. Available online: http://www.theguardian.pe.ca/News/Local/2013-06-05/article-3270012/Residents-upset-province-handing-buffalo-park-to-Buddhist-group-for-$1/1 (accessed July 10, 2014).
Shaw, R. and C. Stewart (1994), "Introduction: Problematizing Syncretism," in R. Shaw and C. Stewart (eds.), *Syncretism/Anti-Syncretism: The Politics of Religious Synthesis*, 1–24, London and New York: Routledge.
Shields, J. M. (2012), "Blueprint for Buddhist Revolution: The Radical Buddhism of Senoo Girō (1889–1961) and the Youth League for Revitalizing Buddhism," *Japanese Journal of Religious Studies*, 39 (2): 333–51.
Shirasu Jōshin (2002), *Ōtani tankentai to sono jidai* [大谷探検隊とその時代 The Ōtani Expedition and its Time], Tokyo: Bensei Shuppan.
Śivaprasād, R. ([1874] 1880), *Itihās Timiranāśak* [इतिहास तिमिरनाशक History as the Destroyer of Darkness], Pt. III. Ilāhābād: Gavarnmenṭ ke chāpekhāna.
Skilling, P. (2009), "Theravada in History," *Pacific World: Journal of the Institute for Buddhist Studies*, Third Series (11): 61–93.
Smith, J. Z. (1978), *Map Is Not Territory: Studies in the History of Religion*, Chicago: University of Chicago Press.
Snelling, J. (1993), *Buddhism in Russia: The Story of Agvan Dorzhiev, Lhasa's Emissary to the Tsar*, Longmead: Element Books.
Snodgrass, J. (1998), "'Budda no Fukuin': The Deployment of Paul Carus's 'Gospel of Buddha' in Meiji Japan," *Japanese Journal of Religious Studies*, 25 (3/4): 319–44.
Snodgrass, J. (2009), "Discourse, Authority, Demand: The Politics of Early English Publications on Buddhism," in N. Bhushan, J. L. Garfield and A. Zablocki (eds.), *TransBuddhism: Transmission, Translation, Transformation*, 21–41, Amherst: University of Massachusetts Press.

Soucy, A. (2012), *The Buddha Side: Gender, Power and Buddhist Practice in Vietnam*, Honolulu: University of Hawai'i Press.
Soucy, A. (2014), "Buddhist Globalism and the Search for Canadian Buddhism," in J. S. Harding, V. S. Hori and A. Soucy (eds.), *Flowers on the Rock: Global and Local Buddhisms in Canada*, 25–52, Montreal: McGill-Queen's University Press.
Soucy, A. (2016), "Constructing Modern Zen Spaces in Vietnam," in M. Dickhardt and A. Lauser (eds.), *Religion, Place and Modernity: Spatial Articulations in Southeast and East Asia*, 125–45. Brill Publishing.
Soucy, A. (2017), "Global Flows of Vietnamese Zen," in J. Borup and M. Q. Fibiger (eds.), *Eastspirit: Transnational spirituality and Religious Circulation in East and West*, 149–71. Leiden: Brill Publishing.
Statistics Canada (2006), "Visual Census: Ethnic Origin and Visible Minorities, Prince Edward Island," Available online: http://www.census2006.ca/census-recensement/2006/dp-pd/fs-fi/index.cfm?LANG=ENGandVIEW=CandPRCODE=11andTOPIC_ID=11andformat=flash (accessed June 27, 2019).
Statistics Canada (2012), "Prince Edward Island Continued to Lead in Potato Area," Available online: http://www.statcan.gc.ca/pub/95-640-x/2012002/prov/11-eng.htm#N4 (accessed September 8, 2016).
Stewart, D. (2012), "Warm Coats, Warm Hearts," *The Guardian Newspaper*, December 22. Available online: https://www.theguardian.pe.ca/news/local/warm-coats-warm-hearts-95359/ (accessed April 23, 2019).
Stewart, D. (2016a), "Buddhist Monks at Little Sands Repay Kindness by Baking Rolls to Help Feed Hungry Islanders," *The Guardian Newspaper*, April 3. Available online: https://www.theguardian.pe.ca/news/local/buddhist-monks-at-little-sands-repay-kindness-by-baking-rolls-to-help-feed-hungry-islanders-101309/ (accessed April 23, 2019).
Stewart, D. (2016b), "Major Supermarket Chain in Taiwan Opens Store in Charlottetown," *The Guardian Newspaper*, June 28. Available online: https://www.theguardian.pe.ca/business/major-supermarket-chain-in-taiwan-opens-store-in-charlottetown-108234/ (accessed April 23, 2019).
Stewart, D. (2017), "Monks' Monastery Growing, While Same is Planned in Brudenell for Nuns," *The Guardian Newspaper*, September 30. Available online: https://www.theguardian.pe.ca/news/local/monks-monastery-growing-while-same-is-planned-in-brudenell-for-nuns-58558/ (accessed April 23, 2019).
Sueki Fumihiko [末木 文美士] (2004), *Kindai Nihon to Bukkyō* [近代日本と仏教 Modern Japan and Buddhism], Tokyo: Toransubyū.
Sueki Fumihiko [末木 文美士] (2013), "Lingmudazhuo Lijie de Ribenshi yu Zhongguoshi" [铃木大拙理解的日本式与中国式 Japanese and Chinese as Understood by D.T. Suzuki], trans. Liu, Lijiao [刘丽娇], *Academic Journal of Fudan University*, 4: 1–8.
Sugunasiri, S. (2006), "Inherited Buddhists and Acquired Buddhists," *Canadian Journal of Buddhist Studies*, 2: 103–42.
Sun Yat-sen [孫中山] (1924), "Sanmin Zhuyi" [三民主義 The Three Principles of the People]. Available online: https://zh.wikisource.org/wiki/三民主義 (accessed March 5, 2018).
Suzuki, D. T. (1927), *Essays in Zen Buddhism, First Series*, London: Luzac Press.
Suzuki, D. T. (1933), *Essays in Zen Buddhism, Second Series*, London: Luzac Press.
Suzuki, D. T. (1934), *Essays in Zen Buddhism, Third Series*, London: Luzac Press.
Suzuki, D. T. (1938), *Zen Buddhism and Its Influence on Japanese Culture*, Kyoto: Eastern Buddhist Society.

Suzuki, D. T. (1953), "Zen: A Reply to Hu Shih," *Philosophy East and West*, 3: 25–46.
Suzuki, D. T. [鈴木 大拙] (1968), *Suzuki Daisetsu Zenshū* [鈴木大拙全集 The Collected Writings of D. T. Suzuki], 30 vols, Tokyo: Iwanami Shoten.
Suzuki, D. T. (1970), *Shin Buddhism*, New York: Harper and Row.
Suzuki, D. T. [鈴木 大拙] (1987), *Chan yu Ribenwenhua* [禅与日本文化 Zen and Japanese Culture], trans. Tao Gang [陶剛], Beijing: Sanlian Press.
Suzuki, D. T. (2008), "Impressions of Chinese Buddhism," *Zaidan hojin Matsugaoka Bunko kenkyu nenpo*, 22: 81–123.
Suzuki, D. T. (2015), *Selected Works of D. T. Suzuki, Vol II*, J. C. Dobbins (ed.), Oakland: University of California Press.
Suzuki, D. T., Soga, R., Kaneko, D., Nishitani, K. and M. Unno (1985), "DIALOGUE: Shinran's World," *The Eastern Buddhist*, 18 (1): 105–19.
T'ai hsu (Taixu) (1928), *Lectures in Buddhism*, Paris: publisher unknown.
Taixu [太虛] ([1930] 2017), "Foxue gailun" [佛學概論 Introduction to Buddhist Studies], in Yinshun (ed.), *Taixu Dashi Quanshu* [太虛大師全書 Collected Works of Master Taixu], vol. 1: 1–21. Available as CD-Rom, version 5.0, *Yinshun fashi foxue zhuzuoji* 印順法師佛學著作集, Hsinchu, RoC: Yinshun Foundation.
Taixu [太虛] ([1936] 2017), "Zenyanglai jianshe renjian fojiao" [怎樣來建設人間佛教 How to build Pure Land on Earth], in Yinshun, (ed.) *Taixu Dashi Quanshu* [太虛大師全書 Collected works of Master Taixu], vols. 14: 431. Available as CD-Rom, version 5.0, *Yinshun fashi foxue zhuzuoji* 印順法師佛學著作集. Hsinchu, RoC: Yinshun Foundation.
Taixu [太虛] ([1936] 2017), "Zhongguo shifou you sengqie wenti zhi bianlun" [中國是否有僧伽問題之辯論 The Debate About Whether There is Sangha in China], in Yinshun (ed.), *Taixu Dashi Quanshu* [太虛大師全書 Collected Works of Master Taixu], 17: 790–96. Available as CD-Rom, version 5.0, *Yinshun fashi foxue zhuzuoji* 印順法師佛學著作集, Hsinchu, RoC: Yinshun Foundation.
Taixu [太虛] ([1937] 2017), "Foli yaolue" [佛理要略 Brief Summary of Buddhist Theory], in Yinshun (ed.), *Taixu Dashi Quanshu* [太虛大師全書 Collected works of Master Taixu], vol. 1: 71–87. Available as CD-Rom, version 5.0, *Yinshun fashi foxue zhuzuoji* 印順法師佛學著作集, Hsinchu, RoC: Yinshun Foundation.
Taixu [太虛], (2005), *Taixu Dashi Quanshu* [太虛大師全書 The Collected Writings of Master Taixu], 35 vols, Beijing: Religious Culture Press.
Tamura Kōyū [田村 晃祐] (2005), *Kindai Nihon no bukkyōshatachi* [近代日本の仏教者たち Buddhists of Modern Japan], Tokyo: Nihon Hōsō Shuppan Kyōkai.
Tan Chee Beng, ed. (2007), *Chinese Transnational Networks*, London and New York: Routledge.
Taylor, C. (2007), *A Secular Age*, Cambridge: Harvard University Press.
Taylor, C. (2011), "Western Secularity," in C. Calhoun, M. Juergensmeyer and J. VanAntwepen (eds.), *Rethinking Secularism*, 31–53, New York: Oxford University Press.
Taylor, P. K. (2007), "Modernity and Re-enchantment in Post-revolutionary Vietnam," in P. Taylor (ed.), *Modernity and Re-enchantment: Religion in Post-revolutionary Vietnam*, 1–56, Singapore: Institute of Southeast Asian Studies.
Thelle, N. R. (1987), *Buddhism and Christianity in Japan: From Conflict to Dialogue, 1854–1899*, Honolulu: University of Hawai'i Press.
Thích Niệm Châu (1937), "Chừng nào Diệt trừ Hết Sự Mê tín Của Các Phật tử" [When Will the Superstition of Buddhists Be Eradicated], *Tạp chí Duy tâm Phật Học* [Mind Only Magazine of Buddhist Studies], 18 (1 March): 318–21.

Thích Thanh Ân (2012), *Luận giải Chính tín và Mê tín* [An Explanation of Orthodoxy and Superstition], Place unknown: Giáo hội Phật giáo Việt Nam.
Thích Thanh Từ (2000), *My Whole Life*, trans. Tu Tam Hoang, Westminster: Tu Tam Hoang.
Thích Thanh Từ (2010), *Mê tín Chánh tín* [Superstition and Right Belief], Hanoi: Nhà xuất bản Tôn giáo.
Tolz, V. (2011), *Russia's Own Orient: The Politics of Identity and Oriental Studies in the Late Imperial and Early Soviet Periods*, New York: Oxford University Press.
Topmiller, R. J. (2002), *The Lotus Unleashed: The Buddhist Peace Movement in South Vietnam, 1964–1966*, Lexington: University of Kentucky Press.
Tsukamoto, Z. (1985), *A History of Early Chinese Buddhism: From Its Introduction to the Death of Hui-Yuan*, trans. L. Hurvitz, New York: Kodansha America.
Tsunemitsu Kōnen [常光 浩然] (1968), *Meiji no bukkyōsha* [明治の仏教者 Buddhists of the Meiji Period], Tokyo: Shunjūsha.
Turnbull, D. (2000), *Masons, Tricksters and Cartographers: Comparative Studies in the Sociology of Scientific and Indigenous Knowledge*, Amsterdam: Harwood Academic.
Turner, J. (2014), *Philology. The Forgotten Origins of the Modern Humanities*, Princeton: Princeton University Press.
Tweed, T. A. (2006), *Crossing and Dwelling: A Theory of Religion*, Cambridge: Harvard University Press.
Tweed, T. A. and S. Prothero, eds. (1999), *Asian Religions in America: A Documentary History*, Oxford: Oxford University Press.
van den Bosch, L. (2002), *Friedrich Max Müller: A Life Devoted to Humanities*, Boston: Brill.
van der Veer, P. (2001), *Imperial Encounters: Religion and Modernity in India and Britain*, Princeton: Princeton University Press.
Verchery, L. (2010), "The Woodenfish Program: Fo Guang Shan, Canadian Youth, and a New Generation of Buddhist Missionaries," in J. S. Harding, V. S. Hori and A. Soucy, *Wild Geese: Buddhism in Canada*, 210–35, Montreal: McGill-Queen's University Press.
Verchery, L. (2015), "The Avatamsaka Sagely Monastery (華嚴聖寺) and New Perspectives on Globalized Buddhism in Canada," in J. Zuidema (ed.), *Understanding the Consecrated Life in Canada*, 361–76, Waterloo: Wilfred Laurier University Press.
Verhoeven, M. J. (2004), "The Dharma Through Carus's Lens" [Introduction], *The Gospel of Buddha According to Old Records*, author, P. Carus, 1–101, Chicago and LaSalle: Open Court, Carus Publishing Company.
Vertovec, S. (2009), *Transnationalism*, London: Routledge.
Victoria, B. D. (2006), *Zen at War*, 2nd ed., Lanham: Rowman & Littlefield.
Vivekananda Vedanta Society of Chicago (2018), "The 1893 World's Fair," https://chicagovedanta.org/1893.html (accessed June 6, 2019).
Wakeman, F. Jr. (1978), "The Canton Trade and the Opium War," in J. Fairbank (ed.), *The Cambridge History of China*, 163–212, Cambridge: Cambridge University Press.
Wang Enyang [王恩洋] ([1940] 2006), "Du yuanshi fojiao sixianglun" [讀原始佛教思想論 Reading the Discussion of the Thoughts of Original Buddhism], in Huang Xianian [黃夏年] (ed.), *Minguo Fojiao Qikan wenxian jicheng* [民國佛教期刊文獻集 Collected Literature of Buddhist Journals in Republican Era], vol. 85: 430–32, Beijing: Quanguo tushuguan.
Wang Leiquan [王雷泉] (1986), "Abu Zhengxiong de Chan yu Xifangsixiang" [阿部正雄的禅与西方思想 Masao Abe's Zen and Western Thoughts], *Dushu* [读书 Reading], 5: 143–45.

Wang Leiquan [王雷泉] (1995), "Fojiao zai Shichangjingji Zhuanguizhong de Jiyu yu Tiaozhan" [佛教在市场经济转轨中的机遇与挑战 Opportunities and Challenges for Buddhism in the Transitioning Moment of Market Economy], *Research of Buddhism*, 4: 1–9.

Warner, M., J. VanAntwerpen and C. Calhoun, eds. (2010), *Varieties of Secularism in a Secular Age*, Cambridge: Harvard University Press.

Weiye [末也] (1989), "Yihouji" [译后记 Translator's Epilogue], in D. T. Suzuki, trans. Weiye [末也], *Chanzhe de Sisuo* [禅者的思索 The Thoughts of a Zen Thinker], 228–29, Beijing: Chinese Youth Press.

Welch, H. (1967), *The Practice of Chinese Buddhism* 1900–1950, Cambridge: Harvard University Press.

Welch, H. (1968), *The Buddhist Revival in China*, Cambridge: Harvard University Press.

Wikipedia (2019), "Swami Vivekananda at the Parliament of the World's Religions (1893)," June 6. Available online: https://en.wikipedia.org/wiki/Swami_Vivekananda_at_the_Parliament_of_the_World's_Religions_(1893) (accessed June 6, 2019).

Wilkinson, G. (2015), "Taishō Canon: Devotion, Scholarship, and Nationalism in the Creation of the Modern Buddhist Canon in Japan," in Jiang Wu (ed.), *Spreading the Buddha's Word in East Asia*, 284–310, New York: Columbia University Press.

Williams, D. R. and T. Moriya, eds. (2010), *Issei Buddhism in the Americas*, Champaign, IL: University of Illinois Press.

Williams, P. (1989), *Mahāyāna Buddhism: The Doctrinal Foundations*, London and New York: Routledge.

Wilson, J. (2014), *Mindful America: The Mutual Transformation of Buddhist Meditation and American Culture*, New York: Oxford University Press.

Woodside, A. B. (1976), *Community and Revolution in Modern Vietnam*, Boston: Houghton Mifflin Company.

Xie Siwei [谢思炜] (1989), "Yizheqianyan" [译者前言 Translator's Foreword], in D. T. Suzuki, trans. Xie Siwei [谢思炜], *Chanxue Rumen* [禅学入门 Introduction to Zen Buddhism], 6–9, Beijing: Sanlian Press.

Xing Dongfeng [刑东风] (2012), "Lingmudazhuo yu Zhongguoguanxi Gaishuo" [铃木大拙与中国关系概说 On D. T. Suzuki and His Relationship with China], *Chinese Chan Studies*, 6: 353–66.

Xuyue [虚云] (2009), *Xuyunheshang Quanji* [虚云和尚全集 The Collected Writings of Master Xuyun], 9 vols, Zhengzhou: Zhongzhou Classics Press.

Yack, B. (1986), *The Longing for Total Revolution: Philosophic Sources of Social Discontent from Rousseau to Marx and Nietzsche*, Princeton: Princeton University Press.

Yanagida Seizan [柳田 聖山], ed. (1975), *Hushi Chanxuean* [胡適禪學案 Documents for Hu Shih's Chan Studies], trans. Li Naiyang [李迺揚], Taibei: Zhengzhong Book Bureau.

Yang Wenhui [楊文會] (2000), *Yang Renshan Quanji* [楊仁山全集 Collected works of Yang Renshan], Hefei: Huangshan shushe.

Yasumaru Yoshio ([1979] 2003), *Kamigami no Meiji ishin: shinbutsu bunri to haibutsu kishaku* [神々の明治維新：神仏分離と廃仏毀釈 The Meiji Restoration of the Kami: The Separation of Kami and Buddhas and the Movement to "Abolish Buddhas and Destroy Shakyamuni"], Tokyo: Iwanami Shoten.

Yinguang [印光] (1997a), *Yinguangfashi Wenchao* [印光法師文鈔 Writings of Master Yinguang], Taibei: Hua Zang Buddhist Library.

Yinguang [印光] (1997b), *Yinguangfashi Wenchao Canbian* [印光法師文鈔參編 Supplemental Writings of Master Yinguang], Taibei: Hua Zang Buddhist Library.

Yinshun [印順], ed. (1950), *Taixudashi nianpu* [太虛大師年譜 Chronology of Master Taixu]. Available online: http://yinshun-edu.org.tw/Master_yinshun/y13_02_24 (accessed January 20, 2017).

Yinshun [印順] (1993), "*Nanquandazang duizhongguofojiaode zhongyao*" [南傳大藏對中國佛教的重要 The Importance of Tipitaka from Southern Tradition to Chinese Buddhism], *Huayuji* [華雨集], vol. 5. Available online: http://yinshun-du.org.tw/en/Master_yinshun/y29_04 (accessed January 20, 2017).

Yinshun 印順 (2005), *Pingfandeyisheng* [平凡的一生(重訂本 An Ordinary Life], revised edition, Taipei: Yin-Shun Cultural and Educational Foundation. Available online: http://yinshun-edu.org.tw/en/Master_yinshun/y41_01 (accessed January 20, 2017).

Yoshida Kyūichi (1959), *Nihon kindai bukkyōshi kenkyū* [日本近代仏教史研究 Studies in the History of Modern Buddhism in Japan], Tokyo: Yoshikawa Kōbunkan.

Yoshida Kyūichi (1967), "Meiji jūnen zengo no Shimaji Mokurai (sōritsu yonjūnen kinen ronbunshū)" [明治十年前後の島地黙雷 Shimaji Mokurai in the Late 1870s], *Taishō daigaku kenkyū kiyō, bungakubu, bukkyōgakubu*, 52: 351–62.

Yu Xue (2016), "Buddhist Efforts for the Reconciliation of Buddhism and Marxism in the Early Years of the People's Republic of China," in J. Kiely and J. B. Jessup (eds.), *Recovering Buddhism in Modern China*, 177–215, New York: Columbia University Press.

Yuan Jiuhong [袁久紅] (1990), "Foxingzai Dangdai de Shanguang, Lingmu Dazhuo Chitian Dazuo de Fojiao Rendaozhuyi Sixiang" [佛性在当代的閃光，铃木大拙与池田大作的佛教人道主义思想 The Light of Buddhism at Present, The Buddhist Humanism in the Thinking of D. T. Suzuki and Daisaku Ikeda], *Fayin* [法音 Dharma Voice], 8: 13–20.

Zhang Chunjie (2008), "From Sinophilia to Sinophobia: China, History and Recognition," *Colloquia Germanica*, 41 (2): 97–110.

Zhao Puchu [赵朴初] (2007), *Zhaopuchu Wenji* [赵朴初文集 The Collected Writings of Zhao Puchu], 2 vols., Beijing: Sinoculture Press.

Ziolkowski, E. J., ed. (1993), *A Museum of Faiths: Histories and Legacies of the 1893 World's Parliament of Religions*, Atlanta: Scholars Press.

Ziyan [自衍] (2009), "Taiwan diqu nanchuanfojiao feiyingli chubanpin xiankuang fenxi (shang)" [台灣地區南傳佛教非營利出版品現況分析(上) The Contemporary Analysis of Non-profit Making Publications of Southern Buddhism in Taiwan District (A)], Management for Buddhist Libraries [佛教圖書館館刊] 50: 15–21. Available online: http://www.gaya.org.tw/journal/m50/50-main2.pdf (accessed November 17, 2016).

Zumoto, M. (2004), "Bunyiu Nanjio: His Life and Work," *Pacific World*, 3rd series, 6: 119–37.

Zürcher, E. ([1959] 2007), *The Buddhist Conquest of China: The Spread and Adaptation of Buddhism in Early Medieval China*, Leiden: Brill.

Index

Abhidhamma 104, 112, 179 n.10
Āgamas 111–14, 117–18
agency 3, 26, 35, 80, 88, 137, 150
    Asian 3, 6, 26, 121, 129, 176
    Buddhist 6, 88, 95, 129, 135, 137, 152, 157, 164
agriculture 164, 170–4
    organic 7, 166
ahimsa, see non-violence
All Ceylon Buddhist Congress 112
alliances, political 84, 167
Amaterasu 3, 20–1, 25, 31, 33
Ambedkar, Bhimrao 73, 85
Amida, *see* Amitābha
Amitābha 29, 30, 91, 93–4, 101, 127, 130, 133, 153
    recite name (*see* nenbutsu)
    vows 137, 148
ancestor 16, 21, 52, 63, 69
animal welfare 7, 163–4, 170–4, 176
anitya/anicca, see impermanence
Aoki Shūzō 133–5
Appadurai, Arjun 2–3, 62
Asia
    as backwards 11, 74, 89
    as culturally superior 157
    as non-rational 41, 89, 92
    as passive 2–3, 5, 46, 164, 182 n.5
atheism 12, 40, 51–2, 63, 80–2
Australia 104, 155–6, 160, 164, 167
authenticity 17, 36, 99, 145, *see also* tradition
    Biblical 17
    Chan/Zen 96, 101
    religious 23, 177 n.2
authority 10, 28–9, 36, 57–9, 67, 105, 145, 152, 184 n.15, *see also* authority, scientific
    Biblical 4, 15, 25
    Buddhist 30, 66, 91, 106, 118
    Papal 12, 71
    political 85, 123, 131
    scientific 12, 49
    state 20, 62

Bailin Temple 101, 110, 115–16
Bakufu 123–5, 128–9, 131–2
Bible 4, 14–15, 17, 25
binary codes 58–9
Bliss and Wisdom Foundation, *see* Fu Chih
Bodhgaya 4, 60–1
Bodhidharma 29–30
bodhisattva 54, 62, 65, 105, 113, 118
boundaries 36, 59, 66, 152
    of Buddhism 47, 68
    metageographical 27, 28
    secular 42, 48, 50, 52, 54, 59, 66, 68
Britain 4, 18–19, 78, 88, 107, 136, 141, 145, 149, 179 n.6
Buddha, the 1, 23, 29, 31, 56, 61, 72, 74, 78–81, 90, 145
    authenticity of 104, 106, 111, 148
    humanity of 52, 113
    revolutionary 72, 82, 84–5
    supplication of 56, 61, 64–5
    teachings 6, 23, 47–9, 82–3, 91, 102, 144, 147, 179 n.5
buddha nature 91, 93, 146
Buddhism
    Asian 1, 5–7, 144, 152
    Chinese 2, 6, 53, 69, 89–95, 99, 102–4, 106–10, 112–13, 118–19, 121, 141, 156, 158, 166
    corruption of 7, 23, 42–3, 81, 92–5, 106
    decline 54, 61, 108, 129
    demythologized 92, 105
    global 4, 58–9, 112, 151, 161, 165, 179 n.6
    globalization of 6, 10, 26, 47, 57–8, 104, 107, 151, 157, 163, 165

Index

Indian   71, 74, 109, 113
Indian origins   1, 15, 29–34, 49, 85, 104, 137, 143, 147
Japanese   6–7, 81, 87, 89–90, 95, 102, 126, 129, 137, 139, 141–4, 146–9
lay   1, 30, 47, 94, 114, 116–18, 159–61, 167–70, 173–5, 180 n.18, 184 n.16
and Marxism   6, 71–5, 78, 80–5
modernist   4–5, 26–7, 37, 41–2, 59, 61–2, 65, 68, 73, 79, 151, 178 n.4
original   1, 6, 22–3, 60, 81, 105, 109, 111, 113–14, 119, 139, 144–5, 147
patronage   30–1
and politics   32, 35, 46, 53–4, 57, 67, 71–3, 80, 84, 108, 113, 115, 123–35, 167, 172, 178 n.7
Protestant   69, 183 n.8
Pure Land   7, 24, 56–7, 93, 137, 142, 145, 148–9, 183 n.10, *see also* Shin
rational   23, 40–1, 43, 53, 83, 105
reform   4–5, 79, 81, 90, 92, 98, 101, 106–9, 111–13, 115, 119, 132, 143
as a religion   6, 22, 40, 45, 49, 52–6, 60–5, 68, 72, 81, 83, 118, 136
revival   43, 51, 61, 95, 100–2, 106, 108, 110, 115–17, 132, 145
scholarship   22, 43, 105–7, 119, 137, 140, 142–3, 147, 150–2, 157, 166, 178 n.1
and science   41, 45–6, 52–5, 75, 80, 89, 94, 107–8, 146
sects   21, 66, 125, 141, 149
and secularism   10, 45–6, 53–5, 181 n.15
as technique   39, 40, 47
Tibetan   5, 53, 104, 109–10, 114–16, 163, 166
transformation   3, 29–31, 38–9, 49, 121, 165
transmission   26, 28, 29, 31, 33–4, 36, 114, 155
true   6, 42–3, 60, 111, 145, 159, 161
Vietnamese   56, 62
Western   1, 40, 152
as world religion   2, 4–5, 9–11, 23–5, 37–8, 40, 57, 60, 108, 141, 144, 147–9
Buddhist Association of China   52, 111, 115

Buddhist Association of the Republic of China   113, 165
Buddhist Reform Movements   4–6, 26, 45, 58–62, 66–70, 81, 92, 98, 101–2, 106–15, 119, 129–32, 143
Buddhist Studies   1–2, 4, 6, 22, 27, 39, 88, 107–8, 115, 137, 139–43, 151, 181 n.9
global approach   2–3
in Japan   143–5, 149
Burma, *see* Myanmar

Canada   7, 99, 121, 156, 160, 163–4, 166–8, 171, 174
capitalism   51, 76–8, 84, 98, 164–5, 176
Carus, Paul   35–7
caste   72, 82
Catholic Church   12–13, 16, 63, 66, 134, 175, *see also* Jesuit
bias against   7, 23
causality   4–5, 45
Ceylon, *see* Sri Lanka
Chan   29–30, 94–7, 101, 158, 161–2, 180 n.18, *see also* Zen
"fever"   100, 116–17
lineage   96, 98, 100–1, 183 n.10
patriarchs   154–5, 162
popularity   100, 116–18
temples/monasteries   94, 110, 115–16
Chấn hưng Phật giáo, *see* Buddhist Reform Movement
charity   7, 16, 94, 109, 114, 163–4, 166, 168, 170–1
China   2, 4, 6–7, 13, 18, 31, 92, 97, 164, 167–9, *see also* Jesuits, in China; People's Republic of China; Republic of China
central power   29, 88
Communist revolution   60, 98
corrupt   92, 159
European impressions   3, 14–18, 25
and Japan   6, 32, 35, 87–8, 93, 100, 102
Japanese invasion   90, 109–10
Middle Kingdom   29–30, 33
modernization   89–90, 92, 97
religion in   43, 46, 51–3, 55, 98, 101, 116
secular   51–2, 55, 161, 177 n.5

and Sri Lanka   112, 115
  temples/monasteries   115, 117
Chinese (language)   15, 100, 140, 142, 156, 158–9, 171
Chinese Buddhist Association   98, 101
Chōshū   123
  authorities   123, 125, 127
  and Buddhism   123, 125–7, 130, 132, 135, 180 n.5
  military   123–9, 131, 180 n.2
Christianity   9, 16, 43, 45, 69, 133, 149, 157
  conversion   14, 20–1, 134, 144
  in Japan   19–21, 126–7, 132, 134, 177 n.2
  missionaries (*see* missionaries, Christian)
  as model religion   2, 9, 12, 24
  worldview   14–15, 45
class   15, 73, 77–8, 103, 117, 124, 127, 174
  perspective   82, 97
  struggle   75, 98–9
Cold War   95, 99
colonialism   2–3, 5, 7, 9, 18, 24–5, 28, 45–7, 57, 60, 74, 79, 121, 140, 145, 152, 164, *see also* India, colonial
Communist Party
  Chinese   53, 55, 95, 98, 100–1, 154, 166–7, 178 n.7
  Indian   76, 82
  Vietnamese   62–3
community   58, 62, 65–6, 160, 165, 170, 176
  Buddhist   96, 106, 118, 152, 155–6, 163–4, 166, 169, 183 n.13
  global   6, 160, 165
  lay   164, 170
  monastic   106, 111, 168
compassion   47, 69, 93, 100–1, 149, 160, 169, 173
Confucianism   2, 14–17, 25, 88, 117, 166
Confucius   14, 16–17, 22–3
craving   77–8
Cultural Revolution   98–101, 115, 184 n.16
culture   6, 25, 39, 44, 54–5, 60, 66–7, 78, 99, 167, 183 n.9

  American   52, 99, 153
  Buddhist   42, 53, 57
  Chinese   3, 15, 17, 53, 88, 90, 101–2, 116, 150, 154
  Japanese   6, 21, 89, 91, 97, 100, 102, 147, 149
  material   29–30, 32
  other   14, 21
  Western   1–2, 5–6, 13, 15, 60, 92, 123, 138, 156–9

Dalai Lama, The   53, 76
Dhammapada   112, 114
Dharma Drum Mountain   69, 113, 160
Dharma Realm Buddhist Association   7, 34, 150–61, 182 nn.1, 2, 5, 183 nn.6, 13, 184 nn.16, 17, 18, 20, 21, 22
Dharmapāla, Anāgārika   4, 24, 45, 107, 112
discourse   28, 43, 55, 97, 145, 151, 157
  academic   141, 143
  Buddhist   35, 37, 46, 53, 59, 88
  global   27, 33–5, 37, 40–1, 60, 90, 112, 178 n.5
  nationalist   89, 91, 145
  reformist   57, 61–3, 65, 67
  scientific   46, 49
  secularist   54, 64, 66, 68
disenchantment   12, 42
divination   21, 57, 63
Đổi Mới   63–4
duḥkha, *see* suffering

East-West   28, 32–4, 39, 69, 102
  binary   1–2, 5, 11, 17, 19, 25–7, 30, 33–9, 41, 60, 152
  reified categories   26–7, 35
  signifiers   26, 35
education   15, 90, 138, 148, 166, 173–4
  Buddhist   92, 96, 107, 168–9, 171
  monastic   61–2, 109–11, 115, 129, 168
  morality   109–10, 154, 156
elite, political   124, 140
emperor worship   3, 20–2, 25, 123, 129, 132
Enlightenment (Buddhist)   56, 105, 113, 146
Enlightenment, The (European)   2, 9, 12–13, 17, 23, 43–4, 91, 147

ethics   15, 17, 21, 51, 116, 172–3, 176
  secular   53
Eurocentrism   87–9, 182 n.3
Europe   3, 12, 18, 25, 30, 34, 37, 88, 106, 109, 141, 149, 178 n.1, 184 n.22
  and Asia   3, 14–7
  and communism   74, 83
  exploration   13–4
  secular   42–3, 51, 53, 149
  Theravāda Buddhism in   104, 114
  visits to   106–8, 114, 124–5, 132–8
evolution (theory of)   45, 81, 135
experience   48, 97, 99, 144
  spiritual   44, 117–18

Fafang   108–13
Fa Gu Shan, *see* Dharma Drum Mountain
family   58, 62, 64–6, 125, 128, 138, 148, 174, 184 n.15
Faxian   29, 105, 107
field (Bourdieuian)   53, 58, 64–8
Five Precepts   47, 103
flows (global)   5, 27, 34–5, 37–9, 69–70, 121, 160, 165
Fo Guang Shan   69, 160–1, 166
force, political   54, 67, 74, 127
Fu Chih   7, 121, 163, 166
function systems   58–9, 62, 65–7, 178 n.5
funerals   63, 65, 69, 106, 129, 154, 180 n.11

Gandhi, Mohandas K.   60, 71, 76–9
Gelug (tradition)   166, 168
gender   5, 64, 68, 167–8, 174, *see also* masculinity; women
  structures   57, 64–5
Gesshō   127–8
ghosts   62, 69, 106, 108, 113
global and local   71, 88, 151, 165, 167, 176, 184 n.19
global approach   2–3, 7, 41, 140, 176
globalization   27, 42, 51, 57–9, 71–2, 89, 102, 104, 150–2, 159–60, 164–5, 176
  of Buddhism   6, 10, 26, 39, 47, 57, 59, 68, 88, 95, 102, 107–8, 143, 150, 157, 163
  of religion   58–9, 63, 65
glocalization   7, 15, 71, 165, 176

Goenka, S. N.   5, 47–9, 51, 114, 116
Gospel of Buddha   36–7
Great Enlightenment Buddhist Institute Society (GEBIS)   7, 163–4, 167–71, 173–5
Great Wisdom Buddhist Institute (GWBI)   163–4, 167–70, 173–5
Guomindang, *see* Kuomintang

Haichaoyin   108–9, 112
Hanoi   56, 61, 63–4, 66–7
health   48, 56, 58, 65, 77, 116, 166, 171, 173
hegemony   1, 5, 7, 57–8, 60, 65–6, 121, 163
Hīnayāna, *see* Theravāda
Hinduism   2, 9, 10, 24, 49, 72, 74, 78
Hong Kong   18, 112, 114–15, 155, 158, 180 n.16, 184
Honganji (temple)   126–7, 135
  Higashi Honganji   137–8, 145
  Nishi Honganji   36, 126, 129–33, 180 nn.10, 11
Hsi Lai Temple   155, 162
Hsuan Hua   7, 34, 121, 150, 152–62, 182 n.2, 183 nn.10–12, 184 nn.16, 17, 184 n.22
Hui Neng   154, 162
Huisong   111, 113
humanism   81–2, 85, 92, 100–2
humanistic Buddhism   61, 69, 92–3, 97, 100–2, 108, 113, 116–19, 179 n.10
Hu Shih   87, 95–9, 101

identity   5, 32–3, 56–8, 65, 81, 99, 110, 121, 147, 156, 165, 184 n.15
  cultural   26, 32, 41
  global   151, 159, 161
  national   21, 31, 33, 90, 159
  religious   9–10, 40, 59, 104, 150–1, 160, 184 n.20
  sectarian   56–7, 68
immigration   99, 150, 169, 171, 174, *see also* migration
imperialism   28, 72, 78, 89–90, 93, 124
impermanence   47, 81
India   5, 10, 18, 28, 34, 53, 69, 77, 85, 96, 111–12, 139
  Buddhist decline   77, 81, 105, 148

Buddhist revival   4, 80, 107
colonial   32, 71, 73, 76, 84
homeland of the Buddha   1, 15, 29, 32, 104, 142–3, 147
Marxism   72–3, 76
secularism   49–52, 55
as West   29–31, 33
Indology   137, 140–3, 145, 149
institutions   19, 49–50, 53, 59, 62, 72, 76, 80, 178 n.1
  academic   109, 145, 182 n.13
  Buddhist   36, 47–9, 53–8, 60, 64, 66–8, 81, 85, 92, 126, 129–30, 132, 138, 150
  political   22, 113
  religious   12, 23, 40–1, 44, 48, 82

Japan   3–4, 26, see also Meiji; modernization; religion; Russo-Japanese War
  and China   6, 31–3, 35, 87–8, 90, 92, 98–100, 102, 109, 110
  culture   91, 95, 100, 102, 147, 149
  emperors   3, 20–1, 25, 31, 33, 123–4, 127, 129–32, 134, 148, 180 n.14
  imperialism   89–90, 92–4
  isolation   18, 20, 123
  Jesuit mission   14, 22
  Marxism in   71, 81
  modernization   3, 19, 25, 87–8, 97, 123–4, 127, 130, 133, 136, 140, 180 n.4
  myth   3, 20–1, 25, 31–3, 89
  nationalism   87, 91, 129
  opening   18, 123, 127
  religion   6, 19–22, 38–9, 125, 133–4, 136, 148, 177 n.2, 181 n.15
  as sacred East   31–3
  society   20, 146
  state   20, 135
  as superior   148–9
  unequal treaties   18–20, 88, 124, 141
  Western pressure   45, 140
Japanese Buddhism   6, 19, 24, 31–3, 36–7, 107, 139, 141–3, 145, see also Shin
  Chinese view   90, 95
  delegation to World's Parliament of Religions   24, 35–6, 89, 157
  mission to Europe   133–6
  reform   81, 87, 95, 108, 146–7
  scholarship   112, 137, 141–4, 149
  temples   89, 126, 142
  universalization   147–9
  Western pressure   123–4
Japanese (language)   19, 140, 179 n.7
Japanese Buddhist Studies Society   109
Japanese Constitution   3, 19–22, 25, 134–5, 145, 180 n.13
Jesuits
  in China   3, 14–17, 22, 25
  cultural accommodation   14–16
  in Japan   14, 22
Ji Zhe   53–4, 178 n.7
Jih-Chang   163–4, 166–8, 173
Jinghui   100–2, 115–16
Jōdo Shinshū, see Shin sect

Kabat-Zinn, Jon   50–1, 177 n.4
kami   3, 20–2, 25, 33, 130, 133, 148–9, 180 n.14
karma   45, 57, 93–4, 147–9, 171
Kasahara Kenju   138–9, 141, 143, 145
Kido Takayoshi   128, 133
Kisān Sabhā   82, 179 n.7
knowledge   30, 43, 54, 82–3, 105, 138, 146–7
  of Asia   14, 75
  Buddhist   83, 106, 109, 117, 142, 147
  of China   14, 17
  local   140–1, 143
  production   140, 146
  scientific   46, 78, 107, 127, 137, 139–41, 143, 146
  secular   47–8, 53
  of the world   27–8
koan   30, 180 n.17
Korea   31–3, 88, 99, 105, 109, 115
Kosambi, Dharmanand   71–9, 81–2, 85, 178 nn.2, 3, 4, 5
Kōshōji (temple)   125–6, 131
Kuomintang   81, 95, 97–8, 107, 109, 112–14, 166

Lam Rim Chen Mo (text)   166, 169
language   27, 29, 50, 72, 84, 96, 104, 107, 111, 141–2, 146, 161, see also Chinese; Japanese; Pāli; Sanskrit

Buddhist   37, 47, 73, 79, 111, 137, 140–1
  classical   22, 116
  English   37, 110
  European   14–15, 22, 38, 139–40
  Marxist   72, 79, 81
  science of   139, 141, 144
  scientific   14, 24, 41, 45, 48, 51, 146, 181 n.4
  secular   20, 47–9, 51
  study of   14, 139, 143, 181 n.4
lay Buddhism   47, 160
  communities   163–4
  leader   7, 94, 107, 116, 167
  life   69, 115
  organizations   47, 163, 170–4
Ledi Sayadaw   47, 49, 69, 114
Leezen   163, 166, 173–4
Life Chan   101–2, 116
lineage
  Buddhist   90, 111, 117, 155, 159, 166, 183 n.10, 184 n.17
  Chan/Zen   30, 96, 98, 100–1, 116
  imperial   21, 31, 33

Mādhyamaka   105, 111, 113
Maha Bodhi Society   24, 61, 73, 80
Mahāyāna Buddhism   53, 109, 113, 148–9
  bias against   7, 23, 105
  in China   103–4, 110, 112, 118–19
  spread   105, 179 n.4
  superiority   104–5, 111, 118
  teachings   145, 148–9
  texts   104, 107, 111, 167
mapping   5, 9, 26, 29–30, 32, 41
maps   27–8, 39, 177 n.1
marginalization   5, 43, 51, 57–8, 64–7, 118, 152
Marx, Karl   3, 78–9, 83
  writings   71, 80
Marxism   71–85, 97
  thought   5, 69, 71–2, 74, 81–2, 84–5
masculinity   58, 64–5, 68
materialism   46, 81, 84, 97–8, 156
media   51–3, 62–4, 66–7, 160, 166, 170–1
meditation   6, 39, 47–8, 50–2, 54, 91, 109, 114, 174–5, 177 n.1, 185 n.1, *see also vipassana*

Chan/Zen   30, 50, 68, 116
  retreat   103, 117, 158, 169
  scientific study of   50, 53, 55
  secularization of   5, 44, 47–51
  as technique   47, 49–50, 177 n.4
  Theravāda   6, 70, 103–4, 112–19
  as "true" Buddhism   42, 48
mediumship (spirit)   56–7, 63, 66, 178 n.2
Meiji   3, 6, 19, 21, 36, 69, 140, 146
  Constitution   20–2, 25, 145
  Emperor   124, 131
  government   125, 128–33, 145, 148
  religious policy   138
  Restoration   3, 19, 89–90, 107–8, 123–4, 129–31, 138, 180 n.4
merit   93–4, 171, *see also* karma
metageography   27–8, 33–5
method, scientific   9, 45, 139, 143, 146
migration   36, 99, 164–5, 169, 172, 174–6
military   27, 50
  Chinese   92, 94
  European   18, 45, 105
  Japanese   123–6, 128, 131–2, 147
  monks enlist   92
mind   48, 52–3, 56, 93, 158
  -body   116, 119
  religious   146
mindfulness, 5, 39, 47, 50–1, 103
missionaries
  Buddhist   36–7, 80, 89–90, 107, 110
  Christian   10, 14–17, 20, 57, 60, 106, 109, 127, 138, 144–6
modernity   2, 6, 39, 46, 60, 62, 66, 68, 74, 88, 121, 145, 151
  Chinese   46, 89, 98, 159
  discourses   57, 59, 62, 65
  features   9, 125, 136
  global   41, 91, 178 n.1
  Japanese   90, 97, 123, 124
  multiple   42, 72, 81, 150
  structures   58–9, 67
  Western   1, 7, 25, 136, 154
modernization   2–3, 25, 43, 49, 135
  Asian   3, 5, 19, 25, 87, 89, 96
  Buddhist   1, 4–6, 11, 21, 40, 43, 45, 47, 54, 58, 69, 87, 102, 106, 108, 110–11, 118, 121, 123, 130, 136, 165, 181 n.15

equivalent to Westernization   1, 11, 19, 25, 88
   linear   21, 43, 49
   movements   7, 20, 26
   precondition   4
   and rationalism   12, 23
   two-sided process   25
morality   9, 15–17, 48, 85, 93–4, 97, 101, 108, 147–9, 154, 156
movements (political)   100, 115, 119
Müller, Max   4, 6–7, 22–34, 106, 141–2, 179 n.6
   approach to religion   139, 144–6, 149, 182 n.10
   and Nanjō Bunyū   121, 137–9, 143, 149
   science of language   139, 181 n.4
Murata Seifū   127–8
Myanmar   1, 45, 47, 49, 69, 73–4, 84, 103–4, 109, 112, 114–15, 117–18
mythology   3, 6–7, 25, 31–3, 78, 86, 92, 105

Nanjō Bunyū (南条文雄)   4, 6, 106–7, 121, 138, 143, 179 n.7, 181 nn.1, 2, 7, 8, 9, 182 n.13
   in Europe   107, 138–43, 149
   Mahāyāna   148–9
   and Max Müller   121, 139–46
   and religious studies   146, 148–9
   scholarship   137, 141–3, 146
   universalism   141, 145–7
Narada   110–11
nationalism   35, 77–9, 150–1, 157
   Chinese   90, 100, 108
   cultural   87, 95
   Hindu   10, 74
   Japanese   35, 87–9, 91, 95, 100, 145, 148–9
nenbutsu   94, 126
networks   5, 26, 39, 160, 163, 176, 184 n.21
   Asian   4, 26
   Buddhist   35, 109–10
   global, 3, 35, 37, 39–40, 61, 84, 107, 160, 165
   transnational   4–5, 104, 111–13, 115, 118–19

New Buddhism   69, 89, 92
nianfo, see nenbutsu
Nikāyas   74, 111
nodes   2–4, 26, 41
non-violence   76–9
North America   4, 6, 34, 37, 51, 89, 95, 115
   Buddhism in   26, 36, 98–9, 121, 150, 155–6, 159, 182 n.2, 183 n.13
   D.T. Suzuki's influence   88, 99, 100
   Theravāda   104, 114
nuns   22, 56, 69, 103, 106, 115–17, 155–6, 160, 163, 166–8, 170, 175, 180 n.18, 184 n.16

offerings   56, 64–5, 155
Opium Wars   18, 88, 123
ordination   30, 80, 83, 111, 115, 154, 183 n.12
organic, *see* agriculture
organizations   44, 50, 156
   Buddhist   24, 50, 67, 73, 93, 112–13, 115, 121, 132, 155, 164–6, 175
   charitable   163, 168
   global   160, 164, 167, 176
   lay   170, 173–4
   monastic   150, 163
   religious   21, 40, 50, 66
   socialist   71–2, 82
Orientalism   1, 53, 72, 75, 121, 137, 151, 157, 183 n.7
   paradigm   11, 152, 158, 164
   reverse   34, 158
   scholars   22–3, 80, 85, 104–5, 118
   scholarship   6, 80, 105–7
   view of Buddhism   7, 23, 107, 111, 152
orthodoxy   5, 10, 57–61, 64–8, 75, 81, 150, 157, 159, 161

Pāli   22, 73, 103, 107, 111, 179 n.3
   language of original Buddhism   23, 111, 141, 179 n.5
   scriptures   22, 79–80, 104–5, 107–11, 114
   study of   4, 75, 85, 108, 110, 112, 143
   translation   112–14, 118
Pāli Text Society   22, 105
People's Republic of China   88, 95, 115

Perry, Commodore Matthew C.   18, 123
philology   51, 137, 139, 141, 144–5
philosophy   9, 16–17, 23, 46–7, 54, 79
   Buddhist   40, 42, 83, 85, 94, 170, 179 n.10
   Western   94, 110
pilgrimage   28–30, 37, 61, 117
political strategies   73, 78
political structures   51, 57
political theory   76, 82
political turmoil   12, 110, 116
politicians   20–1, 79, 163, 172, 179 n.10
politics   42, 44, 46, 52, 71, 98, 109, 113, 124, 128, 130, 161, 184 n.15
   and Buddhism   32, 53, 135, 147, 178 n.7
   Indian   5, 74, 76, 79–80
   secular   9, 54–5, 134
power   27–8, 43, 57–8, 67, 74, 85, 121, 124, 131–2, 178 n.5, 184 n.15, *see also* hegemony
   Asian   7, 29–32, 89, 92
   asymmetric   140–1
   colonial   28, 45, 89, 145, 152
   discourse   55, 68
   divine   91, 127, 148
   institutional   60, 129
   local   62, 90, 92–3
   military   18, 105, 125
   secular   127–8
   self   93, 148
   Shin Buddhist   125, 127
   spiritual   146–7
   state   63, 84
   Western   3, 7, 18, 105
practice   9, 16, 42–4, 49, 54, 61, 151, *see also* koan; meditation; *vipassana*
   Buddhist   49, 56, 58, 62–9, 93, 103–5, 115, 148, 159–60, 164, 166, 171, 183 n.6, 185 n.1
   non-religious   47, 59
   religious   55, 63–4, 119, 133, 159
   spiritual   50–1, 54, 57, 113, 117
   therapeutic   50–1, 177 n.4
   women's   58, 64–7
precepts   158, 160, *see also* Five Precepts
Protestant Buddhism   69, 183 n.8
Protestantism   12, 20, 44, 106, 134, 145, 175, 177 n.2

psychology   46, 52, 91, 93–4
Pure Land   29–30, 56, 91–4, 101, 113, 138–9, 148
   on earth   92, 94, 101, 108

qigong   116, 119
Qing Dynasty   18, 89, 92, 106–7

race   18–19, 96, 99, 174
rationalism   12, 23, 46
rationality   12, 21, 44, 96–7, 147
   of Buddhism   52, 82, 91
reason   12, 15, 80, 91, 97
   Buddhism and   74, 80
rebirth   45, 91, 113, 148–9
reform
   Buddhist   4, 6, 45–6, 60–7, 69, 73, 92, 104, 106–8, 111–12, 119, 143, 151
   economic   100, 127
   land   98, 115
   Marxist   79–84
   political   108, 129
   religious   74, 90, 101, 143, 149
   sectarian   129, 130
   socioeconomic   77, 99
religion   19, 55, 74, 90, 139, *see also* world religions
   Asian   17, 25, 182 n.6
   as category   9, 13, 15, 21, 40, 42, 44, 46–8, 52, 66, 149, 177 n.1, 178 n.3, 182 n.3
   Christian model   9, 12, 24, 44, 146
   classification   19, 21–3, 25, 58–60, 63, 144
   comparative   24, 144, 146, 149
   concept   3, 9, 11–24, 55–6, 133, 149
   decline   42, 51
   defining   48, 51, 146–8, 182 n.12
   freedom of   3, 19, 20, 25, 108, 113, 126, 145, 147, 168
   as function system   59, 62, 65–7, 178 n.5
   globalization   58–9
   heathen   11, 13, 15
   institutional   23, 40, 48, 82
   Japanese conception   6, 19–22, 125, 133–6, 177 n.2, 182 n.12
   modern invention of   2, 9, 12, 23–5, 56, 59, 65, 67

monotheistic 2, 15, 133
national 19–22, 52, 133–6
natural 12, 15–16
non-Christian 5, 9
opiate of the masses 77, 98, 101
premodern 5, 11–12, 24–5
primitive 13, 21, 46, 53, 133, 146, 177 n.2
private 20–1, 42–4, 51, 177 n.2
rational 10, 17, 23, 40, 74, 97
reform 90, 92, 95, 101–2, 143, 145, 149, 183 n.8
repression 52, 63–4, 75, 98
resurgence 43, 51, 116
revealed 2, 16, 82, 144
revival 90, 102
science of 23, 144, 182 n.10
and secular 2, 4, 9–10, 12–3, 20, 25, 39, 42–6, 48, 51–5, 59, 66–7
and state 6, 20, 25, 50, 55, 89, 125, 134–5, 145
study of 6, 13, 20, 23–4, 27, 137, 139, 144, 149, 150
and superstition 64, 183 n.8
tolerance 13, 16, 23, 48, 81, 147
true 12–3, 17, 24–5
in United States 49, 52
universal 7, 46, 48–9, 141, 143–9
Western roots 2, 3, 11–19, 135
religious studies 27, 59
Republic of China 89–90, 95, 113, *see also* Taiwan
retreat 47, 101, 103, 115–18, 129, 138, 158, 168–9
Rhys Davids, Caroline 22, 105
Rhys Davids, T. W. 22, 105
ritual 16, 21–3, 44, 48, 54–6, 63–4, 66, 106, 115–17, 154–5, 165
specialists 9, 184
Russia 3, 5, 18, 75, 77, 85, *see also* Soviet Union
Buddhism in 5, 69, 71, 73, 80–2
Communist Revolution 60, 72, 75

Sacred Books of the East 22–3
Śākyamuni, *see* the Buddha
salvation 9, 12, 59, 65–6, 93
Salvation Army 170–1
saṅgha 73, 108, 111, 116, 155, 167

disappearance in India 77, 179 n.8
early 74, 82–5
Sankrityayan, Rahul 71–3, 79, 83, 85, 179 nn.6, 8
Sanskrit 106, 139, 144, 179 n.3, 181 n.8
scholarship 73, 76, 104, 106–7, 109, 112, 137–45
scripture 4, 22, 80, 105, 107, 109, 137–42, 145, 147
Sanskritization 6, 142–3, 149
science 11–12, 16, 18, 21, 42, 44–53, 58, 83, 97, 107, 116, 136, 140–1, 146–7, *see also* religion
advent 11–12
age of 21, 144
and Buddhism (*see* Buddhism; language; religion)
of the mind 48, 52–3
natural 139, 146
secular 44, 46, 53, 59
worldview 45, 149
sectarianism 21, 44, 46, 48, 56–7, 60, 66, 68, 78, 113, 162
sects, *see* Buddhism, sects
secular 9, 12–14, 16, 23, 42, 52, 59, 67, 128, 136
boundaries 42, 48, 50, 52, 54, 59, 66, 68
institutions 22, 48–50, 53–5
practice 47, 49
state 2, 5–6, 20, 22, 44, 49, 51, 136, 145
secularism 2–3, 5, 9, 12–13, 16, 24–5, 43, 177 n.2, *see also* laïcité
codependent with religion 4, 10
differentiated from religion 9, 66, 68
discourses 2, 45–6, 49, 54, 68
dominance 39, 55
globalized 39–40
ideological 22
in India 49, 53
in Japan 21–2
linear 43, 49
and modernity 54, 68, 125
multiple 5, 42, 44, 55
narrative 42
naturalization 44
porousness 42, 54
scholarship on 42

separation of church and state   12, 21, 50, 145
   universal   48–9
   validity   125
secularization   145
   debate   182 n.12
   linear   43, 49
   narrative   42–3, 55
   non-uniform   43
   thesis   12, 43
Seikōji (temple)   125–6, 128–9
Shaku Sōen   24, 35–6, 45, 89, 91
Shambhala   185 n.1
Shimaji Mokurai   6, 124–6, 128–9, 132–5, 180 nn.8, 11
shin bukkyō, see New Buddhism
Shin sect   6, 24, 36, 38, 89–91, 93–5, 129, 133, 138, 142, 148
   in Chōshū   6, 123–30, 180 n.4
   Higashi   126, 130, 137–8, 145
   in Meiji period   129–32
   missionaries   36, 133–5
   Nishi   126, 129–33, 180 nn.10, 11
   priests   124–9
   strength   126–30
   Suzuki's view of   91, 94
   temples   124–6
   Yinguang's critique   93–5
Shintō   2, 21–2, 89, 128–30, 132–3, 138, 145, 149
Siddhartha Gautama, *see* The Buddha
Sinocentrism   88–9, 102
Sino-Japanese War   90, 95–7
socialism   5, 72–3, 75, 101, 149, *see also* Marxism
   Buddhist   71–2, 74, 79, 81
sonnō jōi movement   123, 127–8, 130–1
Sonoda Shuye   36–7
soteriology   51, 56, 59, 64–5, *see also* salvation
Soviet Union   43, 72, 75, 79–81, *see also* Russia
space   3, 80, 118, 185 n.1
   secular   44, 55, 117–18
spirituality   46, 54, 101, 119
   not religion   40, 59, 177 n.3
Sri Lanka (Ceylon)   4, 29, 45, 69, 73, 80, 83–5, 104, 107, 109, 179 nn.3, 9
   Buddhist meetings in   61, 106

visit by Chinese monks   105, 108, 110–12, 115, 118
Stalin, Joseph   72, 75, 81
suffering   47, 73, 77, 79, 84, 85, 170–1, 173
Sun Yat-sen   90
supernatural   9, 12, 23, 47, 52, 56, 62, 65, 67, 154
superstition   55, 74, 97, 177 n.2
   as corruption   7, 46, 65
   distinct from Buddhism   5, 21, 57, 61, 65–6, 92
   distinct from religion   43, 46, 55, 62, 64, 183 n.8
   suppression   44, 62–3, 66, 108
Suzuki, Daisetsu Teitarō   6, 35, 37–8, 87
   and Carus   35, 37
   and Hu Shih   95–7
   influence in China   37, 98–102
   influence on the West   37, 87–8, 98
   at Mt. Hiei   38–9
   nationalism   6, 87, 95
   and Taixu   90, 92–3, 109
   view of Chinese Buddhism   94–5
   visits China   90, 95
   writings   87, 89, 91, 93, 99–100, 121
   and Yinguang   93–4

Taiwan (Republic of China)   95–6, 99, 117, 156, 161, 164, 168–9, 173–4, 183 n.12, 184 n.20
   Buddhist organizations   7, 69, 113, 121, 163, 165–6
   Theravada Buddhism in   114–15
Taixu   2, 4, 45–6, 69, 98, 109, 112, *see also* humanistic Buddhism
   Buddhist reform   87, 92, 104, 107–8, 112
   dialogues   90, 92–4, 109–12
   and education   109–10
   and Japan   95, 109
taṇhā, see craving
temple   13, 75, 94, 101, 115, 125, 127, 129, 142, 155–6, 165
   American   150, 155–6, 160, 183 n.13, 184 nn.16, 21
   branch   89–90, 130, 132, 150, 159, 184 n.21
   destruction   21, 69

DRBA 160, 183 n.13, 184 nn.17, 20, 21, 22
Fo Guang Shan 155, 161
local 21, 90
requisitioning 90, 92, 106, 108, 131
Shin 124–6, 128, 130
Vietnam 56, 61–7
text 16, 23, 38, 61, 114, 118, 139–40, 179 n.12, see also Lam Rim Chen Mo; Mahāyāna; Pāli, scriptures; Sanskrit, scriptures; translation
  Chinese 17, 107, 109, 111, 114, 141, 163
  Confucian 14, 22
  early 118–19
  emphasis on 46, 105, 111, 144, 168
  India as source 29, 105
  publishing 94, 106, 114, 117
  recovery of 107, 113
  sacred 2, 21–2
  Tibetan 108–9, 163, 166
Theravāda Buddhism 103–5, 111, 121, see also meditation
  China 6, 70, 103–4, 109–17
  "Hīnayāna" 105–6, 111, 118
  inferior 104–5, 111, 118
Thích Thanh Từ 61, 65
Three Refuges 57, 60, 103
Tibet 5, 53, 108, 110
  China and 52, 71, 85
  Diaspora 53–4
  language 53, 105
  studies of 80, 110
Tipiṭaka, see Pāli scriptures
Tokugawa 20–1, 123–31, 180 nn.2, 9
Tokugawa Ieyasu 125, 180 n.2
Tokugawa Yoshinobu 124, 131
trade 17–19, 29, 74, 78, 87–8, 123, 133
tradition 1, 37, 46, 54, 89, 151–2, 178 n.3
  authentic 60, 159
  fossilized 25, 43
  as religion (or not) 2, 59
  textual 25, 42, 105, 140–1, 163
  transmission 5, 10, 31
translation 14, 29, 36, 38–9, 61, 73, 84, 100, 111, 146–7, 184 n.22
  to Chinese 29, 37, 105, 109, 111–14, 117–18, 137–8, 140
  to English 111, 139, 142–3, 155–6, 178 n.4
  to Indian languages 107, 178 n.4, 179 n.10
  to Japanese 37, 108, 145, 179 n.11
  mistakes 138, 140
  of Pāli Canon 22–3, 105
  of "religion" 19–20
transmission 5–6, 26, 28, 31, 33–4, 41, 114, 139–40, 155, 159, 162
  direction 6, 38, 140
  India to China 29, 33
  lineage 155, 159, 162, 183 n.10, 184 n.17
transnationalism 6, 150–1, 160, 164–5
treaties 18–19, 28, 88, 124, 133, 141, 145
tṛṣṇā, see craving
Tse-Xin Organic Agriculture Foundation 173–4
Tsong-kha-pa 166
Tzu Chi 69, 113, 160, 166

union (workers') 74, 76
United States 18–19, 28, 50, 74, 88, 95, 97, 109, 155, 183 n.13
  Buddhism in 36, 50, 156, 164, 166–8
  religion in 49, 52
  secular 50–1, 53, 55
universalism 48, 141, 143–4, 146, 148–9

Vatican 63, 66
Vedas 74, 82, 139
vegetarianism 7, 93–4, 153, 163, 169–72, 174
Vietnam 4–5, 56–7, 60, 62–3, 67, 69, 88, 105, 156, 182 n.1, 183 n.13, 184 n.22, see also Buddhist Reform Movement
  Buddhism in 56, 58, 60–8, 178 n.5
Vietnamese Buddhist Association 62, 67–8
Vinaya 111, 183 n.10
violence 28, 57, 75–8, 85, 94, 130, 138, 144, 157
vipassanā (meditation) 47–50, 69, 103, 114, 116–17, 119
Vipassanā, (movement) 47–9, 114
Visuddhimagga 73, 112, 114, 118
Vivekananda 24, 72

Wanfo Sheng Cheng (temple)   150,
    155–6, 160, 183 n.13
wastefulness   63, 65, 178 n.2
Wesak   60–1
West, the   7, 11, 13, 25, 29
    imaginaire   150, 152–4, 156–7, 159
Westernization   19, 87, 97, 151
    paradigm   6–7, 25, 123, 125, 152, 154,
        157–8
women   57, 77
    and Buddhism   5, 56–8, 63–8, 117,
        180 n.18
    gender structures   64–5
World Buddhist Conference   108–9
World Buddhist Forum   52, 115–16
World Fellowship of Buddhists   85, 106,
    112
world religion   4, 11–12, 143–4
    appearance of term   10, 23–4, 27, 37,
        40, 181 n.6
    category   2, 40

Christian model   2, 24
classification   23, 57
World's Parliament of Religions   24–5,
    35–7, 69, 89, 157

Xuanzang   29–30
Xuyun   98, 100, 115–16, 179 n.15

Yang Wenhui   4, 104, 106–8, 112, 179
    nn.6, 7
Yijing   29, 143
Yinguang   87, 90, 93–5, 102
Yinshun   109, 112–13, 118–19, 179 n.13
Yogācāra   46, 94, 105, 107, 111

Zen   6, 35, 38, 87, 89, 91, 94–7, 99–100,
    102, 125, *see also* Chan
    identity   57, 61
    meditation   50, 68
    school   29–30
Zhen Ru   7, 164, 166–8, 170, 172–3, 175

www.ingramcontent.com/pod-product-compliance
Lightning Source LLC
Chambersburg PA
CBHW052039300426
44117CB00012B/1888